WHITE HOUSE
DAZE

WHITE HOUSE DAZE

The Unmaking of Domestic Policy in the Bush Years

CHARLES KOLB

THE FREE PRESS
A Division of Macmillan, Inc.
NEW YORK

Maxwell Macmillan Canada
TORONTO

Maxwell Macmillan International
NEW YORK   OXFORD   SINGAPORE   SYDNEY

The Free Press
A Division of Macmillan, Inc.
866 Third Avenue, New York, N.Y. 10022

Maxwell Macmillan Canada, Inc.
1200 Eglinton Avenue East
Suite 200
Don Mills, Ontario M3C 3N1

Macmillan, Inc. is part of the Maxwell Communication Group of Companies.

Printed in the United States of America

printing number

1   2   3   4   5   6   7   8   9   10

Library of Congress Cataloging-in-Publication Data

Kolb, Charles.
    White House daze : the unmaking of domestic policy in the Bush
years / Charles Kolb.
      p. cm.
    ISBN 0-02-917495-3
    1. United States—Politics and government—1989–1993.   2. Bush,
George, 1924–   —Friends and associates.   3. Presidents—United
States—Staff—History—20th century.   I. Title.
E881.K65   1994   93-33175
973.928—dc20   CIP

For Ingrid
and my parents

Rationalists, wearing square hats,
Think, in square rooms,
Looking at the floor,
Looking at the ceiling.
They confine themselves
To right-angled triangles.
If they tried rhomboids,
Cones, waving lines, ellipses—
As, for example, the ellipse of the
　　halfmoon—
Rationalists would wear sombreros.

　　　　　　　　　—WALLACE STEVENS
　　　　　"Six Significant Landscapes"

CONTENTS

Introduction xi

1. Doing It Differently 1

2. Playing Tennis: It's All Form 27

3. "You've Been Darmanized" 51

4. Darmanomics at Work: "We Can't Lose!" 85

5. The "Ed-Chew-KAY-shun President" 125

6. The Week Bush Fired Cavazos:
   Sununu Knows Best 165

7. Empowerment and the "New Paradigm" 185

8. In Search of Domestic Policy:
   "Kinder, Gentler" Gridlock 231

9. Campaign Mode: Ready to Fight? 263

10. Omens of the Reckoning 307

11. Looking Beyond 337

   Epilogue 355
   Notes 357
   Index 364

Acknowledgments

Many friends have contributed to the development of this book. All made valuable suggestions, most of which I have followed. Some called me on their own, unsolicited, to offer thoughts, observations, and relevant anecdotes about the Bush Administration. Everyone I contacted for information graciously and enthusiastically offered their assistance.

I would especially like to thank the following individuals, many of whom read portions of the book or offered their suggestions as I was researching and writing: Tim Adams, Martin Anderson, Jane Barnett, Randolph Beales, Rich Bond, Todd Buchholz, Tom Butts, Chino Chapa, Shannon Christian, John Cogan, Diana and Harold Furchtgott-Roth, Austen Furse, Arlene Holen, Jay Lefkowitz, Larry Lindsey, Nancy Mitchell, Richard Porter, Richard Rahn, Catherine Russell, Gene Schaerr, Jeremy Shane, Russell Shields, and Allen Weinstein. Still others, including several senior Bush–Quayle presidential and vice presidential aides at the Assistant-to-the-President level, willingly offered assistance but preferred anonymity. They know who they are, and they have my lasting gratitude.

Two close friends, Richard D. Komer and George A. Pieler, read the entire manuscript closely and suggested several valuable changes.

I am indebted to Robert H. Bork, Jr., for introducing me to Erwin Glikes at the Free Press. In addition to reviewing the text, he and Diana Culp Bork have been extremely encouraging throughout the entire process.

At the Free Press, Marion Maneker provided skillful editorial suggestions, for which I am grateful.

Throughout my nearly ten years in government my confidential assistant, Peggy Smith, kept me on time and organized. She also experienced much of what is written in these pages, and I am grateful to her for her dedication and professionalism during this period.

Cornelius J. Golden, Jr., of the law firm of Chadbourne & Parke, guided me through the legal formalities associated with this project, and Neil offered many helpful comments on the manuscript.

Sue Sommerfield served as an exceedingly capable and patient research assistant in tracking down dozens of sources and loose ends.

Mike Horowitz, General Counsel to OMB Director David Stockman during the first Reagan Administration, brought me into government nearly a decade ago. I continue to learn from Mike, who was there on my first day in government and on my last. He remains a close friend and mentor, a man who believes that ideas do matter and that one's time in government should be spent trying to get things done.

During my time at the White House, Jim Pinkerton was a good friend and, despite his relative youth, a mentor. If more "Bushies" had listened to Pinkerton, Chelsea Clinton would still be attending a public school.

The Office of Policy Development staff at the White House was the best, most talented group of professionals with whom I've been fortunate to be associated. They made the place worth it.

My wife, Ingrid, encouraged me during countless nights and weekends at the word processor. During the editing phase, she saved considerable time by handling the almost daily revisions. It is but small comfort for her many sacrifices that I also dedicate this book to her.

Alexandria, Virginia
August 22, 1993

INTRODUCTION

There are days when the nation's capital really does resemble what Ronald Reagan liked to call a shining city on a hill. Leaving my home in Alexandria, Virginia, I would drive to work shortly after sunrise, always relishing the still glory of dawn as it broke over the Potomac River.

Crossing the Fourteenth Street bridge I could see the majesty of the city arrayed across the horizon, from the National Cathedral atop Mount St. Albans to the Kennedy Center along the river's bank and the Jefferson Memorial at the Tidal Basin. On those days of clarity, the city not only shimmered in the river's reflection but evoked in me an awe-inspiring sense of pride, even excitement, at being part of the country's government.

Then there were other days when the view and the vision were far less clear, when the Washington Monument was almost totally obscured by dense, low-lying clouds. On those days, Washington would almost appear to rise up from the mist and haze that often lingered on the Potomac.

On May 29, 1990, I traveled this route for the first time to my new job as a member of the Bush White House. I was headed for the White House to join the staff of an immensely popular President who had pledged to continue the economic boom launched by Ronald Reagan.

As I drove I became almost physically conscious of what the morning meant in my life. I was eager, filled with a sense of expectation about my new opportunity. The White House would be a place of clarity and precision. There would be direction and a sense of purpose. Gravitas. The nation's future awaiting my input.

As I drove it began to sink in: "Today I'm going to work at the White House as Deputy Assistant to the President for Domestic Policy." At approximately 6:55 A.M. the Southwest Gate will swing open, and I will drive my car inside on West Executive Avenue to parking space 42, some 150 feet from the entrance to the West Wing. Not the Old Executive Office Building next door. The West Wing—just paces from the Oval Office.

I was going to work in the Bush White House, joining the ranks of really talented, top-flight people. Men and women who knew what they were doing.

Or so I thought.

This book is about the internal workings and politics of the Bush White House. In addition to several members of Bush's Cabinet, the main actors are the top fifty or so "staffers" who enjoyed truly remarkable power and discretion—the Assistants and Deputy Assistants to the President of the United States. These are the people who would sift through options papers long before a short list made its way into the Oval Office. They are the presidential gatekeepers who often determine whom he sees, where he'll speak, and what he'll say; whether his Cabinet will meet with him and when; what the topics will include; and what his major and minor foreign and domestic policy initiatives will entail.

Getting a job in the White House is more often than not the result of luck. Right place, right time. I did not invent some grand plan to end up working on domestic policy in the White House. I started out in Washington in 1979 as a young international lawyer at the city's largest law firm, Covington & Burling. At that time I had no inkling that I would ever work in government, let alone occupy a senior-level position in the White House.

But serendipity took its course, and a series of domestic policy appointments in the Reagan Administration altered my career plans and took me first to David Stockman's Office of Management and Budget (part of the Executive Office of the President) as an Assistant General Counsel and then to the U.S. Department of Education under Secretaries William Bennett and Lauro Cavazos, where I served as Deputy General Counsel and finally as Deputy Under Secretary for Planning, Budget, and Evaluation. A heavy dose of education budgeting and policymaking experience was what ultimately led me back to the White House complex under George Bush.

To end up where I did, it was usually necessary to have played a major role in a presidential campaign. I had not. In fact, during the Bush–Dukakis campaign, when I was still at the Department of Education, I was technically "Hatched," precluded by law from any active campaigning.

From my position at the Education Department, I came to know and to work closely with Roger B. Porter, a former professor at Harvard's John F. Kennedy School of Government who was on leave serving as George Bush's Assistant for Economic and Domestic Policy. Porter was the first person to hold this position for *both* economic and domestic policy. He was to become a most important figure in the Bush White House, not so much for what he did as for what he chose not to do.

My immediate predecessor was Dr. William L. Roper, a health policy expert who was also a licensed pediatrician. After a year as Porter's deputy, Roper bailed out of the White House in February 1990 for Atlanta, where he headed the Centers for Disease Control. Before long I would come to understand why Dr. Roper left when he did.

One month before Roper departed, both he and Porter contacted me separately to see if I was interested in being considered for Roper's position. I had worked closely with both men in shaping Administration education policy from the first week of the Bush presidency. Porter had also asked me to join Roper and Larry Lindsey (then another Office of Policy Development staffer) to serve as a rapporteur in the closed meetings between Bush and the nation's governors at the September 1989 Charlottesville Education Summit.

Although my initial reaction to Porter's inquiry was favorable, I did not exactly jump for joy at the prospect of a White House position. The job, after all, entailed a Faustian pact—lots of prestige in exchange for exceedingly long hours, a grueling pace, and a fundamentally uncertain future. I was wavering, and it was my wife who urged me to accept Porter's offer.

The only problem was that I didn't have an offer. After Roper's and

Porter's inquiries in early February 1990, I didn't hear anything further until late March, when Porter asked me to come over for an interview. Followed by silence. He specifically asked me not to mention our discussion to my boss, Secretary of Education Lauro Cavazos, since he didn't want to alarm Cavazos with the perception that he was "stealing away" one of the Secretary's senior aides. I also asked Porter not to say anything yet to Cavazos. He agreed not to.

But then he did anyway. About two weeks later Porter called me to say that he had just told Cavazos after a Cabinet meeting that he was thinking of bringing me to the White House. I had wanted to be the one to break the news to Cavazos. That Porter jumped the gun was not accidental or a slip of his memory. (It also wasn't the last time he said one thing but did another.) He and Cavazos were constantly struggling over who was to set education policy in the Bush Administration, the Education Department, or the White House. Press accounts had already referred to Porter as the *de facto* Education Secretary, given the perception that Cavazos was relatively weak and ineffective. I did not want to become a pawn in their power squabble.

Another month went by, and I ran into Porter shortly before I was to give a speech in the Roosevelt Room (the main conference room in the West Wing, just across from the Oval Office). He took me aside and asked me when we were "going to do this."

"Do what?"

"Come to work here, of course."

So that was my offer. What I didn't realize then was that Porter's taking nearly three months to offer me the job was all too characteristic of his own decisionmaking style on virtually everything from personnel to policy.

My first day at the Bush White House was unforgettable—but not for the reasons one might think. I woke up that morning to find that the *Washington Post*'s "Style" section featured a front-page profile about "workaholics in the White House." George Bush took the prize as the biggest workaholic in the West Wing (after all, he lived nearby, had no commute, and enjoyed plenty of servants). My new boss came next:

On a Saturday night the lights in Roger Porter's office are burning. Porter, the president's adviser on domestic and economic policy, can beaver like nobody's business. Inexplicably, he keeps the longest hours of all, according to an informal poll of his White House peers. "I'd put Roger Porter in the Vampire Category," says [Andy] Card [Bush's Deputy Chief of Staff and later Transportation Secretary]. "I don't think he ever sees daylight."

"He's Mormon. He can't even drink coffee or smoke," says a fellow staffer. "Without caffeine or nicotine, how does he do it?"

"A known insomniac," answers a third.[1]

But I'd already been warned. Another profile of Porter that had appeared two months to the day previously in the *New York Times* had allowed that Porter's dedication to detail merited him "a black belt in white paper." A colleague had even gone so far as to describe him as being "born to process."[2]

In a sense, the *Post* article was reassuring. People did work hard at the White House, and for what struck me as an obvious reason: It was a place to get things done for the country. If there was process, then I was certain that it must be process with a purpose.

First days in the federal government usually involve tedious routine: lots of paperwork, orientation, fingerprinting, photographing, and other necessary details. The White House is no different. But the most important, and eye-opening, event that day was the impromptu staff lunch I attended—impromptu in that it included almost the entire Office of Policy Development senior staff minus their leader, Roger Porter.

We gathered over sandwiches and chips from the Mess in Larry Lindsey's Old Executive Office Building quarters. A brilliant Harvard economics professor in his early thirties on leave to the Office of Policy Development, Lindsey (now a Governor of the Federal Reserve Board) had developed a well-deserved reputation as one of the most able and articulate defenders of the Reagan era's growth-oriented supply side economic theory. Around Lindsey's table was gathered some of the finest talent in the Bush White House. Bright, likable people like my co-deputy Jim Pinkerton, Deputy Assistant to the President for Policy Planning; Rae Nelson, who handled education and drug policy; Hans Kuttner, an irrepressibly witty Princetonian who managed health policy for the Office of Policy Development; Emily Mead, a charming New Englander who kept the complete record on every George Bush policy statement uttered since the late 1960s; Bradley Mitchell, Porter's executive assistant; Michael Klausner, OPD's White House Fellow; as well as several others.

At lunch on my first day, I listened as one by one my new colleagues told astonishing stories of Roger Porter's ineffectiveness within the White House: his predilection for avoiding controversy, his preoccupation with mind-numbing and pointless detail, his love of lists and fact sheets, his desire not to incur the wrath of Budget Director Dick Darman, and his basic inability to make decisions or delegate authority. Pinkerton was, as usual, to the point: "At least Roper did the smart thing and left town after a year." I was hearing all this for the first time, and the staff was hoping, almost pleading, that as Porter's new deputy I could do something about it.

On Day One I found a terribly frustrated and dejected staff who felt that Porter treated them like peons while simultaneously regarding mid-level Office of Management and Budget officials, to whom he was unquestionably far senior, as on a par with himself. Curiously, it never occurred to Porter how this posture devalued not only his own staff but himself as well. The overall gloom of the meeting lifted slightly when someone lightheartedly suggested psychotherapy as a cure, only to have that idea shot down as improbable and, at any rate, unlikely to change Porter's strictly ingrained habits.

I was stunned. I simply couldn't believe the degree of dejection and frustration, the sense of hopelessness and helplessness among such intelligent and capable people! They had indeed given me a sense of the dynamics inside the Bush White House; it was a far cry from the picture Porter had painted, and I had fondly imagined, when he approached me about the job.

As I left Lindsey's office that afternoon I comtemplated Porter's chummy description a month earlier of how he, along with Chief of Staff John Sununu and OMB Director Dick Darman, basically ran domestic policy as a troika, occasionally augmented by Michael Boskin, Chairman of the Council of Economic Advisers. What I'd heard described at lunch was anything *but* chummy. Darman had already elbowed aside Porter and Boskin, and in late May 1990 he was near cementing his lock on policy with Sununu.

What my new colleagues said suggested that it didn't really matter what the exceedingly capable Office of Policy Development staff managed to do, because very few innovations ever got beyond Porter's six in-boxes. When it came to the development of domestic policy, the Bush White House had produced what came to be a fatal impasse.

This memoir of my White House days is an attempt to explain why the Bush Administration accomplished so little and ultimately collapsed, thereby winning a place for Bush in the history books along-side William Howard Taft, Herbert Hoover, Gerald Ford, and Jimmy Carter. Some of the people mentioned in these pages will not be flattered, and for good reasons.

The focus of this book is relatively narrow and modest. It is not intended to be a history of the Bush Administration, an impossible undertaking so soon after George Bush has left office.

Moreover, no one person who served in that Administration can tell that story, especially given that it was essentially an Administration where people went to considerable lengths to conceal things from each other. As will become increasingly clear, too much of what constantly went wrong and led to the unmaking of domestic policy can be attributed to the systematic denial of the truth about what was actually happening around George Bush and his senior aides. Critical information was denied not only to the President of the United States but to the American people as well.

Far too often—whether the issue was the economy, the budget, or extending unemployment benefits—the paramount goal in the White House was daily spin control. It is clear now that this lunatic obsession with spin control in Washington has not ended with the departure of the Bush Administration. The multiple examples of Bill Clinton's early missteps and attempted recoveries illustrate that a preoccupation with spin control has now become truly bipartisan.

Be that as it may, when it comes to the collapse of the Bush Administration, we can continue to expect prodigious efforts in blame-shifting as the history of the departed Republicans comes to be written. Some of the key players themselves will begin to lay the blame for 1992 elsewhere. That's why I believe it is important now to offer this memoir of the daze—the confusion and inaction—that came to characterize and ultimately overwhelm George Bush's presidency.

While grateful for the rare opportunity to serve on a President's staff, I became increasingly dismayed by the principal advisers surrounding George Bush. I was not alone in this feeling. Some of those advisers, like John Sununu, thought they knew everything and were openly dismissive of attempts to pursue an aggressive domestic agenda emphasizing such ideas as economic opportunity and empowerment. Others, like my boss, Roger Porter, were basically decent people but essentially miscast in roles that required political action rather than endless analysis and reflection.

One of the President's senior advisers, Gregg Petersmeyer, who headed the Office of National Service (the "Thousand Points of Light" office), said to me a few months before the 1992 election that this President's "staff was screwing him over. They've cut him off and isolated him from the American people. That was the chief crime of John Sununu." The problem was that no one at a senior level in the White House was willing to do anything about this, and the President himself really didn't seem to care. Some wondered whether he even noticed.

A true and proper history of an administration will do its work best by stepping back—far back—and viewing that administration from above, to achieve a broad historical perspective of world issues and the long-term economic and political forces at work. This cannot be that book. My intention here is far simpler: to offer a picture of what it was like to work in the White House during the fleeting moments of the Bush Administration.

Did the "Bushies" intentionally forget about Ronald Reagan? How did Bush's domestic policy office become a nonplayer in policy development? How did the strictures of the 1990 budget deal crowd out other domestic policy initiatives? How well did Dick Darman serve George Bush? Did Bush earn any part of the title he sought as "the education president"? How did the White House handle domestic crises? Why did the concept of empowerment keep appearing and disappearing throughout the entire four years? Why did the President fail to advance a domestic agenda when his popularity peaked just after the Persian Gulf War? Did the Bush Administration really want another four years?

These questions matter, and the Bush years are important ones. Assessing them correctly—the achievements and lack of achievements of the White House in which I served—is critical to determining whether the Bush years represented the end of conservative rule for a long time to come in America or, instead, constituted a unique act of bungling that only interrupted what may continue to be a growing conservative tide in the affairs of the nation.

My friend Arlene Holen, who had served in senior positions in both the Reagan and Bush Administrations, asked me shortly after the 1992 election whether I would have written this book had George Bush been reelected. Her question reminded me of what motivated me to write in the first place: My intention—as I made personal notes starting in late 1990—was to keep a record of what went wrong in the first term so that a second Bush term would avoid making the same errors. As I began shaping those notes into a manuscript after the 1992 election, nothing was sadder than having to delete repeated references to that nonexistent "second term."

From that first day in the Bush White House, however, I realized that all was not well. The opinion polls hadn't registered this fact yet: The President's popularity was remarkably high, and Ronald Reagan's stunning economic expansion was still continuing. In late May 1990 I was only beginning to learn just how my colleagues felt about the Bush White House—its policies, its people, and its problems—although I didn't yet entirely understand why. Nor in the generally placid economic and political environment in the second year of the Bush Administration could I know what the consequences of everything I took in that first day would be.

1

Doing It Differently

Shirley MacLaine . . . thinks I was Martin Van Buren
in a former life.

—George Bush,
Looking Forward[1]

Not since Herbert Hoover succeeded Calvin Coolidge to become
President in 1929 had there been a two-term succession like the
transition from Ronald Reagan to George Bush. The pundits called it
a friendly takeover.

After eight years of a clearly successful presidency accompanied by
unprecedented levels of national economic growth, personal prosperity, and international peace, George Bush inherited what in effect was
Ronald Reagan's third term. Or so his supporters hoped and his opponents feared.

But as George Bush and his inner circle saw it, the challenge soon
became to define the incoming President's differences in relation to
his supremely popular predecessor without alienating that solid core
of Reagan Republicans and, especially, the Reagan Democrats who
gave Bush his margin of victory over Governor Michael Dukakis of
Massachusetts.

Defining the difference from one's predecessor is the first preoccupation of virtually all incoming Presidents. In some instances, as

1

with Franklin Roosevelt, the differences defined themselves. In 1932 the electorate rejected the failed economic policies of Herbert Hoover and the Great Depression. On occasion, new Presidents have announced policies and programs designed to put their own stamp on America's future. Virtually all of Roosevelt's Democratic successors have sought to follow his New Deal policies by espousing an overarching theme that encompassed their programs. Thus, Truman's Fair Deal; Kennedy's Arthur Schlesinger- and Ted Sorensen-inspired "New Frontier"; and Lyndon Johnson's "Great Society."

Republicans, on the other hand, have tended to be less global and inclusive in their thinking about the role of government, preferring instead to manage their administrations on a day-to-day basis inspired by the central tenet that free-market economies and decentralized government—not grand public works schemes or hundreds of new federal programs—reflect what the people want most.

Ronald Reagan, however, changed the political landscape for Republicans. Although he never announced a unifying theme like Roosevelt, Johnson, or Kennedy, Reagan nonetheless campaigned on and governed with reference to three relatively simple and straightforward principles—core convictions—that he had honed over the years and that his loyal supporters knew by heart: reduce taxes, strengthen defense, and get big government off the backs of the American people. After Jimmy Carter's malaise and stagflation, Reagan, despite his age, appeared a sunny optimist. His clarity and focus were epitomized in the phrase "Morning in America"—the quest for that "shining city on a hill."

Reagan's supply side tax policies put resources in the pockets of the American people rather than in government coffers. He steadfastly believed that individuals and families could spend their own money more efficiently than the federal government. During the 1980 primary campaign, candidate George Bush derided Reagan's supply side theory as "voodoo economics." Then he spent the next eight years assisting in its implementation and watching it work.

The success of Reaganomics effectively forced Vice President Bush to campaign on the same theme in 1988: "no new taxes." While Ronald Reagan had presided over several major tax increases between 1982 and 1988, it never hurt his fundamental popularity, thanks largely to his remarkable communications skills plus the fact that each of those tax increases was usually buried deep in the bowels of some other, more technical and elaborate piece of legislation. Since 1977 employer-based Social Security taxes had increased roughly nine times, with some of the largest increases coming on Reagan's watch. And yet, because of his "Teflon" presidency, coupled with the general recognition that he was a president with strong convictions, Reagan was always forgiven when taxes went up and managed to avoid political liability for these generally large and economically regressive tax increases. George Bush would not be so lucky.

While it was natural for George Bush to look for ways to differentiate himself from Ronald Reagan, Bush's approach to doing so was fundamentally flawed at the outset. He inexplicably downplayed and virtually ignored two factors that had contributed mightily to Reagan's success: the importance of presidential rhetoric and the creation of a well-oiled propaganda machine for swaying public opinion.

Almost from the beginning, George Bush's presidency was an antirhetorical operation. According to one of his senior aides, it was even borderline anti-intellectual: "Remember, the movie actor's White House was the one that was hospitable to new ideas. Not the Yalie's." This assessment came from a long-standing Bush partisan who served in the West Wing and believed that many members of the Bush team had little more than "generalized social contempt" for the Reaganites. Some Bushies even went to great lengths to add credence to the charge that Reagan had been simply lazy. They would emphasize with relish that George Bush got to the Oval Office by 7:15 each morning, almost two hours before Reagan. The focus soon became not how well Bush communicated or what he actually achieved but how long he worked.

Rather than build on Reagan's strengths, Bush systematically dismantled them. First came his treatment of the White House speechwriters and then his intentional understaffing of the Office of Public Liaison.

Perhaps nothing so exemplified the differences between the two Presidents as Bush's approach to speeches and speechwriting.

Whereas Franklin Roosevelt had skillfully used his fireside chats to explain complex issues in fairly simple terms, George Bush saw little need for speeches to explain much of anything. His public remarks lacked content, depth, inspiration, and, frequently, even elementary grammar.

Bush abhorred soaring rhetoric and emotional speeches. While Ronald Reagan could readily move an audience with carefully crafted words spoken in his soft, mellifluous voice with gently cocked head, Bush instead chose a more pedestrian style that was almost deliberately flat, characterized by broken, incomplete sentences and steadfast avoidance of the word "I."

Reagan's most gifted speechwriter, Peggy Noonan, quickly noted and understood this tendency.[2] Noonan observed that Bush intentionally resorted to incomplete sentences to make it easier to avoid bragging about himself. He would actually cross out the first-person pronoun or even delete a sentence that included it. As Noonan put it, "I became adept at pronoun-less sentences. Instead of 'I moved to Texas and soon we joined the Republican Party.' it was, 'Moved to Texas, joined the Republican Party, raised a family.' " She even worried whether, come Inauguration Day, Bush would take the oath of office on the Capitol steps by saying: "Do solemnly swear, will preserve and protect . . ."[3]

The success of Noonan's book on the Reagan years itself undoubtedly was a factor in Bush's penchant for a more modest role for rhetoric. Bush assumed the presidency with a desire that staff remain staff. Whereas Reagan's speechwriting shop included recognized conservatives like Peggy Noonan, Peter Robinson, Tony Dolan, and Josh Gilder, Bush's office was essentially an afterthought. Speechwriters (and other staff, too) should never achieve a notoriety that, in some instances, meant outshining their principals. Accordingly, the Bush speechwriting operation was intentionally downgraded. The small staff was initially headed by Chriss Winston, a pleasant but relatively nonideological woman who saw her role as manager of the process. Winston herself did not write speeches so much as edit them.

To add insult to demotion, the speechwriters were deliberately denied use of the White House Mess, a fact which—aside from the personal affront—ensured their isolation and insulation from the staff's open roundtable, where junior White House aides in the Reagan years had exchanged ideas, schemes, policies, and frustrations. The Reagan speechwriting operation had been a center of ideological ferment inside the White House, a focal point for the debate over presidential policy. Bush preferred anonymous wordsmiths, toiling out of sight, removed from whatever meager discussion of issues might be occurring, while crafting passionless prose to convey the message handed to them.

Ronald Reagan used his rhetorical skills to articulate a new direction for the nation. Actually achieving his goals required Reagan to undertake an extraordinary and sustained attempt at coalition-building that would generate support for his proposals in Congress. To do this, Reagan established a zealous band of lobbyists and skilled persuaders inside his Office of Public Liaison, the unit that served as the White House's eyes and ears with the American public.

According to Wayne Valis, a well-connected lobbyist who had served with Richard Nixon and Gerald Ford as well as in Reagan's Public Liaison Office, Bush decided early on—even before taking office—to downplay the type of coalition-building that Reagan had deployed so artfully. Valis and a small group of his clients met with Bush, Sununu, and Darman in December 1988 in the Roosevelt Room, where the President-elect and his advisers made it obvious that there'd be no more coalitions and no bickering with the Congress. Negotiation, not confrontation, was the new style. "We were stopped in our tracks," Valis explains. "It was unilateral disarmament in the face of George Mitchell and company." By 1992, Reagan's well-oiled machine, capable of mustering support across the country, had grown rusty with disuse.

Under Reagan, there was cacophony in the West Wing as various outside groups—business, conservatives, special interests—played Jim Baker, Mike Deaver, and Ed Meese against one another. As a result, a wide array of constituents had access to the Reagan White House. Bushies, however, disliked ferment and debate. Our White House would be a quiet place, a neat and tidy operation.

Bush placed both his speechwriting and Public Liaison operations under the centralized control of David Demarest, a former Labor Department spokesman during the Reagan years. Demarest had no idea whatsoever about how to make the linkage between presidential rhetoric and actually moving the American public to support a presidential initiative. He acknowledged that formal presidential speeches were "only one piece of the pie" and explained that the White House was relying on speeches, press conferences, trips, and unscripted appearances by the President to create a "mosaic" of the Bush presidency.[4]

The communications jigsaw puzzle envisioned by Demarest never added up to a whole picture, and the reason was simple: Unlike Reagan, who had a clearly defined roadmap of where he wanted to go and what he wanted to accomplish, George Bush replaced substance with form. Perhaps this approach is understandable in retrospect, because, from the very beginning, Bush had little of substance to communicate.

Instead of an action agenda, Bush began his presidency with . . . a list. All over town in late January 1989, members of the new Administration's team were framing and hanging on their office walls the President's nine-point credo, which reflected Bush's own governmental, bureaucratic, and managerial experience as distinguished from Reagan's ideological, outsider, and conviction perspective. George Bush wanted his Administration to observe the "Golden Rules":

1. Think Big.
2. Challenge the system.
3. Adhere to the highest ethical standards.
4. Be on the record as much as possible.
5. Be frank.
6. Fight hard for your position.
7. When I make a call, we work as a team.
8. Work with Congress.
9. Represent the United States with dignity.

This was not just the new team's management philosophy; it was our whole agenda!

Bush's "Golden Rules" were all process. They offered no hint about what to think big about or fight hard for. After all, while the 1988 election campaign was supposedly about "ideology" rather than "competence," now it was time to govern. "Campaign mode" was over for another four years.

No one put it better than a Bush transition team aide who observed, "Our people don't have agendas. They have mortgages. They want jobs."[5] This remark was perhaps more revealing than the aide (who later became head of Presidential Personnel) intended it to be. Reagan's two-term presidency had seen relentless ideological ferment and struggle—over taxes, government spending, and defining contests like his battle with the striking air traffic controllers. Bush had signaled a different beginning with his reference to a "kinder, gentler" America at the 1988 New Orleans GOP convention and in his Inaugural Address, when he acknowledged a desire not to "bicker" with the Congress.

The only problem was in figuring out precisely what Bush's

"kinder, gentler" distinction meant when it came to domestic policy. "Kinder and gentler" than what? Loyal Reaganites were beginning to grumble.

Demarest had it right when he spoke of a Bush communications mosaic that would gradually become apparent to the American people with the passage of time. Not so with Reagan, who announced his bold tax and spending cuts as part of a hundred-day agenda intended to stun the Congress into acquiescence. People knew what he wanted to achieve and where he was headed. Bush had his "Golden Rules" of process: "Think Big" and "Be Frank."

It became obvious that George Bush would reject Reagan's model and refuse to announce a bold hundred-day agenda within the first weeks of his presidency. After an uninspiring Inaugural Address, Bush launched into preparing a speech to the Congress scheduled for February 9, 1989. Reagan had delivered a final State of the Union Address, so Bush's first speech to the Congress was intended to set the tone for his new team. Along with the speech he would also emphasize his own budget themes for the coming fiscal year.

The February 9 address was as close as George Bush came in his first three years in office to articulating a serious, comprehensive domestic agenda. Accompanying the speech was a 193-page document, "Building a Better America," prepared by his White House staff. The speech would outline the broad framework of his presidency and his priorities. "Building a Better America" supplied the details, along with proposed modifications to the last Reagan budget, submitted just a few weeks before Bush took office.

Rereading Bush's "Building a Better America" speech to the Congress after his one-term presidency is a strange experience now. Considerable portions of the text were devoted to domestic themes: education, the environment, drugs, crime, and future investment. His emphasis on education and the environment was designed as a clear departure from the Reagan years. Bush also listed as critical priorities reducing the federal budget deficit, meeting urgent priorities (unspecified), investing in the future, and, of course, the pledge that got him elected in the first place, "no new taxes." Furthermore, Bush himself laid out the contours of his economic empowerment agenda when he said: "I believe in giving people the power to make their own lives better through growth and opportunity. And together, let's put power in the hands of people."

But there was also something else at work behind the scenes in the crafting of Bush's "Building a Better America" speech that would prove a curious omen for the future of his presidency. Right from the beginning a battle was under way for George Bush's mind.

Sir Isaiah Berlin, the British historian of ideas, wrote memorably about the distinction between the hedgehog and the fox: "The fox knows many things, but the hedgehog knows one big thing."[6] Ronald Reagan was unmistakably a hedgehog—someone who lived by a "single, central vision, one system more or less coherent or articulate, in terms of which they understand, think and feel." Bush, by his own express contrast, was a fox, a man who would "pursue many ends, often unrelated and even contradictory, connected, if at all, only in some *de facto* way."[7]

No one should have been surprised by what turned out to be an early fight between the "hedgehogs" and the "foxes" inside the Bush Administration. The "hedgehogs" were the political and ideological heirs of Ronald Reagan, leaders like Jack Kemp, Bush's Secretary of Housing and Urban Development; Drug Czar William Bennett; and my fellow deputy Jim Pinkerton, who repeatedly urged that Bush advance a bold domestic agenda characterized by economic growth and opportunity, empowerment, and institutional reform. The reform theme was critical, since it would position Bush—like Reagan—as an outsider determined to bring change to a Washington dominated by special interests. A slogan from Bush's 1988 campaign even summarized this attitude: "We are the *Change*!"

The "foxes," by contrast, were represented by OMB Director Dick Darman, Roger Porter, and David Demarest. These were the process "pragmatists," true believers in the efficacy of government who wanted Bush to define himself not by advancing a strident, confrontational ideological message but by presenting a pastiche whose principal contours would emerge over time. The pragmatists stressed good government and sound day-to-day management. They spoke in terms that expressly distinguished campaigning from governing. Most important, they saw themselves as insiders, not outsiders, and in many respects—background, breeding, mostly Ivy League education—they were like George Bush himself.

As Bush prepared for his first major address to the Congress, Pinkerton reviewed the draft prepared principally by a former Bush speechwriter, then a Darman aide, Bob Grady. Pinkerton added language that had Bush emphasizing the importance of various reform themes. Pinkerton's additions were crafted to provide an emotional crescendo with a big buildup to a line that Bush would articulate with gusto and determination: ". . . for I am a reformer!"

Bush deleted Pinkerton's suggestions. In fact, the text came back with the following marginal comment in Bush's own handwriting: " 'for I am a reformer'? Strains credulity."

"We are the *Change!*" was long abandoned. It was never taken seriously.

From the earliest days of the Administration it would be "go along to get along." Ideology had lost out to competence.

But competence at doing what? Who would take the lead in charting the new Administration's future course?

The 1988 election saw the lowest voter turnout in any presidential election since 1924. Candidate Bush, if he galvanized the public with any of his campaign themes, did so with the one that most harked back to Reaganism: "Read my lips: no new taxes." The rest of the 1988 Bush campaign had been little more than a pollster's collage of themes—not agenda items or policy proposals, and certainly not promises—such as crime, race, the American flag, Willie Horton, and the line-item veto.

The triumph of competency and its companion, slavish adherence to process, meant a policy vacuum at the heart of Bush's presidency. Whereas Ronald Reagan had surrounded himself with advisers like Ed Meese, Jim Baker, Mike Deaver, Martin Anderson, and others who were constantly scheming among themselves, Bush placed a premium on politeness and collegiality. People were not expected to disagree with each other.

The absence of ideology coming from the Oval Office signalled an Administration lacking in direction. Even Gregg Petersmeyer, long a staff aide to Bush, remarked to me that George Bush was "a President who, intellectually, needed to be led." There was always lots of energy and motion in the Bush White House—early morning meetings, late nights, lots of press briefings, countless fact sheets announcing the details of one policy proposal after another. What was lacking, however, was a sense of purpose and direction. There was no focus.

Another noticeable and significant difference between the Reagan and Bush Administrations was the latter's persistent efforts at defining its differences with the wrong people. In his Inaugural Address Bush extended a hand to congressional Democrats. There was nothing wrong with this, especially given the fact that Bush lacked a majority coalition in both houses of Congress.

The principal difficulty was that the Bush White House far too often forgot to include congressional *Republicans* and others in the GOP who, had they been asked, would have been delighted to lend a hand. Frank Wolf, a Republican Representative, would recount to some of us how he had repeatedly written Darman and others at the White House urging a more activist pro-family agenda. Months passed before he received even a perfunctory reply. And then nothing happened. Not only were skilled former Reagan operatives like Ed Rollins and Lyn Nofziger virtually ignored or systematically derided by the Bushies, but Reagan's economic team—people like Martin Anderson, Martin Feldstein, William Niskanen, William Simon, Beryl Sprinkel, and Murray Weidenbaum—were intentionally excluded from the Bush Administration's policy discussions.

The fruits of this curious predilection—the need to coddle the Democratic opposition while simultaneously ignoring or even vilifying the Administration's natural GOP supporters—were abundantly present by the second year of the Bush Administration. During the 1990 budget deal talks at Andrews Air Force Base the Bush negotiating team of Treasury Secretary Nicholas Brady, Darman, and Sununu placed a premium on compromising with House and Senate Democrats. When some Republican congressmen, led by Representative Newt Gingrich, balked at the tax increases contained in the first deal, the Bush White House branded those renegade Republicans—not the tax-raising Democrats—as the villains.

Over time, the Administration's inability to undertake coalition-building also found expression in the way the Bush Administration conducted its relations with the Congress. Rather than define what he *favored*, Bush's strategy was to highlight what he *opposed*. Nothing illustrated this more than the way in which Bush exercised the presidential veto of legislation he didn't like.

Governing by veto—or, more precisely, governing by the *threat* of veto—came to be a hallmark of the Bush presidency. The veto threat was, after all, used sparingly in part because of the number of Democrats on Capitol Hill. Sustaining a veto in the House of Representatives meant holding 146 votes for the President, a difficult task given the margins between Democrats and Republicans. The numbers were somewhat more favorable in the Senate but kept getting significantly worse (especially after the 1990 elections), not better.

Given those congressional party divisions, a veto strategy became a game of chicken. Surprisingly, congressional Democrats and moderate-to-liberal Republicans never figured this out. If they had—and if they had been clever enough—they could easily have called the President's bluff more often or could even have mustered sufficient votes to override his vetoes.

Bush would rarely veto legislation unless he knew in advance that he had the votes necessary to sustain the veto. The issue was counting heads, not standing on principle. If Fred McClure or Nick Calio, his two assistants who headed his legislative shop, told him he was shy on votes, Bush rarely applied the veto. Simple as that.

What the Democrats failed to appreciate was that with each newly sustained veto, George Bush was becoming the captive of a no-override strategy. As his personal popularity soared in the polls, his advisers became increasingly addicted to preserving an unbroken string of sustained vetoes. To the public, this standard initially conveyed an aura of invincibility. To anyone concerned with principled policymaking, it often appeared supine and weak-willed. Occasionally it even meant an unfortunate break with perfectly sound positions taken by Ronald Reagan.

One minor but revealing example of how this passion for an unbroken string of vetoes overrode more prudent and consistent policy considerations was Bush's decision to sign the so-called kid-vid legislation regulating the number of minutes of commercial advertising on children's television programs. As enacted by Congress in September 1990, the "Children's Television Act" would have required the Federal Communications Commission to enforce strict limits on the number of minutes of commercial advertising that could be aired on children's television programs. During weekdays, no more than twelve minutes per hour were permitted. On weekends, particularly during the Saturday morning television period, only 10.5 minutes were permitted. The rationale for federal intervention was the fear that television commercials were influencing children to bedevil their parents to buy them all the various toys, cereals, candies, and other goodies dangled before them by the sponsors. In one way or another, the federal government just had to step in to address a situation that parents were deemed unable to handle.

Ronald Reagan—quite properly—had vetoed almost identical legislation in 1988. His veto statement explained that this legislation was unnecessary and that while it may have had "laudable goals," its provisions raised serious constitutional issues about the ability of the "Federal Government to oversee the programming decisions" of broadcasters. Consistent with his desire to keep the government out of matters of personal taste and individual decisionmaking, Reagan vetoed the bill on November 5, 1988, noting that the legislation might "discourage the creation of programs that might not satisfy the tastes of agency officials responsible for considering license renewals."

The facts and the Constitution had not changed in the intervening twenty-two months, nor had the details of the legislation, and yet, here was George Bush—for eight years during the Reagan Administration supposedly the archfoe of excessive government regulation—poised to sign this bill into law. What could possibly explain this reversal of Reagan's stance? I strongly objected to Bush's signing the bill and decided to find out why the President's "senior advisers" were recommending this clear break from Reagan policy.

So I went to see Roger Porter and handed him a memorandum I'd drafted explaining why signing the bill would be a mistake. First off, he acknowledged we lacked sufficient votes to sustain a veto. I said, so what? We were bound to lose a veto at some point, so why not lose it over a relatively small issue now and get the superstition behind us? Otherwise, our fear of losing would continue to distort our adherence to sound principle.

Porter told me politely that I didn't really appreciate or understand the problem. After all, he had four kids, and those Saturday morning ads on TV were awful. Something had to be done about them.

"Roger, it's simple," I argued. "Why not turn off the television set if it's a problem? After all, kids don't buy TVs, parents buy them."

Porter said it *wasn't* that easy: "Children visit their friends and watch the shows at their homes. I can't very well turn off those TVs too, can I?"

"Sure you can. Talk to those parents if it's really that bad. If the situation's out of control—which I seriously doubt is the case—keep your kids at home. Furthermore, a few seconds more or a few seconds less of advertising hardly makes a difference. We've preached stronger parental involvement as a hallmark of this Administration's education policy. If we sign this bill, it sends a contrary signal, particularly since Reagan vetoed it. Why does a paternalistic government—in this case the FCC—have to step in to deal with a problem that should be dealt with by parents?"

That's when the telephone rang and Porter, looking relieved, had to take the call, but only after noting again that we lacked the votes to sustain a veto. So much for the principle of parental involvement.

Bush did not actually sign the children's television legislation but instead let it become law without his signature. This was perhaps worse. The *New York Times* had endorsed the legislation and had specifically urged Bush "to take a careful look at what the market has wrought in children's television and come to a different conclusion" than Ronald Reagan. On October 17, 1990, Bush issued a statement indicating that he had "decided to withhold . . . approval from H.R. 1677, the 'Children's Television Act of 1990,' which will result in its becoming law without my signature." The President's statement applauded the bill's goals but decried its imposition of content-based restrictions on programming, the constitutional uncertainty of the limits imposed, and the quantitative advertising restrictions that applied to cable television operators. For all those reasons—plus Reagan's precedent—Bush should have vetoed the law. He didn't because he knew he would have been overridden.

The fate of the Republic hardly turned on this obscure statute. The major news media organizations never covered the story in much detail after the bill became law, with the exception of William F. Buckley's *National Review*, which criticized Bush for abandoning Reagan's staunch and principled opposition. What the kid-vid legislation signaled, however, was a willingness on Bush's part to sacrifice principle—even one consistent with his own emphasis on parental involvement in children's education—when he knew he lacked the votes to prevent a veto override.

By such instances was finger-in-the-wind "pragmatism" defined and stratospheric approval ratings maintained, at least initially. This mindset gave birth to a central characteristic of the Bush presidency: It would be a hesitant, timid, and reactive Administration, one which governed largely by thwarting the congressional Democrats' efforts through the skillful use of the presidential veto pen. Still, Bush's use of the veto in his first three years in office was relatively less frequent than that of many of his modern predecessors. By the end of 1991 Bush had vetoed some twenty-five bills, and the Congress had failed to override a single veto, although it had tried to do so thirteen times.

Domestically the Bush Administration, faced with a need to differentiate itself from Ronald Reagan, embarked consciously upon a strategy in which it defined its differences with the wrong people. Haunted by Reagan, Bush constantly looked backward to make sure that his Administration would be seen as somehow different from his predecessor's. He could have achieved the same result had he instead articulated a forward-looking vision and an agenda that would define his differences with the congressional Democrats. But he didn't, and the result was fratricidal warfare.

Congressional Democrats became the good guys with whom people like Dick Darman and Roger Porter could cut deals. Republicans like Jack Kemp, Newt Gingrich, Vin Weber, and Ed Rollins were readily dismissed as ideologues, loose cannons who lacked any appreciation for the art of compromise, which was seen as essential to the ability to govern. Whereas Reagan's popularity had a bedrock foundation in democratic populism, the Bush Administration identified almost reflexively with the important and powerful. Senior aides in the West Wing were profoundly uncomfortable when dealing with real people outside the Beltway.

Ronald Reagan entered Washington in 1981 as an outsider riding a populist wave that had its origin in the antitax and antigovernment movements at the state level, particularly California. Even during his eight years in Washington, Reagan always managed to position himself as a Washington outsider—someone working on behalf of the little guy against big government and the special interests that thrived "inside the Beltway."

Bush was the exact opposite, a man whose patrician upbringing and preference for elites was only masked, but hardly extinguished, by his preference for pork rinds, country music, and a voting address in a downtown Houston hotel room. In his autobiography, *Looking Forward*, George Bush describes his New England upbringing: "Maine in the summer was the best of all possible adventures. We'd spend long hours looking for starfish and sea urchins, while brown crabs scurried around our feet. . . . Then there was the adventure of climbing aboard my grandfather's lobster boat, *Tomboy*, to try our luck fishing." As the young Bush matured, he "graduated from outboard motors to powerboats" so that "[h]andling boats became second nature."[8] He and Barbara Bush moved to Texas after his graduation from Yale in an effort to "break away" from that upbringing[9] in order to avoid doing "anything pat and predictable."[10] But Bush's move to Texas was more a studied exercise in breaking with his own upbringing, a way to strike out on his own and make some money. Yet he never lost sight of his New England roots and continued to return to Kennebunkport—and boats, the sea, and lobsters—throughout his life.

By contrast, one could not imagine such sentiments coming from Ronald Reagan, whose own childhood was characterized by an alcoholic, often unemployed father and relative poverty in comparison with Bush's privileged background. The Reagan biographer Lou Cannon describes how Ronald Reagan

> . . . worked his way through an obscure, church-affiliated college, where his grades were never more than mediocre. Most of his classmates sought to become ministers or teachers, and his own ambitions to be a sports announcer or an actor seemed hopeless fantasies beyond his training and abilities.[11]

Given their backgrounds, the world views of these two future Presidents were at polar opposites. Bush felt the need to differentiate himself from his investment banker father—to make it on his own—as a means of legitimizing his own continued participation within that same world into which he had been born and where he would always be welcome. Reagan, by contrast, sought to leave his past behind and, braced by his fundamentally sunny disposition and relentless optimism, believed he could make a better world for himself.

Ronald Reagan had the easier task. With his past an unpleasant memory, Reagan was free to break entirely new ground, and he did repeatedly—becoming a sports announcer, an actor, a union president, a television spokesman, a two-term Governor of California, and, ultimately, President of the United States. For George Bush, on the other hand, the challenge to define his own separate identity had plagued him throughout his life. The *Boston Globe*—no admirer of George Bush—asked five months before the 1992 election whether Bush would "now say who he is." Specifically, the columnist Martin Nolan observed that "Bush faces a decision he has ducked for decades: whether to be more Texas or more Yale."[12]

George Bush's pattern of favoring the status quo is present in many aspects of his domestic policy. This predilection explains why initiatives like "economic empowerment" never made it to the forefront of Bush's policy agenda. Even his much-touted education reforms were shaped primarily with elites in mind, rarely with the desires of real people taken into consideration. Bush almost never missed an opportunity to take what should have been a populist crusade and turn it into an activity for the elites. Those contradictions were almost invariably lost on the President.

In April 1991, for example, Bush and Education Secretary Lamar Alexander launched their "America 2000" national education strategy to help the country meet the six education goals that Bush and the governors had announced in the months after the Charlottesville Education Summit. "America 2000" was conceived as a populist crusade to inspire communities across the country to work hard at improving their education systems. Its direction was to be, appropriately, bottom-up, not top-down.

Part of the strategy, however, was to involve the business community. The way that was ultimately done was a classic example of the Bush Administration's penchant for seizing a populist initiative and turning it topsy-turvy. Bush and Alexander urged the creation of a nongovernmental entity called the New American Schools Development Corporation (NASDC), which was to be privately incorporated and instructed to raise up to $200 million from corporate America—most notably from Fortune 500 firms. The donations were to finance revolutionary new "break-the-mold" school designs that could then be emulated or replicated by communities across America. David Kearns, Alexander's exceedingly capable Deputy Secretary and the former head of Xerox, oversaw NASDC's activities.

Membership in the New American Schools Development Corporation read like a *Who's Who* of corporate America: Lou Gerstner of RJR Nabisco, James Baker of Arvin Industries, Walter Annenberg of the Annenberg Foundation, Norman Augustine of Martin Marietta, and Kay Whitmore of Eastman Kodak were just a few of the nearly two dozen CEOs constituting NASDC's Board of Directors. At the corporation's first meeting in Washington, these luminaries of business gathered at the White House to meet with the President. Ushered into the Roosevelt Room, the board members eagerly awaited their opportunity to brief the President on how their efforts at school reform—once presumably all the money was raised—would transform American education. The President entered the room and spent some thirty minutes hearing about the general activities of the corporation to date. He praised the members for having raised $40 million so far.

But before long Bush's natural inclination to socialize with people like himself had kicked in. In a flash he was exuberantly inviting the NASDC board to visit with him and Barbara up at Camp David when they next got together in Washington. And bring along your spouses, too, he insisted. Which they did for sure just a few months later.

The point about this episode is not to criticize the President for being sociable or for wanting to share with others perquisites of the presidency like Camp David. But it does show that when left to his own devices, George Bush naturally gravitated toward elites and away from the populist masses. The same instinct explains why he doggedly followed the erroneous economic advice of men of vast inherited wealth like Brady and Darman while ignoring populist entrepreneurial capitalists like Jack Kemp or Vin Weber.

When a scheduling proposal was made for Bush to meet with some nonelite group—nonunion "independent" teachers, for example—a reflex against doing anything with a populist flair frequently kicked in. The concept of using the presidential "bully pulpit" to credential some nonestablishment (but otherwise pro-Republican) entity was foreign to the Bush White House.

Occasionally, there was even downright fear inside the West Wing when it came to the public. I can remember when Kimberly Bergalis, a young Florida woman who had contracted AIDS from her dentist, came to Washington to testify before Congress. Leigh Ann Metzger, a Special Assistant to the President in Public Liaison, called me one afternoon to ask if I would be free to meet with the visitor. I said, of course. My door was always open. The young woman was dying and wanted to have a chance to share her thoughts with someone at the White House as well as to see the Oval Office.

The next day Metzger called me back. Everything had been canceled. No meeting. No tour. No nothing at the White House for Miss Bergalis. When I asked why, I was informed that the meeting had been nixed at a higher level because of fear of adverse publicity!

As David Broder has remarked, the Bush Administration's penchant for dealing with elites manifested itself not only in domestic policy but in its foreign policy as well.[13] The collapse of Communism will probably be seen as the most significant event in the last decade, if not the last half, of the twentieth century. And once again, as with the economy, George Bush inherited Ronald Reagan's investment and proceeded to squander it.

The pressure—economic, political, and military—that Reagan brought against the Soviets gradually took hold and wore down their economic and political will. Coupled with Gorbachev's own efforts at *glasnost* and *perestroika* and furthered by continuing communications and technological advances, which made it harder for the Communist party to monopolize information and thereby retain authority, Reagan's policies reached fruition with the "Revolutions of 1989" throughout Eastern and central Europe.

The delegitimizing of Communist authoritarian and totalitarian regimes was accompanied by an odd reaction in Washington. The ruling foreign policy elites—the White House, State Department, and National Security Council staff—sought to bolster and preserve the legitimacy of their counterparts, the ruling Soviet elites. As it became increasingly evident that the old Communist order was indeed collapsing, the Bush Administration took the curious stance of seeking complicity with Gorbachev instead of encouraging the democratic reformers. Our "foreign policy" President was, once again, a passive observer of events unfolding around him, reacting rather than leading. Afraid of the new and unknown, the Bush Administration pointedly distanced itself from the reformers. The issue had once again become one of competence, not ideology.

Nothing illustrates this passive posture more than Bush's relationship with the leading Russian democratic reformer, Boris Yeltsin. During his first unofficial visit to Washington in 1989, Yeltsin was virtually ignored—snubbed by the Bush Administration—and openly slandered by Presidential aides, who participated in a whispering campaign against Yeltsin. Leaks about Yeltsin's reported drinking and other supposedly boorish habits found their way into the press. When Yeltsin visited the White House, Bush himself declined to receive him in the Oval Office, deciding instead to "drop by" the office of his National Security Adviser, General Brent Scowcroft, with whom Yeltsin was meeting informally.

Yeltsin next returned to Washington in June 1991, exactly one week after having been popularly elected president of Russia in a stunning landslide, the first democratically held election in Russia in a millennium. Bush met with him only after the congressional leadership and his own Vice President had extended cordial invitations. By now it was obvious to everyone—even to those in the West Wing of the White House—that Yeltsin was significantly more popular and more powerful than Gorbachev. This time, he could not be so readily ignored.

Yeltsin's visit was sponsored and coordinated in part by Allen Weinstein, head of the bipartisan Center for Democracy in Washington. Weeks prior to Yeltsin's visit and before his remarkable electoral victory, Weinstein had called me one afternoon with what he called "an offer you simply cannot refuse." Andrei Kozyrev, Yeltsin's foreign minister, was coming to Washington and was willing to speak to our White House "Empowerment Breakfast Group," which met every Friday morning in the West Wing basement. The question was whether I could persuade the National Security Council staff to approve such a visit.

Beginning in the fall of 1990, about twenty members of the White House staff gathered together for breakfast each Friday morning to hear from an outside speaker on the subject of domestic policy reform. We had met with Bill Bennett, Irving Kristol, Jack Kemp, Hernando de Soto, and many other notable and outspoken advocates of political and economic reform. We had extended our sessions to include foreign policy as well, having also heard from Ognian Pishev, Bulgaria's newly appointed Ambassador to the United States; Kazimierz Dziewanowski, the Polish Ambassador; and Weinstein himself. As it turned out, the NSC clearance—much to my surprise—went smoothly. The only problem was that Kozyrev had to change his schedule at the last minute to return to Moscow and canceled the breakfast. The fact remained, however, that the only direct link to the Yeltsin forces that I was aware of in the West Wing was my effort through Weinstein. Don't forget: I did *domestic*, not foreign policy.

But my role with Weinstein was not the only activity under way in the White House complex. Vice President Quayle and his staff, less reluctant about meeting with Yeltsin, quietly began making more favorable comments about how he should be handled during his forthcoming visit. That should have been a perfect opportunity for the Bush White House to open its arms to Yeltsin. By then the auguries about Gorbachev's future were clear, and yet Bush and his aides were in no hurry to begin ensuring at least a degree of continuity should Yeltsin ever replace Gorbachev.

As Weinstein explains his dealings with the Bush White House, "They had their antennas closed. It was a 'stand by Gorbachev' mentality. Whenever I needed to speak to someone at the White House I'd call Kolb, or Quayle's staff, Bill Kristol or Karl Jackson. The State Department actually objected to Quayle attending a dinner for Yeltsin that June." The Vice President ultimately attended and made exceedingly obvious his warmth and enthusiasm for Yeltsin.

As it turned out, Bush's June 1991 meeting was a godsend two months later when it was Yeltsin—the so-called drunk and bully— seen standing atop a Soviet tank preserving both democracy in the rapidly disintegrating Soviet Union and Mikhail Gorbachev's neck. The Bush Administration, preferring to deal with existing elites, had nearly blown it once again. Weinstein had also met with Yeltsin as recently as a week before the August 1991 putsch. As the drama was unfolding and Yeltsin's and Gorbachev's fates were unknown, Weinstein received numerous faxes and other communications directly from the Russian White House and from Foreign Minister Kozyrev. He shared them immediately with the Bush White House, where he got no reaction.

It was, after all, Ronald Reagan who had stood before the Berlin Wall and exhorted Mikhail Gorbachev to dismantle the barricade. By contrast, it was George Bush who delivered a speech in the Ukraine urging the reformers to cease their efforts and support the continuation of the Soviet Union.

A similar predilection for dealing with elites rather than real people also explains the curious position the Bush Administration took on democratic reform in China and later its benign neglect of the worsening situation in Yugoslavia. Bush's personal experience as U.S. Ambassador to China reinforced his loyalty to a regime that was systematically violating international human rights agreements, not to mention murdering its own people who were agitating for democratic reforms. The Administration's lame explanation of its policy hardly comported with Bush's lofty rhetoric on human rights or his principled articulation of a New World Order after the Persian Gulf War.

When it came to Yugoslavia, the same patterns evident with respect to the elites in the Soviet Union and China began to repeat themselves. In this case, however, the Bush Administration's inexplicable reluctance to endorse Croatian and Slovenian independence would return to haunt it during the 1992 reelection campaign.

The worsening crisis in central Europe made George Bush's decisiveness in the Persian Gulf look like an aberration. In retrospect, even his marvelously successful Persian Gulf War effort could not have been accomplished had it not been for the Reagan Administration's defense and arms policies. Yes, George Bush masterminded, coordinated, cajoled, and sustained a remarkable alliance among a disparate collection of countries—including the former Soviet Union—but the actual muscle and high-tech firepower needed to win were the direct consequence of the Reagan-era defense buildup, which bought and paid for the weapons. Investments in new weapons systems made during the 1980s paid off in the first major military engagement during the 1990s. Bush depleted the inventory and sent aloft the Stealth bombers, Tomahawk cruise missiles, and jet fighters to soften up the Iraqi enemy before launching the troops during the 100-hour battle. His crowning achievement as President was but one more reminder of how much his Administration owed to Ronald Reagan. And yet, with one Communist regime after another crumbling, the President's reluctance to support those emerging democracies led many to question whether the Administration truly understood the significance of what was happening and whether, with the Cold War ending, they were intellectually equipped to deal with these new situations.

Throughout his 1988 bid for the presidency, George Bush had Martin Van Buren very much on his mind. In the introduction to his autobiography, *Looking Forward*, George Bush acknowledged his familiarity with history:

> Martin Van Buren served as Andrew Jackson's vice president from 1833 to 1837. When Jackson left the White House, Van Buren succeeded him, defeating William Henry Harrison in the election of 1836. Since that time, reporters reminded me, no incumbent vice president has ever been elected to the presidency.[14]

Expecting to break the historical jinx, Bush noted that past campaigns, particularly the one in 1836, had "little or no bearing" on his own race in 1988. He then added the following prophetic observation: "even if [past campaigns were relevant], I have an ace in the hole: Shirley MacLaine—so I've been told—thinks I was Martin Van Buren in a former life."[15]

Bush became the first sitting Vice President since Van Buren in 1837 to succeed his predecessor to the presidency by election. But there were more ominous—and apparently overlooked—similarities between the two Presidents. Each was considered an aristocrat more in touch with Eastern moneyed interests (Bush presided over the massive savings and loan cleanup; Van Buren championed a national bank, which was opposed by Eastern workingmen and populists who were part of the Jefferson–Jackson tradition) than agrarian or working-class concerns. Both had been preceded by extremely popular men (Andrew Jackson and Ronald Reagan) who made lasting impressions on the political life of their generation. Interestingly, both faced political rivals named Clinton.

The historian Arthur M. Schlesinger, Jr., wrote of the Jacksonian reform period, "The driving energy of Jacksonian democracy, like that of any aggressive reform movement, came from a small group of men, joined together by essential sympathies in a concerted attempt to transform the existing order."[16] Schlesinger could as easily have been describing the Reagan years.

George Bush might have spent more of his time worrying about his similarities with Martin Van Buren than his differences from Ronald Reagan. Bush's principal hurdle had been to break the historical trend and get elected in the first place, but he had obviously neglected the full import of Shirley MacLaine's quip. For neither Martin Van Buren nor George Bush was capable of sustaining the momentum of his predecessor, and each was ultimately challenged for reelection by an opponent who championed fairness, class power, and the need for economic change. In many respects, each tried to "do it differently" in ways that effectively undermined his predecessor's records and his own success as well. Each man was limited to a single term by a populist challenger promising a new direction.

No other President in our history was as well prepared to assume the presidency as was George Bush. Yet Bush's lifetime of preparing for the nation's highest office translated into an Administration whose sights were aimed unnecessarily low and whose expectations and aspirations for America's future rarely advanced beyond uninspired platitudes.

The Bush Administration was a polite, not a political, operation. Compromise, camaraderie, and collegiality were the trademarks of Reagan's successors. Nowhere was this limited horizon more apparent than in the development of domestic policy.

The absence of ideological commitment—the lack of direction accompanied by an innate desire to respond to others rather than to initiate something itself—meant that the Bush Administration was often adrift without a rudder. In the Reagan days there were zealots—Jim Pinkerton affectionately called them the "nuts"—like Elliott Abrams, Assistant Secretary of State for Human Rights and later for Latin America, or Brad Reynolds, Assistant Attorney General for Civil Rights, with principled beliefs for which they paid dearly.

Men like Reynolds and Abrams and my former boss at the Education Department, Bill Bennett, were constantly battling inside the Administration to achieve Ronald Reagan's social and political goals. Don Regan, while a disaster as White House Chief of Staff, was a strong Treasury Secretary with sufficient clout to block efforts by David Stockman and Dick Darman (even then!) to raise taxes. There were also thoughtful, gifted people like Peggy Noonan and OMB General Counsel Michael Horowitz, whose energy and moral direction infused the Reagan Administration with agendas, options, and strategies for the social revolution it sought to achieve. Those people set the tone of the Administration and were indispensable to the policy and political successes achieved during the Reagan years.

Among the people nearest to George Bush, however, only Chief of Staff John Sununu came close to filling their shoes. And even his natural combativeness and disdain for internal debate was seriously eclipsed by an overall tone of "let's get along" with the opposition to achieve, if possible, marginal successes rather than bold triumphs.

The often-repeated excuse for these compromises was the need to govern rather than to pursue some abstract or abstruse ideological agenda. When it came to governing, Bush relegated ideology to the back seat and sometimes left it on the curb. Competence was indeed what mattered most, but the Bush Administration did nothing with the many talented officials it managed to attract.

According to Martin Anderson, Ronald Reagan's first domestic policy adviser, there were clear differences in the way policy was made in the early Reagan years and under George Bush:

"First of all, it was a misnomer under Reagan to speak of the Office of Policy Development. It wasn't that at all, notwithstanding the name. Remember that Ronald Reagan had spent ten or fifteen years developing and honing his message, and he locked it in during the campaign.

As a result, when we took over the White House in January 1981 there was not a hell of a lot of *new* policy for us to develop. Reagan had already done it. I thought of OPD as the Office of Policy *Implementation*. It wasn't going to be a supermarket of things to choose from like it was under Jimmy Carter.

"Ronald Reagan knew what he wanted to do. From the outset he set the priorities which everyone knew: national security and economic growth, and in the first eighteen months, 90 percent of our efforts were on economic policy."

Anderson was also emphatic in explaining that nobody inside the Reagan White House questioned the President's priorities. There were lots of arguments and debates, but they were mostly over details and were confined to the seventy or eighty working groups on policy that were established simultaneously while the two main themes were being pursued.

"We worked very hard on this," Anderson recalls. "I had ideas of my own, and I knew that Ronald Reagan liked them. So we were driving them. We were ruthless at it."

Once again, the contrast between the Bush White House and his predecessor's could not have been clearer. Bush enshrined process through his "Golden Rules" and ultimately substituted a flurry of activity for Reagan's more focused, principled development of policy. Reagan was the hedgehog, and the various working groups of foxes were established to complement the President's laserlike focus on the big picture. For Bush, there was no big picture, only foxes. There were multiple working groups operating in a vacuum without any overarching focus. Like our communications policy, domestic policy had become another mosaic. This structure became even worse when Sam Skinner replaced John Sununu. Martin Anderson put it succinctly when commenting on the various ways in which the Bushies set about to distinguish themselves from Ronald Reagan's successes: "That's dumb."

In the Bush White House everyone was, essentially, nice. People rarely disagreed or argued over matters of substance. Roger Porter, in particular, liked things that way.

At one of our daily OPD staff meetings, Porter read at length from a letter he'd received from one of our former colleagues, Andy Sieg, who'd returned to graduate school at Harvard. Sieg had attended an evening seminar at the Kennedy School of Government on the presidency where someone in the press had characterized the Bush Administration as consisting of relatively junior aides who were extremely loyal to the President and never engaged in the type of personal infighting and leaking of stories to the press that occasionally occurred in the Reagan years. Porter read the letter to us with considerable pride. Later I said to Pinkerton: "Yes, that's all true. But the reason there are no leaks is easy to understand: There's nothing to leak."

Ours was an Administration whose expectations were so low as to be virtually invisible. Policy disagreements rarely occurred, because there was a constant premium placed on harmony, inclusiveness, and, above all, politeness.

We were undoubtedly doing it differently from Ronald Reagan when it came to developing policy. The question, however, was what were we really doing? What kind of game were we up to when it came to developing policy in the Bush White House?

2

Playing Tennis

It's All Form

Young Bingo, you see, is one of those fellows who, once their fingers close over the handle of a tennis racket, fall into a sort of trance in which nothing outside the radius of the lawn exists for them. If you came up to Bingo in the middle of a set and told him that panthers were devouring his best friend in the kitchen garden, he would look at you and say, "Oh, ah?" or words to that effect.

—P.G. Wodehouse,
Very Good, Jeeves![1]

For the first three years of the Bush Administration, Roger Porter occupied the prestigious dark-panelled southeast corner office on the second floor of the West Wing. The notorious John Ehrlichman had worked there under Richard Nixon; Stuart Eizenstat occupied the office under Jimmy Carter; and Martin Anderson, Ed Harper, and conservative activist Gary Bauer served there under Ronald Reagan. Finally, it was Porter's.

On the wall just inside the door of Porter's office hung two seemingly identical framed black-and-white photographs, one above the other. The date was 1974, the location the White House tennis court: doubles with President Gerald Ford and George Bush on one side, and another individual and Roger Porter, then a thirty-year-old White

House Fellow on leave from Harvard to serve as staff secretary to Ford's Economic Policy Council, on the other. According to the *New York Times*, that was the first occasion on which George Bush met Roger Porter.

The top picture bore the following inscription: "To Roger Porter in appreciation of your warm kindness and loyal supporter [sic] and with admiration for your career accomplishments. Warm regards, Gerald Ford." The other picture is dated August 15, 1989, and is signed by George Bush with the following handwritten message: "Roger—Eye on the ball, Bend your knees! Same place, 15 years later."

The photographs are indeed identical. Bush had inscribed a duplicate of the 1974 picture to Porter as a memento of their long friendship. And while Porter and Bush—sometimes accompanied by Michael Boskin and Gregg Petersmeyer—still enjoyed playing doubles, things had very much changed during the intervening fifteen years for both men.

The tennis motif, memorialized on Porter's wall, was not incidental or accidental. Along with the tenets of his strict Mormon upbringing, reinforced by his four years as an undergraduate at Brigham Young University, the game of tennis played a central role in Roger Porter's outlook on life. Here's how the *New York Times*'s Maureen Dowd presented it in her 1990 profile of Porter:

> Roger Porter has a theory that you can learn a lot about people by watching them on the tennis court.
>
> Take Mr. Porter himself, an expert player who often plays doubles with President Bush.
>
> "A lot of players play impatiently," he says, talking about tennis and about life. "And it is not easy in tennis unless you're much better than your opponent, to score a lot of outright winners. My point is to win the point, but not to do it in any particular time frame."[2]

And what a point, indeed! Why rush? Why hurry? Take your time, and if you're lucky you can play a full four-year term, perhaps even eight years. Maybe the court also has lights, so the game can continue at night. (Unfortunately, the one at the White House doesn't, so the tennis—at least the tennis played outdoors—stops at sundown.)

Tennis was so essential to Porter's outlook that he used to regale his staff each year with stories from his weekend spent selecting the next crop of White House Fellows who would devote a year to gov-

ernment service working at the right hand usually of some Cabinet
Secretary, Deputy Secretary, or senior White House aide. Each year
he would select a Fellow to serve in the Office of Policy Development, and we would hear how he judged prospective Fellows on the
basis of their tenacity on the tennis court.

Did any of this make a difference in the White House Fellows
selection process? It's hard to tell, but what was interesting was the
fact that during my first year at the White House, Porter asked me to
help in the selection process to determine which Fellow should be
offered a position in OPD. The incumbent Fellow who'd been selected the previous year—a bright young lawyer who'd also clerked
for a Supreme Court Justice—and I both agreed on the same candidate, who was a quadriplegic. Our choice happened to be an expert on
health care for the disabled with a proven record of published articles
and academic achievement. He was, needless to say, someone who
had also overcome immense obstacles. But Porter chose someone
else, also an exceptionally talented person. Porter told us how he was
taken with this young man who, while demonstrating absolutely no
tennis form whatsoever, revealed an aggressive intensity in running all
over the court to retrieve the ball. This would have been difficult, no
doubt, for someone in a wheelchair.

Porter joined the Bush Administration at its outset, once again
leaving behind his tenured position at Harvard's Kennedy School.
Having sat out the Carter presidency, Porter returned to Washington
during the Reagan years to hold a series of junior and mid-level
economic and domestic policy staff positions under more senior Reagan advisers such as Martin Anderson and Ed Harper. In each instance Porter played second fiddle to someone else: He was the
consummate staff member devoted to ensuring the integrity of the
process rather than the content of the policy. As one former member
of the Reagan Administration remarked, "Roger is great when it
comes to following process, in making sure that all sides are faithfully
represented in the deliberations and summarized in the staff memorandum that ultimately gets to the President. But don't expect a lot of
innovation or creativity coming from him. That's just not his forte."

"Eye on the ball" is one way to put it, and keep the ball within the
lines of the court. Don't really look for winners. Lob a lot. Stray a little
too far in any direction and you lose the point. Maybe even your job.

The game of tennis came to characterize much of what happened in economic and domestic policymaking at the Bush White House, and Porter, a nationally ranked tennis player during his college days in Provo, Utah, and later while a Rhodes Scholar at Oxford, brought a tennis mentality to the conduct of economic and domestic policy in the Bush Administration. Rather than set a new, bold, imaginative, or politically relevant agenda, Porter preferred to continue to play the role of loyal staff member, an unfortunate attitude, given his considerable talents and experience, that left him at the mercy of more aggressive colleagues like Richard Darman. Rather than play a leading role in developing most of the Bush Administration's domestic and economic policy initiatives, Porter was content to operate within the confines of somebody else's rules. He worked on whatever Sununu, Darman, or the President told him to work on. Except for national education policy (principally at the K–12 level), Porter preferred to hew to a safe script and systematically avoided areas— such as civil rights or the Administration's inert economic opportunity agenda—that would prove divisive, controversial, ideological, or ultimately partisan.

Bush placed Porter in charge of one of the most critical White House Offices, the Office of Policy Development. OPD was "an office meant to matter," according to Jim Cicconi, a senior Bush aide who had been instrumental in recommending Porter for the job. Porter had been offered, and was on the verge of accepting, a position as principal deputy trade representative under Carla Hills when the senior White House staff position came his way. Having always been a deputy to someone else, Porter eagerly accepted this more elevated assignment. Bush also gave him the dual title of Assistant to the President for Economic and Domestic Policy. Porter, in fact, insisted on the title as a condition of taking a position in the Bush White House. From the beginning of the Administration, Porter assembled an exceptional team of policy analysts, lawyers, and experts, many selected from among his former Kennedy School students.

Porter brought back to the White House as his first Deputy for Domestic Policy Dr. William L. Roper, a former White House Fellow who was also a licensed pediatrician. During the Reagan years, after his fellowship had ended, Roper played an increasingly central role in formulating Administration health care policy. One of his key assignments was heading a task force on medical malpractice liability reform, and thereafter serving as Administrator of the massive Health Care

Financing Administration, where he oversaw the multibillion-dollar Medicare and Medicaid programs. During the first year of the Bush Administration, Roper worked closely with C. Boyden Gray, the President's legal counsel, to secure passage of the Americans with Disabilities Act. After thirteen months at the White House, Roper and his family moved to Atlanta, where he took charge of the Centers for Disease Control.

Roper was typical of the people Porter chose to join the Office of Policy Development staff: quiet, self-effacing, extremely capable, experienced in public policy, and low-key in style. Virtually all of the people recruited for OPD enjoyed one or more of the elite credentials that Porter displayed himself: Ivy League, Oxford, Rhodes Scholar, Supreme Court clerk, or White House Fellow. The problem, however, was that all this talent was chained up, shackled, and ultimately squandered by a passion for staff-level trivia and minutiae that lost sight of the big picture. Porter's own previous White House experience and timid makeup gave him a much narrower focus than might otherwise have been suspected given his title and supposed closeness with the President, not to mention Porter's own experiences and judgment.

In a speech on the presidency delivered nearly a decade earlier during the years of exile under Carter, Porter had warned about becoming preoccupied with minutiae: "[T]he President must not be gripped by what the historian Thomas Bailey had called 'the tyranny of the trivial.' "[3] Yet Porter would send his staff a memorandum on September 7, 1990, on "OPD 'Source Reduction,' " which began as follows:

> I very much appreciate the efforts each of you has made to comply with the new White House recycling program. Your assistance in separating newspapers and aluminum cans for recycling enables the White House to conserve natural resources and set an example for the country.

When it came to the issue of setting an example for the country on an important issue like family and parental leave, however, Porter was rarely heard from.

The Bush Administration had consistently taken a firm stance against congressional legislation that would mandate family and medical leave. This was sound policy: More than 80 percent of employees covered by collective bargaining agreements already received job-protected medical leave of eight weeks or more, and many employers had their own family leave policies. Moreover, there was no need for another one-size-fits-all government mandate on American businesses. Many companies were heading in this direction already and didn't need the heavy hand of government to make them do the correct thing.

In July 1990 Porter sent a memorandum to Sununu following up on a suggestion by Bobbie Kilberg, a fellow Deputy Assistant to the President, that both the Office of Personnel Management and, more particularly, the White House itself issue their own voluntary family leave policy statements. This was a smart idea: At the same time we were opposing a mandate on the ground that the leave policy was happening anyway, we would have behaved consistently with the premises of our own policy and set our own house in order.

Porter's memo went to Sununu, to Andy Card, to Ede Holiday (the Cabinet Affairs Secretary), and even to the President. Nothing ever happened. Everyone agreed that the suggested policy was correct, but the issue and the memos went round and round. Every six months or so someone would raise it—usually in conjunction with the latest congressional effort to revive the legislation—but neither Porter (supposedly in charge of domestic policy) nor anyone else would see the matter to fruition.

Porter treated himself as if he were still junior White House staff. He was all over most of his staff when it came to hands-on micro-management of his and their daily affairs. Delegation didn't exist, even when it came to simple matters like hiring a secretary for an OPD staffer. Consequently, his staff was trivialized and demeaned even further. By the morning I got to the White House in May 1990, the staff was seething in frustration, a fact totally lost on Porter. Eye on the ball . . .

Porter's other deputy was 6-foot, 7-inch Jim Pinkerton, who occupied a spacious corner office on the second floor of the Old Executive Office Building adjacent to the White House. While most real estate agents believe that "location is everything," Pinkerton soon convinced me that working in the West Wing had some definite downsides. Being farther away from Porter meant that it was easier just to forge ahead and *do* something. Permission (or an apology) could come later.

Because of his work in the 1988 campaign on opposition research, Pinkerton was accorded a position within the Bush Administration that permitted him to focus less on the day-to-day development of policy and more on long-range planning. His mini-think tank in the Old Executive Office Building comprised two or three staff members who helped him in researching and writing issue papers, speeches, and articles that took a more extended view of the Bush Administration's agenda. Not being in the West Wing ensured that he would not have to spend much time working on Porter's favorite pastime, the development of detailed "fact sheets" whenever a new policy initiative was launched. Pinkerton once warned me about the downside of having an office next to Porter's: I would always run the risk of becoming "Roperized"—having my time squandered on relatively useless exercises that produced paper, summarized a meeting, or satisfied some internal process but had virtually no meaningful consequences.

Porter was extremely jealous of access in the White House—to the President, to Sununu, even to the speechwriters. He was a borderline control freak, insisting that almost every piece of paper leaving the Office of Policy Development be routed through him. He became worried lest some more junior staffer develop an independent relationship with a high potentate in the complex or, especially, the West Wing.

In part because of his location and his campaign work, Pinkerton had done precisely that when it came to reviewing the President's speeches, and it drove Porter crazy. Staff Secretary Jim Cicconi, who knew Pinkerton well and encouraged his involvement in crafting presidential language, routinely sent Pinkerton advance copies of Bush's speeches for review. Cicconi also enjoyed the full backing of Sununu in keeping Pinkerton in the loop. The comments, usually drafted by Pinkerton or his assistant Austen Furse, bypassed Porter and went directly back to Cicconi or the speechwriters.

When Cicconi left the White House in late 1990 to return to his law practice, he advised incoming Staff Secretary Phil Brady to continue the practice. Pinkerton and Furse—two of the cleverest minds in the entire complex—made vast improvements in presidential speeches. They were no threat to their speechwriting colleagues; they offered always welcome help.

Porter saw it differently. No sooner was Cicconi out the gate than Porter asked that Brady stop the practice. Brady did, and Pinkerton and thereafter Furse rarely saw a draft presidential speech unless it had been first routed to them expressly by Porter.

A prime example of Porter's ability to trivialize himself and his staff was his hopeless addiction to the "memcon," the memorandum of conversation. Whenever a significant meeting had ended, especially one he had been unable to attend, Porter usually asked the staff member who attended it to prepare a memorandum of the meeting. Of course, everyone knew the main purpose of this exercise: to produce a document that Porter could then place in his elaborate personal filing system to form the background material for his next book about White House decisionmaking. Porter himself kept detailed notes on every meeting he attended, starting with a list of the people attending and including verbatim quotes.

The earliest fruits of these efforts may be seen in Porter's book *Presidential Decision Making*, published in 1980 by Cambridge University Press. The book describes in detail the operation of Gerald Ford's Economic Policy Board. Interestingly, the book's index includes fifteen references to Porter himself. Most of the references, however, are to the fact that Porter was present at a particular meeting. Only five include something substantive that Porter actually said or contributed.

Porter evidently saw his role in the Bush Administration as that of managing the process, not advocating any particular approach, outcome, or direction. His Reagan Administration precedessors, on the other hand, had been *zealous* partisans in developing policies that reflected Ronald Reagan's governing principles. Since Bush himself lacked a concrete domestic vision, Porter was left with virtually nothing to manage except the discrete assignments his superiors asked him to undertake. The thought of actually initiating something himself was just not part of his intellectual, emotional, or experiential makeup.

One of Porter's closest friends in Washington, his mentor and boss in the Ford Administration, L. William Seidman, was serving Bush as Chairman of the Federal Deposit Insurance Corporation. In *Presidential Decision Making*, Porter describes his mentor's role under Gerald Ford in terms that were completely applicable to himself fifteen years later. Take the following passage and replace "Seidman" with "Porter," and you'll have an accurate depiction of how Roger Porter functioned in the Bush White House:

Seidman's willingness to accept relative anonymity surprised and per-
plexed many other White House and executive branch officials. He
resisted the lure of becoming a principal spokesman for and defender
of the administration's economic policies by maintaining a low public
profile. . . .

Seidman felt that if he became an active public spokesman for the
administration's policy, it could limit his ability to preside impartially
over the policy development process. In short, Seidman viewed the
roles of advocate and, to a somewhat lesser extent, public spokesman as
conflicting with his most important responsibility of honest broker and
policy manager.[4]

Given this philosophy, the obvious question, then, was *who* developed
the various substantive options? Porter's honest-broker mentality left
him wholly at the mercy of more ambitious and aggressive players like
OMB's Darman (and Darman's chief aides) or William Reilly, the
Administrator of the Environmental Protection Agency.

What few outsiders realized about Porter is that he was actually
quite frustrated in the job as domestic and economic policy adviser.
Although he never admitted it publicly, he had fervently hoped Bush
would name him Director of the Office of Management and Budget.
Instead, he found himself in charge of an office that had relatively
undefined responsibilities and virtually no power. That didn't have to
be the case. The Office of Policy Development in the Reagan years
enjoyed both a higher profile and considerably more clout. It came as
no surprise, then, to discover Porter quietly and embarrassingly de-
ferring to Darman or others whenever contentious issues arose. It was
always safer to play the dutiful scribe, retreating to one's office to
spend countless hours in drafting a White House fact sheet describing
whatever the latest policy initiative (developed by someone else, of
course) might be. Porter was simply unwilling to do or say anything
that would result in controversy. Matters could have been dramatically different for Porter had he chosen to show some gumption and
turn loose his staff.

In late 1991 Porter took a rare and unexplained week's leave, reportedly to undergo surgery. He went to great lengths to explain to his
staff and others around the White House that his medical problems
stemmed from a bad back. His absence prompted one Administration
wag to remark that Porter had undergone back surgery to have a spine
inserted.

According to Pinkerton, "Porter's approach [to his White House job] makes sense if your ambition in life is to be domestic policy adviser to every Republican president in the latter years of the twentieth century." If, on the other hand, the goal was to advance a solid agenda, Porter's strategy was an abject failure.

For all his meticulous attention to detail and process, Porter had relatively little to show for his efforts. His long hours were legendary, and he almost always found an excuse to announce at staff meetings that he'd left the office at 2 A.M. or arrived at 4:30 A.M. (or occasionally both on the same day). Porter was famous for having multiple in-boxes (as many as six) in his office to handle his massive paper flow. One of his White House peers quipped: "The only problem was that Roger never had an out-box."

Porter's operating style was a literal example of letting the perfect be the enemy of the good. For example, on the day of Bush's second State of the Union Address in January 1990, Porter dithered so long over the speech's fact sheet that it was of relatively little use to the White House press corps covering the address. After all, they had the text in advance. Porter was famous for calling his more junior staff at all hours of the day or night or on weekends, keeping them in his office until the wee hours of the morning (while he worked and watched C-Span or televised tennis matches throughout the night), and calling them in to the office on Super Bowl Sunday with nothing of substance for them to work on. When it came to White House fact sheets (particularly such big ones as those accompanying a State of the Union address), Porter would spend countless hours worrying over such trivia as font sizes and the width of page margins. He would have one staff member, usually Hanns Kuttner (affectionately nicknamed the "Fontmeister"), run seemingly endless trials of different page formats, over and over again, before finally settling on the most aesthetically pleasing format. The exercise was then repeated for the next year's State of the Union address as if it had never been done before.

Porter was not lazy. He was, however, unimaginative, an apparatchik whose first passion was process. Some members of his staff joked occasionally about printing lapel buttons saying "Born to Process" and then wearing them around the White House and Old Executive Office Building corridors. When it came to substance, on the other hand, he was so reticent as to be literally a nonplayer.

An example:

For months during late 1990 and early 1991, I had been urging Porter to focus on child adoption policies as a critical Republican issue for the 1992 election. If, after all, the GOP platform was to continue its staunch anti-abortion position, then it seemed to me a wise move to temper that message with a more affirmative position on adoption. If mothers were expected to carry unwanted pregnancies to term, then it made sense to eliminate barriers to adoption, either through proposing a nonpreemptive model state statute or by focusing on specific ways to provide incentives for easier, speedier adoptions all across the country.

Each of the memoranda I sent to Porter came back with his usual handwritten comment, "Interesting. Let's discuss." I had learned after a few weeks on the job that this response was code for "Interesting. Forget it."

Which, of course, I did not. I peddled the concept elsewhere in the West Wing, eventually interesting some of the Cabinet Affairs staff in pursuing the idea.

In late January 1991, however, Porter went by himself to the Capitol to meet with the minority Senate staff to hear from them what they expected the principal legislative items to be during the coming year. Afterward, Porter returned to the White House and rattled off his findings at one of our staff meetings. I sat there stunned to hear Porter indicate that—only because Senator Lloyd Bentsen was expected to come up with some pro-adoption proposals—we should begin thinking ourselves about how to deal with this issue!

This example was but one of dozens demonstrating the remarkably reactive posture of the Bush White House when it came to domestic policy. By that time we had wasted some six months because no one above him had told Porter to investigate the issue. The implication was clear: If you want to move forward on a domestic policy initiative in the Bush Administration, forget trying to persuade someone in the West Wing of the White House. First get some Democrat (or, later, Pat Buchanan) to introduce your idea, then the scramble would set in at 1600 Pennsylvania Avenue.

By contrast, there were occasions where Porter could be both forceful and didactic. He had an ability to chew up innumerable hours lecturing his staff about some tedious aspect of policy. In countless meetings, Porter would pontificate for thirty minutes or more in a pointless monologue describing to his audience (usually our staff) the history of education reform in the Bush Administration, beginning with the Charlottesville Summit. But this endeavor, after all, offered Porter a safe harbor: There were virtually no federal dollars involved and therefore little opportunity to clash with Darman.

Porter once made the mistake of lecturing Diane Ravitch (a distinguished education historian who headed the Education Department's research office) and David Kearns (the former head of Xerox, whom Bush recruited as Deputy Secretary of Education) on education policy. Ravitch and Kearns sat patiently and politely through Porter's monologue, which served only to divert discussion from its intended purpose: setting achievement standards for America's children and schools. There was no need for Porter to lecture two eminent experts on subjects they already knew well. Ravitch left the West Wing beside herself with anger. She called me the next day with an observation and a question about Porter: "I certainly don't think much of your boss. Is he always like that?"

Porter could waste endless staff hours on meaningless activities. He could even totally ignore critical issues like higher education policy, but he had all the time and patience in the world when it came to PEPAC. In fact, you might say that Porter had a veritable passion for PEPAC.

You ask, "What's PEPAC?" The President's Education Policy Advisory Committee, which consisted of twenty-some high-powered corporate executives (David Kearns before he joined the Administration in 1991, Paul O'Neill from Alcoa), education experts (Checker Finn, Joe Nathan), and prominent political or public figures (former New Jersey Governor Tom Kean and the incumbent Education Secretary) among others. They were charged with advising Bush on national education policies. PEPAC also included the leaders of the two major teachers' unions, Al Shanker of the American Federation of Teachers and Keith Geiger of the National Education Association.

By and large PEPAC's membership was distinguished. It just never did anything of consequence. Its members would meet in the Roosevelt Room or in Room 180 of the Old Executive Office Building (Nixon's old hideaway office) and debate the merits of the national education goals, school choice, standards and assessment, or some other aspect of national education policy. At most, the members of PEPAC endorsed what we were already doing, but the fact that

PEPAC was largely irrelevant never stopped Roger Porter from de-voting hundreds of hours of staff time (including his own) in prepar-ing for and attempting to script its meetings, which were held every three or four months.

At the end of 1990, as PEPAC's initial charter was about to expire, I suggested to Porter that we change its membership by replacing Shanker and Geiger with people actively working to further the Pres-ident's education agenda—people like Milwaukee's Polly Williams, Pat Rooney from the Golden Rule Insurance Company, or other school-choice advocates.

Porter disagreed. There was a real benefit, he told me, in having Geiger and Shanker on the Committee, even though they were con-stantly criticizing the Administration in public. At least we would always be able to say we had consulted with them on various educa-tion policies. That point was lost on me. Geiger and Shanker each wrote weekly newspaper columns in which they almost invariably skewered the President or his Administration. As I saw it, all we were accomplishing was to give them a more effective bully pulpit to use against us. Why not use PEPAC appointments and other presidential advisory committees to help credential people who could actually help advance *our* agenda?

Porter won out, and both Geiger and Shanker remained. A year later, late in 1991, Keith Geiger became the first major union leader to declare that Bush should not be reelected in 1992. And we were still welcoming him into the White House! It was dumb.

In the end, however, PEPAC wasn't a total waste of time, although its biggest success had nothing at all to do with domestic or education policy. It came in foreign policy or, more precisely, military *dis*infor-mation.

Operation Desert Storm was launched in the early evening hours of January 16, 1991. The only scheduled public event on the President's calendar that afternoon was a 2 P.M. meeting with PEPAC in the Cabinet Room. The President showed up on time and also made sure that the White House press pool was summoned to photograph and videotape him flanked by Paul O'Neill and Education Secretary-designate Lamar Alexander. The film footage ran on CNN through-out most of the afternoon. Here was the Commander-in-Chief surrounded by his education policy experts, conveying the unmistak-able message that cruise missiles headed for Baghdad were the farthest thing from his mind. By dinnertime, Saddam Hussein—reportedly an avid CNN watcher—was receiving somewhat different signals as the sea-launched Tomahawks were beginning to reach their targets in Iraq. PEPAC had finally accomplished something of substance.

I soon learned that sending a memorandum to Porter with a suggestion was the kiss of death. So I developed a healthy circulation list of "blind copies" that I sent all over the White House to try to engage others in pursuing a particular proposal. The "usual suspects" who received these missives were Jim Pinkerton and Richard Porter; John Schall in Cabinet Affairs; Tony Snow, the chief speechwriter; Alan Hubbard, who served as the first executive director of Dan Quayle's Council on Competitiveness; and Quayle's chief of staff, Bill Kristol. While this cumbersome approach to policy development occasionally led to some notable successes, it was an extremely inefficient and frustrating way of trying to promote reform ideas in an Administration that through 1991 was becoming increasingly identified with the status quo. For those of us looking ahead to the 1992 reelection campaign, a do-nothing first term would brand George Bush as little more than a twelve-year incumbent with few ideas about where to take America as it approached the end of the twenty-first century. A lingering economic recession would only reinforce this impression.

As long as the economy remained robust, however, the public would probably never even know that the Administration was repeatedly missing several opportunities to advance a new agenda. In fact, even as late as the aftermath of the Persian Gulf War in February 1991, President Bush was talking explicitly about maintaining the status quo. Even when he had a tremendous opportunity to advance his legislative agenda before the Congress, in the wake of his Persian Gulf victory and soaring popularity, Bush called upon the Congress to pass only two measures in the succeeding hundred days: crime and transportation bills that were offered without any convincing rationale.

Another example of how the internal policy development process worked in the Bush White House under Porter is the way we decided to make legal reform one of the Bush Administration's principal domestic policy ideas. Shortly after arriving at the White House in May 1990, I wrote Porter a memorandum proposing several new ideas for domestic policy initiatives, one of which included reforming the legal system. In particular, I was keen on advancing the so-called English Rule—the practice followed in civil litigation in England and other countries whereby the losing party in a lawsuit pays not only his own costs and attorney's fees but those of his opponent as well. Adopting a "loser pays" approach in the United States would represent a fundamental—indeed, radical—change in the way lawsuits were filed and would, in my judgment, alter the calculation a suing plaintiff made *before* filing a complaint. The most probable result would be a dramatic reduction in the number of lawsuits filed.

As usual, I got no reaction from Roger Porter, so I began shopping the idea elsewhere. Frankly, Porter's nonreaction was somewhat surprising, because he had been influential in advancing the Administration's "tort reform" package consisting of state-level modifications to the handling of medical malpractice claims. A much broader set of legal reforms would have popular appeal going well beyond the narrow, albeit important, audience of the nation's medical profession.

When Porter failed to respond, I mentioned it one day over lunch with Alan Hubbard. An Indiana businessman whom Quayle had brought to Washington to run his Council on Competitiveness, Hubbard held both M.B.A. and J.D. degrees from Harvard. Aware of how much the American people disliked lawyers, Hubbard liked the idea. Advancing an appropriately American version of the English Rule in a well-chosen set of cases would vastly improve the operation of justice in America by curbing our seemingly endless appetite for lawsuits. Such reform would also represent a major populist initiative.

Hubbard pitched the idea to Quayle, who liked it immediately and took the unusual step of asking Solicitor General Kenneth Starr to head a Working Group on Legal Reform to make recommendations to the Competitiveness Council. A former federal appeals court judge, Starr served as the federal government's chief litigator before the Supreme Court. In such a position—which placed him at the top of many people's short list for filling the next Supreme Court vacancy— Starr ordinarily would not have been asked to undertake a task likely to take on a partisan coloring for the Administration.

After eight months of deliberation, Starr produced some two dozen recommendations, which included a limited version of the English Rule to be tried in federal diversity cases. Along with discovery reforms, the expanded use of alternate dispute resolution mechanisms, and several other new ideas, the Starr proposals were hard-hitting and likely to generate substantial controversy among members of the bar.

While I sat on the Staff Working Group and repeatedly urged adoption of a version of the English Rule as well as various other reforms, Porter played no role in the process. It was evident to me that he failed to see how important these ideas could be, especially as we moved closer to the 1992 election. Aside from medical malpractice legislation, the only other legal policy issue Porter became engaged in was the Administration's crime bill, a rather limited legislative proposal that emphasized reforming the *habeas corpus* law, extending the reach of the death penalty, and modifying the Fourth Amendment's "exclusionary rule." While all of those reforms were substantively sound, they didn't exactly galvanize massive popular support, in part because Porter and others never succeeded in explaining them in ways that related to the average man or woman on the street. Terms like *"habeas corpus"* and "exclusionary rule" don't exactly stir the masses, although they would no doubt spark a rip-roaring debate at Harvard's Kennedy School.

Legal reform—or civil justice reform, as it became known—caught on almost from the start. When Quayle unveiled his proposals in August 1991 at the Atlanta convention of the American Bar Association, he received the expected negative reaction from the organized bar, but the reforms played well throughout the rest of the country. Not only had Quayle found a serious issue that captured the fascination of many Americans who loathed lawyers, but he had begun to give shape to one of the key "reform" ideas that, along with health care, welfare, education, and government, would constitute the centerpiece of George Bush's 1992 campaign theme.

Again, Roger Porter remained blissfully unaware of just how powerful the reform theme was to become in the months ahead. Shortly after Quayle announced his package of civil justice reforms, I had lunch in Washington with Dorothy Moss, Director of Federal Affairs for the American Medical Association. Most of our discussion that afternoon involved the ongoing dispute between the Bush Administration and the nation's doctors over physician payment procedures in the massive and complex Medicare program, as well as the prospects for an Administration-sponsored health care reform package sometime in 1992.

Relations between the Administration and the AMA had grown strained because of the recurring disputes over physician payments.

Nonetheless, I believed that when it came to civil justice reform— after all, who detested lawyers any more than the country's physicians?—there was a strong identity of interest between the AMA and the Administration. So I proposed to Moss that she talk with AMA Executive Vice President James Todd about the possibility that the AMA might explicitly endorse the Administration's legal reforms. If we could perhaps forge an alliance on something in which we both felt a strong interest, perhaps other differences could be settled as well.

Moss liked my suggestion and carried it directly to Todd. Within a few weeks, the AMA had not only endorsed the Bush Administration's civil justice reforms but had invited me to attend its annual convention in Los Angeles to participate in two seminars on the proposals. I was pleased. So was the AMA.

But Roger Porter wasn't. The AMA conference was scheduled for mid-January 1992. Announcements had been printed indicating that I would be on a panel to discuss civil justice reform. Approximately three weeks before the conference, I told Porter what had been arranged. Much to my surprise, he vetoed my attending. As he put it, "Why should we be helping out the AMA? All they've been doing is giving the Administration grief."

I was incredulous. So was Dorothy Moss when I telephoned to explain that I couldn't attend. The official excuse I gave her was the pressing need to stay in Washington to prepare for the President's State of the Union address, scheduled for January 28, 1992. (The Office of Policy Development was again on its annual State of the Union fact sheet alert.) Not wanting the AMA left speakerless, I turned to Quayle's legal counsel, John Howard, explained to him Porter's ridiculous reaction, and asked him if he was interested in attending for me. Shaking his head and expressing his disbelief, Howard graciously took my place in Los Angeles. Otherwise, we would have blown a splendid opportunity to explain the President's civil justice reform proposals to a major organization that could have helped us advance our legal reform agenda.

Another legal issue—implementation of the Supreme Court's *Beck* decision—was supposedly an Administration priority, but Porter never engaged in this battle either. In 1989 the Supreme Court had ruled that nonunion members working under a collective labor contract did not have to contribute funds to unions when the money went for purposes other than collective bargaining. In short, these members could demand the refund of any of their dues that went to support lobbying or political activities unrelated to official collective bargaining representation. Enforcing this decision could have meant the loss of tens of millions of dollars used by the nation's labor unions to pursue political causes in Washington and elsewhere throughout the country.

Implementing the *Beck* decision required the Labor Department and the National Labor Relations Board to force unions to notify their members of their rights to request dues refunds, but no senior official in the Bush White House actively began pursuing the issue until after Pat Buchanan, the conservative challenger, began pushing Bush to the right in early 1992. Reportedly in 1991 Bush had himself read an article in the *Wall Street Journal* about the need to move ahead with implementing the three-year-old Supreme Court ruling. The fact remains: nothing happened.

White House Counsel Boyden Gray also had long supported *Beck* implementation, but until Bush needed a more conservative agenda after Buchanan's strong challenge in the New Hampshire primary, Bush's policy advisers simply refused to promote the issue, even after the President had raised it himself. Fred Barnes, a *New Republic* writer, explains the hilarious way in which *Beck* implementation finally got some momentum when Jay Lefkowitz, an extremely able but also at the time a relatively junior staffer, literally ran into Chief of Staff Sam Skinner in the White House basement. According to Barnes, their fateful collision produced the following exchange between Lefkowitz and the Chief of Staff:

> "What are you working on?" Skinner asked. "I want to get this *Beck* decision implemented," Lefkowitz replied. Skinner perked up, knowing Bush's long-standing interest. The Supreme Court had ruled in 1988 . . . that a non-union worker is not required to pay the part of union dues that goes for political activity. Lefkowitz told Skinner that Harry Beck, the electronics technician who won the case, and actor Charlton Heston, who'd lobbied Bush to follow through on the ruling, were available for a White House appearance. So Skinner instantly arranged a Rose Garden event for April 13, when Bush signed an executive order instructing federal contractors to inform non-union workers that they don't have to pay for union politicking."[5]

Exaggeration? Only slightly. The fact is that the President had sent Porter a note about *Beck* implementation the previous August after seeing a *Wall Street Journal* article on the fact that the White House under Bush had done nothing. But even after Bush raised the matter again, months passed before anything happened. Incidentally, that Barnes article sparked anger on the second floor of the West Wing. On the ground floor, however, Sununu's successor as Chief of Staff, Sam Skinner—according to one of his aides and Quayle's Chief of Staff, Bill Kristol—thoroughly enjoyed the piece!

Another central Republican issue inexplicably ignored was the family. This time the vacuum left by the failure of the White House to act was ultimately filled not by the Democrats but by more right-wing elements in the Republican party. During the 1992 election campaign the Bush–Quayle team attempted to make "family values" an important part of George Bush's agenda. The tactic was sound, especially if the message was positive and inclusive of diversity rather than exclusive. Family values would contrast nicely with Bill Clinton's alleged record of womanizing and with his wife's history of supporting left-leaning feminist causes. At the Houston Convention, however, speeches by Pat Buchanan and the religious fundamentalist Pat Robertson were so negative, strident, and exclusionary in tone that what should have been an important Republican theme worked against the President. As with so many other aspects of its domestic policy, the Bush Administration's approach to basic family issues was one of intentional neglect, in part because it had been so closely identified with the preceding Reagan Administration.

Roger Porter's immediate predecessor under Reagan had been the conservative activist Gary Bauer, an attorney and former Education Department under secretary during the tenure of William Bennett. Bauer, who left government in 1989 to head the Washington office of the Family Research Council, had drafted Ronald Reagan's Executive Order on the Family. Among other things, this order instructed Bauer's—now Porter's—office to prepare an annual report on the American family. The order also called on government agencies and departments to review all their rules and regulations to ensure that they had no adverse effect on families through, for example, creating perverse incentives in certain income assistance programs that served to break up rather than unite families.

Under Porter's stewardship of the Office of Policy Development, Reagan's Family Executive Order was almost completely ignored. During my first week at the White House Porter handed me a draft report more than fifty pages long prepared by the Department of Health and Human Services. The document was intended as the first annual report on the family as mandated by Reagan's Executive Order, which was still on the books and still to be implemented. The draft needed substantial revisions, and Porter asked me to review it carefully and put it in releasable shape.

I did precisely that, with assistance from Hanns Kuttner and a family policy expert, Patty Farnan, with whom I'd worked at the Education Department. The draft went back to Porter, where it sat for weeks without comment. Whenever I'd ask about it, he'd return it to me with a few comments scribbled on the first page and ask me to review it again in light of some new policy wrinkle. This pattern went on for well over a year, until it became obvious that Porter had no interest whatsoever in issuing the report envisioned by his predecessor.

Family policy did not go away or wait for Porter to take action. Many aspects of what became the Administration's economic opportunity or "empowerment" strategy had direct and important consequences for the family. But even as some of us in the Bush White House attempted to highlight those issues, it was abundantly clear that there was no serious interest.

The President himself, however, became actively involved in one family-related issue in late 1991 when he instructed Porter and others to include the creation of a new Commission on America's Urban Families in his January 1992 State of the Union message. The President had met with several urban leaders in December 1991, and they had urged him to focus on the grave predicament of urban families. They were right to urge presidential involvement, but I told Porter that establishing yet another commission was a bad idea, primarily because we already had the Reagan Family Executive Order on the books and had done absolutely nothing about it. He agreed and told me he'd tried unsuccessfully to dissuade Bush from creating the commission. On January 28, 1992, Bush announced the new commission and named Missouri's Governor John Ashcroft and former Dallas Mayor Annette Strauss to head it.

Ashcroft, one of the brightest lights in the Republican party, was a superb choice for the job. (Porter was pleased, because the two had a good relationship which included frequent rounds of tennis on the White House court whenever Ashcroft was in Washington.) But weeks went by without action. Porter, and later Ashcroft, approached me about serving as the commission's Executive Director, and it took me at most five seconds to turn them down: given the total neglect of the family to date by the Bush Administration, I had no desire to accept such an assignment. It wasn't until April that Porter and Ashcroft, on my recommendation, chose HUD Assistant Secretary Anna Kondratas, herself a nationally known expert on antipoverty policies and a former Heritage Foundation official, to staff the commission.

A month later the Los Angeles riots occurred in the wake of the acquittal of the police officers charged with severely beating Rodney King. Given the timing, the Bush Administration's actions looked prescient indeed. The sorry fact was that for more than three years, other than expanding the Earned Income Tax Credit, the Administration had done little to advance a comprehensive family-oriented policy agenda. Porter couldn't be bothered to initiate it himself, and nobody above him asked him to work on it until Bush did in early 1992. By the time the Republican Convention rolled around in August 1992, the decision to highlight family values was borderline laughable. It was just another indication of the Bush White House's tendency to treat issues seriously when it came to campaign rhetoric but to ignore them while actually governing the country.

Porter was by no means reluctant, however, to seek credit for an accomplishment, whether or not he actually deserved it. One of the more amusing incidents involving Porter and his low-profile West Wing style involved the mini-flap over whether the President should hold a signing ceremony for the Clean Air Act Amendments. For months Porter had been deeply involved in negotiating, primarily with the Senate, to iron out complex legislation amending the Clean Air Act. Success would have meant breaking a twelve-year stalemate between Republicans and Democrats on Capitol Hill. Bush wanted a bill, although he appeared reasonably indifferent as to its contents. The legislation he sponsored was part of a mushy desire to be an "environmental president." So Porter and Darman's aide Bob Grady were dispatched to Congress as the lead negotiators, and Porter was fond of recounting to his staff in elaborate detail the central role he played going head-to-head with the likes of Senate Majority Leader George Mitchell and others. (These incidents prompted John Schmitz, Boyden Gray's deputy in the counsel's office, to remark that each time George Mitchell complimented Roger Porter or smiled at him it cost the American taxpayers another $25 million.)

If he is anything, Porter is persistent. He did George Bush's bidding and reached a monumental accord, which the White House agreed to sign. Normally, for major legislation reached on the basis of a bipartisan compromise, the President would hold a bill-signing ceremony in the Rose Garden or the East Room, during which he would invite the key members of Congress who had helped shape the legislation to stand by his side as he signed the bill into law. The members got photo ops with the President, and one or two were even recipients of presidential pens used to sign the legislation. By those criteria, the Clean Air Act Amendments would have easily warranted similar treatment.

But there were two important obstacles: Sununu and Darman. Neither wanted a ceremony, since they prided themselves on detesting any environmental legislation or regulation that imposed high and unwarranted costs on the American public. Sununu was adamant: He would not allow a ceremony that would have the Senate Majority Leader standing at Bush's side on the platform.

Porter and at least one other Assistant to the President felt differently, but rather than confront the short-tempered Sununu directly, each went separately to see Staff Secretary Jim Cicconi. Knowing full well that Darman and Sununu opposed a signing ceremony, Cicconi, who personally agreed with Porter, decided to raise it at one of the 7:30 A.M. senior staff meetings in the Roosevelt Room.

When he did, all hell broke loose. Sununu started yelling that this was a dumb idea and just wasn't going to happen. Sitting at the opposite end of the table from the Chief of Staff was Dick Darman, who decided to heap more scorn on Cicconi. Did anyone at the table come to Cicconi's aid? Of course not. Roger Porter just sat there quietly taking notes, as did the other person who had spoken with Cicconi.

Bruised but undeterred, Cicconi went to see Sununu immediately after the senior staff meeting and told him he was being ridiculous and not serving the best interests of the President. "You're letting your own personal views and biases get in the way of serving the President. After all, the Clean Air Act was one of his major priorities, and it makes eminent sense to have a signing ceremony. You're just wrong on this one, John."

Sununu listened to Cicconi's reasoning and agreed. He changed his mind and okayed the signing ceremony. Later that day Roger Porter spoke to Cicconi in the hall of the West Wing and told him that he, Porter, had gone to see Sununu and was the one who had managed to persuade Sununu to change his mind about the signing ceremony! Porter avoided all responsibility if it meant being yelled at by Sununu or Darman, but he was more than eager to assume the credit. "Craven" was how one of Porter's colleagues described his behavior on this occasion.

Porter's timid approach to substantive policymaking permitted the unmaking of whatever domestic agenda might have evolved during George Bush's presidency. Porter ran the policy office by keeping his head down, taking lots of notes at meetings, and not making waves. He allowed himself to be consumed with process while making certain that his staff was kept occupied in pointless tasks. We were always busy—too busy to do anything that mattered.

Just as Bush brought to the nation's highest office perhaps the most extensive experience in government of all Presidents, so too did Porter bring a wealth of experience to the West Wing out of his service to Gerald Ford and Ronald Reagan. The problem was that he was afraid to act. Whenever the Office of Policy Development staff suggested controversial domestic policy proposals—on subjects ranging from budget process reforms to curb entitlements and school discipline to automobile insurance reform, an information superhighway, privatization, and economic empowerment—Porter steadfastly refused to become engaged.

Porter's errors were sins of omission. Having few policy principles, he allowed himself to be sidelined and refused to fight for much of anything. And yet, he didn't get to the sidelines all by himself. Someone else muscled Porter, among others, off the playing field. If Porter ended up administering an office devoted almost exclusively to process, it was not he who insisted that process be the principal function of his staff. That insistence came from somewhere else.

3

"You've Been Darmanized"

For something sufficiently toad-like
   Squats in me, too
Its hunkers are heavy as hard luck
   And cold as snow,
And will never allow me to blarney
   My way to getting
The fame and the girl and the money
   All at one sitting.

—Philip Larkin, "Toads"[1]

The blackest day of the Bush Administration for me (other than when the President abandoned his "no new taxes" pledge) was November 16, 1990. That's the day I realized that Richard G. Darman, the Director of the Office of Management and Budget and a key adviser to the President of the United States, could not be trusted. Richard Nixon had Watergate. George Bush had Dick Darman.

For those of us busy promoting the Administration's economic empowerment agenda, November 16 stands out as the afternoon when Darman gave his National Press Club speech on "neo-neoism" and attacked Jim Pinkerton's "New Paradigm" proposal as nothing new, even mocking it with the wisecrack, "Brother, can you paradigm?" As Darman came to recognize and no doubt regret a few days later, his heralded and well-publicized public appearance—his first since the great budget deal—was not a terribly smart move.

51

We had seen it coming for months. Roger Porter's weakness as Director of the Office of Policy Development had created a power vacuum at the heart of Bush's presidency. With Porter marginalized by his own risk-averse behavior and Darman's aggressiveness, something fundamental in the White House power structure had happened.

Porter had let himself be pushed out of the way by one of the most power-hungry men ever to have served at the highest levels of American government.

To appreciate Richard Darman's Dickensian dimensions, one need only meet him in person. Had he lived in England, Darman might have been looked upon as one of those cultivated eccentrics frequently found in Oxford or Cambridge senior common rooms. But his eccentricity was spiced with a poisonous temper and a relentless vindictiveness toward anyone who disagreed with him.

Those wrists. Thick, barrel-like, clumsy wrists. That's what I remember about first meeting Darman over breakfast in the Executive Dining Room shortly after I had started at the White House. He was not a friendly or outgoing person. Warmth and magnetism were not natural to him. He could be all charm and smiles if he needed something from you. I came ultimately to appreciate his wit, but even that was almost always calculated, or so he would have you believe.

Darman was one of those who lived to see stories about themselves in the *Washington Post*'s "Style" section, the quintessential Washington insider who reveled in building an aura of complexity about himself. Behind his carefully contrived veil of deception, however, it became readily apparent that Dick Darman was little more than a clever but extremely insecure Wizard of Oz.

The term "Darmanesque" evolved during the Reagan years to characterize a convoluted tactical approach to an issue on which Darman was reportedly working. The tactics often turned out to be smoke and mirrors. For someone who was always described as having something up his sleeve, Darman actually produced relatively little. He had managed to create a mystique to mask the fact that there was actually very little there.

During the Bush Administration, his most noted triumph was the completely disastrous 1990 budget deal in which Darman (plus Sununu and Treasury Secretary Brady) were outmaneuvered by Congressional Democrats like Senator Robert Byrd of West Virginia.

Darman had been running the best three-card monte game in Washington. As one former colleague described him, he was "a poseur of world class order . . . the biggest con artist of them all." The trouble was that Darman, almost singlehandedly, cost Bush his reelection. Clayton Yeutter, the former Republican National Committee Chairman and a Bush counselor, openly acknowledged three days after Bush's defeat that Darman's 1990 budget deal was the principal reason why George Bush was a one-term President.

How did one man come to dominate the internal workings of the entire Administration and crowd out other senior advisers to the President of the United States? To answer this requires an understanding of how Dick Darman got to be OMB Director in the first place.

According to one longtime Bush aide, George Bush had once actually detested Darman, who had been suspected as the source of negative stories about Bush leaked to the press during Ronald Reagan's 1984 reelection campaign. By 1988, however, Darman had managed to patch things up with Bush and had proved himself indispensable during Bush's campaign debate preparation. As that same senior Bush aide put it, Dick Darman is "the best suck-up there is. He's someone who is capable of convincing people who actually despise him."

Darman, having played no role in Ronald Reagan's 1980 election, nonetheless managed to work his way into the Reagan Administration in 1981. He had served with Jim Baker in the Nixon Commerce Department, and reportedly he wrote Baker an obsequious letter to solicit a position in the new Administration. Baker brought him to the White House as his deputy but made sure that Darman had sufficient adult supervision to prevent him from doing much harm. Either Baker would ride herd on him, or other Reaganites who were downright hostile toward or suspicious of Darman were able to keep him in check. In the Bush White House, John Sununu failed to exercise the necessary control and, in the end, became seduced and ultimately overwhelmed by the man.

For Dick Darman, what mattered most was ensuring his own intellectual dominance. Quick to spot weakness in other potential key players (most notably Mike Boskin, Porter, and Treasury Secretary Brady), Darman moved to fill the political vacuum that he helped to create. In the process, he would run people down through remarkable displays of personal vindictiveness. It didn't matter whether his "enemy *du jour*" was a Cabinet Secretary like Brady (of whom he was openly disdainful by the end of the Administration), Jack Kemp (whom he detested), Louis Sullivan (whom he openly scorned), or a lower-level staffer who dared to offer views that might conflict with Darman's perspective. The unfortunate fact was that Darman's contemptuous nature—his predilection for indulging in personal vitriol—managed to infect Sununu as well, and the two would feed each other's worst intellectual vanities, convincing themselves that only they had the right answer on every issue coming before the President.

Perhaps the most insightful journalistic piece on Darman appeared in the *Washington Post*'s Sunday magazine on July 29, 1990. "The Man With All the Answers: What Makes Dick Darman Run," by Marjorie Williams, portrays Darman as a fundamentally insecure man. It is painfully evident from the Williams story that Darman had yearned for years for such a story to be written about himself. Now he had made it to official Washington insider status. He even counted the *Post*'s Bob Woodward as one of his close friends.

Darman's need for self-promotion was obvious from the way Darman conducted Ms. Williams on a tour of his sprawling suburban house. He had thought carefully about the mementos, photographs, and other carefully placed objects he wanted her to notice—the majestic views from the windows, the pictures he had taken of his two sons, the copy of Eliot's *Four Quartets* lying open on a desk. When asked about the poem (and you can sense that his disappointment would have been indeed palpable had Ms. Williams not asked), Darman felt obliged to tell Ms. Williams that he was "*re*-reading" the famous Eliot work:

> . . . he is going [through the house] at a near jog, as photos, books, personal artifacts—the revelatory details that are red meat to a journalist writing about personality—flash by. He points out what he wishes, and waves away questions about attractions that are not on the tour. The message seems to be that he would like to display his pride in this house, this family; but he would like also to control what is seen.[2]

Unfortunately for Darman, he could not control what Ms. Williams ultimately wrote. The impression she leaves is of a self-centered and driven individual. She recounts how, during the Reagan years, Darman had instructed his staff "to keep a bibliography, with separate sections for mentions of Darman in books, in periodicals and in newspapers; at times when Darman was in the news, the bibliography was updated often—weekly or even every few days. As for the morning newspapers, secretaries were told to clip headlines and only the portions of the stories that dealt with Darman." The secretaries did not save stories that referred to Darman as a mere "aide" to then chief of staff James A. Baker III.[3]

People who have followed Darman over the years will tell you that he is essentially a chameleon. He has demonstrated an ability to change virtually everything in which he supposedly believes to achieve whatever his latest quest may be. Some cynics have noted how he even changed his religion—Darman was born into a Jewish household and even had a bar mitzvah—when he decided to pursue his future wife, Kathleen Emmett, an attractive Radcliffe undergraduate, and an Episcopalian. Williams quotes Ed Rollins to the effect that "getting her was a contest [for Darman] too." One Darman observer notes how much Darman has changed to ape the life-style and values of his "Brahmin" mentor, former Attorney General Elliot S. Richardson. Darman bought a house just a few doors away from Richardson's, and then "went the whole nine yards." He moved into the neighborhood, became an Episcopalian, and acquired the obligatory golden retriever.

For one longtime Darman observer, himself a Jew who had served with Darman in the Reagan Administration, the Marjorie Williams story in the *Post* provided a remarkable revelation about the inner makeup of Richard Darman. "Many of us in the Reagan Administration always saw Dick as the ultimate Boston Brahmin, a clone of his mentor Elliot Richardson. He wore cheap clothes, intentionally dressing down. He made sure everyone knew he cut his own hair, and badly at that. And then along comes the Williams story and everything falls into place: this supposed Brahmin was an insecure little boy from Woonsocket, Rhode Island, trying desperately to be something that he wasn't."

He added: "In Dick's case, it was obvious after the Williams story that he wouldn't last a minute before the likes of Bobby Byrd, Leon Panetta, and Dick Gephardt, tough men all, who knew who they were, could exploit vulnerabilities, and could both spot and skewer blowhards from miles away. And that is exactly what they did.

Over time, however, obvious patterns begin to emerge in any person's life, and malleability—plasticity, if you will—has come to characterize Dick Darman. As a man who believes fundamentally in one thing and one thing only—himself—he will do anything, say anything to advance his own standing. The nonsense he tried to spin in the article by Marjorie Williams about his being a "secret good guy" whose chief motivation was the long-term good of the United States was, in Washington talk, an effort to dissociate himself from the conservative policies of his boss.

Darman's advice to Bush on the economy, the budget, and the deficit was often wrong, politically and economically. But perhaps even more significant for Bush was the extent to which Darman's unchecked ego managed (with Bush's acquiescence) to stifle honest intellectual debate inside the Bush Administration. Only near the end of Bush's presidency did it become public, ironically but appropriately through a series of articles written by his *Post* pal Woodward, just how duplicitous Darman had been and how willing he was to sacrifice principle for power.

There is no other plausible explanation for Darman's decision to talk Bush into the 1990 budget agreement, a deal that effectively repudiated Reagan's growth-oriented economic principles in favor of both higher taxes and higher levels of domestic spending. It was Bush's single biggest mistake as President, and it led directly to the unraveling of the Reagan coalition and Bush's eventual defeat. This about-face was especially difficult to understand coming from a budget director who, during the 1988 campaign, sat in on a meeting at Bush's Kennebunkport, Maine, home during the Memorial Day weekend and swore his allegiance to supply-side economics. Richard Rahn, the former chief economist for the U.S. Chamber of Commerce, who also attended the Kennebunkport meeting with Bush, recalled: "Dick Darman sat there and swore that he had learned his lesson and he was a supply-sider. He told that to George Bush in my presence."[4]

On the day after Bush's reelection defeat, Rahn told me that, contrary to what Darman had said to the *Post*'s Bob Woodward, Darman actually agreed with the "read my lips: no new taxes" pledge and did *not* want it stricken from Bush's 1988 New Orleans acceptance speech. Just to make sure that I'd heard Rahn correctly, I reconfirmed this information a few weeks later.

"That's right," said Rahn. "Dick Darman was an enthusiastic supporter of the 'read my lips: no new taxes' pledge."

I pressed further: Are you sure that Darman wasn't perhaps just acquiescing in the "no new taxes" part but really did oppose the "read my lips" emphasis as making it too hard to backtrack later?

"No," Rahn answered. "Given the actual history at the time, everybody rather liked the phrase. It was a dramatic expression. It was attention-getting. If you just said 'I'm opposed to raising taxes,' no one would've remembered it. They wanted to get people to remember the President's pledge."

I asked Rahn to tell me more about that Memorial Day at Kennebunkport in 1988. "I remember it so vividly," he added. "Bush was there. So were Sununu, Marty Feldstein, Pinkerton, Barbara Bush, Teeter, Kathryn Eyckoff, Don Sundquist, Lynn Martin, and Debbie Steelman. I'm looking at the picture right now on my office wall. Darman told us all how he'd learned by his mistakes. Remember, the Republican platform at the time called for a flexible budget freeze, regulatory restraint, and no new taxes. Taken together, these policies were to have produced a balanced budget by 1993.

"Bush was clearly pro-supply side, too. After all, Beryl Sprinkel had been lecturing him on the subject for weeks. After the meeting was over, I remember returning to Washington and telling Newt Gingrich how Darman had changed his ways. Gingrich laughed at me for being so naïve. I guess I was."

During the Reagan years, Darman had never been considered a "Bushie." In fact, he had consistently discounted Bush's abilities and was, in turn, viewed with suspicion by Bush. A Bush victory in 1988, however, would leave Darman out in the cold unless—working through his other mentor, Jim Baker—he could ingratiate himself with the nominee and prospective President. That's precisely what he systematically did in the summer of 1988, pledging his fealty to Reaganomics and to George Bush. No sooner had Bush named him OMB Director than Darman set about once again to posture as the master of the grand deal that would save Bush from the follies of that same supply side theory to which Darman had sworn allegiance only a few months before.

Change a religion, change an ideology, change your economics—it was all the same to Dick Darman.

My own first serious encounter with Darman occurred that November afternoon in 1990 shortly after he'd concluded the budget agreement and launched his verbal attack on Jim Pinkerton. What happened that day involved a relatively minor budget issue, but it nevertheless left me convinced beyond any doubt that one of the senior advisers to the President of the United States was someone who would stop at nothing to achieve victory for himself. Ironically, although I couldn't have known it at the time, that little incident would have greater consequences for Darman than he could appreciate then.

On November 15, 1990, I received a copy of a presidential document for review and comment. The document was a bill report intended for the President on a recent piece of legislation that, among other things, included an $8 million sole-source grant award—essentially "pork barrel" dollars—to Loyola University of Chicago. Ordinarily a document of this kind would have been no big deal, but in this case the report indicated that Education Secretary Lauro Cavazos was recommending that Bush sign the bill, notwithstanding the pork-barrel project for Loyola University.

The report could not have been correct. Having served under Cavazos for almost two years as his budget chief, I knew that he detested sole-source grants. I had never known him to support one, since he believed fervently that they broke with the Department of Education's long-standing position favoring competitive grant awards. I made a few telephone calls and soon discovered that every office in the Education Department that reviewed the issue of the Loyola grant—the General Counsel, the Legislative Affairs office, and my old budget shop—had recommended vetoing the bill.

Only one officer, Under Secretary Ted Sanders, supported the bill. He had overruled everyone else and had authorized use of the "autopen" to sign Cavazos's name to a bill report sent to OMB recommending that the President sign the bill. Sanders had authorized the autopen while Cavazos was in Paris attending a meeting of education ministers at the Organization for Economic Cooperation and Development. I later discovered that Sanders had never checked with his absent boss before authorizing the signing of a recommendation of which Cavazos would have vehemently disapproved. (Before coming to Washington, Sanders had been the Illinois Chief State School Officer.)

Upon further checking, I discovered that the Loyola University pork was no ordinary piece of legislative fat. Loyola University was the alma mater of Illinois Congressman Dan Rostenkowski, the powerful chairman of the House Ways and Means Committee, with whom Darman had just finished negotiating the 1990 budget agreement. The two men had apparently agreed to slip in this little goody as a personal favor to the chairman, who could then bring home the bacon to his old school.

I decided to take some action. Late that afternoon I called the Cavazos entourage in Paris and reached Chino Chapa, the Secretary's chief of staff. Chapa confirmed what I had suspected: Cavazos had no idea that the letter had been sent to OMB supporting the sole-source grant. It was nearly midnight Paris time, and Chapa asked me if I thought he should wake up Cavazos with the information that night. I said no, just to tell him the next morning and then let me know if he wanted to do anything about it.

My home telephone rang at four the next morning with Chapa on the line from Paris. He had told Cavazos the story about the autopen at breakfast, and Cavazos was furious. The Secretary wanted me to direct my successor in the Education Department's budget office, George Pieler, to prepare another letter to OMB revoking the unauthorized Sanders letter. Pieler was to take the letter himself to Cavazos's secretary, have her autopen his signature, and then forward it to OMB. Sanders was not to be informed or provided with a copy of Cavazos's new official letter until after it had arrived at OMB.

I followed Cavazos's request and took the additional step of informing Bush's Staff Secretary's office that the recommendation on the bill being processed by OMB inaccurately reflected the Education Department's views. Rather than recommend that the President sign the bill, Cavazos would urge a veto and would explain that his earlier letter had been sent inappropriately, the product of an internal "administrative mistake." By informing the Staff Secretary's office I managed to block speedy transmittal of the OMB recommendation to the Oval Office, since the Staff Secretary could not in good conscience forward to Bush a document he knew to be either incomplete or in error.

By the time the new Cavazos letter arrived at the White House, OMB had gotten wind that the Department of Education was reversing its position. Darman was livid. He would now have to represent to the President that a Cabinet Secretary was recommending a veto of the bill (and of Rosty's pork, agreed to by Darman). In midafternoon I ran into Darman as I was coming down the steps of the Old Executive Office Building and heading toward the West Wing. A shouting match ensued. Darman yelled at me that we weren't going to veto a piece of legislation over a small bit of pork like this, regardless of what Cavazos wanted. I said that wasn't the issue. The real concern was the integrity of the process. A Cabinet department's views had been misrepresented through a conspiracy between Darman and a willing accomplice at the Education Department.

Darman now had to tell Bush of Cavazos's amended recommendation. Not that it really mattered; Bush signed the bill anyway. By that evening I had learned from Roger Porter that because of my actions—expressly following a request from a Cabinet Secretary—I was now in trouble with Sununu and risked being dismissed. According to Porter, Darman had given this account to Sununu: I had misrepresented the White House position on the bill and had implied that Sununu himself wanted it vetoed, I had talked Cavazos into supporting a veto, and I had generally acted out of spite. Each of those assertions was false. I learned from this that Darman was willing to misrepresent to the President's Chief of Staff what had happened in order to neutralize me as a threat to his own schemes.

I could not have cared less whether I was fired, but I was determined to set the record straight with Sununu and let Darman know that he didn't scare me in the least. Porter suggested that I call Sununu or walk down to his office and explain what really happened. I decided not to, because Sununu was leaving with Bush for an overseas trip to Europe within the hour, and the last thing he needed to worry about then was the justification for what I had done. I sent Sununu a memorandum explaining precisely what had happened. Darman received a copy. I never heard another word from Sununu, and I obviously wasn't fired.

A few days later I recounted this episode to my Cabinet Affairs colleague, Steve Danzansky, whose reaction was immediate and intended to be comforting: "Charlie, don't worry about it. You've just been Darmanized." Danzansky went on to explain that what I'd experienced was the typical Darman *modus operandi*. To get his own way on something—regardless of how inconsequential—Darman would try to blackball anyone who stood in his path. That explained the misrepresentations of my motives to Sununu. By sullying an individual's character, reliability as a team player, and trustworthiness, Darman would increase the likelihood that the individual would no longer be invited to attend meetings and participate in work on sensitive issues. As a result the number of people who might challenge Darman's dominance on the issues would steadily shrink.

Danzansky had been on the receiving end of similar treatment from Darman while serving on the National Security Council staff in the Reagan Administration. Another friend who had tangled with Darman told me of a related incident. In his case the consequences were far more severe and carried potentially criminal liability. Darman apparently had a hand in fingering him (incorrectly) as the possible culprit who during the 1980 presidential campaign had somehow managed to purloin the presidential debate briefing book being used by those preparing President Jimmy Carter for his debate with challenger Ronald Reagan.

One example of just how low Darman would stoop in his effort to terrorize anyone he saw as thwarting his wishes was his attempt to intimidate a young, exceedingly bright, dedicated economist who served on Vice President Quayle's staff as an expert on the impact of economic deregulation. Nancy Mitchell was twenty-eight when she left Senator Bill Armstrong's committee staff to join the Office of the Vice President. She also happened to be the wife of Dan Mitchell, a Heritage Foundation economist who had been outspoken in the *New York Times*, the *Washington Times*, and *National Review* in criticizing the failures of Darman's economic policies.

At one point Mitchell was to be shifted from Quayle's payroll onto that of the Office of Management and Budget's Office of Information and Regulatory Affairs and then "detailed" back to Quayle. When Darman learned of this—as well as who her husband was—he decided to launch a series of attacks against this staffer. First he tried physical intimidation. At a meeting in the office of Quayle's Chief of Staff, Bill Kristol, Darman walked in late, looked directly at Mitchell, and picked up a chair. Before sitting down, he moved the chair right into her, setting it down almost on her feet.

Later, he tried to yank her detail and banish her to the New Executive Office Building, a relocation that would have made it virtually impossible to carry on her work for Quayle. The issue of the detail was subsequently resolved when Quayle moved Mitchell directly onto his payroll. Shortly thereafter she went to Darman's office to deliver a document. The OMB director stared at her and abruptly asked where she was employed now and on whose payroll she was listed. As Mitchell told me, "Dick Darman is someone who read *Winning Through Intimidation* and believed it."

All that is the behavior of a man racked by doubts about himself and his abilities. One former Darman aide even suggested that this explained the 1990 budget deal process: "You have to understand that Darman sees the world in a conspiratorial fashion. He doesn't see the president like Terry Eastland does as a leader of the American people.[5] Darman is a self-aggrandizer who relishes the backroom deal. That's his theater. He doesn't trust anybody. That's why he arrived at OMB without bringing a cadre of loyalists with him."

For Darman, everything had to be done in secrecy. Once, when the budget was to include a major increase in funding for Head Start, Darman ordered the wrong numbers sent to the Department of Health and Human Services in its budget passback so it would not learn the truth until the very last minute. Darman was unwilling even to share information with Dr. Louis Sullivan, the Secretary of HHS and a member of Bush's Cabinet!

There are times, of course, when a backroom, closed-door strategy in government is appropriate. To Darman's credit, such an approach worked for him beautifully to produce an "immaculate conception," in which both political parties took the blame and the President was left untouched, in the repeal of the catastrophic health insurance legislation in 1989. But it was sheer folly to believe that a similar approach could be used successfully to reverse a crucial promise of George Bush's 1988 campaign. According to one former Assistant to the President, "Dick was consistently out-thought and outmaneuvered by the Hill Democrats, who had both a better sense of timing and understanding of what the American public would buy. Dick was out of touch with average people" in the country.

In short, Dick Darman always had to be in control. When dealing with possible Administration rivals, Darman tried to elbow them out of the way, deprive them of access to necessary information, impugn their integrity, and make certain that his own actions were shrouded in secrecy. Darman managed to make sure that only a handful of aides were privy to his plans.

Unlike his immediate GOP predecessors at OMB, David Stockman and Jim Miller, Darman surrounded himself with policy lightweights and political hacks. Stockman had talented assistants like economist Larry Kudlow (now chief economist at Bear, Stearns) and John Cogan (a labor economist and budget expert now at the Hoover Institution). Darman replaced the exceedingly competent economist Arlene Holen, a Miller holdover who resigned her position in Darman's OMB, with Tom Scully, a lawyer-lobbyist and a former Bush campaign worker. As Program Associate Director (PAD) for Labor, Veterans, and Human Resources issues, the young Scully (he was in his early thirties when he took office in 1989) was responsible for more than half the nondefense portion of the federal budget. An amiable, fast-talking individual, Scully consistently demonstrated such shallowness when it came to the complexity of various education and health programs that his own career staff nicknamed him "Cliff Notes."

Bob Grady, a former protégé of New Jersey's Governor Tom Kean and a Bush speechwriter while Bush was Vice President and during the 1988 campaign, was the PAD who handled the environmental and natural resources accounts. Widely viewed as a closet "green" inside the Bush Administration, Grady was responsible not only for coining Bush's disastrous and confusing "no net loss of wetlands" pledge but also was frequently credited with doing the bidding of EPA Administrator William Reilly, who was often at odds with the White House over environmental policy. Grady was the OMB official who repeatedly provided Reilly with "cover" inside the White House. When Darman's first Deputy OMB Director, Bill Diefenderfer, left government in 1991, Darman shocked many in the White House by persuading the President to nominate Grady (at the time thirty-four years old) for the position. The Senate, however, never got around to confirming him, which left Darman without a deputy for almost half the Bush Administration.

Darman's third PAD, Janet Hale, primarily handled matters involving the Departments of Justice and Housing and Urban Development. A former HUD official herself, Hale had managed to escape the scandals associated with Ronald Reagan's HUD Secretary, Samuel Pierce, and kept a low profile at OMB. Her chief role was to hold up action on a variety of initiatives ranging from crime and immigration reform to peak load pricing in airports.

Together with his trio of domestic PADs (plus the very capable Bob Howard in defense-related programs), Darman ran OMB as a closed shop, involving very few of the OMB career professionals. The fact that each of his top three aides was wholly dependent on him and lacked any other professional standing only enhanced Darman's ability to maintain centralized control. He liked it that way. What was striking about OMB under Darman's tenure was the number of senior *political* positions Darman could have filled but decided to leave empty. There was no General Counsel, no chief legislative lobbyist, no senior economist, no deputy for almost two years, and no administrator of the Office for Information and Regulatory Affairs. Margaret Heckler, who served as Ronald Reagan's second Secretary of Health and Human Services, once said OMB stood for "One More Barrier." Under Dick Darman, the acronym more appropriately stood for "One Man Band."

Darman had two fairly well-developed techniques for discrediting his enemies: either misrepresent their acts or accuse them of being a leaker of some sensitive issue or decision to the media. The latter tactic was ironic, in view of Darman's own propensity for leaking to the press, which prompted some staffers to dub him "Mr. Speed Dial." Aside from my personal distaste for his tactics, I was saddened and stunned that the President of the United States would rely on an adviser whose personal ego stood in the way of serving his President and his country with dignity and integrity. Ever since November 16, 1990, I have associated the term "Darmanesque" with deceit. It would take almost two more years before my conclusion would be confirmed publicly, primarily by Darman's own words.

Although Bush had signed Rosty's pork, the story did not end in 1990 but continued to return and haunt Darman almost a year later. It turned out that Darman's own budget deal of that fall had an unforeseen—and hilarious—impact on Loyola University's $8 million grant.

The bill Bush signed only *authorized* the $8 million. It did not, however, *appropriate* the necessary funds. Until the funds were actually appropriated by the House and Senate appropriations committees, the school enjoyed nothing more than a mere promise to pay, at best. The problem for Rostenkowski was that under the provisions of the budget agreement, the funds for his alma mater now had to be offset by cuts in spending elsewhere. The question was where.

Originally, funding for Loyola University was to come from the defense portion of the budget deal, one of the three distinct categories in which nonentitlement spending had to be classified: defense, international, and domestic discretionary. Loyola had urged Rosten-kowski to switch funding for the $8 million from the defense category to the Department of Education's budget, which meant the domestic discretionary account. The school, which intended to use the money to expand its business school, feared that if the dollars were taken from the defense account, its defense research funds might be reduced to offset the new grant award.

When Darman opposed Rostenkowski on this technical accounting matter, the powerful congressman responded by blocking House consideration of trade agreements with the Soviet Union, Bulgaria, and Mongolia until Darman could identify where the offsetting dollars would be found to cover the estimated $22 million revenue losses associated with the three agreements. Rostenkowski was hoisting Darman on his own petard.

Darman was forced to acquiesce in Rostenkowski's accounting gimmick and agreed to shift the spending to the domestic discretionary account. Unfortunately for Darman, the spending caps established by the budget deal were so tight that the addition of the extra $8 million in Rosty–Darman pork broke the bank, exceeding the spending limit by $2.3 million! Unless additional offsets could be found, Darman had no choice under the law but to impose a spending sequester on *all* domestic discretionary spending across the entire federal government.

To pay for the $2.3 million excess occasioned by the $8 million grant, then, all domestic discretionary spending throughout the entire federal government had to undergo a sequester (or reduction) across the board of 0.0013 percent. For the hundreds and hundreds of domestic programs run throughout the federal government, hundreds of bureaucrats in all the various budget offices of the federal government had to calculate budget totals that showed the necessary reduction. The federal government would possibly spend substantially more than $2.3 million in staff time and other associated costs just to calculate and impose Darman's mini-sequester! Although a relatively small example, this scenario was typical of Darman's handiwork when it came to mastery over the details of the federal budget.

While Darman's agreement to the Rostenkowski pork occurred in November 1990, it wasn't until almost a year later, in October 1991, that Darman's "sole-source sequester" took place. Perhaps the humor of this incident will be appreciated only by budget aficionados, but for anyone who has followed Darman's career, this little story is rich in delicious irony. His initial insistence on preserving Rosty's pork came back to haunt him through the very strictures of his own budget deal—the agreement meant to reduce the ability of Congress to waste the taxpayers' money on useless pork. Not only did Darman promote such pork-barrel spending himself, but he also ended up preserving it through his own deal and then wasting more taxpayer dollars through the sequester that he had no choice but to implement—given the constraints he himself had imposed on the federal budget.

When news of the incident broke in the *Washington Post* in October 1991, curiously enough the reporter noted that the "usually loquacious Darman had 'no comment' on the issue," according to a spokesman.[6]

Darman's "sole-source sequester" paled in comparison with another occasion when Darman's involvement—more precisely, his intentional noninvolvement—proved disastrous for Bush. When it came to government regulation, Darman studiously looked the other way.

One of the cardinal beliefs of Ronald Reagan's followers was the need to "get government off the backs of the American people." When George Bush became President in January 1989 he not only inherited Reagan's antigovernment legacy but had been the principal overseer of Reagan's entire deregulatory effort. One of the few areas in which Bush himself had a substantial proven and substantive track record in domestic policy was deregulation. For eight years Bush had served faithfully as Ronald Reagan's deregulation czar while heading the Task Force on Regulatory Relief. As Task Force Chairman, Vice President Bush—assisted by his legal counsel, C. Boyden Gray, and Gray's deputies, Richard Breeden (later head of the Securities and Exchange Commission) and Frank Blake (later Education's General Counsel)—had been a stalwart opponent of the numerous burdensome, ill-conceived, or poorly justified regulatory schemes that departments and agencies often hatched, even during the heady years of the "Reagan Revolution."

Conservatives and deregulation advocates cheered when, shortly after his inauguration, Bush announced that the Task Force would be succeeded by a new Council on Competitiveness to be headed by Vice President Dan Quayle. In his February 9, 1989, "Building a Better America" speech to the Congress, Bush stated emphatically,

"We need fewer regulations. We need less bureaucracy." With Quayle succeeding him as regulatory czar, at least organizationally it appeared that Bush would continue his emphasis on regulatory review. The nomenclature of its newest incarnation, the Council on Competitiveness, implied that the effort would focus more specifically on matters affecting the abilities of business and industry to compete. Although the structure and bureaucracy changed somewhat, to the outside world at least, President George Bush was starting out as a deregulator well aware of his eight years as Task Force chairman and determined to continue the effort.

By the end of 1989, however, that impression had all but evaporated, the result of several legislative and regulatory initiatives that cast an altogether different light on the Bush Administration and its interest in regulation. As Bush and his aides became deeply enmeshed in legislative negotiations over a new Clean Air Act, a civil rights bill, and a new law to protect the handicapped (what became "the Americans With Disabilities Act"), the country's business community grew unsettled over the projected costs for implementing those major pieces of legislation.

How George Bush went from being a foe of government regulation to presiding over one of the most regulation-intensive administrations in history is a remarkable story of deceit and insubordination. At the center, once again, was Dick Darman.

On November 27, 1989, the *Wall Street Journal* published a story with the headline, "Unlike Reagan Aides, Many Bush Officials Expand Regulation." The story spoke of "creeping regulation" and quoted Murray Weidenbaum, Reagan's first chairman of the Council of Economic Advisers, to the effect that the "steam for regulatory reform seems to be fully dissipated, and we're reversing course, expanding regulation."[7]

George Bush read the story himself and later that day personally typed the following note to John Sununu: "Maybe you could have someone do some checking on this. Surely our people are not *re-regulating.* I read the entire story and it wasn't too bad, but *if* there is a problem maybe I should mention at Cabinet meeting" (Bush's emphasis). Later that same day, Staff Secretary Jim Cicconi sent Bush's note along with the following cover memorandum to Darman: "The attached is really in your area—could you please have an OMB response prepared for President?"

Darman passed the request to Jim MacRae, an experienced and loyal careerist, who was the acting head of the Office of Information and Regulatory Affairs (OIRA). During the Reagan Administration OIRA had been led by such first-rate talents as Jim Miller (later OMB Director), Chris DeMuth (later head of the American Enterprise Institute), Doug Ginsburg (later a federal appeals court judge and Supreme Court nominee), Wendy Gramm (later head of the Commodity Futures Trading Commission), and, finally, Jay Plager (later a federal appellate judge). It had exercised a choke hold on excessive departmental and agency regulation. Along with Vice President Bush's Task Force, OIRA came to be feared as a powerful office that frequently blocked regulations deemed too costly, inadequately justified in terms of their cost and benefit, or just plain goofy. MacRae had been acting OIRA head since 1989, and the Bush Administration's initial nominee, James Blumstein, a Vanderbilt University law professor, was left dangling in the confirmation process because of congressional animosity toward OIRA.

MacRae complied with the request and eleven days later forwarded to the OMB Director a detailed memorandum for Darman to present to the President in response to his November 27 request. In his cover note to Darman, MacRae noted: "Although the memo has a tough tone, it is accurate."

MacRae's response to Darman included a three-page cover memorandum to the President accompanied by twelve pages of detailed examples from various departments and agencies to support the memorandum's conclusions. What was the "tough tone" MacRae alluded to? The opening paragraph could not have been more direct or frank:

> The recent article on "re-regulation" in the Wall Street Journal is largely on target: the pace of regulation has intensified during the Administration's first year. This represents a retreat from the regulatory principles established by the Presidential Task Force on Regulatory Relief which you chaired.

In cogent and dispassionate prose, MacRae's memorandum explained how "[r]egulatory strategies look increasingly attractive when opportunities for direct government spending are limited." Noting that these reregulatory trends were evident in such areas as environmental protection, occupational health, energy, and transportation, the document also concluded that those trends extended throughout the federal government, as reflected in the twelve pages of detailed analysis and examples.

MacRae wrote further that there has been "a significant retreat from regulatory decision making founded upon sound policy analysis." Not only did many regulations fail to meet the minimum standards of Reagan's Executive Order 12291 (which mandated careful cost-benefit analysis before promulgating rules and regulations), but many "betray[ed] contempt for its analytical requirements and philosophical principles." "Costs often overwhelm any conceivable social benefits. Agencies continue to favor traditional command-and-control regulations and shun market-based alternatives." The document further explained that other important deregulatory initiatives—mostly agenda items left over from Vice President Bush's Task Force—had been "stalled" and that departments and agencies had "developed a variety of techniques for evading OMB oversight." Examples included agencies that ignored the review process and simply announced regulatory initiatives on their own or manipulated judicial deadlines in order to expedite regulatory actions, thereby preempting OMB or OIRA review. The memorandum concluded by noting that an intensified regulatory pace would be to the "detriment of economic growth, jobs, and America's international competitiveness."

To the best of my knowledge, Bush never saw the MacRae memorandum.

After sitting on MacRae's detailed response for nearly *three months,* Darman sent the document back to MacRae with a handwritten note stating that the material was not to go forward at this time and in this form. He'd explain later. That was it. Nothing further happened, and Bush never got an answer to his inquiry. My colleague, Larry Lindsey, saw the memorandum from Darman and raised the matter directly with Chief of Staff John Sununu. Darman, reportedly outraged, announced that Lindsey's actions meant that the information would now be leaked (a curious testimonial to Darman's faith in Sununu!). That was one of the few moments when Porter showed emotion, no doubt because Lindsey's transgression of going around rather than through Porter placed Porter squarely in Darman's sights.

By the time Darman got around to returning MacRae's work, it was the end of February 1990, and the Bush Administration was on the verge of entering into serious negotiations with the Congress over major modifications to the Clean Air Act. At the same time Darman was continuing his maneuvering to reach his long-sought "deal of the century," which would reduce the mushrooming federal budget deficit, cut back drastically on federal spending (especially entitlements), and make Darman a national hero—at least among the handful of budget cognoscenti who might exist inside the Beltway around the capital.

Darman's failure to send the regulatory memorandum forward to Bush was not accidental. Doing so might have prompted Bush to take further action, and that might have undermined Darman's ability to negotiate with Congress. As a result an emerging regulatory schizophrenia was coming to characterize the Bush Administration. On the one hand, the President wanted to avoid imposing substantial regulatory burdens on the American public, while on the other he endorsed such legislative initiatives as renewing the expensive Clean Air Act of 1970 and passage of the Americans With Disabilities Act. Both initiatives passed the Congress in 1990, and a year later they were being characterized as significant drags on the country's economic recovery. Some critics even pointed to those bills as factors contributing to the economic downturn that began in the summer of 1990.

Bush, however, reminded his Cabinet repeatedly that he did not want to engage in excessive regulation that lacked a sound cost-benefit basis. On June 13, 1990, Cabinet Secretary Ede Holiday issued a memorandum to Cabinet and agency heads reiterating Bush's view that his Administration must not engage in reregulation.

Again, nothing happened in response to Holiday's memorandum. There was no follow-up and no serious enforcement mechanism, except for the ongoing controversy between the Administration and the Congress over the role of OIRA and whether the entity would ever be reauthorized. By the summer of 1991, moreover, Vice President Quayle's Competitiveness Council was beginning to attract Congressional hostility for its role in blocking, amending, or otherwise thwarting several ill-conceived EPA regulations that would have imposed costly and unwarranted burdens on American industry and the fragile economy.

Throughout all those events, Darman, who technically oversaw OIRA, remained silent. Just as he ultimately let John Sununu take most of the criticism and blame for the failed 1990 budget deal, so it became increasingly obvious that Darman was willing to let Quayle take the blame for the OMB director's failure to give OIRA the political backing and resources it needed to accomplish its job. In a *Washington Times* column in early December 1991, Warren Brookes blew the whistle on Darman's benign neglect of OIRA and its political impact on the Vice President. Brookes titled his article, "Will Iago Win Again?"

> [E]arly in this administration, OMB Director Richard Darman made his own private pact with the congressional devils to neutralize OIRA in return for making nice-nice on the budget. In two years, he hasn't even sent up a nominee to direct this agency.
>
> But when the president was confronted in October 1990 with a Clean Air Act that Congress had turned into an economic catastrophe (and should be vetoed), Mr. Bush was assured by Mr. Darman among others that OIRA could fix it in the rulemaking process.
>
> This left the entire responsibility for cleaning up Clean Air in the hands of the Council on Competitiveness under Vice President Dan Quayle, who was only too happy to leap into the vacuum and reinvigorate OIRA's operations.[8]

Although Brookes couldn't have known it, Bush himself had once again become exercised over the "reregulation" issue in late November, and the scenario that began in November 1989 in response to the *Wall Street Journal* article repeated itself two years later in yet another curious fashion. And once again—in response to a direct query from the President of the United States—nothing happened.

On November 30, 1991, the cover of the *National Journal* carried a picture of a stern-looking, tight-lipped George Bush with the following headline: "The Regulatory President." The article further explained that "President Bush's first term has witnessed the broadest expansions of government's regulatory reach since the early 1970s."[9] Bush had read the article, and at the end of a domestic policy briefing in the Oval Office with Roger Porter, but without Darman being present, the President mentioned the article and asked Porter about it. Bush wanted Porter to review the article and advise him whether the allegations were, indeed, correct.

Porter returned to his office from the briefing with Bush, called me in, and told me about the President's request. First, Porter asked whether I had seen the *National Journal* article. I told him that I had. In light of his conversation with the President, I immediately volunteered to prepare an analysis of the allegations. Porter gave the go-ahead but openly worried over how to get the information back to Bush without it having to be cleared first by Darman.

"If I send a memorandum to the President," Porter said, "it will have to go through the Staff Secretary process, which means that Darman will review it." Porter had indicated to me that his session with Bush had been good. Without Darman in the Oval Office he had enjoyed a greater opportunity for discussion with the President. It was also evident that Porter still lived in fear of Darman, so I suggested that I prepare a memorandum from me to Porter, which Porter could either give directly to Bush—with the usual disclaimer that a staff member had prepared it—or could distill the gist of my findings into a separate memorandum (or, more likely, a one-page memorandum lacking the usual "To" and "From" markings), which he could present to Bush the next time he was alone with him, perhaps on Air Force One or during some future Oval Office meeting with Darman absent.

In this situation, Porter reinforced the by now inescapable conclusion that he was unwilling to take any position that might involve him in a confrontation with Darman. It also underscored the pathetic state of communications in the West Wing of the Bush White House. Here was a senior presidential adviser unsure of how he should respond to a direct request from the President of the United States because his response might incur the ire of the President's budget director!

I went ahead and prepared a memorandum for Porter analyzing the *National Journal* piece. My findings—similar to those of the December 1989 MacRae memorandum—were that the allegations about costly reregulation were true. After making a few telephone calls I discovered that the *National Journal* article was based on facts gleaned from the public files of OIRA itself.

The *National Journal* contended that by virtually every measure, regulatory activity under Bush was increasing: the number of pages in the *Federal Register* was at the highest level since Jimmy Carter left office in 1981; regulatory spending (adjusted for inflation) would be 22 percent higher under Bush than during the last Carter year; and the overall number of rules issued was significantly higher under Bush than under Reagan. Whereas Reagan was an ardent deregulator, Bush was virtually silent on the subject and, more disturbing, failed to block significant measures that would extend government regulatory activities. Legislation passed with Bush's support during the first two years of the Administration had included the Clean Air Act Amendments (with an estimated $30 billion minimum price tag); the Americans With Disabilities Act; the Nutrition Labeling and Education Act (implemented through a 700-page regulation); and the Pollution Prevention Act. Finally, passage of the Civil Rights Act of 1991 added yet another burden on businesses throughout the nation by altering the burden of proof in discrimination cases and vastly expanding the situations in which costly lawsuits could be filed.

The *National Journal* article also made explicit the nature of the ongoing battle being waged by congressional Democrats who were trying to block the legitimate prerogatives of a President in exercising regulatory review over his own administration. What was so stunning was that Bush's own budget director was a witting accomplice. Darman had cleverly managed to shift the focus—and the blame—when it came to the Bush Administration's regulatory oversight from his own OIRA to the Vice President and his staff.

This was no longer a comical romp or one of Darman's cute bureaucratic squabbles. Lives and careers were being ruined. Congressional overseers like Representative Henry Waxman charged Quayle himself with a conflict of interest because he held stock in a company that owned a paper mill that would have been affected by rules on voluntary recycling. Alan Hubbard—the Executive Director of Quayle's Competitiveness Council—was investigated by Congress in late November 1991 for alleged conflicts of interest based on his holdings in two Indiana companies that may have been affected by Clean Air Act implementation and the Council's efforts to influence those regulations. Even OIRA career staff had their financial disclosure statements requested by subcommittee staff who were probing for possible conflicts. One senior career OIRA staffer was raked over the coals simply for holding a small amount (less than $2,000) of Dow Chemical Company stock in trust for his daughter, the result of the daughter's inheritance!

It all happened on Darman's watch, and he did virtually nothing to fight back or to stop it. Little wonder that OIRA career staff were both disgusted and dejected. It was clear that their top political leadership was unwilling to go to bat for them. Indeed, some even suspected that Darman was willing to let OIRA be emasculated so that he could continue to conduct his "let's make a deal" routine with congressional Democrats.

Fortunately for Darman, the *Washington Times*'s Warren Brookes died suddenly of pneumonia on December 28, 1991. One of Darman's sharpest, most relentless and most accurate critics was no longer around to blow the whistle on "Deficit Dick."

I never heard another word about my memorandum on regulations from Porter. Whether it ever went to Bush in whole or in part I'll probably never know. But I did make sure that others in the White House complex had the document. Ultimately, as was the case with underground *samizdat* publications in the former Soviet Union, one hoped the information would get through.

While Porter feared a blowup with Darman if he sent my memorandum forward to the President, two other Bush aides were less deterred by the staffing process or by Darman's likely wrath. Boyden Gray and Mike Boskin were determined to press forward and sent a memorandum to Bush on December 23, 1991, almost two weeks after I gave my initial analysis to Porter. The Gray–Boskin memorandum was short, only two pages, and recommended that Bush engage in a major new antiregulatory effort to counter the impression that his Administration was massively reregulating. They advised Bush to announce a moratorium on new regulations that were not mandated by law or judicial deadline and to expedite those regulations that promoted economic growth.

Bush read the memo, initialed it on December 27, and sent it back to the authors with the authorization to proceed.

Shortly after New Year's Day 1992 I again asked Porter whether he'd ever discussed my memorandum with Bush. As I suspected, he hadn't: "Since Skinner's arrival, we haven't been having domestic policy briefings with the President, so I haven't had an opportunity to get the information to him."

That didn't stop Boskin and Gray. Although Darman reportedly saw their memorandum in the clearance process and made comments on it, the memorandum ultimately went to Bush with few changes in the authors' suggestions.

To implement this new deregulatory initiative, several staff members assembled shortly after the New Year. The immediate goal was to devise a list of significant, specific deregulatory steps to be implemented that would positively affect economic growth and jobs. Some eighteen possibilities were identified, ranging from reducing and streamlining export controls to expediting the federal drug approval process and scaling back large portions of the new Clean Air Act that had an adverse impact on the automobile industry. Procedurally, discussion focused on Bush announcing a freeze on new regulations in his forthcoming State of the Union speech, to be followed by a ninety-day review period in which each department and agency would scour its regulations for ways in which to reduce the burden on the American public. Only growth-enhancing rules were to be published, and these, in turn, were to be expedited. Each agency was also to appoint a new "regulatory czar" who would report to Quayle's Council on Competitiveness on the agency's success in implementation.

The policy was correct, notwithstanding the inherent cognitive dissonance. We were, after all, the people running the Executive Branch who oversaw the government's regulatory machine. If there were too many regulations, the blame lay with *us*.

Informed of Gray's and Boskin's initiative, Porter asked me to become involved but neglected to share with me the December 23 memorandum. As happened so many other times in my stay at the White House, I got the document from more junior staff (in this case, Counsel's office staff), who had already approached me directly about participating in the initiative. Here was yet another example of the inability and unwillingness of senior aides in the Bush White House to communicate directly with one another.

At a preliminary planning session with staff from the Counsel's office, the Council of Economic Advisers, Cabinet Affairs, and the Vice President's office, I raised the issue of OIRA: If we were to undertake this endeavor and do it successfully, OIRA had to have more clout in bringing the agencies and departments to heel. Everyone agreed, and Gene Schaerr, one of Boyden Gray's attorneys and a former Supreme Court clerk, suggested that we could recess-appoint a new head of OIRA and thereby end-run what would clearly be a bruising confirmation fight during the 1992 election year. If handled properly, such an appointment would be good for two years, longer than the average tenure of most presidential appointees.

Our work culminated in a Roosevelt Room meeting with the Vice President on Monday, January 6, 1992. Porter had told me about the meeting the previous Friday and had invited me to go along. What he hadn't told me was that he was planning surgery the following week and that I'd be representing our office at the meeting with Quayle on my own.

Shortly before the Monday afternoon meeting with Quayle, Boyden Gray approached me to ask if I would feel comfortable raising the question of a recess appointment for the OIRA administrator at the meeting. Gray knew Darman would not be keen on this (to say the least), and "for personal reasons" he himself didn't want to raise the issue. Since I concurred with the approach and was already planning to raise the issue, I told Boyden he could count on me to bring it up.

Had Porter been at the meeting, he would never have allowed the subject to arise. He was too much in dread of Darman. My colleague Jay Lefkowitz, who was also participating in the work on the deregulation initiative, remarked that without Porter in the White House for an entire week I must have felt like the little kid in the hit movie *Home Alone*.

During my chat with Gray, I also shared a copy of the 1989 materials Darman had refused to pass on to Bush. Gray and his deputy, John Schmitz, thought the materials constituted a "smoking gun" against Darman's claim that whatever reregulation had been occurring was the result of statutory mandates—the Clean Air Act and the Americans With Disabilities Act—over which he had exercised no control and in which he had relatively little involvement. Gray saw the 1989 materials as clear evidence that even *before* passage of the Clean Air Act and the ADA Administration reregulators had been hard at it, and Darman's OIRA had been essentially neutered. Here, at last, was evidence pointing to Darman's own acquiescence in new regulatory activities. He could no longer place all the blame on Gray (the leading sponsor of the ADA) or Roger Porter (the chief negotiator for Bush on the Clean Air Act).

The principals gathered that afternoon in the Roosevelt Room directly across from the Oval Office: Gray, Boskin, Darman, Ede Holiday, and Bill Kristol. The Vice President was the last to arrive and took a seat reserved for him in the center of the table. Representing Porter, I sat down at the oblong conference table immediately to the left of the Vice President. Darman sat diagonally across from Quayle. Scattered around the room on couches and chairs along the wall were various junior staffers from the different offices represented. This meeting had obviously gotten a good buildup around the complex, which meant attendance would be high. Even Skinner's chief aide, Cam Findlay, decided to join us for the discussion.

As we reviewed the details of the initiative—what it would include and how it would be presented—I made the suggestion that it would be difficult to run it directly from the White House. We would need strong, determined allies in each of the departments and agencies, and I urged that we consider naming someone in each department and agency to oversee the effort (Ede Holiday termed it a regulatory "mole"), someone who could keep the momentum going and the effort on track. Quayle asked me if I thought there were many examples of discretionary regulations on the books that might be eliminated or revised, and I gave him examples from my own work as Bill Bennett's regulatory "czar" at the Department of Education. I further urged that people not underestimate the difficulty of carrying out such an effort.

At that point Darman interrupted to clarify that most of the work on the moratorium would be conducted by Quayle's Council on Competitiveness. This was not a casual observation but a calculated move to head off any significant involvement of OIRA (and thus OMB and Darman) in what was bound to be a highly visible and controversial activity that was likely to rile Darman's friends in Congress. The late Warren Brookes had been right: Darman's style was to find others to be his fall guys. Just as Sununu took the heat for Darman's budget deal, so Darman was maneuvering Quayle to take the blame from Congress over the deregulatory initiative.

I took Darman's interjection as my cue to raise the OIRA issue. The next time Quayle called on me I noted that the number of issues we were contemplating was both diverse and complex, which raised the question whether the Competitiveness Council's modest staff was sufficient to handle not only those issues but the many more that would arise when each government department and agency began scrubbing its owns portion of the Code of Federal Regulations. More expertise would be needed, and I suggested that we "give consideration to reconstituting OIRA, perhaps by recess-appointing a new administrator," who would send a signal that our efforts were, indeed, serious this time.

Darman's reaction—more precisely, his temper tantrum—was better than I could ever have expected. Pulling his chair up to the table and puffing himself up in his chair, he looked across Quayle directly at me and declared, "*Reconstituting* OIRA! Now I know who's been the source of all these leaked press stories about me recently on the issue of regulations." (I had met Warren Brookes only once and had never spoken a word to him about Darman.) He then proceeded to explain why the OIRA appointment was a dumb idea, especially since no candidate would accept a job for which he'd never be confirmed by the Senate. Darman lectured me about how the OIRA career staff was already working hand-in-glove with Quayle's staff, and the notion of "reconstituting" OIRA was ridiculous.

I told Darman that he'd missed the point: By making a recess appointment to OIRA the President would avoid the confirmation process altogether. But Darman clearly wanted no further talk about the subject, which would tend to lay the blame for reregulating directly at his door, precisely where it belonged.

Darman's performance was extraordinary, but it achieved the purpose of getting the issue squarely on the table, which, I hoped, was enough to get it in to Bush. The next day Ede Holiday took me aside and told me that Darman's outburst was "completely uncalled for." Cam Findlay, who had sat behind Quayle on a couch during the meeting, confided to me that it was the first time in the few short weeks they'd been at the White House that the Skinner crew had seen the "real" Darman in action. Darman had embarrassed himself not only in front of the Vice President but in front of Skinner's people as well, all over a minor point.

The Administration's deregulation efforts *did* get under way with the President's announcement in his January 28, 1992, State of the Union Address. For ninety days the government was to refrain from publishing regulations—except those mandated by statute or court order—unless they had a positive effect on economic growth. The bulk of the work was handled by Boyden Gray and Mike Boskin, with the day-to-day heavy lifting undertaken by the small staff of Quayle's Competitiveness Council. No further mention was made of the OIRA recess appointment, and OIRA, despite its excellent career staff, remained what Dick Darman had wanted it to be: a toothless tiger. After 1989, no OIRA administrator was ever nominated. It appeared as if everyone in the West Wing of the White House—including George Bush himself—was afraid to incur the wrath of Richard G. Darman.

If Darman got his way here, it surely was not because his stance was correct. On the contrary, his policies, suggestions, and stonewalling were proving disastrous to Bush's popularity. But no one was willing to take him on. Bush, an avid reader of the newspapers, must have known the problems Darman was creating for him, and he certainly must have realized that Darman had failed to respond to his query about reregulating in 1989. The only plausible explanation for Bush's tolerating Darman lies in the fundamentally passive attitude the President took toward his own agendaless Administration. George Bush was not a man who would press hard for information. That failing revealed itself starkly in the circumstances surrounding his briefing on the 1990 budget deal.

Bush's biggest blunder as President was the decision to renege on his "no new taxes" pledge and to accept the 1990 budget deal that not only raised taxes but sent a weakening economy further into the tank. At one stage during the extended negotiations, when the contours of the final deal were emerging, Bush, who was traveling at the time on Air Force One, relayed a message back to the White House through Staff Secretary Jim Cicconi that he wanted a rack-up of the budget deal's pros and cons. It was altogether understandable that the President of the United States should be fully versed when it came to the strengths and weaknesses of such an important political and economic decision.

Darman prepared a list for the President, but it included only the *positive* aspects of the deal. Darman had refused to include any negative information whatsoever about his handiwork.

So George Bush—like John Sununu before him, who never understood the enormity of Bush's June 26, 1990, decision to renege on "no new taxes"—was never informed that the so-called spending restraints of the Darman budget deal also included enormous spending *increases* on top of base-level spending and that those increases were scheduled to receive inflationary adjustments upward in future years. All those features taken together made George Bush—who a few weeks after the deal was signed and took effect woke up to the fact—not only a reregulator but one of the biggest-spending Presidents in America's history!

The runaway budget deficit, the original rationale for entering into negotiations, had actually been exacerbated. As for the much-touted spending caps, whenever Bush praised these restraints on congressional spending he conveniently neglected to note that the caps had been bought and paid for by swallowing the largest increases in domestic discretionary spending in almost four decades and by leaving entitlements virtually untouched. No doubt Bush didn't know this, because Darman hadn't told him.

To Dick Darman, independently wealthy through family inheritance, government was just a game, a fascinating experiment with himself at the controls. Not only did he thumb his nose at direct requests from the President of the United States, but he also exhibited contempt for his peers in government and manifested an appalling distrust of the good sense of the American people. Darman's arrogance was so profound that he dismissed the role of the American electorate in deciding things for themselves. The *Wall Street Journal* late in 1991 quoted Darman saying that "I think you get a better outcome from the political system in a non-election year than in an election year."[10] Clearly Darman's view of the ideal government was one without elections or interference from real people. In his mind, the country would be far better off if important matters were simply left to "experts" like himself who would resolve everything through backdoor deals with the Democratic Congress. No need to put anything to a vote! And with Darman at Bush's side to the end, no one should have been surprised that George Bush was ultimately humiliated by a massive tide of populist discontent.

Jim Dyer, a senior official who served in the White House Office of Legislative Affairs, once told me that Darman was the "most destructive" person in the entire White House complex. Darman's willingness to misrepresent the facts to get his own way was becoming legendary. The problem was that no one in the White House with access to the President was willing to blow the whistle on this guy. But then, they really didn't have to. The newspapers, particularly the *Washington Times* and the *Wall Street Journal,* periodically carried stories or editorials calling for Darman's replacement. As time dragged on, it was obvious that Bush, who carefully read numerous morning papers, just didn't care and wasn't in the least prepared to dump Darman. Clayton Yeutter summed up the situation astutely in the summer of 1992: "The President is simply addicted to Darman."

Darman saw himself as the maestro of George Bush's overall legislative strategy on every issue and every policy. This meant that in his eyes he could crowd out not only other White House players, like Roger Porter, but Cabinet secretaries too. According to one former top Darman aide, if the OMB Director was scheduled to meet with members of Congress, before attending he was adamant about knowing in advance who would be present, how the table would be set up, and where he'd be sitting. If he wasn't satisfied that he would occupy the center of attention, he'd refuse to attend.

By the spring of 1992 Darman's antics were prompting more and more Republicans—now clearly worried about Bush's reelection prospects—to call for Darman to be sacked. As I learned from Debbie Steelman, Bush's domestic policy adviser during the 1988 campaign, John Sununu had informed Peter Grace, the government waste "czar" and head of the W. R. Grace Company, that Darman would be gone by June. I subsequently confirmed the Sununu–Grace discussion with two senior Grace executives. Unfortunately, Darman kept hanging on, even in the face of continued gloomy economic news that underscored the manifest failure of his policies.

Throughout the summer of 1992 Darman's influence over Bush, the White House, and the Bush–Quayle campaign only grew. When senior campaign officials prepared detailed analyses rebutting the budget numbers behind many of Governor Bill Clinton's campaign promises, Darman systematically blocked their release for weeks. The effect was an overall failure of the Bush–Quayle campaign to rebut many of the Clinton proposals. The impression left by Darman at Bush–Quayle headquarters was that if it wasn't Darman's idea, his numbers, or his memos, it wouldn't be used.

Darman's final folly, his ultimate act of betrayal toward George Bush, came less than a month before the November 3, 1992, election. The *Washington Post* columnist Bob Woodward unveiled a stunning four-part series starting on October 4 explaining many of the details surrounding George Bush's four-year economic record, going back to and including the origins of the 1988 "read my lips: no new taxes" pledge.

At the center of everything, of course, was Dick Darman, who clearly was one of Woodward's main sources and, apparently, the only official in the entire Bush Administration to get everything right. The 1988 tax pledge was branded "irresponsible"; Treasury Secretary Brady was ridiculed and dismissed as a "dolt"; and the President's decision to renounce the 1990 budget deal in March 1992 was labeled "sheer idiocy."[11]

The irony of the Woodward series will not be lost on longtime Darman observers. Aside from the devastating impact it had on Bush's campaign—coming at a time when one of the key issues was the President's own credibility in domestic and economic matters—there was an eerie similarity to the 1981 transgressions of Darman's friend and mentor, David Stockman. Reagan's first OMB Director nearly lost his job after giving a series of candid background interviews to William Greider, a writer. Stockman essentially labeled Reaganomics a "trickle down" fraud, and Greider published Stockman's musings in the *Atlantic* early in Reagan's first term.

Now it was Richard Darman, whose own mission was essentially derivative, namely, to complete David Stockman's plan to repeal Reaganomics with large tax increases, making the same error of judgment that his friend and predecessor had made. Republicans across the country were furious, but the President himself didn't seem to care much, for even after the Woodward series Darman remained within Bush's inner circle, helping to prepare Bush for his debates against Bill Clinton.

The only explanation I've heard from those close to Bush during this period is that while the President was indeed furious over Darman's remarks to Woodward, he saw no reason to panic and dump him. Up until the last weekend before the election, the President honestly believed he would be reelected, notwithstanding the fact that none of the polls showed him even close when it came to electoral votes.

To the end, the President simply chose not to believe the reality staring him in the face. Whether it was Darman's outrageous behavior or his impending electoral rout, George Bush kept looking the other way. Apparently he'd been doing this for years with respect to Dick Darman.

The day after the last Woodward article ran in the *Post*, Jude Wanniski, a supply-side economist, issued the following statement through his consulting firm, Polyconomics, Inc.:

In February 1984, I met Richard Darman for the first time, in his West Wing office where he served as Secretary to the Office of the President (Reagan). For about an hour we talked economics and politics, a pleasant meeting, as he confided his enthusiasm for supply-side economics and his admiration of Jack Kemp. I expressed surprise, saying I'd always believed that because of his long association with Jim Baker he was a Bush supporter. He scoffed and said, "I've never worked for George Bush for one minute." He said Baker had asked him in 1979 to be issues director in the Bush campaign for President and he had flatly refused. Why, I asked. "Because I had such little regard for the man's intelligence," he replied. At that moment, he clearly believed there was no chance Vice President Bush would ever be elected President, but that Kemp might. It subsequently became clear to me that Darman has a low opinion of the intelligence of practically everyone.

Wanniski wrote further in his memo: "The President, I hear, is said to be confused by the Woodward series, perhaps unable to grasp the enormity of the damage he has sustained at the hands of his Budget Director. Psychologists call this process *denial*."

Darman had managed to consolidate his power early in the Bush Administration. Porter was neutralized as a threat, and Darman's next move was indeed the cleverest step of all: By reorienting White House economic policy *away* from economic growth in favor of deficit reduction, Darman helped set the stage for his own takeover of both economic and domestic policymaking under George Bush. Roger Porter and others at the White House may have had big titles, but by mid-1990 all the power was effectively flowing in Dick Darman's direction.

4

Darmanomics at Work

"We Can't Lose!"

Deficit reduction is contractionary fiscal policy.

—James Tobin, Nobel economist[1]

George Bush inherited from Ronald Reagan a robust economy that was still expanding in what would ultimately become the longest peacetime period of sustained economic growth in American history. "Darmanomics" is the story of how the Bush Administration's economic and budget policy—crafted principally by OMB Director Richard Darman—reversed Reaganomics, failed even to defend its unambiguous triumphs, abandoned economic growth in favor of unrealized deficit reduction, stifled the development of innovative domestic initiatives, and ensured that George Bush would become a one-term President.

By virtually every indicator imaginable—Gross National Product growth, industrial output, almost nonexistent inflation, low interest rates—Americans enjoyed a period of prosperity and economic stability during the 1980s that had not been experienced since the Eisenhower Administration. Reagan's revolutionary supply side tax cuts helped ensure that, during his presidency, the economy as a whole would grow by some 32 percent, creating more than 20 million new jobs. At the same time, real average household incomes rose by over 12 percent, while the national poverty rate declined from roughly 15 percent to approximately 12.8 percent.[2]

It was also true that while the budget deficit had ballooned under Reagan, the Gramm–Rudman–Hollings law was steadily reducing the deficit as a percentage of annual GNP. If the trend continued, then Ronald Reagan would have been vindicated on his fiscal policy as well as on his defense policy. Just as we ultimately forced the collapse of global Communism, we would have grown our way out of the budget deficit.

For his first eighteen months as President, George Bush essentially stayed the course of Ronald Reagan's economic policies. That was, after all, one of the principal reasons he was elected President in 1988. In fact, some cynics quipped that Bush was never even elected in 1988; it was really Ronald Reagan who won a third consecutive term. The 1988 election was dismissed the way comedians had summed up George Bush's patrician background: "He was born on third base and went through life thinking he'd hit a triple."

The country seemed satisfied with four more years of Reaganomics. Articles and studies appeared touting the triumph of the supply siders when it came to advancing economic growth. One of the most significant analyses was written by one of our staff members at the White House, the Harvard economist Lawrence Lindsey. An unorthodox way to approach an understanding of Bush Administration economic policy is to follow Lindsey's activities within the White House. In many respects Lindsey's experience up until he left the White House in late 1991 to join the Board of Governors of the Federal Reserve Board represents in a microcosm what was happening to economic policymaking in the Bush White House.

As a protégé of Martin Feldstein (Chairman of Reagan's Council of Economic Advisers), Lindsey had served as a staff member on the President's Council of Economic Advisers for three years during the Reagan Administration. Before returning to join Roger Porter's policy operation in early 1989 as a Special Assistant to the President for Domestic Economic Policy, Lindsey had published the most thoroughgoing transactional analysis of supply side economics.

Lindsey's book, *The Growth Experiment*, was written just before he left Harvard to join the Bush Administration in 1989, but the study was not published until early 1990. *The Growth Experiment* was not designed for the average reader, but it was not aimed exclusively toward the quantitative economics profession, either.

Lindsey developed a model, which he used to examine tens of

thousands of actual taxpayer returns filed in the years after the 1981 tax reduction act. Lindsey's model reviewed the specific investment decisions actually made by real taxpayers in light of the reduced tax rates. He discovered that people indeed had responded to the new incentives by moving their assets out of tax dodges such as art and collectibles (which often produced nontaxable paper gains) and into activities that tended to boost the overall amount of taxes upper-income individuals paid even when their tax rates were lowered. As Lindsey demonstrated, under the stewardship of President Ronald Reagan the 1980s had witnessed an unprecedented period of sustained economic growth in which the rich did get richer—but so did everyone else! All groups in the economy at every income quintile did better economically and financially.

Supply siders around the country cheered Lindsey's book, but the national media virtually ignored it. Curiously, Lindsey's supply side arguments and findings were both ignored and rejected by most of Bush's policymakers (except for Vice President Dan Quayle). More than one White House aide told me that nobody at a senior level in the Bush White House cared about supply side economics because nobody there believed in Reaganomics! Lindsey himself was warned to stay off the talk shows, as there was no inclination to trumpet the past successes of Ronald Reagan. The only defenders left of Reaganomics were a handful of congressional Republicans like William Archer, Dick Armey, Newt Gingrich, and Vin Weber, who weren't afraid to remind people that tax policy during the Reagan–*Bush* years was characterized by lower marginal rates, increasing revenues, and growing prosperity.

During those years the income taxes paid by the nation's top 1 percent of taxpayers rose from $66 billion to $106 billion, a 60 percent increase. The top 10 percent of taxpayers saw their tax bills rise from $177 billion to $237 billion, a 34 percent increase. Meanwhile, the remaining 90 percent of taxpayers paid some $4 billion *less* in taxes in 1988 than in 1980, a 2.5 percent decline. All that was accompanied by strong economic growth. The notion that during the 1980s the rich got richer and the poor got poorer was sheer nonsense, but you wouldn't have gotten this message from the Bush White House.

One of Ronald Reagan's most steadfast soulmates, Britain's Prime Minister Margaret Thatcher, was also an ardent believer in supply side economics and deregulation. Lindsey had praised Thatcher's policies, noting in his book that "history will likely credit the world-wide resurgence of free markets and lower taxes to Margaret Thatcher as well as Ronald Reagan."[3]

I suggested to Lindsey that he send a signed copy of his book to Mrs. Thatcher. If he would give me a copy, I told him that I would pass it to a friend, Sherard Cowper-Coles, who was a senior aide at the British Embassy in Washington. He had promised to forward it directly to the Prime Minister.

Which he did. Lindsey received a gracious letter from the Prime Minister dated October 9, 1990, which closed with the following prophetic line: "President Reagan's policy of tax cuts helped give the United States more than eight years of steady economic growth and there is a lesson in that for everyone."

Except, apparently, for Americans and particularly for a Bush Administration that appeared to suffer collective amnesia when it came to remembering and practicing this "lesson." For at precisely the time Margaret Thatcher was reinforcing Reaganomics, George Bush's budget director had already gone "wobbly." He was on Capitol Hill negotiating a budget agreement that would dismantle and destroy Ronald Reagan's legacy.

By the end of June 1990 George Bush had placed the country's economy in the safekeeping of three top advisers: Nicholas Brady, Richard Darman, and John Sununu. Neither Roger Porter nor Mike Boskin was a key player. Porter's role in economic policy development was virtually nonexistent, and Boskin's was essentially to deliver updates on various leading economic indicators to Bush. With Porter bearing a lengthy title but exerting no influence, Lindsey found himself marginalized as well. Porter insisted that Lindsey report directly through him and chastised him for communicating directly with Sununu.

Conventional wisdom has it that George Bush's biggest economic policy disaster was his decision in June 1990 to renege on his "no new taxes" pledge and his subsequent signing of the 1990 budget deal. Conventional wisdom is correct on that point, but it could also benefit from some background, specifically another situation early in the second year of the Administration, a seminal event that set the stage for Bush's abandonment of "read my lips."

For twelve years the Republican Party had been identified as the party favoring lower taxes. Ronald Reagan had been elected and reelected on that premise, and opposition to higher taxes was, by the late 1980s, bedrock Republicanism. Walter Mondale learned this lesson the hard way in 1984, and as a result most national Democrats, while openly criticizing supply side theory as "trickle down economics," nonetheless kept their mouths shut about *raising* taxes.

At the same time few Democrats advocated cutting taxes, that is until early 1990, when Senator Daniel Patrick Moynihan of New York proposed scaling back the regressive Social Security tax rates by $55 billion to restore an even greater degree of progressivity to the country's tax laws. Moynihan's rationale was clever: He sought to force Republicans to confront the implications of the growing budget deficit by eliminating the practice of counting the Social Security surplus as a way of reducing the overall size of the federal budget deficit. If Republicans remained consistent to their true belief in lower taxes, they would embrace Moynihan's proposal, but they would then find themselves confronted with an even larger budget deficit! According to one GOP congressional staffer who was privy to the discussions, virtually all the Republican Senate staff favored the idea. As she put it, "there was such an identity of interest on this concept that Pat Moynihan found himself a guest speaker over at the Heritage Foundation! Reducing the payroll tax, perhaps even more than cutting the capital gains tax, would have meant thousands of new jobs."

The reaction to the Moynihan proposal was perhaps the most critical economic policy decision in the Bush Administration, because it signaled that, for the first time in more than a decade, Republicans would now retreat from their fundamental belief in cutting taxes. The decision opened up a fault line that within a few months—June through November 1990—would develop into a political earthquake of enormous dimensions for Bush and the Republican party.

Rather than embrace Moynihan's proposal (which many conservative members of Congress openly urged), Darman and Sununu orchestrated Administration policy in opposition to the idea. They jointly lectured and bullied the Senate Republican Policy Committee and urged the members to oppose the concept. There can be little doubt that Darman knew exactly what he was doing. His plan was to pursue with the Congress a budget deal having as its centerpiece a tax increase (presumably coupled with spending reduction and entitlement reforms) that would substantially reduce the deficit. Administration policy could not champion a tax cut at one point only to turn around a few months later and support a tax increase. So Darman and Sununu went to work to force Republican members of Congress to *oppose* Moynihan's Social Security cut. Back inside the White House, Darman was calling the Moynihan idea "fiscally irresponsible," while publicly the President was warning against tampering with Social Security benefits.

This was incredible stupidity, both as policy and as politics. Moynihan was playing a game of chicken. The issue was who would blink first. Had the Bush Administration and Hill Republicans rushed to Moynihan's support, the Democrats, had they chosen to oppose one of their own senior Senators, once again would have positioned themselves against a middle-class tax cut. Had the Democrats too backed Moynihan, Republicans could have welcomed them as converts to Reaganomics. Meanwhile, Republicans would have remained consistent with their own ideology while driving a wedge between congressional Democrats. As it turned out, Darman not only forced Republicans to blink first but ensured that for the first time in recent history Republicans were opposing a tax cut whereas the Democrats were poised to embrace one! By moving too quickly in opposing the plan, Darman spurred the Democrats to rally behind Moynihan's idea even faster. As for Darman's concerns about the deficit impact, it was by no means certain at the time that Moynihan's idea would have worsened the deficit.

Fortunately for the GOP, the congressional Democrats blew it. Had they been fully awake at the switch, they too would have supported Moynihan. Because of the fierce negative reaction to Moynihan's proposal orchestrated from the Bush White House, the Democrats didn't actually need to pass the New York Senator's plan. They had already achieved what they desired: Through tax policy the Democrats were beginning to reposition themselves as populist champions of the middle class while simultaneously achieving what was once thought impossible—positioning Republicans on the side of higher taxes!

This development, coupled with the administration's retreat on capital gains taxes, set the stage for the 1990 budget deal. When the White House refused in 1989 to fight for the President's capital gains tax cut, in the face of Senator George Mitchell's almost single-handed opposition, it conveyed a clear signal that Bush could be backed off from a major presidential campaign commitment. The Bush White

House was unwilling to fight for the cut: Treasury Secretary Brady had become spooked by the Democrats' specious "fairness" argument, and Darman, according to one Administration official, was pivotal in backing away from the idea. It was always something we could come back to, he reportedly said. Taken together with the hostile reaction to the Moynihan idea, caving in on capital gains was the functional and political equivalent of unilateral disarmament followed by suicide.

Darman, after all, had been plotting actively just after Bush's 1988 election to raise taxes. He had said openly to Jim Cicconi in 1989 that taxes would have to go up the next year.

But it wasn't just taxes that mattered. A former senior Darman aide freely acknowledged to me that "they were spenders, too. Right from the beginning. They thought the American people were not taxed enough. They threw a monkey wrench into supply side economics. They didn't believe it was working. They wanted to accomplish something on their own, but they had no philosophy of the world."

Like his friend and mentor David Stockman, Darman was obsessed with deficit reduction and was determined to address the deficit in part through significant tax increases. Senator Moynihan's plan would have bollixed his efforts to achieve the "deal of the century," and Darman was determined to eliminate anything and anyone who might get in his way. The only question was exactly *when* George Bush should renege on the most important pledge of his 1988 presidential campaign.

The January 1990 budget message prepared by Darman was the final turn of an elaborately orchestrated minuet. It began when Darman took the unusual step of combining what had usually been a budget consisting of four or more volumes into one 1,500-plus-page tome (its combined weight alone was intended to make a point).

Darman took another step that should have set off alarm bells throughout the Administration. In the Reagan years, each budget began with a special message from the President. Darman decided to replace that presidential message with a more extensive message from . . . himself! The President of the United States offered only a brief introductory statement.

Some writing was beginning to appear on the wall.

The focus of Darman's message was almost exclusively on the

perils of the deficit. Using his version of "hip" schoolyard language, he warned of "hidden PacMen" in the form of entitlement programs, which, if left unchecked, would spin out of control and ultimately dwarf the rest of federal spending. With an express bow to Sesame Street and popular culture, the patrician Darman wrote about the budget as the "Ultimate Cookie Monster" and about Washington as a "Wonderland" where the participants played a variety of "games',' such as "spend the peace dividend" game, "cut Social Security" game, and "beat the budget" game. Near the end came this interesting little paragraph nicely tucked away:

> It may be apt to view all this metaphorically as a set of children's games: the Budget as Cookie Monster; its future threatened by hidden PacMen; its path a journey through Wonderland. But at some point, it is appropriate to put games aside—at least for a while. *At some point there is an obligation to be serious.* At some point partisan posturing must yield to the responsibility to govern.[4]

There it was for those who could decipher "inside the beltway" speak: The "no new taxes" pledge was little more than "partisan posturing," something uttered in the heat of "campaign mode" and hardly to be taken seriously. Now we were into serious stuff and had to behave like responsible adults! Darman went on to write: "Sooner or later, the American political system will rise to the responsibility to be serious: to complete the job of fiscal policy correction. It may do this in small steps or large. It cannot do it with side-steps."[5]

This statement was the opening volley in Darman's six-month quest to focus Bush on embracing his grand scheme to tackle the mammoth federal deficit. The only problem was that under the existing Gramm–Rudman–Hollings law (leaving out the costs associated with the savings and loan bailout), the federal deficit already *was* declining. It was therefore arguable whether Darman needed to do anything further: the next "tranche" of Gramm–Rudman spending cuts would kick in later in 1990. If congressional Democrats could not live with the cuts, that was their problem. Forcing them to face up to the continued need for spending restraint (as distinguished from a tax increase) would have been a net plus for Republicans.

Here was a simple yet compelling fact that Darman never acknowledged and the Bush Administration never once chose to drive home, because its veracity confirmed the heart and soul of Ronald Reagan's supply side experiment: From 1980 to 1990, even with the Reagan supply side tax cuts, the U.S. Treasury collected some $1.1 *trillion* in excess of what it would otherwise have collected had tax rates remained at their 1980 level. On top of that $1.1 trillion, Congress authorized borrowing of some $822 billion, which gave the congressional appropriators a whopping total of $1.9 trillion extra to spend! Furthermore, once one factored out savings from programs where budgets were marginally reduced, Congress had some $2.4 trillion in available additional revenues during that period. Only a moron could have been oblivious to the overwhelming message of these figures: Americans were not being taxed too little; Congress just couldn't stop itself from spending.

Later in the spring of 1990, while Housing Secretary Jack Kemp and other supply siders in the Administration were crowing about Lindsey's *The Growth Experiment*, another book on the economy, *The Politics of Rich and Poor: Wealth and the American Electorate in the Reagan Aftermath*, hit the stores. The author, Kevin Phillips, was a longtime supposed Republican loyalist and strategist who had achieved notoriety in the late 1960s for *The Emerging Republican Majority*, which heralded a pro-GOP political realignment. Phillips was lauded as the master schemer whose ideas found implementation in the electoral politics of Richard Nixon and whose predictions for the GOP's future were widely hailed as prophetic—up until the derailment caused by Watergate.

The Politics of Rich and Poor was the opening volley in what emerged as class warfare, as Phillips drew conclusions antithetical to Lindsey's and dismissed supply-side triumphs. Reading the books back-to-back, one might think the two authors were describing entirely different periods in American history. What brought Phillips's book so much attention was his explicit and novel attack, given his nominal Republicanism, on the policies of a popular Republican conservative President, Ronald Reagan.

At one point Phillips quotes from Scott Burns, a conservative economics columnist, to the effect that the "facts suggest that the '80s will be known as the decade of the fat cats, a time when entrepreneurial pieties were used to beat the average worker into cowed submission while America's corporate elite moved yet higher on the hog."[6] Phillips likened the 1980s to the 1920s, a period of excess which led to "populist upheavals" and ultimately the presidency of Franklin Roosevelt. For Phillips, the 1980s had given rise to a "new political economics," which he described as "intensifying inequality and pain for the poor, the unprecedented growth of upper-bracket wealth, the surprisingly related [to what, Phillips never explains!] growth of federal debt, global economic realignment, foreigners gobbling up large chunks of America, the meaninglessness of being a millionaire in an era with nearly a hundred thousand 'decamillionaires.' "[7]

Phillips offered manna from heaven for the Democrats. Here was a well-known Republican strategist—a purported loyalist—supporting their escalating claim that the 1980s was a decade of greed in which the rich got richer and everybody else in America went to hell. With more and more stories penetrating the popular press about the excesses that led to the savings and loans failures and bailouts, the antics of Wall Street as revealed in Michael Lewis's *Liar's Poker*, the President's son's (Neil Bush's) own history with a failed savings and loan, and the billion-dollar earnings of junk bond king (and soon to be incarcerated) Michael Milken, Phillips's analysis fueled populist resentment against those who had prospered during the 1980s. Almost singlehandedly Phillips resurrected class warfare and "fairness" as viable political tools. His flawed but unrebutted populist rhetoric underscored the view that during the 1980s spending on the poor had declined, essential federal programs like education were cut below inflation, and only the wealthy became better off. On each point, Phillips was wrong. The question was whether the Bush Administration would mount a credible defense of economic reality and Reaganomics.

As long as the economy remained sound and continued its record of unparalleled growth, the debate over whose views were accurate, Lindsey's or Phillips's, didn't matter much. While the Democrats were quick to embrace Phillips as one of their own, the differences between the two authors' world views were confined to the op-ed pages of the national newspapers or to magazines like *The New Republic* and *The Nation*.

That debate began to change dramatically when Richard Darman hijacked George Bush's campaign pledge never to raise taxes. This one event more than any other policy decision constituted the defining moment in the Bush presidency. It altered the politics underlying the Republican governing and electoral coalition, giving rise to Pat Buchanan's 1992 challenge to Bush, and it defined Bush's political character as fundamentally inconsistent, craven, and disingenuous. Bush, of course, didn't help matters when he said in a televised interview early in 1992 that he would "do whatever it takes to get reelected."

By renouncing his solemn "no new taxes" promise, Bush effectively sided with establishment Republicans like Darman and Treasury Secretary Nick Brady, who believed that Ronald Reagan's decade of growth was a thinly veiled decade of greed, led by Keynesian deficit spending policies, not the supply-side policies so painstakingly analyzed by Larry Lindsey. Bush's apostasy on taxes was the result of a palace coup orchestrated by Darman. By convincing Bush that the chief threat to the economy was the budget deficit, Darman managed to con Bush away from the one message that had sustained and galvanized Republicans since 1978: economic growth through lower taxes.

Another, institutional effect of the budget deal and Darmanomics is central to understanding why the Bush presidency fell apart in little over a year. After the deal was concluded, Darman and Sununu became locked together in a fraternal death embrace. Anyone who criticized their deal or proposed policies even slightly at odds with the legislation was treated as a leper. Policymaking ground to a halt. In fact, policy was unmade in many respects: Notable advances achieved during the first eighteen months of the Bush Administration simply stalled.

Here's how one senior White House aide, Jim Cicconi, who was there at the time, explained it:

> Our mission coming into office after the 1988 campaign was to refine Reaganism. Take off some of the sharp edges and round it off, particularly in areas like civil rights, the environment, capital gains, day care, and protection for the disabled. Our first year, 1989, was a good year. We got up a good head of steam on those issues in 1989 and then got sidetracked in 1990 on the economic stuff.
>
> If the truth be known, we were beginning to stake out novel, *Republican* solutions in areas like child care, empowerment, and Kemp's revolutionary ideas for housing like vouchers, home ownership, and tenant management.
>
> Childcare was a great example. The hero behind this is Richard

Breeden. In the 1988 campaign he developed a Republican solution, came up with something we could be *for*. Our voucher approach drew loud applause on the '88 campaign stump. Teeter, by the way, had opposed it, afraid that raising it as an issue could expose us to being outbid by the Democrats. Ultimately, Teeter came around and helped move the idea to fruition. Breeden prevailed, and we succeeded in characterizing the Democrats as wanting to regulate day care from Washington and "regulate grandma." Sununu is a hero on this one, too, because he made sure that the Republican childcare language remained in the text of the budget deal.

In fact, the childcare portion of the 1990 budget legislation (even though it was another expanded entitlement) was the only real triumph in that act for George Bush, and when Sununu found the Democrats had deleted it just before passage, he insisted that it be penciled into the margins of the final text.

Thereafter, however, we failed to recognize the lessons and the importance of what had been achieved. According to Cicconi, "We were off to a good start by early 1990. Bush got tremendous foreign policy breaks when Communism collapsed, but we weren't intellectually equipped to follow through. The first year or so we rolled on through with momentum from the 1988 campaign, but there was no follow-through. We were just too slow to perceive the revolutionary nature of Kemp at HUD."

The actual palace coup came on June 26, 1990, when the President made the following announcement at the White House

It is clear to me that both the size of the deficit problem and the need for a package that can be enacted require all of the following: entitlement and mandatory program reform; tax revenue increases; growth incentives; discretionary spending reductions; orderly reductions in defense expenditures; and budget process reform.

With this one assertion, Bush squandered not only his political capital but also his own credibility. Democrats now knew for a certainty that he would compromise with them on even his most fundamental "beliefs." It was the single biggest mistake of his presidency—a conclusion that he finally admitted publicly on March 3, 1992. But that was too late. By then, Bush had already sown the seeds of his 1992 loss.

Bush's statement left the Republican faithful wondering whether he had after all really believed that Ronald Reagan's policies constituted "voodoo economics." The "no new taxes" pledge formed the heart and soul of Bush's 1988 election, the one issue on which he could be said to have received a mandate. By sacrificing that belief, he effectively signaled to the Democrats that everything was on the table and that all he stood for now was business-as-usual Republicanism that stressed deficit reduction.

I first heard the news of Bush's broken pledge while leaving the Capitol Hill office of Peter Smith, a freshman GOP Representative. (He too lost his reelection bid that year, caught up in a brouhaha over the budget deal.) Initially I thought Bush's statement was nothing more than a reiteration of earlier remarks that he stood ready to work with the Congress to address the deficit issue, but when I saw the actual language, it was clear that Bush had gone over a cliff.

Oddly enough, however, Sununu did not interpret the President's statement that way. As Jim Cicconi told me over lunch in the Mess, Sununu firmly believed in June 1990 that the President's statement did not break his "no new taxes" pledge. When Cicconi suggested otherwise, the chief of staff was emphatic: "That's not what [the President's statement] said." How Sununu could square his interpretation with the reality of the President's rhetoric remains a mystery. In any event, the press knew what had happened and from the very beginning hailed the statement as a retreat from Bush's unequivocal 1988 campaign promise.

During the summer of 1990 the budget negotiations continued with very little progress. At one of our morning OPD staff meetings, Pinkerton, Lindsey, and I had raised some skeptical questions about how all of this was going to work out. We were concerned that the President had made a dreadful mistake by permitting Darman to define the central issue as deficit reduction rather than sustained economic growth. With gleeful smugness, Roger Porter explained the brilliance of the strategy: Even if the negotiations broke down, Republicans and the President could not lose. If the talks failed, then we had an issue to use against the Democrats. If they succeeded, then the President got the credit for finally tackling the deficit. "We can't lose. . . . We've got them coming and going."

Pinkerton and I just looked at each other across the table. Lindsey was sitting next to me, so I couldn't see his expression. We could not believe how idiotic Porter's assessment was. Porter's naïve optimism had ignored another critical political reality: Bush had abandoned his "no new taxes" pledge only a few months before the 1990 off-year elections. Moreover, he had done so at a time when dozens of prospective Republican candidates for the House and Senate, incumbents and challengers alike, were also out campaigning on a "no new taxes" pledge. When Bush reneged on his pledge, those party loyalists, among Senate candidates like Representatives Lynn Martin, Pat Saiki, and Claudine Schneider—women all, candidates all, Republicans all, two years before the Democrats' "year of the woman"—who were cut off at the knees, their message preempted by the very leader whose pledge they had proudly and defiantly made their own.

When conservative House Republicans, led by Newt Gingrich, banded together and defeated the first budget deal, the Bush White House—particularly Darman and Sununu—was outraged. An incumbent Republican President had been blocked by his own supposedly loyal troops! But loyalty in the Bush White House apparently ran in one direction only. The President could change *his* mind, and Republicans everywhere were expected to follow in lockstep.

It just didn't happen. Matters grew even more strained among Republicans after the second budget deal was finally concluded and Ed Rollins, former Reagan campaign chairman and head of the National Republican Congressional Campaign, advised GOP candidates for Congress that fall not to hesitate to distance themselves from Bush and the budget deal. Again, there was a firestorm at the White House, but Rollins was giving his clients sound advice. What happened next was unfortunate and would sow the seeds for Rollins's eventual defection to Ross Perot in 1992, because from then on Rollins was *persona non grata* at the Bush White House. But Rollins was ultimately vindicated: Most of those GOP candidates who followed his judgment and put some distance between their campaigns and Bush and his budget deal won handily. Many GOP candidates who had espoused the deal lost.

I attended a dinner with Rollins on October 23, 1990, the day after his controversial campaign memorandum was leaked to the press. Among the dozen or so guests present at Washington's Four Seasons Hotel were Rich Bond and Frank Donatelli, two Bush and GOP loyalists who ran a political consulting firm, along with several White House aides. Rollins's message was sobering: Since Bush had traded his "no new taxes" pledge for the budget deal's emphasis on deficit reduction and new taxes, contributions to the GOP campaign chest had dropped substantially, even dangerously. (This would prove another bad omen for 1992!) What Washington insiders like Brady, Darman, and Sununu ignored was just how central the tax issue was to GOP harmony, solidarity, and credibility.

The November 1990 budget deal signaled that Bush had no political principles whatsoever. If he could so easily relinquish the central plank of his 1988 election campaign and cave in to the Democrats, then what did he really stand for? The moment Bush defined economic policy as deficit reduction rather than sustained economic growth, he not only alienated a substantial part of his core constituency but also ensured that the months ahead would be characterized by poor economic performance and a halting, sluggish recovery from a recession that was becoming increasingly evident by late 1990, official Administration optimism notwithstanding.

Another aspect of the budget deal deserves mention: the fact that it was reached behind closed doors, involving little more than a handful of insiders from Washington's political establishment. Most people in America dislike elitism, and the budget summit held at Andrews Air Force Base was the quintessence of elitism. Recall that in early 1990 Darman had called for "the American political system" to be "serious" in rising to the occasion to "complete the job of fiscal policy correction." Instead of an open process, Darman and his Capitol Hill cronies orchestrated a behind-closed-doors agreement that had no support among the American people. Paul Gigot, the *Wall Street Journal* columnist, captured the atmospherics best when he wrote that in Darman's view, "the essence of government is tinkering with mechanisms, not persuading voters; manipulating insiders, not changing the public mind. No wonder he was no match for serious politicians like Democratic Sens. George Mitchell and Robert Byrd."[8] One of Darman's former Reagan Administration colleagues explained to me: "Dick likes the global conceptualizing, thinking the big political thoughts, but when it comes to the details, he gets his pants taken off every time."

Another unusual event occurred shortly after the conclusion of the budget deal. When conservative House Republicans, led by Newt Gingrich, blocked the first budget deal in October 1990, Darman and Sununu were outraged. As a further indication of just how far the worm was turning, we now had a situation in which the Bush Administration had just agreed to raising taxes, renouncing Reaganomics, and acquiescing in major domestic spending increases, while simultaneously castigating GOP members of Congress who were willing to stand up for real spending cuts, economic growth, and lower taxes! As a political party, we were now at war with ourselves.

The bad blood between Darman and Sununu, on one side, and people like Gingrich (including HUD Secretary Kemp, who had also opposed the deal) on the other, was spilling into the media and could not continue. Darman began to send visible and public make-up signals to Gingrich, although deep down he continued to seethe with resentment over his perceived perfidy. Gingrich had, after all, voted against the second deal too and, to Darman's lasting chagrin, had boycotted the Andrews meetings after the first deal collapsed.

While Darman was pretending publicly that everything was forgiven, he was privately cursing Gingrich and others. Mike Horowitz, who had also served in the Reagan Administration's OMB as General Counsel, ran into the OMB Director in the halls of the Old Executive Office Building shortly after the budget deal. To his surprise, Darman spontaneously invited him into his spacious office and opened the discussion pointedly: "So, Mike, I hear you're against the budget deal." Horowitz was, but the former Stockman aide also acknowledged that the architecture of the deal—the equally shared pain of entitlement cuts *and* tax increases—made some sense. The cuts, however, never materialized, as the congressional Democrats forced through more taxes and more spending.

Horowitz now found himself a captive in Darman's office, in a scene which the former Reagan aide describes as "eerie." Darman proceeded to demean both Gingrich and Kemp. For nearly an hour Darman lashed out against the two men, shouting, his arms flailing in the air.

Darman had less to say about Kemp, whose opposition to the deal was not as vocal as Gingrich's. "I'll get Kemp fired," Darman said of the HUD Secretary.

Darman treated Gingrich with the scorn and the contempt reserved for a congressional peon: "He's only worth thirty votes."

Horowitz interrupted: "And how many votes are *you* worth, Dick?"

Darman exploded. "This meeting is over." And it was. The two men have spoken only once—briefly in the Mess—since that encounter.

The circumstances surrounding the budget deal point to a broader and fundamentally more serious problem that goes to the heart of George Bush's presidency: Was the President of the United States being systematically misled by one of his most senior advisers? If John Sununu honestly believed in June 1990 that George Bush's statement that launched the negotiations that ultimately led to the budget deal did *not* amount to a reversal of Bush's "no new taxes" pledge, what in God's name had he and Bush been told?

They apparently hadn't been told the truth. According to one observer, at the heart of the decision to sign the disastrous budget deal lay a monumental breakdown in the legal advice provided to the President of the United States. It was perfidy—or ineptness—of the greatest magnitude.

According to one insider, Darman never explained to Bush that a budget summit with the Congress was wholly unnecessary. There was never any reason to compromise at all with the Democrats, much less on their terms. With the prospect of major budget cuts called for under Gramm–Rudman–Hollings beginning in October 1990, there was a legitimate practical concern about what would happen to the government if the cuts were made according to the law. There was also serious political concern about the impact such spending reductions would have on an array of affected interest groups. Under the Gramm–Rudman law, the burden was on the Congress to amend the statute if it felt the cuts were too draconian. Bush didn't have to do anything. If no agreement was reached on the level of spending for the 1991 fiscal year, which began on October 1, 1990, Bush could simply close down the federal government while ensuring that essential services—air traffic controllers, prison guards, food safety inspectors, the processing of Social Security checks—were maintained.

The stage was apparently set by a series of Darman memos to Bush throughout the spring of 1990 setting forth the dire, apocalyptic consequences that would befall the nation if later that fall the country had to endure a Gramm–Rudman–Hollings sequester. During that period, however, Darman presented only one side of the story, the blackest picture of what would happen if Bush failed to cut a deal with Congress. Apparently no one presented a different interpretation of the legal options available to Bush that, if pursued, could have given the President another set of options beside signing on to a tax increase.

During the spring and summer of 1990 Darman provided Bush with briefing papers that were never vetted through the normal West Wing circulation process. Traditionally, the staff secretary's office handled the paper flow into and out of the Oval Office, in part to ensure that Bush was not receiving biased advice. In this case, the staff secretary saw what came out but not what went in.

One senior Bush aide familiar with the situation recalled, "Darman had the papers going in." Of course, memo or no memo, no one could control what Darman actually said once inside the Oval Office. "The Gramm–Rudman–Hollings dynamic was in our favor. The question was whether the Democrats would blink first. Darman had to change this dynamic by portraying, rightly or wrongly, the deficit as getting much, much worse than expected very quickly."

Not only did Darman not present the entire picture as to what might happen if no deal were reached, but, as already noted, he also ignored a direct request from Bush to explain to him the positive as well as the negative aspects of the proposed budget deal. A White House aide familiar with the episode says, "Dick Darman just provided [to Bush] what he wanted to provide."

It is therefore arguable that George Bush made the biggest blunder of his presidency based on misinformation from his own budget director. Instead of forcing the Congress to blink first, Bush blinked on the basis of arguments that he was responsible for governing and could not, as President, allow a massively dislocating Gramm–Rudman–Hollings sequester to occur.

Throughout his tenure as OMB Director, Darman never installed a permanent political General Counsel. Instead, he named a career attorney, Bob Damus, as acting OMB General Counsel. While Damus was a competent lawyer, the chief OMB counsel's job was a key position. During the Reagan Administration when it was held by the brilliant and energetic Mike Horowitz, it had been a focal point for many critical domestic policy initiatives. Early in the Bush Administration a Darman protégé at OMB reportedly announced that Darman didn't want a "Mike Horowitz or Lloyd Cutler [Jimmy Carter's White House Counsel] kind of lawyer." And they didn't get one, not in the sense of an independent legal presence who could stand up forcefully to Dick Darman.

The result for George Bush was the flip side of Reagan's 1981 showdown with the air traffic controllers. In this instance, however, it was Bush—following Darman's advice—who blinked, essentially caving in to the Democratic leadership in Congress, which outsmarted Darman.

Darman apparently never told Bush that the apocalyptic scenario of a Gramm–Rudman–Hollings-induced sequester never had to occur. Assuming sufficient strength in the Congress to sustain presidential vetoes of either separate appropriations bills or an omnibus continuing resolution (an assumption that was by no means extravagant, as the passage of time showed), Bush could have forced the Congress to make the necessary reductions in domestic discretionary spending and entitlements. Instead of a "draconian" Gramm–Rudman–Hollings sequester, Bush could have presided over an old-fashioned Ronald Reagan shutdown, forcing the Democratic leadership in the Congress to come to the table on his terms. In fact, given the absence of appropriations bills, Darman's much feared Gramm–Rudman sequester was impossible: you cannot sequester a nonexistent budget. Instead, had Bush made effective use of the shutdown process, he—not Congress—would have held the upper hand.

A look at the final budget deal showed that the Administration had apparently scrapped deficit reduction as a goal too. The so-called budget reforms of the budget deal replaced real spending cuts with adherence to a process. The actual *size* of the annual deficit didn't really matter any more under the law, so long as the annual appropriations ritual adhered to the new spending caps for discretionary spending in military, international, and domestic programs and abided by the "pay as you go" principle for entitlements. It was the ultimate triumph of process over reality, with reality showing both rising spending in real terms and an exploding budget deficit.

As for the spending cuts, nothing of substance was accomplished to rein in mandatory entitlement spending. While it was true that new spending had to be offset by reductions elsewhere, spending on existing mandatory programs kept chugging right along. Once again, Republicans had swallowed tax hikes and had failed to hold the Democrats to the promised spending reductions. Darman told the Cabinet that the budget deal produced the largest deficit reduction package in history. In truth, it was almost all tax increases, no spending cuts, and phony entitlement reforms.

Meanwhile, Darman was bragging in the media about how all of this was a big victory for the President over Congress. This was about as convincing as Alexander Haig's infamous "I'm in charge here!" line. If you have to brag about it, it probably isn't so.

And it wasn't. The new law actually undermined existing presidential authority under Gramm–Rudman and the Anti-deficiency Act.

Congress rewrote the old Gramm–Rudman process to deny the President authority to allocate spending reductions among various programs. OMB now had to report to Congress on August 20 (well ahead of the next fiscal year) as to how any mini-sequesters would apply. If Congress then disagreed with the new scorekeeping, it could simply thumb its nose at OMB and rely on estimates from the Congressional Budget Office and the General Accounting Office, both of which were creatures of the Congress.

Darman, of course, saw matters differently. Bob Woodward wrote in the *Washington Post* just a month before the 1992 election that it was evident as early as shortly after the 1988 election that Darman had a plan for a grand strategy, to include raising taxes, domestic spending cuts, and serious entitlement reform as a means to address the budget deficit. According to Woodward, Darman was motivated by a desire to maximize his own leverage as an Administration player. Bush had behaved irresponsibly ("sheer idiocy" was what he'd later called the President's decision to repudiate the budget deal) in making his "no new taxes" pledge, and the Congress was equally irresponsible for its failure to curb entitlements.[9]

This attitude left Dick Darman at the center of the action, the only one who could save the President, the Congress, and the country from each other. The power! The glory of it all!

To minimize the risk of any dissent, Darman hijacked not only Administration budget policy but objective legal policy as well. The interpretation of what would happen without the grand deal served Darman's purposes in achieving his ends, and nobody—not the White House Counsel's office, not the Department of Justice—was prepared to contradict him.

The net effect on Bush was to condition him—manipulate him, if you will—to believe that the country would fall apart unless the President signed a tax increase. (According to one former senior OMB official in the Reagan years, this was, after all, the same Dick Darman who, along with David Stockman during the 1980s, used to joke about Ronald Reagan as "Dummy Number One.")

As Bush's chief negotiator with the Congress, however, Darman ended up applying pressure, but to his own side, to his own principal, the President of the United States. Congressional Democrats knew full well—after all, they were politicians and had felt the potential wrath of the electorate, whereas Darman had nothing but contempt for the electorate—that Bush would take the resulting heat for raising taxes, welshing on his promise, and ultimately for presiding over a worsening economy once one of the largest tax increases in history kicked in.

The sad part of the story is that none of it worked to help George Bush. He got absolutely nothing out of the 1990 budget deal. To conclude the deal in the first place, Darman benignly neglected ballooning domestic discretionary spending and creeping reregulation throughout the economy. Furthermore, there were no entitlement reforms; the 1990 "Budget Enforcement Act," as the deal was formally dubbed, actually codified additional entitlements involving childcare and Medicaid.

And what about the much-touted spending restraint imposed by the "pay as you go" offset formula? This, too, was a sham. According to one practical (and cynical, but totally correct) interpretation, all the "pay-go" limitation did was codify the existing political convention of relying on budget gimmickry and phony savings to justify whatever new expenditures were desired. Years later, when the savings never materialized, people like Darman could blame the error on "technical" problems with the original forecasting model or estimates.

None of it actually worked as policy or as politics. The ink on the budget deal was hardly dry when it became apparent to OMB and others that the economy was stalling and that a growing economic downturn would mean a ballooning federal deficit. While Darman was still touting his successes as a negotiator and trying to get the media to portray his handiwork as his "deal of the century," OMB's career staffers were advising that the hemorrhaging was likely to continue and even worsen.

One of Darman's senior career staffers, David Kleinberg, confided to me shortly after the budget deal that the loss of revenue in the federal Medicare and Medicaid programs alone was so great that the fiscal year 1992 deficit would probably approach $400 billion! When I mentioned this assessment in a subsequent staff meeting, Porter raised his eyebrows. Even Larry Lindsey expressed shock. (As it turned out, the official OMB projection for the fiscal year 1992 budget deficit, released in the fiscal year 1993 budget announced in early February 1992, was $399.4 billion! The actual deficit clocked in at $290 billion after nearly $100 billion in S&L cleanup costs were postponed until the next fiscal year.)

When it came to economic policy, what did Bush stand for? At least as defined by the November 1990 budget deal, it meant a preoccupation with deficit reduction (versus economic growth), tax increases, and a near total renunciation of Ronald Reagan's supply side experiment. Within just a few months after the deal was concluded it became apparent that Republicans had been snookered once again. Darman and Bush both crowed about how they had swallowed modest tax increases in exchange for $500 billion in real spending restraint over the next five years. They would repeatedly point to the "pay as you go" requirement and the so-called enforceable spending caps.

But the public was never told until much, much later that the projected $500 billion in savings was a fiction, premised on wildly optimistic assumptions about interest rates, unemployment, and economic growth. The worsening economy caused federal expenditures to expand rapidly for income maintenance programs, but even without the adverse effects of the emergent recession Bush had capitulated to real spending *increases* as demanded by Senator Robert Byrd of West Virginia. Under the 1990 budget deal, domestic discretionary programs would enjoy the largest baseline increases in spending in years, if not decades, and the agreement then ensured that this base would be inflated thereafter. That is what Senator Byrd (whose creed was that West Virginia would work better if only he could move more federal dollars and employees there) meant when he pointed out in the floor debate that the spending caps were crafted so that the appropriations committees would have no trouble at all living under them from 1991 through 1993.

Darman's January 1990 budget message had warned against a "Wonderland" of current services budgeting where "a 'cut' may really be an increase, and a deficit said to be going 'down' may really be going up."[10] The country learned in the next year that the budget deal had itself created a "Wonderland" in which George Bush would extol $500 billion in theoretical savings, while the headlines kept announcing record-level and growing budget deficits.

The importance of answering the question of what George Bush stood for in economic policy—fortunately, for Bush—was overshadowed by the Persian Gulf crisis. The President's January 1991 budget message for fiscal year 1992 spoke of the need for economic growth as well as research and investment in America's future, but the winter and spring months of 1991 saw virtually no activity from the White House or the Treasury Department to address the country's growing economic and fiscal worries.

Darman's January 1991 budget message showed a marked departure from his cavalier jauntiness the previous year. His tone was explicitly "somber," recognizing that the economy was weakening. Darman blamed three factors: excessively tight monetary policy, an unfolding "credit crunch," and the adverse effects of the Persian Gulf crisis. The budget deal, however, was seen as a bright spot, an accomplishment that would "reduce . . . the previous baseline deficit by $72.9 billion for 1992 and $138.1 billion for 1995."[11] Darman's budget message also praised the budget deal for having eliminated several "perverse incentives" for the Administration "to err in the direction of rosy [economic] projections."[12] The sorry fact is that such projections tended to be relatively accurate *before* the budget deal. Afterward, Administration economic forecasting went haywire.

The Persian Gulf War was over by late February, and by the spring of 1991 the economy was obviously not rebounding, even though our coalition partners made substantial contributions to offset the cost of both Desert Shield and Desert Storm. Blaming the recession on the Gulf War seemed less and less plausible.

As the slump continued and worsened, the Administration's focus turned to economic growth. As with many other aspects of domestic policy, Bush's preferred tactic here was to put a few ideas out on the stump, walk away from them, and then see what the Democrats did. When nothing happened—which should have come as no surprise to a White House that had failed to rally its troops both in the Congress and in the electorate—Bush just dropped the issue rather than fight.

A recurring example of Bush's reluctance to engage the Congress over issues of substance on his economic agenda is the strange fate of his proposal to cut the capital gains tax rate, perhaps the keystone of his effort to spark economic growth and renewed entrepreneurial activity.

The 1986 Tax Reform Act further lowered individual tax rates but at the same time substantially raised rates on capital gains. Bush had proposed significant cuts in those rates in the 1988 campaign and again in his February 1989 message to Congress. By the summer of 1989, the House had passed Bush's proposal, and the Senate stood ready to follow suit: Bush's legislative team had assembled more than a majority of Senators to vote in favor of the capital gains tax cut.

Senate Majority Leader George Mitchell, however, recognizing that a Bush victory would mean yet another triumph for supply side economic theory, worked successfully to block Senate passage on procedural grounds. No vote was ever taken.

Instead of railing against Mitchell (after all, Bush placed a premium on maintaining cordial relations with his former congressional colleagues), Bush simply walked away from the issue. Only after the 1990 budget deal, where Bush maneuvered himself to accept a tax increase, did he decide again to champion the capital gains tax cut, in part to reestablish his support for lower taxes after his capitulation to Darmanomics.

This time his proposal emerged half-baked. In his 1991 budget message and State of the Union address, instead of continuing to assert aggressively that lowering the capital gains tax would produce revenue, Bush apparently accepted the idea that the jury was still out on whether such a cut would be a revenue-loser or would actually generate tax dollars (as supply siders claimed it would). To resolve that question for good, Bush proposed cutting the rates only after a bipartisan study of the issue led by Federal Reserve Board Chairman Alan Greenspan. Bush invited the Democrats to appoint their own members of the Greenspan panel so that the inquiry could begin.

Once again, Bush's preference for the politics of consensus over the politics of confrontation got him nowhere. The Democrats never accepted his idea. In fact, they ignored it altogether, and the matter was dropped. By that spring, even Bush's own Treasury Department had omitted capital gains cuts from its listing of priority agenda items that it sent the White House Office of Cabinet Affairs every quarter.

While the President and his advisers periodically talked about the need for economic growth, the economy continued to falter. As the weeks and months passed, that much-vaunted budget deal looked less and less successful. Although it technically constrained new discretionary spending through its spending caps, and new entitlements through its pay-as-you-go principle, existing entitlement spending was virtually out of control. It was becoming increasingly clear that the deal's heavy tax increase was hurting the economy and, moreover, failing to constrain a burgeoning deficit. As the economy worsened throughout the spring of 1991, Bush finally admitted the country was in a recession but added that it would be short-lived. By late spring and early summer, Administration spokesmen like Marlin Fitzwater and Michael Boskin were proclaiming that the recovery was at hand.

What was construed as a moderate economic expansion in the spring of 1991 prompted Administration economists to believe that a recovery had arrived. On that assumption, Bush would initially resist a Democratic proposal to extend unemployment benefits to millions of Americans whose assistance had run out after twenty-six weeks and who were still unemployed as the recession dragged on. The White House made the correct initial decision, although again it was never properly explained to the public. The perception of an out-of-touch and uncaring President only worsened as the economy flattened out and remained sluggish through the rest of 1991. As the recession touched more and more middle-class and white-collar Americans, Democrats found that their message of economic populism and their Kevin Phillips-like portrayal of the Reagan years as a "decade of greed" were gaining credence. Both Ronald Reagan's and George Bush's popularity was plummeting; remarkably, Jimmy Carter's was on the rise.

The Congress would repeatedly vote to extend unemployment benefits, which Bush would veto, up until the late fall. By that time, it was too late for Bush to receive any political credit for his grudging acceptance that the recession was still lingering. On the last day of October, Bush signaled he would sign an extension of benefits because "people are hurting and they ought to be helped." Any extension, however, would have to be temporary, be self-financing, and not raise taxes. Even though Bush was now doing the correct thing (in part to arrest his rapidly eroding popularity), he did so in a context constrained by the strictures of the 1990 budget deal. He was trying to reposition himself as Santa Claus, but the relentless logic of the politics he had been trapped in cast him as the Grinch.

At the end of October 1991 the Commerce Department announced that the third-quarter real growth rate for the nation's Gross National Product was 2.4 percent, a promising figure but still below the 2.5 to 3.0 percent expected. At the time it was the best quarterly increase in the Bush Administration, but there was no cause for real celebration. Most of the GNP increase could be traced to a decline in the rate at which businesses were reducing their inventories rather than a solid, broad-based expansion. Inflation was still under control—always a good factor—but consumer demand, the traditional leading indicator of an economic recovery, was flat.

Preparing for a speech I had to give on November 20 to the American League of Lobbyists, I requested some economic data from the Council of Economic Advisers. I wanted to be as upbeat as possible in my remarks, and the CEA's "talking points" were cautiously optimistic—"while not yet fully recovered, the economy is moving in the right direction, the recession has ended and the expansion has begun." The next day I received talking points from our own staff that told a different story: "Statistics released in recent weeks indicate that the economic recovery, which seemed strong in the summer, may be faltering." If the economists in the White House were uncertain about our current situation, it was little wonder that the American public was confused. My new talking points ticked off the reasons for concern: unemployment claims were rising; leading indicators were falling again; orders for manufactured durable goods were declining; home sales and housing starts were down; and industrial production was almost flat. It was also true that interest rates were declining, along with the inflation rate, and the stock market was still relatively buoyant. A weaker dollar meant a significant rise in the country's export sector, but no one seemed to care much. The Conference Board reported that its index of consumer confidence (on a downward path for the previous six months) fell sharply by 12.5 points in October 1991, from 72.9 to 60.4.

Throughout this period, the White House offered no credible explanation of what was happening to the country's economy. One year after the much-vaunted budget deal, it was evidently not working. The economy was in the tank and the deficit was rising, not falling. With each passing day it became harder to blame the downturn on Saddam Hussein's invasion of Kuwait more than a year before.

Essayists of all political stripes were starting to write convincingly and frequently about a new American economic malaise. Paul McCracken, a former CEA chairman, warned that slow economic growth was "the big domestic issue,"[13] while Bush's arch-foe George Will (who once called Vice President Bush a "lap dog") began to ask whether middle-class America was really better off after four years of Bush economic policy. Will observed that real disposable income was lower in late 1991 than when Bush became President. As for the merits of the 1990 budget deal, Will correctly noted that "[t]wo-thirds of the budget—entitlements and debt service—are exempt from its spending caps."[14] The conservative columnist Warren Brookes fingered stagnant job growth as likely to create a permanent decline in America's standard of living should Bush win a second term.[15] Christopher Byron, writing in *New York Magazine*, explained that the budget deal imposed a $165-billion tax hike that "has turned out to be the dopiest economic move since Richard Nixon adopted wage and price controls twenty years ago."[16] According to Byron, *after* the 1990 agreement the budget deficit grew by almost 40 percent; unemployment shot up by almost 23 percent; inflation was rising slowly by some 3.8 percent; housing starts dropped by more than 6 percent; and car sales plummeted by more than 11 percent.[17]

What emerged was a stubborn recession affecting a group of people traditionally untouched by bad economic news: America's white-collar, service-sector middle class, which also included people in the media, or people the media knew personally. It was not a pretty picture, and all that was really on the mind of the White House was getting the Congress to adjourn for the year and leave Washington.

But before Congress could adjourn, two significant things happened, one in Pennsylvania, the other in Washington. Both events were to prove fateful for the Republican party. The first was an unusual Senate race in which the incumbent, Senator Harris Wofford, appointed to the Senate on the death of John Heinz, retained his seat in the face of a challenge mounted by former Pennsylvania Governor Dick Thornburgh, who was also George Bush's former Attorney General and Chairman *pro tem* of his Domestic Policy Council. The second was a surprising, although fleeting, flirtation with a middle-class tax cut offered by House Ways and Means Committee Chairman Dan Rostenkowski.

Thornburgh's loss shocked Republicans across the land. First, he managed to blow a 44-point lead primarily by running an issueless campaign in which he touted his Washington insider status—precisely the wrong message to convey to an electorate that was growing increasingly frustrated with Washington politicians. Second, Wofford stressed such middle-class concerns as the sluggish economy, job creation, and the need to overhaul the nation's health care system. Wofford's campaign was short on details, but for the first time in more than a decade Democrats began to believe they had a potential road map, based on Wofford's trial balloons, for broadening their message to the entire country.

Wofford campaigned as "the kind of Democrat who believes health care isn't a matter of privilege but a fundamental right." His goal was "to represent the people who pay taxes, do the work, foot the bill, struggle to save and often come up a little short at the end of the month . . . to fight this administration's proposal to cut college aid for middle-class families . . . to provide federal tax relief for the middle class." Mark Shields, a columnist, explained perceptively that Wofford won because he was able to reach real people: He "did not run as a Democratic liberal; he won as a Democratic middle-class populist." Less than one year before the 1992 presidential contest, the overarching question was "whether the Democrats can learn from the leadership and example of Sen. Wofford."[18]

This was something altogether new, an approach by a Democrat that appealed directly to Reagan Democrats, many of whom were now beginning to fear for their job security (those who were still employed) and worry about their future—about their ability to own or keep their homes, send their kids to college, pay for quality health care, and plan for their retirement. Traditional "liberal" issues—abortion rights, funding for the National Endowment for the Arts, gun control, civil rights—were ignored in favor of the pocketbook and family concerns of average American breadwinners.

By contrast, back in Washington the Bush Administration was incapable of inspiring confidence or ensuring a consistent message about the economy. What emerged was pure muddle.

The Administration's chief economic strategy—preserving the budget deal on the pretext of reducing the deficit—precluded doing virtually anything that would stimulate the economy and aggravate that same deficit. "Sit and wait" was not only the attitude, it was also the policy prescription. It was a stark, gloomy contrast to the Democrats' emerging message that they were an energetic party that really cared about real people. They were the ones portrayed as serious about changing America.

Back at the White House, the effect was daze. Inaction. Confusion. Lack of direction. Silliness.

On the one hand, the Administration urged people to spend money on consumer goods, cars, and housing to stimulate the economy; at the same time it also urged higher savings levels through tax incentives to boost savings and investment. Clearly you can't put money into your pocket or your savings account and spend it simultaneously. The public as well as the country's financial markets were growing confused.

To make matters worse, the President gave a speech during which he made an offhand remark urging the country's credit card companies and associated banks to lower the interest rates they charged consumers from the 18 to 20 percent they currently levied. It was an ill-advised, naïve suggestion that no one had thought through. In a rare moment of non-gridlock, the Senate decided to turn the President's hortatory *suggestion* into a regulatory *mandate* that would limit credit card interest rates to 14 percent (just four points above the IRS penalty interest rate).

The market reaction to this craziness was swift. The Dow Jones Industrial Index dropped 120 points on November 15, the fifth worst day in market history. The stock price of one of the country's biggest credit card companies, Maryland's MBNA, dropped 25 percent. Citicorp, one of the country's largest issuers of credit cards, said that if the bill became law it would probably have to eliminate nearly half of its customers, which would obviously contract rather than expand consumer credit. The flap over Bush's credit card rate remarks was a telling sign that economic policy in official Washington was out of control.

The Wofford victory had heartened the Democrats about their prospects for toppling George Bush in 1992. Within a matter of days after the Pennsylvania senate race, the Democrats were presented with yet another opportunity to take the high ground on taxes, in much the same way Senator Moynihan had tried in 1989. The race was on as to which party would be the first to embrace a middle-class tax cut.

Congressman Dan Rostenkowski read the tea leaves of the Wofford victory correctly and on November 7 became the first legislator to propose a plan to give 80 percent of American households a $200- to $400-a-year income tax credit that would be financed by taxing the rich. Tax rates would rise to a top level of 35 percent, and Rostenkowski favored imposing a 10 percent surtax on the country's 30,000 millionaires. Texas Senator Lloyd Bentsen had already championed a tax credit of up to $300 per child to benefit some 27 million middle-income families. Rostenkowski's plan, by contrast, was touted as helping some 90 million households.

That was smart politics. Once again the Democrats were positioning themselves as champions of the middle class, defending the average American from being done in by the wealthy. This chapter of their strategy was taken directly from Kevin Phillips and was in marked contrast to previous Democratic proposals (like Walter Mondale's 1984 presidential bid), which usually included *raising* taxes.

Congressional Republicans quickly grasped what was happening, just as they had earlier perceived the potency of Pat Moynihan's proposed cut in the Social Security payroll tax. The day following Rostenkowski's announcement, some sixty-six House Republicans (including Frank Wolf, Vin Weber, Dick Armey, and Guy Vander Jagt) wrote to the President urging him to take a pro-family, pro-middle-class stance by supporting the "Tax Fairness for Families Act of 1991," which would raise the dependent deduction for children under 18 to $3,500. As these GOP cosponsors noted, "Today's families are not hurting because government is too small or because families are not taxed enough. Families are hurting because their own budgets are too small due to Uncle Sam taking a bigger and bigger bite out of the family pie."

The bidding war had begun, and it threatened to break the 1990 budget deal. Interestingly enough, Dan Rostenkowski, one of the chief participants in the Andrews Air Force Base negotiations, obviously felt no reluctance at all about proposing tax cuts, albeit financed by higher taxes on the wealthy. The Bush White House, however, lashed to the mast of Darmanomics, just wanted the Democratic and Republican advocates of tax cuts to get the hell out of town. The debate was seen as highly counterproductive, especially as the Administration was busy putting the finishing touches on the fiscal year 1993 budget to be released in early 1992.

As with so many other aspects of its domestic and economic policy, the Bush Administration again failed to act consistently or coherently. On November 14 the White House announced that the President intended to propose a new economic growth package in his State of the Union speech, scheduled for late January 1992.

To Congress, the message was: Just leave!

To the American people, the message was: Just wait!

Neither worked.

A few days after Bush's statement, the *Washington Post* reported that the Administration was considering its own tax rebate of up to $300 per person. This trial balloon, however, not only fell flat but aroused the ire of GOP conservatives. Gingrich deemed the idea "an unmitigated disaster," and Jack Kemp, calling it "Carteresque," derided the plan as doing nothing to address the country's real economic needs.[19] Coming directly on the heels of the credit card rate fiasco the previous week, the tax rebate idea only underscored the internal disarray at the White House. Additionally, when coupled with the President's "let's just wait until January" attitude, the rebate underscored the appearance that the President just didn't understand or care. Press Secretary Marlin Fitzwater only highlighted this perception when he admitted that the President's "repeated comments that he cares deeply about this problem just hasn't [*sic*] broken through."

Once again, it was rhetoric—and confused rhetoric at that—not action coming from the Administration. Message: I care! Action: the President buys some socks to boost the Yuletide economy.

The same day the *Post* reported the purported tax rebate story, the *Wall Street Journal*'s editorial page chastised the Administration for being spooked by congressional Democrats, behaving incoherently, and failing to keep the spotlight on economic growth: "The world's most important economy is in the grip of economic incompetents."[20]

That same day, the President met in the Oval Office with a handful of reporters to inform them that he had no real plans for a major effort to stimulate the economy. The "fundamentals" were good: low inflation, low interest rates, and declining personal debt. Quality and exports were both up. "So it's not like we're dealing with a totally bad economy," he said. The problem was, once again, attributed to faulty communications:

> I think I've got to do better in making clear what the message is, and I think I can do better. But I think there's so much noise out there that I've got to figure out how to make it clearer that we are for the things that I have advocated that would help.[21]

What would have helped was clarity inside the White House. No wonder there was "so much noise out there," because the Administration had been one of the chief contributors to the confusion. The President didn't help matters much by reiterating his belief that what the economy needed was enactment of his all-but-forgotten capital gains proposal, a banking reform proposal that most Americans could not have cared less about, and passage of a new highway bill that struck many as irrelevant to the fundamental issue at hand. As if to underscore the discrepancy between Bush's optimism and reality, Dun & Bradstreet reported later that same day the results of a survey of 3,000 business executives. Most of them saw sales and profits expectations during the first quarter of 1992 reaching their lowest level since 1983. The next day the Labor Department announced that jobless claims the first week of December had shot up by 79,000, a much higher figure than expected.

The President's credibility was further undercut by the numbers showing a continuing if not deepening recession as well as the confusion coming from his own economic spokesmen. The Congress finally adjourned on November 20, but even then the issue of the economy lingered.

Kemp and other Republicans had urged the White House to keep the Congress in session throughout November and December, if necessary, until it passed the President's economic growth package announced ten months earlier. Darman resisted and persuaded the President to wait until the end of January. Once again Bush listened to Darman, even though by the end of the year Bush's own campaign advisers were urging him to move more quickly on the economy.

As usual, Kemp's instincts were on target: The Bush Administration had a splendid opportunity to retake the economic growth agenda by putting the pressure on the Democrats in Congress to act. Instead, fearful of doing anything that might upset the 1990 budget deal or throw OMB's budget planning off track, the Administration chose to do nothing, thereby ceding the field and the airwaves to the Democrats. All this after the President had explicitly worried that he had a communications problem!

Kemp's strategy would have positioned the President perfectly for the coming election year. Had he pressed the Congress to no avail, Bush could have pointed to the congressional Democrats as the reason why the recovery was delayed. At least he had tried, and he would then have established a record of effort that would have made a Truman-style campaign against a do-nothing Congress credible. If Bush had pressured the Democrats and they had caved in, then he could claim the mantle of leadership and underwrite his optimism with solid achievement. Instead, he not only did nothing, he quit the arena altogether.

The week after the Thornburgh loss, Roger Porter called me into his office one afternoon and handed me a thick sheaf of clippings containing nine articles that had appeared in the *Philadelphia Inquirer* over a two-week period before the Pennsylvania senate election. Written by two Pulitzer Prize winners, Donald L. Barlett and James B. Steele, the series was entitled "America: What Went Wrong?" These articles were but the latest installment in the Kevin Phillips analysis of how the Reagan years saw the rich getting richer and everyone else going to hell.

There were stories by Barlett and Steele about how Reagan–Bush-era policies were "dismantling America's middle class" and how the "rules of the game" were rigged: Those who played by them always lost, those who didn't—the Michael Milkens, the Japanese, the Mexicans, corporate raiders who pursued leveraged buyouts, bankruptcy and tax lawyers, Wall Street, deregulators, and large health insurance companies—always won. The articles were also cleverly crafted to appeal to gut emotions.

For example, after describing how a particular company had been bought out several times by some large, impersonal corporate raider, the authors would zero in on how the maneuvers affected the "little people" who *used to be* employed by the company. The tales of personal misery and desperation were gut-wrenching, a brilliant contrast to the professional politicians, the establishment elites, the Washington rule-writers like the Darmans and Bradys, whose wealth was mostly inherited rather than earned and whose personal world views were now shaping America's economic policy.

As he handed me the Barlett and Steele articles, Porter said, "Charlie, I want you to take a look at these. Spend some time analyzing them and see if you can't put together a rebuttal, because I'm virtually certain that the arguments here will constitute the heart of the Democrats' attack on us next year."

After reading the articles from first to last I was convinced that Porter's assessment about their being a Democratic blueprint for 1992 was correct. The Barlett and Steele series would indeed prove to be an early warning signal for the Bush Administration of what was coming from the Democrats. Little did I realize then, however, that the *Inquirer* series would serve as another example of the Bush Administration's remarkable ability to ignore a disaster staring it squarely in the face.

Working with my research assistant, Jonathan Levey, I spent the better part of the next month assembling and writing a detailed point-by-point rebuttal. The challenge was massive, given the variety of assertions and claims—many of them wrong or skewed—in the newspaper series, so I turned to more than a dozen senior colleagues throughout the Bush Administration to help tell the other side of the story. Harris Weinstein, Chief Counsel at the Office of Thrift Supervision; Larry Lindsey; Kate Moore, Assistant Secretary of Transportation; Ken Gideon, Assistant Secretary of the Treasury for Tax Policy; David Bradford, a Princeton economics professor on leave as a member of the Council of Economic Advisers; Martin Gerry, an exceptionally able Assistant HHS Secretary for Planning and Evaluation; Nancy Mitchell, Associate Director of Quayle's Competitiveness Council and the author of a major study on the positive effects of deregulation; and many others gave generously of their time to review the *Inquirer* series and provide the necessary details to rebut its charges.

On December 16, 1991, I sent Porter my analysis, entitled appropriately, I thought, "America: What Went *Right?*" Levey and I had prepared more than a hundred pages of detailed responses, including more than forty charts and graphs from Lindsey and Bradford.

The Barlett and Steele articles egregiously misrepresented a host of economic and other data, but nowhere was their analysis more flawed (typically of the quality and depth of their overall presentation) than when it came to the supposedly harmful effects of deregulation. Since it was Vice President George Bush who headed Ronald Reagan's overall deregulatory effort, an attack on deregulation was effectively an attack on Bush. The *Inquirer* series focused on the impact deregulatory policies had on the nation's trucking industry, noting that of the top thirty trucking firms operating in 1979, twenty had either folded or merged, with reportedly adverse consequences on the trucking industry overall.

The authors neglected to explain, however, that deregulation forced many of the larger inefficient firms to close down or merge, and that by 1990 there were actually close to 27,000 more carriers in business. Additionally, there were many more smaller carriers, greater competition, higher productivity, greater incentives for cost control, and pricing structures (like just-in-time delivery) that were more responsive to consumer needs. Barlett and Steele would have people believe that the nation's trucking industry was on its deathbed; in reality, the total number of trucking jobs had *grown* by about 30 percent, and the overall savings to the economy from transportation deregulation was some $15 billion per year. Somehow, Barlett and Steele had left those facts out of their story.

Days went by without hearing anything from Porter. Shortly before

Christmas I asked him at a staff meeting if he'd reviewed the binder I'd sent him. Clearly he hadn't (and had probably lost or filed it in his elaborate filing system), because he asked me for another copy. I never heard another comment from Porter about "America: What Went Right?"

Frankly, I wouldn't have cared about ever hearing back on the subject had it not been for the alarming fact that the Barlett and Steele analysis was growing legs. The series had been reprinted in newspapers around the country, and its assertions were beginning to be accepted as gospel truth. Letters were coming to the White House asking for our reaction. Nowhere was the other side of the story being told.

Finally I blew a gasket. On April 16, 1992, four months to the day after I gave Porter the analysis he'd requested, Bill Clinton delivered a major economic speech in Philadelphia at—appropriately—Pennsylvania's Wharton School of Finance and Commerce. Clinton pitched his message squarely to the country's middle class and accused the Bush Administration of "keeping taxes low for the high-income individuals and corporations." At the same time, although "America's rich got richer under a deliberate governmental strategy to see that that was done, the country did not grow. The stock market tripled but wages declined."

Clinton chose his venue carefully, just as carefully as he had crafted his message. According to the Arkansas Governor, Wharton was a breeding ground for the nation's financial elite and was "also a powerful symbol of where our country went wrong in the 80s":

> It was here at Wharton that Michael Milken got the idea to use junk bonds to leverage corporate buyouts, a quick-buck scheme that was supposed to shake up failed management but too often forced corporations to close plants and lay off workers in formerly profitable operations.
>
> Together we have got to work to bring an end to the something-for-nothing ethic of the 80s.
>
> Unless we decide that we want a very different kind of president and a very different economic policy; unless we decide that we're all going to be more responsible citizens, responsible for our common problems, we're in for more trouble.

As it turned out, it was Bush who would be headed for more trouble. On Friday, April 17, both the *New York Times* and the *Washington*

Times carried accounts of Clinton's Wharton speech, and each newspaper ran a picture of Clinton holding up a copy of *America: What Went
Wrong?* as he delivered his remarks.

The nine Barlett and Steele articles had now been compiled in
book form for sale across the country. Not only had we done nothing
as an Administration for over a year to rebut the Kevin Phillips
charges, but now we were standing idly by as yet another wave of
attack was about to be launched. What the hell was going on?

I had had enough of fooling with Porter, so I called Sam Skinner's
office that Friday afternoon and asked if I could drop by. No problem,
just come on in Monday morning.

Over the weekend I bought my own copy of *America: What Went
Wrong?* On Monday morning, when I brought it to Porter's staff meeting and held it up, he just looked at it. Again, no reaction and no
reference to our own rebuttal.

After the staff meeting I went down to see the chief of staff. It was
mid-April and there was a roaring fire going in his fireplace. Skinner,
who had always been extremely cordial to me, welcomed me in and
invited me to sit down. "What's up?" he asked.

"Sam," I said, "I'm worried about something. Have you seen this
book?" I handed him my copy of *America: What Went Wrong?* He
hadn't, so I told him how it came to be written and that several of us
in the Administration and the Bush White House months ago had
prepared what I thought was a pretty solid rebuttal. The only problem
was, nobody knew about it. We needed to get the message out. Then
I handed him a copy of the picture showing Clinton holding up the
Barlett and Steele book during his Wharton speech.

I continued: "Look, Sam, I didn't prepare it alone. Lots of people
helped out. But I gave it to Porter in December and heard nothing.
Gene Croisant has it. So does Clayton Yeutter. But let me tell you
something: If Barlett and Steele becomes a bestseller, we're going to
be in big trouble. The good news, I guess, is that last year, 60 percent
of Americans didn't buy a single book, not a cookbook, not a Tom
Clancy thriller, not even a romance novel. The bad news is that if this
book hits the bestseller list, it doesn't matter whether people buy it or
not, or whether they even read it. The authors go on the talk shows—
Donahue et cetera—and their message becomes more credible, and
we'll be on the defensive."

"Okay, Charlie, I hear you. Let me take a look at what you've
prepared and I'll see."

That was it. I never heard another word from anyone in the Bush White House about *America: What Went Wrong?* or "America: What Went Right?" Perhaps someone in the West Wing was certain it wasn't necessary; we couldn't possibly lose. We were the right kind of people, and surely the voters would remember that.

Three weeks later, on May 3, 1992, *America: What Went Wrong?* hit the bestseller list in the *Washington Post* and shortly thereafter the *New York Times* list as well. In the *Post*, it hit number one! It remained on these lists—usually near the top—until shortly after George Bush lost his reelection bid to Bill Clinton.

Even a cursory comparison between *America: What Went Wrong?* and two other summer bestsellers, Bill Clinton's and Al Gore's *Putting People First* and Ross Perot's *United We Stand*, will show a remarkably similar and effective use of middle-class populist themes. Here was a clear market test of what message was selling. Both the Bush White House and the Bush–Quayle reelection campaign just couldn't be bothered.

As the 1992 presidential campaign continued throughout the late spring and summer, George Bush actually made a virtue out of not responding to these criticisms. The failure to do so was part of a high-risk strategy of riding out the recession. With each passing day, however, the critique of Reagan–Bush–Quayle economic policies went unanswered, making it all the harder for Bush to mount an offensive later that fall.

The good news on the economy never did arrive in time for the November 3 election, and by the time Bush got around to active campaigning—defending his record, challenging his opponent, and presenting his reform agenda for the second term—the public was not inclined to listen.

Many Republicans, particularly among the GOP's conservative base, which included Reagan Democrats, were outraged over what was happening to the economy by the end of 1991: not only was the deficit rising, but so was spending. Richard Darman had sold the President on ratifying the budget deal as the only means to avert the disaster of a runaway deficit or a government shutdown. But the deal practically guaranteed escalation of the deficit. Incredibly, one of the fundamental reasons for entering into negotiations with the Congress in 1990—a desire by the White House to place at least some curb on the growth of mandatory "entitlement" spending—was totally ignored in the final budget deal. The Democrats got their tax and spending increases. All the President got was snookered, by the Democrats and by his own OMB Director.

As the 1992 election drew closer and the economy failed to recover, there was an unfolding sense that the price to be paid for inaction could be incredibly steep. Even people inside the Bush White House began to worry that the President could lose his reelection bid. Some even dared to mention their own worst fear: that we didn't deserve to be reelected.

By the end of November 1991, the fault lines through the Republican ranks had widened. Because of indecisiveness in the White House over taxes, brought on principally by a reflexive and intransigent desire to preserve the budget deal intact at all costs, Republicans had once again lost an opportunity to recapture the tax issue, which had cemented their governing coalition for more than a decade. As it turned out, this was their last opportunity before the February 1992 presidential primaries began. But the on-again, off-again nature of economic policymaking not only hurt the party but revealed clearly to the public that the Bush Administration lacked both economic principles and a sound, carefully crafted blueprint for improving the economy.

The essence of Darmanism—social and economic—was to avoid taking positive steps to stimulate the economy. The President had, in fact, been so counseled repeatedly. If there *was* an economic policy at the time, it consisted in little more than relying on the Federal Reserve Board to lower the discount rate as a means of stimulating an economic recovery. Perhaps the only good news that came during November 1991 was that Larry Lindsey, after waiting almost a year since his nomination, was finally confirmed as a member of the Federal Reserve's Board of Governors.

Many of us below the Assistant-to-the-President level in the White House were seriously worried that the problems were much deeper than personnel or even communications. With the collapse of Communism and the nagging recession, the country was turning inward and was yearning for something more. As one Bush loyalist, a former Assistant to the President who was close to both Bush and Secretary of State James Baker, put it: "We never perceived what was going on until it was too late. The President was consistently counseled *not* to do anything—in November 1990, February 1991, August 1991, and November 1991. We didn't respond in large part because of hubris.

There was no need to rise to the challenge. Moreover, during this entire period we didn't have a clue as to what our economic strategy was."

The cracks within the Administration were increasingly visible to the public. There was a growing sense of populist discontent with the status quo, but the Bush White House reacted with a lack of understanding and clarity. As one former Assistant to the President said, "The President had no clear idea where he wanted to go. We conveyed no certainty, and we had no credibility with regard to our own principles" after the budget deal. The debate about tax cuts in November was followed by the White House staff shakeup and Bush's disastrous trip to Japan, where he rather unsubtly and unsuccessfully tried to convert a foreign policy venture into a domestic effort to promote "jobs, jobs, jobs."

When the Congress left town, matters still did not improve for the Bush White House. The political fallout over John Sununu's arrogant behavior ultimately led to his resignation on December 3 and the appointment of Transportation Secretary Sam Skinner as Bush's new Chief of Staff. As Jim Pinkerton expressed it, Skinner would be good enough to get Bush reelected in 1992, and that was all that mattered. Unfortunately, that was one of the few times Pinkerton was wrong.

5

The "Ed-chew-KAY-shun President"

We must set realistic goals and timetables. The most obvious date on the horizon is the year 2000, a number imbued with almost mythic proportions.

—David Kearns and Dennis Doyle,
Winning the Brain Race[1]

Running for president with Ronald Reagan still sitting in the White House was not easy for George Bush. The need to distinguish his vision of America's future from that of the seventy-eight-year-old incumbent was critical for the 1988 Bush election campaign. At the same time, running against Reagan meant running against eight years of Reagan–*Bush* policies. The challenge was evident. The solution wasn't.

The answer evolved during the early months of the 1988 campaign and came to full public fruition during Bush's acceptance speech at the New Orleans convention in that now famous Peggy Noonan phrase envisioning "a kinder, gentler America." After two terms of relentless budget-cutting debates, Bush was pledging to lighten up.

The beauty, the political brilliance, of "kinder, gentler" was that it offered Bush thematic distance from Reagan without his ever once having to criticize his mentor personally or, for that matter, any of his specific programs and policies. As a means of defining Bush's message, it was poetic, not programmatic. As a phrase for all seasons—each listener could define his or her own version of kindness and gentleness—it would help get him through November 8, 1988. The details could come later.

But "kinder, gentler" by itself would probably not have carried Bush's thematic effort to differentiate himself from Reagan through the campaign. More beef was needed. As it turned out, months earlier Bush had actually offered some specifics about how he would be different from Reagan. On January 6, 1988, Bush declared in a speech in Manchester, New Hampshire, that he wanted to be America's "education president."

The initial reaction was puzzlement. Was this an effort to distance himself from Reagan, who, after all, had campaigned with almost vigilante ferocity against the education establishment? Reagan initially had wanted to abolish the U.S. Department of Education, which his predecessor, Jimmy Carter, had established as a sop to the two national teachers' unions, the National Education Association and the American Federation of Teachers, both of which contribute substantially to the Democratic party. Was George Bush about to become a big spender who supported greater federal aid to education?

The answer was no. But during the campaign Bush never fully explained what he meant by the phrase "education president." It was clear, however, that he thought he could emphasize the issue of educational quality without becoming tied to endorsing higher spending levels in the bargain. That position did not bear fruit until a few weeks after his inauguration, when he began to shape his education policy, which in many respects came to serve as the cornerstone for the rest of his domestic social agenda.

Education is a perfect issue for an American president. It permits—virtually invites—flights of high-sounding rhetoric divorced from responsibility. In matters of education policy, a president can talk about somebody else's money and not just dwell on the federal education budget, because 93 percent of education spending in America occurs at the state and local levels. In 1988 Americans spent some $331 billion on education in the aggregate—at the state, local, and federal levels—but only 7 percent of that money was federal spending.

The predominance of the state and local governments in education spending and policy direction reflected both constitutional and historical trends. The federal office of education dated to 1867, but throughout American history there has been little if any federal involvement in such issues as curriculum content and educational quality. Thus, if Bush were to make a substantial impact as the country's "education president," he faced a fundamental choice: spend more federal money (and hence seek greater federal control) or preach about ways to reform the existing system to produce better results.

The issue posed by the new President in January 1989 was how to spend better, not how to spend more. It came to be the model, incidentally, for several other domestic policy initiatives, from job training to health care.

Bush's claim to the title of "education president" positioned him to assume the credit for selecting the last Secretary of Education named by Ronald Reagan. When the controversial and outspoken William Bennett announced his intended resignation in midsummer of 1988, Bush turned to an old Texas friend, Lauro Cavazos. A Democrat, Cavazos was serving as president of Texas Tech University in Lubbock. Almost twenty years older than Bennett and steeped in years of higher education administration, Cavazos might have seemed an odd choice for a presidential candidate whose focus was on reforming elementary and secondary education.

But Cavazos brought one key credential: his name and striking personal background. If confirmed as Secretary of Education, Lauro Cavazos would be the country's first Hispanic Cabinet member.

Cavazos's background stood in stark contrast to that of the mostly well-heeled white males in the Cabinet. He had been born on the immense King Ranch in East Texas, the son of the ranch's foreman. Cavazos had attended the Anglo school in town, had done well, and had gone on to Texas Tech, where he majored in zoology. After obtaining a doctorate in physiology at Iowa State University, he held various teaching positions in anatomy, ultimately serving as Dean of Tufts Medical School before being asked to return to head his Texas alma mater. The father of ten children, Cavazos was also a devout Catholic. While not precisely rags-to-riches, Lauro Cavazos's biography was one that thousands of Hispanic Americans would appreciate. It meant there was opportunity in America, and people whose first language was Spanish could wind up in Washington's corridors of power. This fact was not lost on the political tacticians and demographers with their eyes on states like Florida, Texas, and California.

The word would leak out that Bush had been instrumental in

selecting Cavazos. More pointedly, when Cavazos was sworn in on September 20, 1988, in a packed East Room of the White House, the man facing Cavazos and reading him the oath of office while a beaming Ronald Reagan looked on was Vice President and candidate George Bush. Although denied at the time, the simple fact was that Bush wanted Cavazos to succeed Bennett for one reason and one reason only: Hispanic votes.

Never the politician, Cavazos nonetheless agreed to stump for Bush, especially throughout the Southwest. Two months later, after the election and shortly before Thanksgiving, Bush asked Cavazos to continue in his new Administration. Bush had no choice; he could hardly have dumped Cavazos less than sixty days after hailing his arrival and personally swearing him into office. So it would be Secretary of Education Lauro Cavazos who would lead the charge to make President-elect George Bush America's "education president."

It wasn't exactly a charge, though. Some might actually call it a retreat of sorts. The problem with Cavazos was twofold: He was seen as lacking an agenda, and as lacking the political compass to implement one.

Amiable, slow to anger but proud, Cavazos was himself an education success story. The majority of American students would never know the barriers he had to overcome—language, status, relative lack of income—and he firmly believed that if he could make it educationally, anybody could. Education was like logic: First you figured out what was right, and then you spread the good word. Everybody was sure to fall in line behind.

Unfortunately, what Cavazos never understood was that education was one of the most contentious ideological issues in modern American political life.

Things got off to a shaky start on his first day in office. At 10 A.M. on September 21, 1988, the new Secretary of Education gathered his senior staff together in the Secretary's Conference Room at the Education Department. Bennett and most of his aides had departed the day before, although several political appointees had remained. After brief introductory remarks and greetings to all, Cavazos launched into a statement of his mission.

Cavazos saw his goal as putting education on the map as a national issue. No one dared tell him that this had already been achieved thanks to Mike Deaver's brilliant use of an obscure report (Terrell

Bell's "A Nation at Risk," the blockbuster report that decried the "rising tide of mediocrity" in American education) and nearly four years of the highly effective challenges of Bill Bennett. The task wasn't to alarm people but to overcome their apathy, to motivate them to do something about our "education deficit."

Rhetorically, Cavazos kept stressing the need to "educate all of our children to their full potential." "Full potential" became his central theme, a somewhat vague and empty counter to Bennett's repeated emphasis on "content, character, and choice." But while "full potential" struck some in his audience as squishy, the room went deadly silent when Cavazos announced that if we only somehow managed to solve our educational needs, America "probably wouldn't even need a defense department, wouldn't need all those missiles and other weapons." No one moved. No one looked around or at anybody else.

Someone obviously talked, however, because a few days later the press had picked up and reported Cavazos's first indiscretion, as if being a registered Democrat weren't enough.

So much for Cavazos's boss, Ronald Reagan, who had just about finished presiding over history's largest peacetime buildup of conventional military forces and who, as a result, would reap the gratitude of millions the following year when the "Revolutions of 1989" saw one Communist regime after another collapse. Cavazos was off to a rocky start.

Throughout the fall of 1988 Cavazos's role was simple: sit there, look Hispanic, visit Texas as often as possible, and don't make any mistakes. As Cavazos assumed the helm at the Education Department, I moved from being Deputy General Counsel to Deputy Under Secretary for Planning, Budget and Evaluation, a position with direct oversight responsibility for the federal education budget and education policy. The move gave me direct access to the new Secretary as well as an opportunity to help shape his education message. Because Cavazos had traveled from Lubbock to Washington without bringing any staff, it had become evident that he would need someone to help him develop his message. For weeks on end he had delivered platitudinous remarks about the need to educate all American children "to their fullest potential." This type of loose, unfocused rhetoric was obviously not going to carry Cavazos—or Bush—very far.

A week after Cavazos learned that he would be staying in the new Bush–Quayle Administration, I found out that Cavazos wanted me to remain as Deputy Under Secretary, assuming the new Administration's personnel office agreed.

I immediately set about trying to shape a message for Cavazos. On November 28, 1988, I sent him a detailed five-page memorandum entitled "The First 100 Days," which described the basic themes plus an implementation plan for his tenure at the Department. Cavazos was grateful for the suggestions, but only later did I discover that hundred-day thinking was not part of the incoming Administration's mindset. Such long-range planning was actually eschewed at the White House.

Cavazos liked my suggestions about raising expectations, ensuring access to quality educational institutions, and promoting accountability for results. Without higher expectations, particularly when it came to achievement, children were unlikely to perform better in school. The emphasis on access to quality educational opportunities served as a hook for postsecondary education policy concerns, although it also reflected such elementary and secondary themes as school choice. Our subsequent emphasis on choice was crafted expressly to appeal to minority (and urban Catholic) parents and families who frequently were denied access to quality schools, finding themselves stuck in an educational environment where spending was high while performance was dismal.

Accountability was the most important of the three themes: the new Administration had a unique opportunity to focus education policy on results rather than resources, especially given the substantial spending increases in education at all levels during the 1980s. The problem was that these spending hikes were rarely matched by comparable performance. Our education system had been relatively stagnant since *A Nation at Risk* was published, and the accountability theme was designed to bring much-needed reform and restructuring by stressing outputs rather than inputs. Cavazos liked the three themes and began using them in the fall of 1988 and well into 1989.

As the new Bush White House began to assemble, I waited to see what role the Education Department would have in shaping the "education President's" agenda. I didn't have to wait long.

During the first week of the Bush Administration, Secretary Cavazos asked me to attend a planning session at the White House in Roger Porter's office. It would be the first of several meetings intended to sketch out the basic education message that Bush would launch in his speech to the Congress less than three weeks later, on February 9. Besides Porter, Jim Pinkerton, Kate Moore, Barry White, Gregg Petersmeyer, Dave Demarest, and Bob Teeter attended.

That was my first extended exposure to Roger Porter's operating style, which involved meetings stretched out to prodigious length (almost four hours in this case) by seemingly endless repetition and wasted time. Nonetheless, Lauro Cavazos's shortcomings as a politician made Porter's involvement a godsend. Until the arrival of Lamar Alexander as Education Secretary in March 1991, Roger Porter was considered the *de facto* Secretary of Education.

Those meetings in Porter's office produced four themes that drove Bush's educational policy through the first two years of the Administration. First, we should find ways through the federal budget and through other reform-oriented activities to recognize, reward, and replicate examples of *excellence and success* in the American education system. While there were plenty of signs in American education that things weren't working well—low test scores, high expenditures, intolerably high dropout rates among certain minority groups, and poor showings on international comparative tests in math and science—we still had many individual schools, students, and strategies that were succeeding. The federal government could play a strong role in making sure that such examples were duly appreciated and shared.

The second animating theme was a call for greater *choice and flexibility* in our education system. Educational choice meant letting all parents pick the public, private, or religious school of their choice. That would disempower the vast education establishment bureaucracy, which denied the privilege of selecting the school of choice for their children to all but the rich. Of the four themes, this was the most controversial and overtly political, a clear and deliberate wedge issue to be used against the Democrats. But choice was also seen as a critical catalyst for education reform. As a favorite agenda item for conservatives, it would win Bush support from his party. *Flexibility* emerged as the code word for deregulating education; the mission was to find ways to remove, relax, or waive existing state, local, and federal regulations that precluded greater autonomy at the local level.

The third theme envisioned *targeting* scarce federal resources on the nation's neediest children. This was not a particularly difficult task, as essentially it described existing efforts. Some 85 percent of the federal education budget was already targeted on needy children and students: programs like the Chapter 1 remedial math and reading program, student loans, Pell grants (i.e., vouchers!), and assistance to the disabled and the handicapped. Stating this theme would accomplish two things: set a priority that would continue to govern how we allocated federal dollars to education programs and take credit for what was already happening.

Porter wanted to stop at three themes. He had developed a habit of thinking in threes because, he would say, most people can remember no more than three points. He would therefore respond to virtually every question or issue—on education or any other topic—by stating that "there are basically three things to note about such and such."

Here, however, three themes weren't enough, and I lobbied strenuously for adding a fourth: *accountability*. Having closely studied education spending patterns, I was convinced that the most critical issue in American education was not money but performance. I told Porter that without accountability we lacked a comprehensive reform message and would be left constantly on the defensive to explain why we weren't outspending the Democrats and others who saw the solution to our educational deficit as simply more and more spending at all levels. Our critics would call this approach a dodge in order to avoid spending extra money. But the fact was that the budget wouldn't permit huge new expenditures. Even if it had, extra dollars would make very little difference. Porter finally agreed, and we added a message that emphasized the importance of focusing not on resources but rather on educational results.

Bush unveiled his education message on February 9, 1989, in the context of his "Building a Better America" speech to the Congress. The four themes, in language crafted by Porter, were articulated as part of the new President's reworking of Ronald Reagan's final budget:

> [T]he most important competitiveness program of all is one which improves education in America. When some of our students actually have trouble locating America on a map of the world, it is time for us to map a new approach to education. We must reward excellence and cut through bureaucracy. We must help schools that need help the most. We must give choice to parents, students, teachers, and principals; and we must hold all concerned accountable. In education, we cannot tolerate mediocrity.

Bush then outlined his plan for a modest increment in federal education spending—$500 million—for merit schools, teacher awards, National Science Scholarships, expanded aid to magnet schools, and support for alternative teacher certification.

The budget hearings that followed in the spring would focus relentlessly on Bush's priorities. The Democrats would seek to embarrass the Administration by constantly pointing out that the self-proclaimed "education President" was turning out to be just as stingy as his predecessor. Our response was to emphasize the facts: Study after study had shown no correlation at all between education spending and performance. The system needed more accountability for results, not endless resources. Any new federal dollars *would* be targeted on the neediest children, and the system as a whole should be made more flexible to accommodate state and local innovation.

It was almost immediately evident that any serious reform of American education was not going to involve the Congress. With only 7 percent of total education spending in the country coming from Washington, it didn't take a Ph.D. (or an Ed.D.) to conclude that the real reform action had to be at the state and local levels, the source of the rest of the funds. Leveraging serious reform—whether through curriculum changes, higher standards, or new assessments—could not begin in Washington; it had to start elsewhere. That "elsewhere" was with the nation's governors.

During the 1988 election campaign, Vice President Bush pledged to convene a meeting with the nation's governors to discuss education reform. Chief of Staff John Sununu made good on that commitment and hatched the idea of a summit between the President and governors to be held at Charlottesville, Virginia, home of the university founded by Thomas Jefferson, the country's *first* education president. As Sununu would later tell it, the Charlottesville Education Summit was a brilliant stroke on two counts.

First, following the rare precedents set by Theodore Roosevelt (who convened the first summit with governors in 1908 to address environmental concerns) and Franklin Roosevelt (who convened the second in 1933 to address the Great Depression), Bush was signaling his leadership in education reform as well as making good on a campaign commitment. Interestingly, the Charlottesville Summit had all the trappings of pageantry that Bush came to relish when he met with foreign dignitaries. The colorful two-day event at Mr. Jefferson's University of Virginia received so much attention that ABC's Peter Jennings even moved his nighttime broadcast from New York City to Charlottesville for the occasion.

The second stroke of genius, according to the ever modest Sununu, was the signal sent to the Congress, namely, "You're a nonplayer" in this issue. Wrapped in flags, pomp, and pageantry unlike just about any other single domestic event in Bush's presidency, the Charlottesville Education Summit was an intentional "back of the hand" to the Congress, and from the beginning members deeply resented (and never forgot) that they were not invited to attend.

Sununu's symbolism was clearly intended to extend beyond education to a host of other domestic issues. Sununu saw Charlottesville as our first attempt at devolving power and authority *away* from Washington and lodging it closer to the American people. That theme would come to characterize major features of the Bush Administration's domestic agenda, such as our proposals on childcare, health care reform, and housing policy. The message was made explicit a year later, following the disastrous 1990 budget deal, when Sununu said, "There's not another single piece of legislation that needs to be passed in the next two years for this president. In fact, if Congress wants to come together, adjourn, and leave, it's all right with us. We don't need them."[2]

Classic Sununu—with a predictable response. While Sununu was substantively correct, he and Bush would have been far better off never articulating such insults. As was too often the case, Bush's lieutenants were constantly blabbing publicly about their strategy, which simply tipped off their opponents and put them in a mood to make things that much harder for the President. Rather than "just do it," the former professor Sununu had to show everyone how smart he was by announcing the strategy. His pie-in-your-face approach enraged Democrats and many Republicans in the Congress.

The Charlottesville Education Summit was not, however, without risks. Porter and Sununu rightly worried that the meeting would degenerate into posturing about spending. They were concerned that Democrats like Arkansas's Bill Clinton, then head of the National Governors' Association's education committee, would use the national platform to call for massive increases in federal education spending.

To forestall that, Sununu insisted that all direct exchanges between the President and the governors be closed to the press. Six closed-door sessions were held, with the only people in the room other than the President and the governors being one or two staff members taking notes. After the first day, which concluded with a "state dinner" for the governors hosted by Bush on the lawn outside Jefferson's Monticello, Porter returned to the Boar's Head Inn and spent most of the evening—until almost 3 A.M.—negotiating with Governors Carroll Campbell of South Carolina, Terry Branstad of Iowa, and Clinton over the text of the final communiqué to be issued the next day. For Clinton and Porter, who had known each other since they were Rhodes Scholars together at Oxford in the early 1970s, the nearly all-night session was a macho endurance contest between two friends and former rivals.

Behind all the ceremony, however, the conference almost fell completely apart over the issue of federal spending. Bush and Sununu wanted the focus on structural reforms—choice, flexibility, alternative certification, the need for high standards that would spur greater educational achievement—which would ratify and complement the President's four-part message delivered in February. Democratic governors, prodded by their own constituencies at home, in the Congress, and among the usual interest groups, did not want to let Bush off the hook so easily when it came to resources.

Bush won. Throughout the morning of the Summit's last day, Bush advisers were huddled in negotiations with Governor Clinton, who was threatening to walk away from the discussions, leaving the Summit without a final communiqué. Clinton, however, backed off from his insistence on language calling for higher federal education spending. Bush and the governors were able to release a "Joint Statement" that called for (1) establishing a process for setting national education goals; (2) seeking greater flexibility and accountability in using federal resources to meet the goals, especially through regulatory and legislative change; (3) undertaking a major state-by-state effort to restructure America's educational system; and (4) reporting annually on progress toward the goals.

The centerpiece of the agreement was the establishment of a bipartisan partnership between the Administration and the governors that would set educational goals for the nation. This was the effort on which most of the subsequent education-reform efforts of the Bush Administration would be focused.

Four months later, as Bush delivered his second State of the Union address on January 31, 1990, and the governors convened for their annual winter session in Washington, the Administration and the governors announced their agreement—based on a series of regional hearings and solicited input from hundreds of individuals from around the country—to pursue six "national education goals" to be achieved by the year 2000:

1. [E]very child must start school ready to learn.
2. The United States must increase the high school graduation rate to no less than 90 percent.
3. [W]e are going to make sure our schools' diplomas mean something. In critical subjects—at the 4th, 8th, and 12th grades—we must assess our students' performance.
4. U.S. students must be first in the world in math and science achievement.
5. Every American adult must be a skilled, literate worker and citizen.
6. Every school must offer the kind of disciplined environment that makes it possible for our kids to learn. And every school in America must be drug-free.

By the time of the next meeting of the National Governors' Association in Mobile, Alabama, in late July 1990, the bipartisan partnership had mapped out the subsequent phase: creation of a National Education Goals Panel that would oversee the measurement process and report to the nation annually on whether progress was being made toward reaching the six education goals. Membership on the Goals Panel included six governors (three Democrats, three Republicans) and four Bush Administration officials (Sununu, Darman, Porter, and Cavazos). Members of Congress and interest group representatives were pointedly *not* included among the participants.

Announcement of the six goals themselves was relatively noncontroversial. While some interest groups—most notably representatives from arts, music, civics, and foreign language associations—groused that they were not included among the core subjects listed in Goal 3, by and large there was a general consensus that the goals represented an appropriate focus on future education priorities.

A striking fact about the goals process was that its development was almost totally dominated by elected politicians. That gave rise to the first serious criticism: that politicians could not be trusted to report honestly on their own achievements—or shortcomings. Obviously, the Bush Administration and the governors had an interest in seeing education performance improve on their watch. Skeptics warned publicly that, with politicians in charge of the reporting and measurement process, it was unlikely that the system would ever entail real accountability.

The fear was not altogether unreal. An interesting but unreported aspect of the education goals process was the resentment many governors openly expressed toward a reporting system that would compare their states against each other. To put it bluntly, the governors were sick and tired of being ranked. A ranking system had the disadvantage of pleasing the twenty-five governors whose states ranked in the top half while enraging the bottom twenty-five. The education goals reporting process was therefore expressly crafted to avoid such political embarrassments. An unresolved issue was whether or not the information to be released annually represented an improvement over past reporting.

"A Nation at Risk" had awakened millions of Americans to the serious shortcomings of our expensive but essentially dysfunctional monopolistic education system. One of the responses to the report was the creation of an annual "Wall Chart," initially prepared by Ronald Reagan's first Education Secretary, Terrell Bell. The Wall Chart ranked the states on ACT or SAT scores, per pupil spending, pupil–teacher ratios, and nearly a dozen other indicators. Bell's successor, William Bennett, used the annual release of the Wall Chart as an occasion to bash the country's education establishment and make his pitch for radical education reform. With Bennett's penchant for bravado, the annual Wall Chart press conference had become the Education Department's most widely covered press event. It also made front-page news throughout the country, and stories rippled across the land and into local newspapers for weeks after the Washington release.

By 1990, most of the governors despised the Wall Chart. After several years of dismal achievement data, accountability for education performance was rapidly becoming an issue of political accountability back home. Ironically, the Wall Chart owed its origins to a request by a handful of governors who met with Terrell Bell and then Vice President Bush in 1983 at Bush's Kennebunkport vacation home. By the time Bush became President, many governors of both parties were actively doing all they could to scuttle the Wall Chart.

Dropping the Wall Chart, however, would have made a mockery of the Bush Administration's emphasis on accountability, for there would be no alternative measurement system to take its place until September 1991. Roger Porter and others in the Bush White House made it clear, however, that after the Charlottesville Summit they did not want to see another Wall Chart press conference. Releasing this comparative data would only undermine the evolving relationship between the Administration and the governors.

It was my office in the Education Department that prepared the Wall Chart, so I was in a difficult spot. While I understood Porter's political concerns, it would have been equally disastrous to have scrapped the Wall Chart in 1990 without a replacement. Consequently, I advised Secretary Cavazos to proceed with issuing the 1990 Wall Chart, in part to keep the pressure on to ensure that a credible successor emerged.

It was the last Wall Chart.

While the governors were griping about yet another Wall Chart, members of Congress were still whining about having been excluded from the Charlottesville Summit and the subsequent process for announcing, measuring, and assessing the education goals. Even Republicans, for example, Bill Goodling of Pennsylvania, ranking member of the House Education and Labor Committee, were miffed about not being invited to Charlottesville and not playing a role in the evolving education goals process. Goodling, himself a former teacher and an early Bush supporter, resented the fact that *he* had not been named Secretary of Education and was a chronic complainer to Bush.

During the year after the Charlottesville Summit, Bush and the governors ironed out not only the six goals but also the beginnings of a measurement and assessment system that would ultimately, if put in place, provide reliable information about whether our schools and children were making progress toward achieving the goals. Through the National Education Goals Panel, members of the Administration, governors, and, ultimately, the Congress oversaw the reporting process that came to replace the annual Wall Chart. Each year, on the Summit anniversary, the Goals Panel released a book-length compendium of information concerning the goals. The report also included state-by-state data for each of the goals.

The National Education Goals Panel was a politicians' triumph, for it enabled the governors to escape accountability—at least until well into the future—for comparative progress in their own state education systems. To begin with, at the outset of the reporting process the available data were sketchy. It would take years before evidence of real performance would make it into the annual report. That short-coming was of little concern to the governors. Governor Carroll Camp-bell of South Carolina, who helped establish the Goals Panel in Mobile, Alabama, in July 1990, spoke for nearly all the governors when he said emphatically: "We don't need any more Wall Charts."

To preserve the façade of accountability, the Administration and the governors agreed, then, to stop comparing states against each other, as was done through the deceased Wall Chart, and to measure instead each state against itself. This made about as much sense as holding the Olympics without countries competing against each other. Rather, each country's team would . . . compete against itself!

This approach got the governors off the hook politically. No longer would there be twenty-five "winners" and twenty-five "losers," as there had been with the Wall Chart. The National Education Goals Panel's annual report now meant that every state could be a winner, so long as over time it showed improvement when measured against itself. The new indicators that ultimately emerged weren't wrong; they were just boring and included far too much detail to be user-friendly. As a result, it was much harder for the public to grasp their meaning, especially as the annual reporting increasingly resembled those bulky and unreadable reports often issued by the Education Department's research office.

With the Wall Chart dismantled, the goals-reporting process estab-lished, and the first report on the goals due on the second anniversary of the Education Summit, the next effort was the elaboration of the standard-setting activity envisioned by Goal 3. This phase, left un-defined at Charlottesville and Mobile, finally offered members of Congress an opportunity to become involved.

When the governors convened in Mobile some ten months after the Charlottesville Summit, Bill Clinton's fellow Democrats raked him over the coals for his softness vis-à-vis the Bush Administration on the issue of spending. To his credit, Clinton avoided the calls for more spending and sided with a greater emphasis on reform instead. Clinton's successor as lead education governor, the often pugnacious and highly partisan Colorado Democrat Roy Romer, vowed never to be "Clintonized" by the Bush White House.

Romer was true to his word. In fact, he earned himself a reputation at the White House as an egotistical, dim-witted pain in the ass. Porter could barely stand dealing with him. Romer shrewdly perceived that the best way to get Bush's goat was to bring congressional Democrats to the table. After all, part of Bush's education strategy was to ignore the Congress and take his pitch for reform (and for spending less money) to the states. Bringing Congress to the table gave the Democrats another opportunity to criticize the Administration for not spending more.

After the national goals were announced, the Bush Administration took more than a year to devise a national strategy for achieving them. Part of the delay stemmed from lack of leadership at the Education Department, but another culprit was a recurring shortcoming of the Bush White House: a total inability to use the presidency for galvanizing popular support for a major presidential initiative.

One of the worst flaws a policymaker can have is tunnel vision, the failure to recognize that the most important thing on his or her plate may be going completely unobserved by virtually everyone else. I was convinced that we were afflicted with tunnel vision when it came to the education goals. We knew about them, the governors knew about them, but virtually no one else in the country outside the education establishment knew or cared about them. In speeches before numerous audiences I would ask how many people had heard of the national education goals. Few hands went up.

Impressed with this feedback, I carried it back to the West Wing, determined to remedy the problem. Why not have the President make a televised address to the nation's schoolchildren to explain the importance of the goals and what they meant for their future? The speech should be preceded by a massive effort—working with education associations, educators, and others—to get copies of the goals to each of the nation's 116,000 elementary and secondary schools and then into each classroom and ultimately before each student. Compared with the mobilization necessary for the Persian Gulf War, this would be child's play. Literally.

So I wrote up the idea. Porter loved it—he called it a "tenstrike"—and put it into the scheduling process for review. In the meantime I shopped the idea with my usual allies in the White House: Cabinet Affairs, speechwriting, and Public Liaison. Everybody liked it and wanted to move forward.

But nothing happened. And oddly, no one could explain *why* nothing was happening. Finally, some fourteen months later, Bush did give such a speech after I subsequently revived the idea, but it was handled without the necessary buildup or preliminary efforts to ensure that the goals actually made it into the classroom. While the speech had a modest impact, it failed to receive the attention it should have and would have, had it been handled with more care inside the White House.

Although the White House concentrated its education-reform efforts in the states, the President did not altogether ignore the Congress. Beginning in April 1989, and each year thereafter, he submitted important legislative packages that included his various elementary and secondary education reform ideas. The first package, dubbed the "Educational Excellence Act of 1989," included most of the ideas announced in Bush's February 9, 1989, "Building a Better America" address to Congress. The legislation went nowhere, and an almost identical version went up to Capitol Hill the next year.

Granted, Bush faced a Democratic majority in Congress, but the White House expended little political capital in attempting to secure passage of these proposals. At least that approach *was* consistent with Sununu's view about where the real action should take place. Still, near the end of the 1990 congressional session we did come close to passage of compromise education legislation that would have allowed us to claim that Congress had adopted key aspects of what Bush sought (in many instances distorted or watered down, but sufficiently recognizable to allow us, on a political basis, to claim a modest victory). During the final hours of the session, as Porter dispatched me to the Senate to end the logjam, we came extremely close, only to find ourselves stymied not by Democrats but by a handful of conservative Republican Senators—principally Senators Wallop, Helms, and Coats—who opposed provisions that they believed promoted abortion counseling (they were correct, and we fixed the language since that result was never intended by the Administration) and permitted funding for the National Board for Professional Teaching Standards. This last, an education establishment pet project, was anathema to Senator Jesse Helms, since it was chaired by one of his nemeses, former North Carolina Governor Jim Hunt. I, too, opposed the idea of funding the Board but had been instructed by Porter to try to resolve the impasse. The President wanted a bill.

Notwithstanding the yeoman efforts of Senator Nancy Kassebaum of Kansas to negotiate a compromise, the conservative Senators blocked final passage through an ingenious device called a "rolling hold." Every time one of them agreed to lift his floor objections to the bill, another would place a hold on the bill. Under the relatively loose Senate rules, as long as one Senator put a hold on the bill, the legislation couldn't move forward. The session of Congress was due to end that evening, and their obvious intention was to run out the clock. They did.

In retrospect our conservative friends did the right thing. What almost passed really did not include much of the President's package, so we had another opportunity in 1991 to submit new legislation, this time recrafted by the Education Secretary who had replaced Lauro Cavazos. Our next legislative attempt reflected the priorities of the national education goals and Lamar Alexander's ingenious "America 2000" plan for actually reaching the goals.

"America 2000" was fashioned principally by Alexander and his deputy, David Kearns, with considerable support from an education expert (and former Bennett protégé), Checker Finn, and from Dennis Doyle and several of us in the White House. In brief, "America 2000" would promote the education goals through a four-track strategy of improving all schools for today's students, investing in a multimillion-dollar privately funded research effort to develop the world's best "New American Schools," making American communities places where all people could learn, and, finally, enlisting the support of "America 2000" communities in promoting local strategies, including report cards, that would help achieve the goals.

Alexander's strategy was sheer brilliance for two reasons. It was bottom-up, not top-down, and it did not depend on congressional action to get started. The "New American Schools" research component did not necessarily involve one cent of federally appropriated money, although federal dollars would be needed to establish one "New American School" in each of the nation's 535 Congressional and Senatorial jurisdictions. By and large, however, the success or failure of "America 2000" turned on whether the President and Alexander could provoke a populist movement supporting higher levels of educational achievement and serious community-level commitment to education reform. The Alexander approach was wholly consistent with the premise behind the Charlottesville Summit: It signaled that the hard work of education reform began not in Washington but rather in places like Milwaukee, Peoria, and Tampa.

Throughout 1991 and 1992, the Bush Administration transmitted additional legislative proposals to the Congress: ideas to expand school choice for public and private schools and a novel "GI Bill for Children"; efforts to coordinate the myriad federal job-training programs into a coherent and workable structure; and legislation dealing with lifetime learning (a policy disaster) and apprenticeships. Congress ignored most of these ideas or reshaped them to make them mostly unpalatable to the Administration. None of this should have come as a surprise, because the President did little arm-twisting of members of the House and Senate to help achieve his agenda. (Education, by the way, was not the only area where this pattern held; then again, most of those other policy areas had not received the major campaign attention associated with the President's election pledge to be the "education President.")

One particular frustration involved school discipline. Randolph Beales, one of my special assistants at the Education Department who later also served with me at the White House, and I made repeated efforts during the entire four years of the Bush Administration to turn school discipline into a major presidential initiative. There were at least three reasons for considering this an important idea.

First, besides being the right thing to do it was a conservative values issue. Parents all across the nation were outraged at having to send their children to drug- and crime-infested schools. When *Newsweek* devoted a cover story to school discipline in 1991, I thought it was high time for the President to be heard on the matter.

Second, "safe, disciplined, and drug-free schools" were part of the national education goals—Goal 6 to be specific. We had devoted substantial effort to the standards and assessment aspects of "competency" Goals 3 and 4 (what our kids should know and being first in the world in math and science), but if our children went to schools where the learning environment was chaotic or disrupted through drugs or crime, all the good work on the other goals would be for nought. Goal 6, like Goal 1's call for "readiness," was a prerequisite without which the other goals were unattainable.

Finally, unlike some of the other goals, this one was absolutely attainable by the year 2000. While controlling a school's environs in the presence of street crime, violence, and drugs might be impossible, a strong principal plus the proper internal resources—physical as well as personnel—could secure the school building and grounds and make it safe for the students and faculty.

Notwithstanding these arguments, and despite memo after memo to Roger Porter and others in the White House (I even raised it over breakfast early one morning with Sam Skinner), there was no interest. Looking forward to the 1992 reelection effort and realizing that the President's conservative base needed shoring up, Beales, Rae Nelson of our staff, and I thought this was a no-brainer, a ready-made issue that even a political imbecile would find appealing. Moreover, school discipline didn't have to cost any money. One could amend existing federal civil rights legislation, which often deterred teachers and principals from punishing unruly students, could disseminate examples of what works, could give speeches, and could implement a host of other ideas. We even went so far as to float ideas with various conservative groups, like the Concerned Educators Against Forced Unionism, all of which were supportive and enthusiastic. Even Al Shanker, head of the American Federation of Teachers, believed in the importance of more school discipline. But among the senior aides inside the Bush White House, however, there were no takers. Anywhere.

While the Bush White House failed to invest the necessary political capital in securing passage of its education reform legislative proposals, at least it was unquestionably a player and to some extent a force, especially in the nonlegislative arena of securing public recognition and acceptance of the national educational goals. When it came to the other half of the education continuum after the elementary and secondary years—namely postsecondary education—the Bush Administration never even walked onto the playing field.

Education policy in the Bush Administration was assuming a bizarre, schizophrenic character, as was most glaringly apparent in postsecondary education policy. The schizophrenia arose because of the mismatch between rhetoric and responsibility, and the mismatch went essentially unperceived for three years, until the Administration's neglect of postsecondary education became increasingly obvious. It wasn't all the fault of Lauro Cavazos.

Crusading as America's "education President," George Bush advocated structural and systemic reforms at the elementary and secondary levels. But he had nothing of substance or lasting importance to say about education after high school graduation. Although First Lady Barbara Bush made literacy her own special initiative, it remained essentially rhetorical, and every time efforts were made to tee up a substantial literacy effort—in the White House, with the Department of Education, or through working with various groups—things went nowhere.

Bush's bully pulpit rhetoric was aimed primarily at the nonfederal players: governors, states, and localities. On the face of it there was nothing wrong with this approach. Our basic educational shortcomings indeed were in the elementary and secondary schools, as reflected in year after year of dismal test scores and comparative evaluations with the kids of our foreign competitors. If he wanted to have the biggest impact in reforming the education system, it made sense for Bush to concentrate his message on that sector.

There was, however, a growing, and hardly explicable, disparity between the Administration's willingness to preach to others about cleaning up their own house and its unwillingness to do something about the mess in its own backyard. Reform and restructuring were not just for states and local city school boards; they had to be applied to the feds as well, and this is precisely where the Bush Administration turned a blind eye. Where was the "education President"?

American postsecondary education is the strongest, most diverse such system of education in the world. No other nation offers its citizens the variety of postsecondary educational opportunities available in America, with its array of traditional institutions of higher education, community colleges, and thousands of vocational, trade, and technical schools. When Bush became President, most of the post–World War II federal education programs—for example, the GI Bill and the system of vouchers available to low-income students known as Pell Grants (named for Senator Claiborne Pell of Rhode Island)—had enjoyed striking success. Millions of young Americans had gone to college by combining loans and grants, thereby achieving what many of their parents had missed. By 1989 over 50 percent of America's high school graduates went on to college.

Access, however, had guaranteed neither quality nor efficiency. Far too many of those starting college didn't finish. By the mid-1980s, student loan programs that had begun almost two decades previously had spawned a vast cottage industry of trade and technical schools (as well as such supporting institutions as loan servicers, accrediting bodies, and secondary markets) living off the federally leveraged loans or direct federal grants. Many of those "proprietary schools" offered training in cosmetology, truck driving, word processing, and other technical skills. At the same time, some were ripping off kids by providing them with inadequate, in some instances nonexistent, training. By 1991 the federal government was spending more than $3 billion annually on defaulted loans, nearly half the amount budgeted for all the student loan and grant programs. What had been a national success was quickly becoming a serious national scandal and an embarrassment.

The banks that made the loan capital available (in large part because of generous federal interest rate subsidies and loan guarantees) were themselves enjoying the fruits of generous federal support. A 1991 study released by the U.S. Department of Education reported that student loans were the third most profitable banking activity after credit cards and commercial and industrial loans. In other words, the nation's commercial banks were doing better from their student loan business than on home mortgages, certificates of deposit, and just about every other form of banking activity.

For those banks that did not want to hold onto the loan paper (particularly where some of that paper was generated by students attending trade schools with a greater propensity for default), a vast secondary market, led by Sallie Mae, the Student Loan Marketing Association, and others, had developed to purchase their loan paper at a discount and then collect the repayments when they began or, in the event of default, collect on the federal guarantee.

As for the other key players—the academic institutions and the guarantee agencies that processed the loan paper before collecting on the guarantee from the federal government—they too were financial beneficiaries of the status quo. Students spent their loan and grant money at academic institutions, keeping their doors open. It was a system in which there were no losers, save for a growing number of ripped-off students and, of course, the American taxpayers, who underwrote the defaults.

Virtually all of these postsecondary education programs were governed by the Higher Education Act. Congress had last reauthorized this legislation in 1986 and had made relatively few changes. By the usual cycle, the next reauthorization would occur in 1991 or 1992. When Secretary of Education William Bennett testified to Congress before the 1986 reauthorization, his attempt to highlight the looming problem of loan defaults was scorned by Ted Kennedy and other liberal Democrats, some of whom were recipients of PAC money from trade schools that were causing much of the default problem. Kennedy and others falsely accused Bennett and the Reagan Administration of using the default issue to deny access to education for minorities, many of whom had no alternative but to attend these vocational schools.

By 1990, however, the student loan programs had become the focus of national attention because of repeated instances of waste, fraud, and abuse documented by *60 Minutes, 20/20,* and scores of articles in the press. Even leading Democrats recognized that the program had to be fixed to curb not only defaults but also the documented abuses at many proprietary schools.

While at the Education Department, I co-chaired a task force to study reauthorizing the Higher Education Act and to develop recommendations for Secretary Cavazos. After more than a year's effort on the project, I was convinced that the loan programs needed radical structural changes. Students and parents found the programs so confusing that some students receiving loan money never even knew they had an obligation to pay back the funds. The program had become unmanageable, unauditable, and unaccountable with the growth of a cottage industry of banks, guarantee agencies, and secondary markets that grew rich off the generous federal subsidy. Every effort was needed to simplify and streamline the program's operation. The best way to do that was to replace the whole structure with a revolutionary approach called "direct loans."

In April 1990, just before leaving the Department of Education for the White House, I outlined in a private discussion with Cavazos how a direct loan program might operate. The federal government would bypass the commercial banks to capitalize the loan program by borrowing directly from the Federal Financing Bank (FFB). Over some twelve years, the government would need to borrow $10 billion to $12 billion annually to capitalize the program as a revolving fund. The banks would be eliminated. Uncle Sam could raise the same money more cheaply by paying only the Treasury bill rate without the additional expenses of interest and special allowance subsidies.

With a direct loan program there would no longer be any need for guarantee agencies either. Secondary market entities like Sallie Mae could still function, primarily as contractors to service the loans. Educational institutions would themselves play a more central role in originating, processing, and certifying individual loans. Much of the complexity and indirect accountability of the existing program would be replaced by a streamlined system that maximized efficiency and minimized cost.

Cavazos liked and encouraged the concept. By the end of 1990, just two weeks before Bush and Sununu fired him, Cavazos informed OMB Director Darman that he would include direct loans as the centerpiece of his Higher Education Act reauthorization proposals.

It may have just been a coincidence, but I find it suspicious that shortly after his discussion with OMB on direct loans Cavazos received his pink slip. It became increasingly clear throughout November and December 1990 that Darman was intensely hostile to the idea. It wasn't his brainchild, and he believed, erroneously, that direct lending from the FFB would increase the federal budget deficit.

Within just a few days of Cavazos's firing on December 12, 1990, Acting Education Secretary Ted Sanders directed Department staff to stop work on the direct loan concept. That step was seen as an attempt to curry favor with Darman as part of Sanders's feverish and futile three-day effort to be named Secretary of Education.

While Sanders's bid to become Secretary failed, it served OMB's purpose of slowing down the debate, or so Darman thought until a front-page *New York Times* article by Robert Pear on January 7, 1991, broke the story that the Administration was considering direct loans.[3]

Darman accused me at the morning senior staff meeting presided over by Sununu of leaking the story to Pear. I hadn't, but I did know how the story got out. My successor at Education, George Pieler, had been sacked by Sanders as one of his first moves as Acting Secretary. For months Pieler had been a thorn in Sanders's side, standing up for Cavazos and thwarting Sanders's often *sub rosa* efforts to cater to the education establishment and the budget director. Pieler also had been instrumental in working with me to develop the direct loan proposal and refused to see it buried without a full debate within the Bush Administration. So Pieler first went to Tom Toch at *U.S. News and World Report* and then to Pear, spilling the beans.

Why was Darman so opposed to direct loans? Besides streamlining and making more efficient a dreadfully run government program, direct federal borrowing, as estimates by the Department of Education, the Congressional Budget Office, and the General Accounting Office all showed, would save at least $1.4 billion the first year alone and some $6.6 billion over five years. Darman was supposedly interested in deficit reduction, and direct loans would help reduce the federal deficit, his erroneous beliefs to the contrary notwithstanding.

Part of the explanation for the OMB Director's intense opposition lies in a quirk in the personality of Richard G. Darman. He could not abide a new idea that wasn't his own.

Darman directed one of his subordinates, OMB Associate Director Tom Scully, to develop a rationale for opposing direct loans. Scully continued to work with Sanders to concoct three reasons why the direct loan reform was a bad idea.

First, direct loans would increase the *deficit*. This was patently wrong. Under the recently enacted (and OMB-blessed) credit-reform legislation, direct borrowing from the capital markets had no net effect—positive or negative—on the federal deficit. Technically, such borrowing would raise the national *debt*, but on top of a $4 trillion national debt such an increase was trivial. Darman and his associates failed to understand the most basic distinction between debt and deficit, and they completely misperceived the implications of their own credit-reform legislation.

Second, some argued that direct loans meant almost immediate and unlimited exposure of the federal government for liability in the event of default. This fear was based upon a misunderstanding of the way the program currently worked. They wanted greater "risk-sharing" by requiring states to commit the full faith and credit of their state treasuries to bear default costs above a certain level. That proposal was a political and economic nonstarter for states, many of which by 1991 were facing serious fiscal problems of their own. At any rate, for a bank or secondary market entity holding student loan paper, direct federal liability existed already. To obtain that federal guarantee, all a bank or holder had to do was satisfy the relatively simple procedural "due diligence" requirements, and the feds would ante up in the event of default. Due diligence meant every so often calling or writing to a student who has failed to pay a loan on time. It didn't matter whether the student actually received the letter, answered the phone, or bothered to pay. Once those hoops had been jumped through and documented, the feds handled the default, and the American taxpayers covered the loss.

Third, OMB contended that the Department of Education was too inept to manage direct loans. This argument was counterintuitive. It was also nonsense. If OMB truly believed that the U.S. Department of Education was incapable of handling direct loans, which entailed a much more streamlined and efficient delivery system, then it clearly could not handle the existing system with its convoluted complexity. Why not give the Department an easier program to manage? The Department of Education's management aptitude or ineptitude was an argument *for* direct loans, not against them.

The Pear article in the *Times* sparked considerable interest and apprehension. Congressional Democrats whispered that if the Bush Administration offered a direct loan program in reauthorization, it would be enacted. They were enticed by the prospect of using the projected savings on the special allowance and interest payments to fund other discretionary education programs that were otherwise blocked by the terms of the 1990 budget agreement's "firewall" between discretionary and entitlement spending. Consumer banks abhorred the idea, as did the fifty-four guarantee agencies around the country and Sallie Mae, all of which would be hurt bigtime if they lost their lucrative middleman position. Some Republicans were attracted to the idea, though, because in addition to streamlining a cumbersome program, the savings could be used to reduce the growing budget deficit.

The direct loan proposal had already been studied in excruciating detail at the Department of Education, but with Sanders as Acting Secretary and Darman at OMB opposed to the concept, the proposal was going nowhere. The Task Force on the Higher Education Act Reauthorization had developed the details about how the program would be structured and implemented. The Department's Office of Planning, Budget and Evaluation—my old office—had crunched the numbers to arrive at the savings estimate of $1.4 billion the first year. Yet none of this information had been made public officially.

Interest in direct loans continued to grow on Capitol Hill, and the Democrats were desperate to learn whether the rumored savings could be verified. The issue then became how to break open the debate even further. At this point I found an ally outside the Administration, the very capable Washington representative of a large Midwestern state university, who felt as strongly about direct loans as did I. We were determined to end the stonewalling.

Shortly after taking over as Secretary, Lamar Alexander was asked about his position on direct loans in congressional testimony. He demurred, saying that he would have to study the concept in detail.

That answer was not intentionally evasive. Alexander's main goal, after all, was not reauthorization of the Higher Education Act, notwithstanding that his most recent previous position had been as President of the University of Tennessee. His goal was to gain support in Washington and across the country for his "America 2000" strategy. As the first few weeks of his tenure passed, it became evident that he was unwilling to spend valuable time on issues or controversies that would distract him from his primary focus or bring him into needless conflict with OMB.

In the wake of the Pear story, however, and in view of congressional interest in direct loans, the Bush Administration had to decide one way or the other. The question was how and when.

My university ally, Tom Butts (who was acting on behalf of University of Michigan President James Duderstadt), kept calling to stress how important it was that the Department of Education's early work on direct loans be made public or, at a minimum, shared with the relevant congressional committees. That's when I hit upon an idea that finally broke the stalemate.

If those Democrats and Republicans in Congress interested in direct loans saw the vast amount of positive work that the Administration's own Department of Education had done in studying direct loans—not to mention the projected budget savings—the issue would rapidly advance beyond the theoretical. So I suggested to my colleague that he talk with Representative Bill Ford, the new Chairman of the House Education and Labor Committee, and Ford's key education staffers, urging them to write Secretary Alexander and ask him to share with them the work already prepared by the Education Department's staff. Although technically stopping far short of a formal subpoena, such a letter would put the Department—and OMB—on notice that Ford knew about the substantial preparatory work already undertaken on direct loans.

As a Committee Chairman, Ford had a right to request this information and could do so more effectively than Butts could by seeking the same information from the Department under the Freedom of Information Act. The new Education Secretary would surely not want to irritate a powerful committee chairman so early in his tenure. I was certain that Alexander would comply if Ford would go for the idea of sending a letter.

He did, and Butts drafted the letter from Ford to Alexander, which

Ford then sent over to the Department of Education in early April 1991. Bear in mind that there was no policy at the time, and it did not look like there would be one until the junior staff got out ahead on this issue, or at least forced it to surface.

More than two months then passed before Alexander responded. In a June 28, 1991, letter drafted primarily by Ted Sanders (now demoted from Acting Secretary to my old job), Alexander basically reiterated the three objections dictated to the Department by OMB. But one thing was critical: The public saw for the first time the estimated annual budget savings of $1.4 billion. Congressional Democrats drooled, while bankers began to worry in earnest about their future in the student loan program.

Congressional staffers working for both Ford and Representative Dale Kildee became increasingly enamored of the concept, which, combined with their desire to expand funding for Pell Grants by turning the program into a new entitlement, would position them squarely on the side of program simplification and expansion of program benefits for the poor and the middle class.

Reaction to the Alexander letter within the education community depended upon what one wanted to read into it. Direct loan opponents crooned that Alexander had slammed shut the door on the idea. Those favoring it argued that he had not but had merely said it needed further study, and the Department of Education was not "at this time" ready to include the concept as part of its reauthorization package. Mike Farrell, Alexander's acting head of postsecondary education, confirmed that the letter had been crafted carefully to leave the door open. In fact, Farrell, a former Reagan Administration official, had long battled with Sanders, who was trying to close the door on direct loans. Farrell had added the language that preserved the ambiguity and thus kept the issue alive. In fact, Farrell was developing into a closet supporter of direct loans.

As the debate continued, another congressman became enamored of direct loans. Freshman Representative Rob Andrews, a New Jersey Democrat who held the seat vacated by Governor Jim Florio, now served on the House Education and Labor Committee. Convinced that the current Stafford loan program needed serious overhauling, Andrews introduced his own "pure" direct loan program in early September 1991.

The Andrews proposal was "pure" in that it was a stand-alone bill, and did not, for example, link direct loans with making Pell Grants an entitlement. The latter was certain veto bait (and properly so) at the White House. Andrews wanted direct loans debated on their own merits.

My White House colleague Jim Pinkerton had gotten to know the thirty-three-year-old Andrews, whom he described as a "New Paradigm" Democrat. Pinkerton said I had to meet Andrews.

"He may be a Democrat and hold their views, but, in many ways, he thinks like us. He knows these programs are messed up and supports the necessary structural reform," Pinkerton told me. I knew I had another ally in Congress, albeit from the wrong party.

Andrews and Pinkerton met for lunch in early September. I was invited but had to skip the meeting because of a speaking engagement. Pinkerton knew about direct loans and supported the concept (as did Larry Lindsey). I told him to make sure Andrews knew what I'd been up to.

Pinkerton called me later that day. Andrews was delighted to hear of my support and wanted to talk. I called the congressman immediately, and after a few moments of conversation I knew why Jim had become so impressed with this freshman Democrat. He knew the details of higher education policy inside and out and had also mastered the nuances of direct loans. We agreed to work together sharing ideas, information, and strategy, which was technically acceptable for me to do, insofar as the Bush Administration had never yet formally rejected the direct loan proposal.

In the meantime, I was intentionally seeking to sow as much confusion and discord wherever possible to delay a formal Administration response (which I now suspected would be negative) until after the October 2 markup of Ford's bill, which included both direct loans and Pell Grant entitlements. Earlier drafts of the Alexander letter were embarrassingly weak. I told Education Department staff that their letter—even if it opposed direct loans—had to be both sophisticated and excellent. I meant what I said, but lurking in the back of my mind was the conviction that if ever there was an occasion for the perfect to be the enemy of the good, it was now!

Alexander decided not to delay and sent his response on October 2. The Alexander letter offered no new arguments against direct loans and merely restated the three-point opposition litany. Anticipating the Department's position, Representative Andrews had released a week previously a five-page "Dear Colleague" letter that rebutted the OMB position point by point and in considerable detail. It was a brilliant piece of work. It sent both OMB and Education Department staffers scurrying to counteract its impact.

With the Bush Administration now on record opposing direct loans, my room for maneuver was somewhat, but not totally, circumscribed. According to Andrews, the Alexander letter (dictated by OMB's Tom Scully) was so shallowly, poorly, and crudely drafted that few on the Hill took it seriously. Since it stopped short of threatening outright veto of a direct loan program, moreover, the Democrats were undeterred. At Ford's request, Andrews began working with a key Republican colleague, Tom Coleman of Missouri, on framing a legislative proposal to include a pilot direct loan program. I continued my back-channel conversations with Andrews and Butts.

By opposing direct loans, the Bush Administration had now positioned itself against education reform and in favor of, as one colleague aptly put it, "welfare for lenders." It was appalling that an Administration preaching reform at the elementary and secondary level could become so wedded to the status quo when it came to postsecondary education. The Democrats could now take the high road on expanding benefits for poor and middle-class students, not to mention deficit reduction and serious structural reform.

How did all of this happen? Why did it happen? It happened because no one in the West Wing of the White House—not Roger Porter, not Ede Holiday in Cabinet Affairs, not anybody at a senior level interested in policy formulation—was willing to take on Darman, who had by now become the unchecked master of domestic policy. Other White House aides—Pinkerton, Lindsey, and Jay Lefkowitz in Cabinet Affairs, to name but a few—liked the concept but got nowhere with their bosses.

It was an appalling display of weakness, and most disappointing of all was Roger Porter's noninvolvement. It was simply incredible that the President's chief domestic policy adviser, a former Harvard University professor who had played a key role in shaping the Administration's education agenda early on, had no stomach for this battle. He let me continue to push the idea until Darman choked off all debate, but he himself refused to take a position. He refused to raise the issue with Darman. He was just afraid.

Both Larry Lindsey and I had explained to Porter the strategy behind direct loans many times. We thought Porter would be interested. We were wrong.

Once when OMB's Scully and I were in Porter's office, I raised the subject of the Alexander letter. Porter looked quickly at his watch, said he was late for something, and asked Scully and me to continue the discussion in my office. Porter made clear his keen interest in avoiding any discussion that might place him at odds with Darman.

While the Bush Administration dragged its feet on direct loans, Representative Andrews maneuvered with remarkable skill and speed through the House Education and Labor Committee. First, after inviting his Republican colleagues to work with him only to find them pressured by the White House and Representative Marge Roukema, a New Jersey Republican, Andrews managed to steer through the subcommittee markup what was essentially the direct loan proposal I'd suggested to Cavazos. Then, much to the surprise of virtually everyone, Andrews prevailed in full committee as well. Direct loans were on the verge of making it intact through the House of Representatives.

Meanwhile, in the Senate, another "strange bedfellows" coalition emerged through an evolving partnership between Democrat Paul Simon and Republican David Durenberger, who were cosponsoring a variant of direct loans. The Bush Administration, shackled by yet another of Darman's political and policy misjudgments, was hewing to a course fraught with folly. By issuing a Statement of Administration Policy opposing *both* direct loans and the conversion of the Pell Grant program to an entitlement, the President was setting himself up for a clear veto override. Darman was insisting that we issue a senior advisers' veto threat for *any* bill containing either direct loans *or* Pell entitlements. His mistake should have been obvious to any political neophyte. It was made abundantly clear to me by Andrews during a private discussion before we appeared together on a C-SPAN call-in show with Wisconsin's Governor Tommy Thompson.

"The fact, Charlie, is that the Democratic leadership in the House will probably recede from pushing Pell as an entitlement. If that's true, then it maximizes the likelihood that we'll see direct loans as a compromise position offered to Bill Ford." According to Andrews, the Speaker of the House was unwilling to press forward with Pell entitlements because doing so would mean breaching the 1990 budget deal. Moreover, Bush would be hard-pressed to veto a higher education bill *and* a K-12 reform bill on the eve of the November election. The Democrats knew that Darman was just blowing smoke: There was no way in the world House or Senate Republicans would sustain a presidential veto over a limited direct loan demonstration program.

Andrews's analysis was right on target. If the Democrats dropped Pell entitlements, then the Administration's public veto threat lost all credibility. No one believed that Bush would veto a higher education bill during an election year merely because Dick Darman disagreed with the need for fundamental reform in a federal program that had gotten seriously out of whack.

For months I had been warning Porter that higher education would become an important election theme in 1992. The reasoning was simple: Being able to send their kids to college was one of the five things most middle-class Americans really cared about, along with owning their own home, holding a job, saving for retirement, and enjoying access to affordable quality health care. Bush's proposed 1993 budget gave some help on college affordability by proposing that interest payments on student loans be deductible once again and that the maximum Pell Grant rise from $2,400 to $3,700. Nonetheless, more and more Democrats were calling for substantial reforms of the federal student loan programs. Republicans, if they listened to Darman, would soon be missing the boat.

To add to Darman's folly, direct loans received national attention just before the 1992 New Hampshire primary in a Jack Anderson and Michael Binstein column, which accurately portrayed the Bush Administration as opposing the reforms and favoring instead "welfare" subsidies for the banks. Anderson and Binstein reported that the nation's banks were frenzied in their opposition to direct loans.[4] Because of Darman, Republicans were about to walk into a trap where once again they would be portrayed as the party favoring country club elites and other moneyed interests.

But some House Republicans were about to depart from GOP orthodoxy and declare their support for direct loans. Tom Petri from Wisconsin had his own variation of direct loans and was unwilling to support a presidential veto. In a talk with Petri I told him he and other House Republicans should make their concerns known directly to the President and, perhaps more important, to Bob Teeter, Chairman of the 1992 Bush–Quayle reelection campaign. Clearly Teeter would appreciate the significance of Bush's failing to sustain his first veto of an education bill in a bitterly fought and probably close election contest.

In the early summer of 1992 Chairman Ford decided to pull a clever switch on the Bush Administration: Rather than complete action on the Higher Education Act in September, Ford decided to move on that bill by June, thereby postponing the elementary and secondary reform bill to the fall, just a few weeks before the November 3 presidential election. The Democrats again guessed correctly that Bush's veto threat over direct loans was hollow. Consequently, since he'd probably sign the higher education legislation, why not try to embarrass him with a possible veto override of the elementary and secondary education bill in late September?

Ford brazenly carried his strategy a step further. While OMB representatives tried to bluster direct loans out of the final conference report on the Higher Education Act, congressional Democrats, led by Ford, suddenly rammed through a provision that *doubled* the size of the direct loan demonstration program that had already survived both Houses of Congress. Instead of a more modest demonstration program limited to a few hundred participating schools and up to $500 million, Ford responded to the OMB-driven veto threat with a splendid "in-your-face" gesture to Darman: Direct loans would now extend to five hundred schools and reach $1 billion!

With OMB's bluff now called, Darman and Scully had to scramble to save face. A quick head count by the White House legislative office showed that it would be utterly impossible to sustain a presidential veto. The calculus now shifted, and I soon discovered another ally who supported direct loans. Nick Calio, Assistant to the President for Legislative Affairs, sought counsel in shaping arguments to counter Darman as to why we should *not* veto the bill over direct loans. Calio's head count had convinced him that a veto override was a virtual certainty, and he just didn't want it to happen over this issue on his watch.

So much for principle! But I was willing to take my supporters any way I could find them. At White House senior staff meetings, Calio argued in favor of signing the bill, even with direct loans as part of the reauthorization. That position infuriated Darman, who by now realized that he lacked the votes. The OMB Director continued to threaten a presidential veto anyway, but he also went back to the conferees to work out another deal.

Meanwhile, the congressional Republican leadership, along with the key members from both chambers' education committees, met with Bush in the Cabinet Room in July. Their message to the President was short and simple: Don't plan on vetoing the Higher Education Act legislation and seeing your veto sustained. Even Republicans were unwilling to vote against a popular education measure that ensured funding for student loans and Pell Grants to needy students. Besides, a veto at this juncture was likely to disrupt the processing of loans and grants just a few weeks before many college-bound kids headed back to school. These people not only were young, they also voted!

Bush listened to the message and worried aloud that the bill in its current form would raise the federal budget deficit. I was told later that although Darman was in the room and had briefed the President before the meeting, he failed to correct the President's misimpression. Bush had somehow gotten it into his head that direct loans were bad for the deficit, and that was good enough for Dick Darman.

The direct loan pilot program stayed in the legislation—a major loss for Darman—but was scaled back to 300 to 400 schools and $500 million, precisely the result Darman could have had earlier had he not engaged in all his false bravado. The Conference Report included this compromise, and the bill passed both chambers by substantial veto-proof margins.

Bush signed the bill into law on July 23, 1992, at a ceremony at Northern Virginia Community College (ironically, as Senator Edward Kennedy pointedly remarked to me just before the signing ceremony, the same college, albeit a different campus, where Jimmy Carter had signed the 1980 Higher Education Act reauthorization just three months before losing reelection to Ronald Reagan).

Like so much of George Bush's presidency, the Higher Education Act Amendments of 1992 represented a continuation of the status quo tempered by only a modest element of structural reform, which in this instance had been resisted kicking and screaming by the White House and Dick Darman. The *New York Times* referred to the direct loan demonstration as the only substantial reform aspect of the legislation. Bush had obviously once again forgotten about "We Are the *Change!*"

Pragmatism, however, rarely waited for consistency in the Bush White House. In the Bush White House, you were in favor of what happened. After the President signed the bill, Bush's Office of Public

Liaison distributed a mass mailing to its "education contacts" around the country in early August trumpeting the newly signed Higher Education Act Amendments, highlighting in particular the presence of the new direct loan demonstration. If you can't have things your way, why not claim some of the credit? As a further irony, I discovered that in its annual midsession review released on July 24, 1992, Darman's OMB included a passage on entitlement savings which at least recognized and gave credibility to the earlier claims that direct loans could save some $6.6 billion over six years.

It turned out that Darman was correct after all: Direct loans would have an impact on the deficit. He just got the direction wrong. Instead of complaining that direct loans would *raise* the deficit, Darman might more accurately have told the President and the public that the opposite was in fact true.

Was Bush an "education President"? Did he live up to his 1988 pledge?

While Bush was never engaged in any serious way when it came to higher education, his efforts at reforming America's elementary and secondary system constituted what was probably the best-developed and most coherent of all his domestic policy efforts. Simply measuring Bush's performance by his personal "input," it was evident that he had done more education "events" than any previous president: photo ops, speeches, school visits, Rose Garden recognition and award ceremonies. From a "bully pulpit" perspective, Bush had very definitely been an activist "education President."

From a substantive standpoint, Bush—with Roger Porter—deserves enormous credit for beginning to effect structural reforms that, if continued and implemented carefully, can radically reform American education. His "America 2000" strategy—a function of Lamar Alexander's shrewdness and enormous ability—envisions world-class standards for what our children should know and be able to achieve. Those standards, in turn, are to be reflected in a companion curriculum that evolves at the community and state levels. Finally, both the standards and the curriculum are drawn together in one or more of what Bush called "voluntary national assessments," tests designed to provide reliable, measurable information about how well American children are doing in school. All these accomplishments, particularly the concept of national assessments, would have been unthinkable just five or six years ago.

The remarkable aspect of what George Bush began is that he managed to carry out most of his agenda in a reasonably bipartisan manner, working first with the nation's governors at Charlottesville and thereafter (albeit because he was forced to) including members of Congress in the measurement-and-assessment process. Activities across the country were beginning to concentrate on ways to achieve the six national education goals. At the same time, through his emphasis on accountability and educational achievement (rather than merely measuring aptitude), Bush began to shape the debate about education reform, moving it from the perennial question, "How much money are we spending?" to the more difficult and important question, "How well are our children performing?"

In the matter of resources, though, Bush did deliver. Spending increased substantially for dozens of federal education programs, perhaps the most notable example being his decision to fund Head Start fully for all eligible four-year-olds whose parents wanted them to participate. Like Reagan, Bush received relatively little credit for this extra spending, and he was routinely criticized for stating that spending was irrelevant. His message, however, went beyond saying that resources do not matter in education. Clearly they do, but Bush managed to motivate educators, politicians, and parents to ask questions about how best to target scarce resources on the neediest students and how to redeploy those education dollars in order to achieve better results.

Unfortunately, few people knew about Bush's role in those positive developments, and for one simple reason: He didn't take any credit. The advisers around him were incapable of shaping his manifold education events into a coherent national education message. Every month, for example, his communications director, David Demarest, would convene special education planning meetings in the Roosevelt Room. The task was to map out the President's education schedule for the next thirty to sixty days. Sometimes as many as twenty-five or thirty people from the White House and the Education Department gathered for those sessions, in which most of the time was spent discussing which event was worth doing or not doing.

On several occasions I decided to be the skunk at the party by objecting that our planning was "bassackwards." Little if any attention was being paid to what Bush would say. The discussion was always over whether to do a school recognition ceremony in one town or a parental choice–related event in another. There was no overall game plan, and I got only blank stares whenever I suggested that it made more sense first to determine the message we wanted to convey and *then* to select the most appropriate event for conveying that message to the American people.

Remember: Education was our flagship domestic policy! No other area of the domestic agenda that I knew of was the subject of such detailed monthly planning sessions. We were like an evolving pointillist painting in which talented artists were placing dots on a canvas wholly at random. Instead of producing a Georges Seurat, we produced a god-awful blur. Nobody knew what we were up to. There was no focus.

Moreover, some staff openly wondered whether George Bush, if ever asked during a presidential debate, would even be able to remember the six national education goals. Roger Porter prided himself on sending Bush one interesting factoid after another about American education, but no systematic effort was made to devise a strategy making persuasive tactical use of the presidential bully pulpit.

Launching "America 2000" gave Lamar Alexander a forum for traveling the country and enlisting almost every state and several thousand towns and communities to embrace the national education goals. Cynics complained that the former Tennessee Governor was merely using federal dollars to crisscross the country in a massive public relations effort, laying the groundwork for his own 1996 presidential bid. There can be little question that Lamar Alexander had his eye on bigger prizes (as he should, given his considerable natural talents), but his efforts to launch a bottom-up populist education reform movement were precisely the right steps needed, and Lamar Alexander was a brilliantly persuasive messenger.

An Education Secretary's voice, however, carries a much shorter distance than a President's. While George Bush fervently embraced "America 2000" and often praised it, it was also painfully evident to us that he had by no means internalized what it meant. "America 2000" was words on a page. The way the President would describe his new "program" was accurate, but the tone was bureaucratic rather than personal. He never succeeded in painting a canvas that presented a vision of where he wanted America to be. We had a means to get there (a process) but we couldn't explain to people in a convincing manner where we were heading.

Education reform ultimately played a minor role in the 1992 presidential campaign. The Democratic challenger, Bill Clinton, after all, had a solid record as an "education Governor." Moreover, he had been present at the creation of the national education goals and knew the education standards issue inside and out. Bush would have made relatively little headway challenging Clinton on K-12 issues, except when it came to school choice. On that issue Clinton had flip-flopped in a highly visible and craven manner.

In 1990 he had written to Polly Williams, a Wisconsin legislator and ardent choice proponent, sounding vaguely supportive of her efforts and those of Governor Tommy Thompson to bring public *and private* school choice to Milwaukee. Two years later, however, to secure the full backing of the two giant teachers' unions, Clinton retreated, indicating that he endorsed only public school choice. Bush could have scored bigtime by highlighting this discrepancy. Not only would he have been plugging choice, an important conservative issue, but he would have been able to underscore Clinton's inconsistency, vacillation, and unmistakable pandering to the teachers' unions. Vice President Quayle zeroed in on the issue during his one debate with Admiral James Stockdale and Clinton's running mate, Senator Al Gore, and the President himself finally took up the issue (but after the Quayle debate). It took several of us weeks to get this relatively obvious zinger into the President's campaign rhetoric.

On higher education we were fortunate that Clinton didn't skewer the President for his noninvolvement. Clinton's own problems in this area stemmed from the fact that his proposals were costly and cumbersome, but at least his concepts involved innovations, particularly in the job-training and national service areas.

In some respects it may be easy to understand the differences between Clinton and Bush on the issue of higher education. In my view, their respective backgrounds and family experiences hold the key to comprehending their approaches. George Bush, after all, grew up amid wealth and privilege. After attending a prestigious Eastern prep school, he went to Yale, where, like his father, he was a member of the elite and secretive Skull and Bones Society.

For Bill Clinton, higher education meant self-improvement, a key to the world beyond Hope, Arkansas. His father had been killed in a car crash before he was even born, and his mother and stepfather by no means enjoyed the affluence of the Bush clan. For the young

Clinton, Georgetown University, followed by his Rhodes Scholarship at Oxford University and then his admission to Yale Law School, opened up new worlds that his parents never knew. Consequently, Clinton saw higher education the way so many other middle-class Americans did: as a path to higher earnings, opportunity, and status. George Bush already enjoyed those, and his own education was only a part of the package. His benign neglect of higher education policy should have come as no surprise.

Three days after Bush lost to Bill Clinton, Clayton Yeutter explained over breakfast that the President was just never able to communicate his message in ways that Americans found convincing. Despite his undergraduate degree in economics, Bush never mastered the ability to explain his economic plans in terms ordinary Americans could understand. Just as the President would refer to " 'America 2000,' my national education *program*," and assume his audience knew what he meant, so he would refer anyone curious about his economic agenda to the pamphlet entitled *Agenda for American Renewal*. It's all in the program, all in the pamphlet. Just read it. You'll see.

In fact, the way Bush handled his education agenda proved to be a harbinger of many other doomed presidential initiatives. While there was considerable, almost constant activity below the surface of the Administration and the campaign—efforts to highlight school choice, higher standards, or discipline—it was lost on the public because of internal squabbles within the Bush Administration or an inability to decide whether to do anything at all. Bush had actually accomplished much in education reform, particularly relating to the type of structural changes—the incentives—needed within the system to encourage students to reach higher achievement levels, but during the campaign he remained focused, if at all, on issues of marginal relevance.

As in many other areas of domestic policy, the President and his imagemakers couldn't connect with the public and its real concerns. George Bush's own words and body language were clear signs of that failing. He would labor awkwardly over the word "ed-chew-KAY-shun" and would refer to his "America 2000 program" generally without delving into any of its specifics. He knew he had a plan, but few outside the White House or the education field knew what he was talking about.

Did George Bush earn the title "education President"? Not in the least, insofar as higher education was concerned. When it came to elementary and secondary education, however, the President did achieve major successes. With one small qualification: he never understood why.

6

The Week Bush Fired Cavazos

Sununu Knows Best

It's the central impulse of the Bush Administration—
why can't everyone be satisfied?

—An adviser to the
White House[1]

Domestic policy in the Bush Administration *after* the 1990 budget deal suffered from benign neglect. Some people said there was no domestic policy. Others called it moribund or, my favorite word, "inert." There can be little question, however, that matters were essentially on autopilot. No need to worry. No need to do much of anything. That's not precisely what John Sununu said, but it's what lots of people—inside and outside the White House—believe he meant.

Notwithstanding Sununu's wishes, the White House or, more properly, the Chief of Staff could not control everything. There were days when things went haywire and people in the West Wing had to act, or at least react.

Regarding the Bush Administration's ability to deal promptly and convincingly with a domestic crisis, there is probably no better case study than the events that began on Wednesday, December 12, 1990, just a few weeks after the budget deal. Lacking any guiding philosophy, the Bush White House repeatedly found itself confused and incapable of swift or concerted action.

Nothing went right that morning—or during that week, for that matter—and the bungling came not partially, but almost exclusively, from the desk of John Sununu. Three domestic crises occurred before noon that day, and the way in which the President's lieutenants responded was indicative of much larger problems: a stunted domestic policy operation, coupled with an insular arrogance, that ultimately helped overwhelm George Bush's presidency.

The crises began with the firing of Education Secretary Lauro Cavazos. That was followed by former Drug Czar Bill Bennett's unexpected decision to decline the chairmanship of the Republican National Committee. Finally, Michael Williams, the gutsy Assistant Secretary for Civil Rights at the Department of Education, announced his decision to ban all federal funds going to colleges and universities that administered or accepted racially based scholarships. There was no word to describe the atmosphere inside the White House but chaos.

Not since Margaret Heckler was "promoted" from Secretary of Health and Human Services to Ambassador to Ireland had a Cabinet Secretary gotten the boot so abruptly and with such humiliation as the ever faithful and loyal Lauro Cavazos. When Heckler was removed from HHS in October 1985, she appeared alongside Ronald Reagan in the White House press room all smiles and full of appreciation as her new assignment was announced. Not so with Lauro Cavazos, George Bush's holdover Secretary of Education whose appointment in September 1988, at the behest of then presidential candidate Bush, was widely heralded as the first Hispanic Cabinet appointment. Cavazos exited quietly and without fanfare, but the entire episode left a mess in its wake.

The Cavazos firing was supposed to go smoothly. The problem was, however, that Sununu had neglected to consult with anyone who knew Cavazos well to learn how he would react. A close-hold decision resulted in an unnecessary surprise and a potential political embarrassment for the President.

The decision to replace Cavazos was made the previous week, when the President was in South America. Sununu's staff had called the Secretary of Education's office to request a meeting with Cavazos at the White House. No details were offered, but the handwriting on the wall should have been apparent: Cavazos was not a regular in Sununu's office or at the White House. Unlike the amiable, chummy Secretary of Transportation, "gee, guys" Sam Skinner, who frequently showed up at the staff dining table in the White House Executive Mess, Cavazos appeared in the White House for official functions only, and then reluctantly. When his scheduling office followed up with the Cabinet Affairs Office to determine the subject of the meeting, it took thirty-six hours to get an answer: personnel. A meeting was scheduled for the afternoon of December 11.

There were a handful of senior-level positions still vacant in the Department of Education (for example, my former position as Deputy Under Secretary), so Cavazos had the impression that the meeting was to review those jobs. A few hours before the Sununu meeting, Cavazos had lunch with Chino Chapa, his chief of staff, and George Pieler, Acting Deputy Under Secretary for Planning, Budget and Evaluation. The Secretary indicated clearly that his thoughts were on the future and the next year's legislative calendar. He was dissatisfied with previous efforts to secure the Administration's legislative agenda on Capitol Hill, and he planned to take a more personal and active interest in that area himself starting in January.

But that was not to be. Just before he left for the White House, Cavazos's Assistant Secretary for Legislation, Nancy Kennedy, rushed in to alert Chapa that she had picked up a solid rumor from a White House contact that Sununu was going to ask for the Secretary's resignation. Cavazos was stunned.

The Education Secretary was ushered into Sununu's spacious West Wing corner office in midafternoon. According to Marlin Fitzwater, the press secretary, the meeting was not pleasant. Sununu told Cavazos he could choose between two ambassadorships, Costa Rica and the Dominican Republic, but his resignation was expected not later than the end of December.

Cavazos, alternatively blind and indifferent to the crosscurrents of politics and with absolutely no inkling that the President was displeased with his performance, demanded to see Bush personally. He was not interested in any other position. For that matter, he had no intention of staying out the month on those terms. A proud man who never hesitated to show his disdain for Washington politics, Cavazos told Sununu that if he didn't want him in the job, he was leaving. "You'll have my resignation tomorrow, effective Saturday, December 15."

Cavazos insisted on seeing the President. To Sununu it was evident that the matter was not going to be a replay of the graceful

Heckler firing. Sununu overlooked one painfully obvious fact: Cavazos had never been and never would be a political animal, hence felt no need to paper over differences for the sake of public appearances. This was, after all, the same Lauro Cavazos who, his first year in Washington, had cavalierly declined an invitation to one of the Capital's most coveted insider events, the Gridiron Dinner, preferring instead to spend the Saturday night in his apartment with wife, Peggy Ann. Sununu's needs and Cavazos's pride failed to blend. Sununu had another crisis on his hands.

It took twenty minutes for Cavazos to get in to see the President in the Oval Office. When he got confirmation directly from Bush that he should move on, that things weren't working out, he left the West Wing immediately and had his chauffeur drive him home, after first stopping in front of the Education Department so that Chapa could hand him his briefcase. Cavazos had no intention of ever setting foot inside the Department of Education.

The next morning Cavazos spoke briefly with the President by phone and then set off with his wife for the long drive to their home in Concord, Massachusetts. He left his chief of staff to work out the final details of the precise wording of his resignation letter, which he never saw and which was autopenned at the Department and then transmitted to the White House.

Sununu knew he had an embarrassment on his hands. How could he or the President explain Cavazos's abrupt departure? The Heckler model was out of the question: Cavazos clearly wouldn't play along. The resignation letter might be composed in a way to put a good face on the situation, but it would be easy to see through: Why was Cavazos leaving abruptly in four days, at the conclusion of a commencement address he was scheduled to deliver in Charlestown, West Virginia, on Saturday?

By the next morning it was obvious that the letter was not going to help. The first autopenned version was abrupt, only three sentences long. Cavazos had spoken by phone with Chapa and wanted to submit merely a one-sentence statement indicating that he was leaving. Chapa, however, conferred with the White House Cabinet Affairs Office and produced a three-sentence version, which was sent back as unsatisfactory—it failed to reflect any of Cavazos's accomplishments as Secretary. So Chapa added a fourth sentence "for posterity" citing Cavazos's efforts on behalf of school choice and Hispanic education.

Ede Holiday, head of Cabinet Affairs, called Chapa back to insist that the letter also thank the President for the opportunity of serving in his Cabinet. She wanted another sentence stating that the departure was basically voluntary, a recognition by Cavazos that the midpoint of a presidency was a good time to bring in new blood and that he had greatly appreciated the opportunity of serving both Ronald Reagan and George Bush for some twenty-seven months.

Cavazos had made a decision to remain in office through Bush's first term, so he would never have agreed to such face-saving rhetoric. Chapa, unable to reach Cavazos in his car, refused to add language that he knew his former boss would not approve. Two days after Cavazos's resignation became effective, Chapa was sacked as chief of staff, and the White House personnel office was content not to lift a finger to help him out.

Sununu's handling of the dismissal revealed a lack of knowledge about or interest in the kind of man with whom he was dealing. I worked almost directly above his office, so it would have been easy for Sununu or his Executive Assistant, Ed Rogers, to have inquired how Cavazos might react to the choices offered to him. Cavazos had often told me that he had not sought his current job, wasn't interested in anything else, and would be pleased to stay as long as the President wanted him. Cavazos was a fundamentally forthright, proud, and honest individual, with no appreciation whatsoever of politics. He paid scant attention to negative stories in the media, and, hearing no criticism from the West Wing—in fact, Cavazos frequently mentioned with pride the warm personal notes of congratulation he had received from the President—he simply assumed that the President and his senior staff were pleased with his performance and that he had a mandate to carry on, bad press notwithstanding.

Sununu's mistake—and the President's—was in not having sent early warning signals that would have prepared Cavazos for the biggest surprise of his career. That would have let Cavazos down gently and would probably have forestalled the abrupt departure, which left the White House in the awkward position of having to deny the obvious.

Bush announced the Cavazos resignation—accepted with "deep regret"—at his 10 A.M. Cabinet meeting on December 12. But before that hour was out, two other big stories would have the White House staff and the GOP establishment up in arms and in what can only be called political panic and chaos.

Sununu and the President had serious problems with Republican conservatives. The disastrous November budget deal, preceded by the equally catastrophic reversal of his "no-new-taxes" campaign pledge, had cost Bush and the party substantially in the fall congressional elections. Although the net loss in the House of Representatives remained below double digits, that "success" only thinly masked the inescapable fact that rare opportunities to pick up House and Senate seats for the GOP had been needlessly wasted.

For the first time in more than a decade there was open warfare among Republicans: Newt Gingrich (a leading budget deal negotiator who had opposed the final package and who himself only narrowly escaped losing his "safe" House seat) had become the *bête noire* of the Sununu–Darman–Brady troika, which was now in full command of the nation's domestic agenda.

Ed Rollins, the Republican Congressional Campaign Committee Chairman and a staunch loyalist, found himself ostracized from the White House. In retribution for his folly in advising Republican congressional candidates in writing a few weeks before election day not to hesitate to oppose their President on the budget deal, the President reportedly was urging his former congressional colleagues not to renew Rollins's lucrative $250,000 contract. One of the President's sons was reported to be so angry over Rollins's behavior that he refused to speak with him for a year.

Despite his continuing wrath over the whining in the party about the budget deal, Sununu had begun to receive that message loud and clear. Something had to be done to calm and presumably satisfy the restless troops.

Shortly after becoming President, George Bush had rewarded his campaign strategist and longtime friend Lee Atwater with the Chairmanship of the Republican National Committee. Atwater had gotten his start in South Carolina politics under the tutelage of Senator Strom Thurmond. At thirty-nine, Atwater was the youngest RNC Chairman in history. His appointment had surprised many; by tradition, the position was supposed to go to establishment types like former Senator Bill Brock, Frank Fahrenkopf, or George Bush himself, not to a campaign footsoldier.

But Atwater had proved himself a brilliant and tough trench warrior, precisely the sort of hands-on tactician Bush needed if he was to secure for his presidency what Ronald Reagan had at the outset of his: at least a Republican majority in the Senate and substantial inroads by the GOP in the House after the 1990 census and congressional redistricting.

Assuming the helm in early 1989, Atwater guided the RNC adroitly, mapping out a detailed campaign to target key House and Senate races for 1990 to help win for George Bush that much-needed working majority in the Congress. Everything appeared to be on track when Atwater was suddenly diagnosed as having a potentially fatal astrocytoma, an inoperable and exceptionally virulent brain tumor, which took him out of commission almost immediately.

While Atwater battled his brain cancer, the RNC's day-to-day operations eventually fell to chief of staff Mary Matalin and a consultant-spokesman, Charles Black. In the summer of 1990, when Bush abandoned his antitax pledge and sat down to negotiate with the Democrats over budget deficits and tax hikes, the Republican party organization fell apart altogether. By late October, the feuding had escalated to near-warfare. The dismal off-year election results that November set off alarms in the White House that could no longer be ignored.

Faced with both political and financial hemorrhaging, John Sununu consulted with Bush over how best to begin mending their ties not only with the GOP conservatives but with the mainstream, which was now going to find its taxes going up in 1991.

Atwater's health was not improving, and it was clear that going into a reelection mode in 1991 would require strong leadership soon. Burned by the budget deal that wasn't his idea in the first place (and, quite possibly, seeking an intellectual heavyweight to counter the bullying tactics of Dick Darman), Sununu convinced Bush that the job should be offered to William Bennett, a bona fide (neo)conservative and a darling of the right.

The problem was to persuade Bennett.

When he had left the Education Department in September 1988, Bill Bennett had arranged a lucrative series of speaking engagements that would begin to build up his personal wealth. Although a lawyer, Bennett had never practiced. Before coming to Washington to head the National Endowment for the Humanities in 1981, he had previously held only academic or think-tank positions at relatively modest salaries. In short, Bennett was hellbent on making some bucks.

Working out of the newly created James Madison Center just off McPherson Square and two blocks from the White House, Bennett was able to sustain his bully pulpit activities to promote education reform—what he called "content, character, and choice"—while also lecturing around the country and fulfilling his book contracts.

Bennett wasn't able to finish his books: In late December 1988, President-elect Bush offered Bennett the newly created position of Director of the Office of National Drug Control Policy; in short, he was to be the first Drug Czar. Bennett readily accepted the offer. In fact, he had reportedly called Bush and asked for the job, having found the lecture circuit and the discipline of writing somewhat tedious. He wanted back in the action. It was clear that the lecture circuit would keep Bennett far from the national spotlight and would dim any future political opportunities, particularly for elective office.

Bennett served as Drug Czar for some twenty months, then resigned to return once again to speaking and to complete his writing responsibilities. When he announced his planned departure in the White House press room, he also announced that he'd be taking up residence at the American Enterprise Institute, the same Washington "think tank" that also hosted Judge Robert Bork. One of the pillars of the neoconservative right wing had found a home.

At least for a few days. For within two weeks of his announced departure, Bennett was back in the headlines: Sununu had asked him to head the Republican National Committee along with ailing "General Chairman" Atwater.

After checking perfunctorily with White House Counsel C. Boyden Gray about the extent to which ethical requirements might hamstring his ability to "lobby" his former White House colleagues from his new political post and receive honoraria for speeches around the country, Bennett accepted. What he didn't know—and couldn't have known at that time—was that Sununu had basically pressured Gray into giving Bennett a thumbs-up signal on the ethics laws.

A lawyer himself, Bennett thought it wise and prudent to seek a second and, in this case, a third opinion. So he turned to two of his most trusted friends, Wendell L. Willkie II, his former General Counsel at the Humanities Endowment and the Education Department, and, most important, his brother, Bob.

Robert Bennett was not just another Washington attorney who happened to have a famous brother. Bob Bennett was himself becoming a celebrity as the dogged committee counsel conducting the Keating Five investigation into allegations of influence peddling in the savings and loan shenanigans of Charles Keating, Jr. By this time steeped in the intricacies of conflict-of-interest law and the new ethics rules covering former executive branch officials, brother Bob was not one to be bullied by Sununu. The ethics guidelines were cloudy in the lobbying area, but it looked as though Bill Bennett would have considerable difficulty contacting his former executive branch colleagues. This restriction would have seriously undermined his ability to fulfill his RNC responsibilities. Another problem for the ex-Drug Czar was the apparent curb on his ability to earn outside income while simultaneously pursuing his RNC responsibilities. While not forbidden by law, such activities could have created serious appearance problems were the RNC Chairman to receive lucrative honoraria from companies or others with interests pending at the Bush White House.

Bill Bennett was not about to spend a couple of years reelecting George Bush, muting his own conservative instincts, and living on his official GOP Chairman's salary of $125,000. He couldn't have his cake and eat it too. The first legal advice had been too rosy. Bennett was now pulling out.

The news hit Sununu like a ton of bricks. Obviously the impact on Republican conservatives would be devastating. After all, Sununu's choice of Bennett had clearly been conceived to help ameliorate matters with Republican conservatives after the disastrous Darman-led budget deal. What better way to right matters than by placing a darling of the neocons and the party's right wing in control of the RNC?

For others in the GOP, however, Bennett had liabilities, which were hardly mentioned by politicians or the press. Those liabilities made his choice by Sununu hard to explain except as appeasement for disgruntled conservatives. The choice was an overreaction, driven by Sununu's need to mend his own fences after the budget fiasco, and it only complicated matters for the party.

Some party regulars quietly questioned whether Sununu knew what he was doing given Bennett's lack of experience or knowledge of the nuts and bolts of electoral politics, and others asked—even more clandestinely—whether Bennett was really up to the job? Did he really want it?

Approximately two weeks before Bennett withdrew from the RNC chairmanship, he appeared as the guest at one of our Friday morning "Reform Breakfast Group" sessions at the White House. To anyone who had previously spent time around Bennett, that Friday breakfast was like the good old days at the Department of Education when Bennett was Secretary. There he was, expounding the virtues of his "Three C's." Bennett was back to quoting from his pantheon of classical heroes, Aristotle, Plato, and Maimonides, with his characteristic short, punchy, halting, and staccato cadences—each phrase a memorable sound bite. The high-blown moral rhetoric and references to great thinkers were what we had come to expect from him during the Reagan years, the no-nonsense neocon prescription of sound values for putting all of America back on the right track, from its schools to its streets, its communities, and its homes.

Then someone in our group asked an unexpected question about taxes and fiscal policy. Not a complicated question, but one calling for a somewhat sophisticated understanding of the dynamics of economic growth and the operation of the tax code. Bennett was silent. No answer. Hadn't thought about it. Would have to look into it before answering.

It was apparent that Bennett's standard rhetoric, honed over the decade when he headed the National Endowment for the Humanities, the U.S. Education Department, and the Office of National Drug Control Policy, would not take him far when the issue became the economy. While Bennett's rhetoric on morals, family values, and education was the best in the business, being chairman of the Republican National Committee was going to require him to develop an entirely new set of skills, not to mention a new vocabulary. His stump lines about values, morals, and education may have been something he could build upon, but Bennett would not be able to get by with his usual routine.

None of this is to take anything away from Bill Bennett, whom I greatly admire and respect. He is an exceptionally talented and quick individual, blessed with a first-class mind and a deep appreciation of America's moral and political decline, as well as the ways to restore our greatness. As RNC chairman, he would have been a formidable intellectual adversary for his Democratic counterpart. But whether Bennett was ready to move beyond the "soft" values and cultural issues, particularly in an election campaign that would focus on the economy and would require a deft tactician at the RNC's helm, someone who knew the precinct workers and could map a concrete electoral strategy, was open to question.

Bennett's abrupt departure was yet another catastrophe for John Sununu. In their choice of Agriculture Secretary Clayton Yeutter, Bush and Sununu picked a solid, if nonflamboyant, longtime Republican to lead the RNC. Yeutter had earned good marks as Ronald Reagan's Trade Representative and had done well as Agriculture Secretary, but he, like Bennett, was relatively unfamiliar with the tactical and strategic aspects of party chairmanship, in which street-fighters such as Atwater had excelled. Yeutter went on to considerable success during his tenure, however, not only for holding the party together as well as possible after the budget deal but also for assembling a competent RNC staff to handle the challenges of Congressional elections in the wake of the 1990 Census and congressional redistricting.

The Cavazos and Bennett departures would have been more than enough for the Bush White House to deal with on any given day. However, by no means were they the most serious and difficult matters to land in the laps of George Bush and John Sununu that mid-December morning. The press stories about the two former Education Secretaries were short-lived by Washington standards, pure inside-the-Beltway stuff further diminished by Bush's unusually quick response by naming talented and qualified successors for both men.

The third fiasco of December 12, however, proved to have more staying power. In fact, it would become a political headache for the Bush Administration for months to come. A thirty-six-year-old black Texas attorney, Michael Williams, was serving as the Assistant Secretary for Civil Rights at the Department of Education. A close friend of the President's eldest son, George W. Bush, Jr., Williams had once campaigned for local office in Texas with the younger Bush serving as his campaign chairman. Williams had lost that election, but had gone on to hold other positions in Texas and Washington before joining the senior Bush's Administration in 1990.

Williams arrived at the Education Department after having served as a local prosecutor and assistant district attorney in Midland, Texas, and having worked in positions at the Justice and Treasury Departments. A protégé of Judge Clarence Thomas, later a Justice of the Supreme Court, Michael Williams was one of a handful of young conservative blacks in the Bush Administration committed to the original concept of a colorblind America as envisioned by the late Dr. Martin Luther King, Jr., and, more recently, by Bill Bennett.

Charged with enforcing the nation's multiple civil rights laws precluding race, sex, gender, and age discrimination in the areas of education policy and administration—particularly in the country's elementary and secondary school districts and at the nearly 20,000 institutions of postsecondary education—Williams took his job seriously. He also strenuously opposed racial quotas of any sort.

In 1984 the Supreme Court had ruled, in a case called *Grove City College* v. *Bell*, that if a department or unit of a college or university were found to have violated the federal civil rights laws, that department or unit within the institution—rather than the entire institution—would lose its federal funding. Congressional liberals and the principal civil rights organizations throughout the country were outraged at the Supreme Court's narrow, legalistic interpretation of the remedies afforded under the federal civil rights statutes. In their view, the laws should have been interpreted to deny federal funding to the *entire* institution and not just the entity within the institution actually found to have engaged in the prohibited conduct. In short, if any aspect of the institution was tainted with a violation of the law, the entire institution ought to suffer.

Senator Edward M. Kennedy and others sought legislation reversing the Supreme Court's *Grove City* ruling. The so-called *Grove City* civil rights bill of 1987—the "Civil Rights Restoration Act"—required that federal funding to an entire institution be denied if any one part of the institution were found to have breached the civil rights laws.

Assistant Secretary Williams was sworn to uphold the nation's civil rights laws, which now included Teddy Kennedy's *Grove City* bill. In Williams's view, the array of civil rights statutes on the books spoke clearly to the subject of racial quotas in education: They were impermissible, not just as a matter of policy but also as a matter of law.

Upon his arrival at the Education Department, Williams had received favorable press coverage, particularly in the education trade press. A September 5, 1990, article in *Education Week* by Julie Miller noted that Williams had "announced that he plans to focus the [Office for Civil Rights'] attention on issues that civil-rights advocates contend were considered 'off limits' under the Reagan Administration."[2] Williams explained that he would target department compliance reviews (investigations initiated by the Education Department without an individual complaint) on such areas as "ability grouping, the treatment of children whose native language is not English, schools' policies toward pregnant teenagers, and racial harassment on college campuses."[3] As far as the education civil rights establishment was concerned, it appeared that Williams was bringing a breath of fresh air to what they perceived to be a moribund and lax enforcement posture adopted during eight years under Ronald Reagan.

Williams settled upon a rigorous enforcement of the nation's civil rights laws, and properly so. His strict constructionism, combined with his dedication to high principle and his personal courage, soon convinced me and many others that he was one of the Bush Administration's best and brightest stars. Within three months of the *Education Week* article, Williams was to earn his stripes in one of the more unusual civil rights battles of the Bush Administration, a battle that undoubtedly tempered the President's willingness to take on the entire civil rights community when it came to passage a year later of the 1991 Civil Rights Act.

The controversy arose in connection with a college football scholarship. In the autumn of 1990 Williams learned through press accounts about a football scholarship offered by the sponsors of the Fiesta Bowl, held each year in Florida. According to the press accounts, the Fiesta Bowl's backers planned to donate $100,000 to each of the participating teams for a Martin Luther King, Jr., Scholarship Fund for minority students at the two contending schools. In effect, the only recipients of the Fiesta Bowl scholarships would be black men, a provision which, in Williams's view, clearly contravened the civil rights laws. Besides, under Teddy Kennedy's bill reversing *Grove City*, any institution of higher education found to be participating in the scholarship program or accepting the scholarship would be legally debarred from receiving all federal funds. The irony of applying Teddy Kennedy's own corrective—ensuring that its internal logic was relentlessly pursued—could not have been lost on strict constructionist conservatives. While they detested the Kennedy *Grove City* bill, a strict reading of the law, on its face, had the effect of hoisting the liberal civil rights establishment on its own petard.

Williams wrote to the Fiesta Bowl sponsors on December 4, 1990, informing them of the possible violation. Specifically, he told them that Title VI of the 1964 Civil Rights Act and its related regulations precluded race-exclusive scholarships except "when mandated to do so by a court or administrative order, corrective action plan, or settlement agreement." Since the Fiesta Bowl itself was a wholly private entity and received no federal funds, the Title VI prohibitions did not apply to the game. They did apply, however, to the universities designated to receive the funds, because—following the requirements of Kennedy's *Grove City* legislation—those institutions would be sure to be recipients of federal financial assistance.

In effect, the Office for Civil Rights' ruling meant that universities were ineligible to participate in actually disbursing the scholarship funds or assisting the Fiesta Bowl in relation to the funds unless the institutions were "subject to a desegregation plan that includes such scholarships." Williams's December 4, 1990, letter actually tried to be helpful by suggesting alternative ways of structuring the scholarship assistance in order to comply with the applicable civil rights laws. His office also offered whatever technical assistance might be required to rewrite the terms of the scholarships so that they would comply with the governing laws and regulations.

At the same time that Williams sent his letter to the organizers of the Fiesta Bowl, his office also released a statement and conducted a press conference detailing the action taken. While soon-to-be-fired Secretary Lauro Cavazos had reportedly been briefed on the proposed action, no senior official at the White House had been made aware of the decision or of the practical consequences of Williams's interpretation. One of Williams's friends, Richard Porter, then serving as Executive Secretary to the Domestic Policy Council, had discussed the matter with Williams, but only Porter had any advance knowledge of what Williams had in mind. In fact, the White House Office of Cabinet Affairs actually received a copy of the Williams letter to the Fiesta Bowl the next day, December 5, but the issue never surfaced politically in the White House until the *New York Times* ran a front page story on Williams's action on December 12.

The *Times* story hit the White House like a bombshell. Chaos reigned throughout the West Wing, and once again a sense of panic set in, accompanied by the typical daze that hit most senior West Wingers whenever a controversial issue took them by surprise.

Reaction from the usual civil rights groups was swift and predictable: They rejected the Williams interpretation, although their criticism sounded somewhat muted, which many attributed to the fact that Williams was black. In subsequent congressional hearings on the Fiesta Bowl decision, some Democratic Members of Congress actually attempted to show that the Williams decision was really the handiwork of Williams's white deputy for operations, Richard D. Komer, a brilliant civil rights attorney who was also a protégé of Clarence Thomas. Komer, coincidentally, was also my best friend from law school, and I am satisfied totally that in no way was Michael Williams functioning as Komer's cat's-paw. Williams knew his own mind; the decision was his and his alone.

The swift outcry from civil rights leaders caught the White House unprepared. To the best of my knowledge, only three people there argued strongly in favor of supporting Williams's decision: Boyden Gray, Quayle's Chief of Staff Bill Kristol, and I. Roger Porter, out of town the morning when the story broke, managed to avoid any substantive involvement in resolving the matter. Cabinet Secretary Ede Holiday was, to quote Boyden Gray, running around "flapping her wings in the breeze" and arguing that we should back off from Williams's decision.

The issue quickly became one of principle (if not one of legal interpretation as well). Was the White House going to support Williams or cut him off at the knees?

The President had known nothing at all about the controversy until it broke in the press. Although he expressed his "concern" over the decision and later that afternoon called Williams personally to discuss it with him, he essentially stood back from the issue. He directed Gray to review the matter carefully with attorneys from the Education Department and the Department of Justice.

What that review was supposed to accomplish was difficult to guess. As a matter of law, Williams's action was perfectly correct. Besides, it had the virtue of making explicit to liberal Democrats in the Congress how their blind faith in the corrective properties of their own civil rights legislation could come back to haunt them.

Attorneys huddled throughout the day, and eventually Sununu was brought into the picture. Sununu made it clear that Williams's decision—its basis in sound law notwithstanding—could not be allowed to stand. He directed Gray and the other attorneys to craft a statement effectively undercutting Assistant Secretary Williams and backing off from the initial decision.

Late that afternoon I received a copy of the statement Sununu was proposing to put out the following morning. The Department of Education would announce that private donations restricted to scholarships for minority students could be administered by universities that also received federal funds but that no public funds could be so used. That position effectively reversed Williams's December 4, 1990, letter and was patently inconsistent with the *Grove City* legislation. The Department went on to announce further that Title VI of the Civil Rights Act of 1964 also precluded private universities receiving federal funds from funding race-based scholarships with their *own* funds. In other words, a university could discriminate with private money but not with its own or with federal money, a distinction that may well have made sense in honoring the will of scholarship donors but had no basis in law. Discrimination is discrimination.

I went to see Roger Porter immediately after reading the draft statement. Entering his office I made a football "time out" sign with my hands.

I told Porter that Sununu's statement made no sense and in fact was wrong as to both law and policy. Moreover, the draft statement, if issued, would only confuse matters and make things worse. It wouldn't end the controversy.

Porter heard me out, thanked me for my counsel, and said nothing more. The next morning the White House ordered the statement released unchanged.

While making its position public, the Education Department bent over backward to soften the impact of the brouhaha. The Office for Civil Rights explained at some length that in implementing the policy it would provide universities with a four-year transition period in which to allow for sufficient review of their potentially affected programs. In an ironic afterthought, the Department indicated that it stood ready to offer whatever technical assistance those institutions might need to ensure full compliance with Title VI.

The effect of the announcement, of course, was to make a fool of Michael Williams. Not only was his first decision reversed on explicit instructions from the White House, but he was forced to express publicly that while his initial decision was "legally correct," his action had been "politically naïve." So much for principled decisionmaking in the Bush Administration. Rather than back Williams, Sununu mandated that he eat crow. Williams's official public position explaining the reversal acknowledged gracefully that the final decision was the result of a "consensus" based on a review by Education Department and Justice attorneys.

A more sensible approach would have been for the White House to take advantage of the confusion surrounding Lauro Cavazos's departure as Secretary of Education earlier that morning. The Williams decision could have been deferred—not reversed—and explained in the context of the Cavazos exit. Any further action could have been postponed until a new Secretary of Education had been named and installed.

On that latter front, the Bush White House did move expeditiously. Bush walked into the White House press room on Monday, December 17, to announce his intention to nominate former Tennessee Governor Lamar Alexander as successor to Cavazos. Alexander showed adroitness in responding to press inquiries about how *he* would have handled the Fiesta Bowl issue when he remarked that a less confrontational approach would have been a far better way to address the matter. That answer had the wonderful effect of defusing the issue for the time being (along with the White House–forced reversal of Williams's position), but there was no question that Alexander's confirmation hearing the next year would include serious probing about his views on minority scholarships. The issue was not going to go away.

Moreover, Bush's own rhetoric on the subject was confused. When asked about the minority scholarships controversy on December 18, 1990, the President said:

> My own view has been all along, in my own life and everything else, committed to this concept of minority scholarships. Clearly it should be valid privately, and indeed, the support that we give to the historically black colleges—maybe someday will get challenged. I hope it isn't, and I hope it would sustain the challenge. Clearly, the support that we give to these institutions privately should be beyond challenge.

Of course. Perfectly clear.

Three apparently separate and discrete incidents—the Cavazos firing, Bennett's withdrawal, and the minority scholarships controversy—all occurred within the space of three hours the morning of December 12, 1990. Were they related? Taken together, do they shed any meaningful light on the internal functioning of the Bush White House?

First and foremost these incidents point to the fundamental short-comings of Bush's Chief of Staff, John Sununu. Not only was he famous for not listening to other people, but he had acquired a rep-utation for arrogance and abruptness that often stood in the way of his ability to deal with people. As one Washington wag put it, the last two engineers to inhabit the West Wing of the White House, John Sununu and Jimmy Carter, were not raving successes.

The Cavazos firing was mishandled because Sununu failed to do his homework in advance. He and the President had misled Cavazos into thinking that his performance was just fine. Bush routinely praised Cavazos publicly in speeches and expressed nothing but ap-preciation for the job he was doing. In fairness to Cavazos, what was obvious to most people from the way Cavazos was being ripped apart in the media was never mentioned directly to him by the White House. There was a failure of accountability, a failure to signal clearly to Cavazos that things were not going well.

The failure of accountability stemmed, in part, from the inability of the Bush White House to decide what it wanted to achieve and then communicate those expectations to the troops. Cavazos, incidentally, was not the only senior Administration official to undergo this treat-ment. EPA Administrator Bill Reilly often found himself in a similar predicament. Without clear guidance about the outer limits of what Bush meant by his desire to be the "environmental President," Reilly was almost constantly getting into trouble as an overly zealous envi-ronmental regulator. One day he'd be reamed out indirectly in the press through a series of carefully orchestrated White House back-ground leaks, only to find himself and his wife invited by the Bushes to a private dinner and movie in the White House family quarters, to State dinners, or to the President's box at the Kennedy Center.

The choice of Bennett as RNC Chairman was undoubtedly a re-action—perhaps even an overreaction—to the conservative unrest in the wake of the 1990 budget deal, but Sununu was blind to the ethical complexities of the Bennett choice. He was hell-bent on having his way, manifesting in the process an inability to accept opinions or advice contrary to his own determination about what was needed. He was a bully, quick to condemn those who challenged him and impa-tient with those whose minds may have moved more slowly than his.

Whether Sununu was dealing with the White House staff, the press, or members of Congress, he could not tolerate opposition any more than Dick Darman could tolerate sharing the intellectual stage with anyone else. His penchant for belittling those who disagreed with him was a character flaw that, unlike smoother previous Chiefs of Staff like Jim Baker and Dick Cheney, would win him few allies when the going got rough. Inside the White House, however, his domineering reign increasingly meant that Bush was deprived of oxygen. Few people wanted to incur Sununu's wrath, hence little in the way of innovative policy was actually undertaken inside the White House during the Bush years. People kept their mouths shut to avoid being yelled at.

A White House staffer who had also worked with the former New Hampshire Governor during Bush's 1988 campaign summed up Sununu's management style in these words: "Sununu never viewed himself as the problem. He also never brought people in for legitimate counsel. There was a sense of arrogance, of imperialism—like Eisenhower's Chief of Staff from New Hampshire. I'm not necessarily a believer in parapsychology, but it's almost as if the soul of that former Chief of Staff, Sherman Adams, entered John Sununu. He'd become a different person from the one we knew in 1988."

The White House reaction to the minority scholarships announcement by the Department of Education revealed an Administration lacking in principle and resolve. Michael Williams was not only correct in his legal analysis, he was also totally consistent with George Bush's own oft-stated antipathy to racial quotas and set-asides. Of course, even this position was muddied by the President's longstanding support for "affirmative action," whatever that meant. When the time came for theory to confront practice, the Bush Administration was unwilling to stand on principle and take the heat from civil rights groups. Bush had long cherished his support for the United Negro College Fund and was determined not to antagonize the nation's establishment black community.

On the issue of racial quotas, however, Bush couldn't have it both ways. His refusal to resolve these conflicting tendencies augured a confused policy, which endeared him to virtually no one. His Administration's performance in December 1990 was a harbinger of the President's decision eleven months later to agree to a civil rights bill that in fact not only promoted racial quotas but spawned additional and costly litigation. The overall reaction of the White House to these events late in 1990 did not bode well for the last two years of George Bush's presidency.

7

Empowerment and the "New Paradigm"

If a paradigm is ever to triumph it must gain some first supporters, men who will develop it to the point where hardheaded arguments can be produced and multiplied.

—Thomas Kuhn, *The Structure of Scientific Revolutions*[1]

For a brief moment in the fall of 1990, economic empowerment, reflected in the ungainly term "New Paradigm," came to characterize the Bush Administration's principal domestic policy agenda. But like many other aspects of our efforts to mount and sustain a domestic message, this activity never advanced much beyond the rhetorical.

Debate about the "New Paradigm" gained prominence first and foremost by default. There was nothing else, no other dominant theme, under consideration. Competition was sparse.

The "New Paradigm" was the brainchild of my fellow deputy, Jim Pinkerton. Jim explained it to me during my first week on the job: "Charlie, here's how our two responsibilities shape up. I'll do all the talking, while you'll do all the work!" Despite Pinkerton's fantasies about our division of labor, we became fast friends—allies and co-conspirators—in developing his "New Paradigm" domestic agenda for the President.

Pinkerton began to advance his ideas in February 1990, when he gave a speech entitled "The New Paradigm" to the World Future Society. Although an inherently awkward term, "New Paradigm" ultimately symbolized what several young White House aides sought to elevate as a central organizing theme for George Bush's domestic vision. While everyone knew that Bush would be unlikely to use such a highfalutin term as a recurrent theme of his presidency, a battle royal took place inside the White House to install "empowerment" as the centerpiece of Bush's domestic policy.

The "New Paradigm" described a radical shift in the political world view. The underlying concept was not Pinkerton's originally. As he acknowledged in his speech, the concept of paradigm shifts came from Thomas A. Kuhn, the noted philosopher of science. Kuhn's 1961 book *The Structure of Scientific Revolutions* argued cogently that scientific progress and the pattern of new scientific discovery often resulted from a fundamental rethinking of the status quo prompted by the need to respond to some new crisis that could not be properly or adequately addressed under the governing explanation, theory, or "paradigm." Classic examples of paradigm shifts were the emergence of Copernican astronomy replacing the centuries-old but outdated Ptolemaic System, or the emergence of relativity theory displacing systems of physics premised on the work of Leibnitz and Newton.

Kuhn's analysis of scientific revolutions was fascinating in many respects, but it was especially relevant for social and political scientists, as Kuhn saw immediate parallels between political and scientific development:

> Political revolutions are inaugurated by a growing sense, often restricted to a segment of the political community, that existing institutions have ceased adequately to meet the problems posed by an environment that they have in part created. . . . In both political and scientific development the sense of malfunction that can lead to crisis is prerequisite to revolution.[2]

Those whose ox would be gored by a paradigm shift would be more than likely to resist the change or perhaps fail to understand it. Old paradigmers would find themselves lost, subject to what the philosopher William James called "a bloomin' buzzin' confusion."[3]

Pinkerton adopted Kuhn's model to explain a way of approaching American social policy, a viewpoint that was best associated with the neoconservative movement of the 1980s and built in part upon the seminal work of the sociologist Charles Murray. In his controversial book *Losing Ground*, Murray, now at the American Enterprise Institute in Washington, D.C., contended that many of the Great Society's welfare programs had been abject failures. Not only had they been unsuccessful in eliminating or alleviating the consequences of poverty, but they had also fostered the continuation of the very conditions they sought to cure. Many of those programs had been flawed from the outset by numerous "perverse incentives," structural deficiencies that led to, encouraged, and perpetuated welfare dependency, one-parent families, unemployment, illegitimacy, and illiteracy. After nearly thirty years of such policies and programs costing more than $2.7 trillion between 1964 and 1990, American public policy had unintentionally spawned a welfare system that was heavily consumption-oriented and whose very conditions of eligibility condemned the poor—particularly the urban poor known as "the underclass"—to a miserable life in which they were trapped in poverty and barred from accumulating any assets. Many of these people became resigned to a system of self-perpetuating poverty.

Pinkerton's New Paradigm identified five approaches to social policy that constituted an express and revolutionary break with the New Deal–Great Society model:

First, "governments are now subject to market forces in a way they haven't been before."

Second, "the New Paradigm is characterized by increasing individual choice."

Third, "the New Paradigm is characterized by public policies which seek to empower people so that they are able to make choices for themselves."

Fourth, "the New Paradigm is characterized by decentralization."

Fifth, "the New Paradigm implies an emphasis on what works."

Taken together, these precepts formed the intellectual framework for imparting real content to George Bush's 1988 convention pledge to create a "kinder, gentler" America. In contrast with the Reagan Administration's focus on program elimination, particularly with respect to welfare and entitlement efforts, the Bush Administration, were it to adopt the New Paradigm, would redefine government in terms of working *for* and *with* people to restore independence and self-sufficiency. The New Paradigm envisioned an activist role for government—not big government, but effective government that worked for people where it was needed.

The goal was to "empower" individuals, not bureaucracies, so that people could decide what was best for themselves. The New Paradigm's activism contemplated a limited, but committed, government, which would perform a clearly defined role and confine itself to activities that really worked. The "Old Paradigm" rejected self-government and entailed a paternalistic approach to government programs and ideology.

Adherents of the New Paradigm were popping up in both American political parties and on virtually every continent. In the United States, they included a Clinton adviser, David Osborne, author of *Laboratories of Democracy* and co-author with Ted Gaebler of *Reinventing Government*; Amitai Etzioni, a communitarian activist and sociologist; Elaine Kamarck of the Washington-based Progressive Policy Institute; and Michael Sherraden of the University of Washington in St. Louis, author of a pioneering antipoverty concept of asset accumulation for the poor. Abroad, such reformers included entrepreneurial capitalists like Peru's Hernando de Soto and Russia's President Boris Yeltsin, who advocated strongly against giving money to bureaucracy. "Do not finance the bureaucracy, either central or Russian. If you wish Russia well, invest in what people do for themselves," Yeltsin pleaded in a speech in Washington on June 19, 1991. While these reformers may have differed over ends and mechanics, they were nonetheless searching for a government which worked efficiently.

The press did not report Pinkerton's remarks widely, but they were circulated informally around conservative Republican circles in Washington. I first learned of his approach in April 1990, just a few weeks before I left the Education Department for the White House, when a story summarizing the speech and the New Paradigm appeared in the *Washington Times*.

Pinkerton's views struck an immediate chord. It was precisely what I'd been trying to accomplish in promoting educational choice and other reforms at the Education Department. I asked my secretary to get a copy of the text and shot off a quick note to Pinkerton expressing my allegiance to his ideas, particularly educational choice, which was beginning to emerge as a central political issue in Bush's education agenda.

When I arrived at the White House a few weeks later, Pinkerton and I sought concrete ways to advance the New Paradigm agenda. One of the bureaucratic vehicles available was the existing Low Income Opportunity Board, an interagency committee lodged in the White House office and headed by my predecessor, Bill Roper. Established during the Reagan Administration, the Board oversaw a waiver process by which state governments could appeal to the White House to relax existing statutory or regulatory burdens to allow more creative approaches to welfare reform. With the change of presidencies the Board had essentially lain fallow, especially after Roper's departure.

Midway through 1989, however, Roper and other Board members began work on the Board's next logical phase, namely, devising a Bush Administration antipoverty strategy. Roper convened meetings with outside experts to obtain recommendations on what the Bush Administration should undertake, particularly in the wake of the 1988 Welfare Reform Act, as it tackled poverty in America. Board members heard about issues ranging from the working poor and the unemployed to housing affordability. Most of the recommendations involved either new programs or massive new expenditures, both of which were inconsistent with budget reality and Bush Administration preferences and policies. By the time I arrived at the White House in May 1990, Roper's noble effort way lying dormant in a series of internal reports destined for oblivion. The budget and the intellectual climate were simply hostile to important initiatives of the sort contemplated in these reports.

At the same time, however, opportunity to move forward on an antipoverty agenda was there, for Bush had approved a Domestic Policy Council options paper in mid-September 1989 authorizing the Domestic Policy Council to pursue welfare reform through the Low Income Opportunity Board. The President had endorsed options favoring greater waiver and demonstration authority as well as expanding the Board to become "a focal point for defining, coordinating, and publicizing the Administration's overall anti-poverty policy." Attorney General Thornburgh, who chaired *pro tempore* the Domestic Policy Council, was directed to discuss the matter further with Governor Sununu.

After Roper left the White House, the Board's leadership fell temporarily to Richard Schmalensee, an economist on leave from MIT and a member of the President's Council of Economic Advisers. It is significant that Roger Porter, as Bush's chief domestic policy adviser, took absolutely no interest in the Board's activities or its future. Along with Porter's natural hesitancy, he took great pains to distance himself from activities initiated by his Reagan Administration predecessors.

During my first week at the White House, Schmalensee had circulated the most recent draft options paper from the Board to the Domestic Policy Council. The document had been developed by the Board's members, primarily White House staff and Assistant Secretaries from the principal domestic Cabinet departments. It contained several options, including promoting large-scale community intervention in high-poverty areas, reallocating and targeting federal resources on high-poverty areas, restructuring the targeted jobs tax credit to provide more incentives for training, unifying and simplifying welfare programs, integrating federal programs, and establishing a child support assistance program.

The unblessed draft document also found its way to a *New York Times* reporter, Robert Pear, who disclosed the nature of the deliberations in considerable detail. The front-page headline over Pear's July 6, 1990, *Times* story was "Administration Rejects Proposal for New Anti-Poverty Programs." Pear explained that Bush's Domestic Policy Council had considered several options but "decided that the options were too expensive or would stir too much political controversy." Pear also quoted an unnamed White House official who, unfortunately, summarized the decision as, "Keep playing with the same toys. But let's paint them a little shinier."[4] That official obviously considered Bush's antipoverty strategy a hoax, an effort at rhetorical sleight-of-hand amounting to nothing new. I couldn't have known at the time, but "no new toys" would become a metaphor for the Bush Administration's overall domestic agenda.

I have no idea who leaked the document to Pear or who made the "same toys" quip. The effect of the leak, however, was to spark immediate opposition and skepticism within the White House over our antipoverty efforts. The fact that this came at roughly the same time Darman was embarking on his ultimately disastrous budget negotiations with the Congress only made matters worse. According to some in the White House, the last thing we needed at that time was a high-visibility antipoverty strategy that could lead to pressure for more domestic spending just when Darman, Sununu, and Nick Brady were trying to negotiate the "deal of the century."

Interestingly enough, before I arrived at the White House Roger Porter never mentioned my role as Chairman of the Low Income Opportunity Board. I discovered this only when Schmalensee invited me to the next Board meeting to review the draft options paper. I walked in and immediately was introduced to the other Board members as their "new leader," a position that didn't last long.

As indicated, Porter took absolutely no interest in the Board's efforts to devise an effective antipoverty strategy for the Bush Administration. In fact, when the Board's sole employee, Peter Germanis (detailed to the White House from the Department of Health and Human Services), sought to extend his term of duty with the Board, Porter told me that would not be possible. Sununu wanted the Board and its activities as far away from the White House as possible.

The signals were clear. How could economic empowerment be a major Bush Administration initiative if no one in the Bush White House would claim paternity? There was evidently no interest. I was soon to be a Chairman without a staff, which made the work of circulating, drafting, and revising the options papers that much more difficult.

While Porter and Sununu distanced themselves from our antipoverty strategy, Pinkerton and I viewed the Board as the perfect vehicle for advancing the "New Paradigm" and economic empowerment. Working with Schmalensee and John Schall of Cabinet Affairs, we reshaped the options paper to reflect the principles of decentralization, self-sufficiency and independence, choice, and reliance on market forces. As we maneuvered the options paper through the bureaucracy during June and July 1990, we encountered initial opposition within the White House. By November of that year the resistance had grown to full-scale warfare.

The problem was the term "empowerment." The opposition was, as usual, Darman.

Darman was a true product of the 1960s and 1970s. Prior to government service, he spent years in various graduate programs at Harvard and Oxford, ultimately securing an MBA from Harvard. Under Elliot Richardson, Darman served at the Department of Health, Education, and Welfare in the early 1970s and believed he had seen everything, both politically and programmatically. Darman was the deputy assistant HEW secretary who oversaw the work on the Allied Services Act, an ill-fated Nixon approach to integrating welfare services through better government management. The idea went no-where. Darman's 1970s effort, as distinguished from what Pinkerton and others were attempting two decades later, was far more limited in scope. It was essentially government- and management-oriented, with little emphasis on ensuring principles of self-sufficiency and independence.

Moreover, as a child of the 1960s, Darman now abhorred "empowerment" as a buzzword once associated with the Black Power political movement. Those of us who embraced "empowerment" did so for exactly that reason: It provided a stark and arresting contrast when a conservative Republican President, often criticized as the ultimate preppie, appropriated the rhetoric of the Left to advance a new conservative approach to antipoverty strategies, welfare reform, and economic opportunity. The term had inherent shock value. It signaled a change, and it was exactly that contrast which sparked the internal Administration opposition to empowerment.

Our efforts considered bureaucracy not as the solution but as a critical part of the problem. Launching a full-scale assault on failed bureaucracy, however, was not going to be easy. Darman had spent most of his professional life thriving in the heart of centralized bureaucracies. He had done well in them; he believed in them. As a former instructor at Harvard's Kennedy School of Government, Darman was a practitioner of government by management, taking the antiseptic view that ideology only gets in the way of good process and even greater deals. Whenever he found bureaucracy faltering, Darman adopted an essentially incrementalist approach based on the belief that bureaucracy could heal itself. As part of the ruling elite, Darman believed strongly in the efficacy of bureaucracy and was loath to change existing bureaucracies or even attack them. The "closet good guy," as he saw himself, was—and remains—an ardent statist.

Darman was apprehensive about the wisdom of resurrecting empowerment as the principal domestic vision of the Bush Administration. To him it smacked of "power to the people." That's why he pooh-poohed Pinkerton's "New Paradigm" with the phrase "Hey, brother, can you paradigm?" Darman never understood that while the "New Paradigm" movement consciously borrowed 1960s rhetoric, it was closely aligned with the New Left's aim of dismantling centralized bureaucracies. What was distinctly new, however, was the fact that the 1990s version of empowerment was premised on the demonstrated bankruptcy—economic, political, and social—of the Great Society bureaucratic model.

At the heart of the New Left's critique of the Great Society was the latter's neglect of the importance of the individual. Where the New Left failed to connect with both the neoconservative movement, which succeeded it, and the 1990s version of empowerment, was in its failure to acknowledge the primacy of individuals *and* market mechanisms in creating a more rational, efficient, and productive ordering of society. The combination of such themes as decentralization, the importance of individuals, participatory democracy, and the critical value of the marketplace cast the 1990s version of empowerment in a wholly new context. As the battle lines were being drawn anew, the fault lines emerging were between advocates of group entitlements, principally through government-sponsored rights or set-asides, and believers in free markets and individual choice.

Pinkerton and a few others in the Administration—Richard Porter in Cabinet Affairs; Anna Kondratas, a Kemp aide; Betsy Brand, who ran federal vocational education programs; Martin Gerry at HHS; Jo Anne Barnhart, who oversaw Aid to Families with Dependent Children; Catherine Bertini, who administered the Food Stamp program—understood the importance of the New Paradigm to the future of the Republican party. Mavericks like Representatives Newt Gingrich and Vin Weber, along with Jack Kemp, believed that the empowerment/New Paradigm model constituted a workable basis for organizing the Bush Administration's entire domestic social policy agenda. The question was how to convince the rest of the White House. The first battle was waged to wrest control of presidential rhetoric to make the empowerment theme more visible.

The stiff opposition to empowerment in the fall of 1990 was in some respects surprising, as Bush had already embraced it from the first days of his Administration. As already noted, his February 9, 1989, "Building a Better America" speech, not to mention his Inaugural Address, had explicitly embraced the concept. But that was basically it. Rhetoric without follow-through. While we consoled ourselves that we had won at least a few presidential nods in our direction, there was nothing more to come from the Oval Office indicating that Bush himself wanted to develop the New Paradigm or the economic empowerment theme in a more visible, consistent, or compelling fashion.

We weren't deterred. Bureaucratically the next step in the process was to send Bush a series of "empowerment" recommendations from the Domestic Policy Council. Before that could be done, however, there was some routine housekeeping: What was to become of the Low Income Opportunity Board?

Because the Board had been established near the end of the Reagan Administration, the Bush White House saw it as a chance once again to show that this Administration was going to be different. John Sununu's desire to put distance between its activities and the White House suggested a new direction for the Board. So no sooner had I assumed the Board's chairmanship than I saw its activities whisked out of my hands. As usual Roger Porter, seeing no need to cross Sununu, gave no support to my efforts to reconstitute the Board as a White House–run endeavor.

As it turned out, however, my "demise" actually worked to my benefit. Darman and others wanted to end the Board altogether, and with it the whole empowerment effort. There was no way in the world that I could have withstood such an onslaught, especially in my first weeks at the White House.

In the meantime, Attorney General Thornburgh had written to me on July 13, 1990, officially designating me as Chairman of the soon-to-be-defunct Low Income Opportunity Board. The Pear story in the *New York Times* had sparked considerable interest in the antipoverty efforts inside and outside the White House, although even as the Pear story hit the streets, the options were being substantially reworked. Pear's story was based on an out-of-date version of the options paper, but the unexpected media attention focused our efforts and heightened our enthusiasm. We felt we might be on the verge of actually defining George Bush's domestic vision.

While the options paper for the Domestic Policy Council and the President was being revised, a furious debate erupted over whether the Board should continue under the direction of a White House staffer (namely me) or whether someone with much more clout, in this case Jack Kemp, should assume the reins of a new body altogether. At both the staff level and the level of the Domestic Policy Council—which is to say other Cabinet members—the recommendation was that a Cabinet member *not* head the activity.

Domestic Policy Council task forces were traditionally staffed at the Assistant Secretary level, with White House participants appointed from among Deputy Assistants or Special Assistants to the

President. Cabinet members ordinarily did not preside at their meetings, because the individual representatives were all at the sub-Cabinet level. There was speculation besides that other Cabinet members did not want one of their own "elevated" by being asked to oversee this new activity.

Those considerations did not, however, deter Jack Kemp, who openly wanted the assignment and went directly to Attorney General Thornburgh and the President to get it. The President was asked to make the unusual decision of getting Kemp in charge of the Board's successor, the Economic Empowerment Task Force. So much for my new role. Again, this possibility hardly troubled me, for I would serve as Kemp's deputy, chairing meetings in his absence and organizing the work which would now be harder to disregard. The Task Force members were serious about their assignments. From the perspective of policy development inside the Bush Administration, this was the only game in town that mattered. Roger Porter's lack of interest in the New Paradigm and economic empowerment effectively gave us carte blanche to proceed.

By the early summer of 1990, several more versions of the economic empowerment options paper had been prepared and revised. Everything now hinged on a June 20, 1990, meeting of the Domestic Policy Council, to be held without the President.

Chaired by Thornburgh, the Domestic Policy Council met in the Roosevelt Room of the White House as scheduled. Although the purpose of the meeting was to reach closure on the process for establishing the Economic Empowerment Task Force, the session included one of the first of many empowerment speeches by Jack Kemp. I began the meeting by outlining how the work done by the Low Income Opportunity Board could be merged into a newly constituted Economic Empowerment Task Force. It was my first presentation in a meeting at which most of the domestic Cabinet was present. To my considerable surprise, the Cabinet members attending had relatively little to say.

The June 20 discussion draft was a vastly scaled-back approach from the ideas debated earlier by the Board. It began by observing that "the principal goal of an effective antipoverty system should be to provide economic empowerment for American families—to enable them to participate fully in the mainstream of the economy." The document then described "the current face of poverty in America" and articulated nine principles to govern our future empowerment efforts:

1. The government must maintain a healthy, growing economy.
2. Employment should be the central operational objective of an economic empowerment strategy.
3. Anti-poverty policies should target three groups: poor children; the working poor; and the long-term poor who face multiple barriers to economic self-sufficiency and participation in mainstream society.
4. The design, implementation, and evaluation of the entire range of programs and policies that affect low-income Americans should be coordinated, so that accessibility and effectiveness of the overall system is enhanced.
5. Anti-poverty programs should enforce the mutual obligations and responsibilities of individuals and public institutions.
6. Social programs and institutions should empower individuals and communities.
7. Financing and decision-making need to be appropriately shared between local, State, and Federal entities.
8. The private sector is an essential partner with government in economic empowerment efforts.
9. The public system of anti-poverty programs should encourage innovation and experimentation, particularly among State and local governments that want to design programs to fit their populations.

The Roosevelt Room meeting was a marvelous exhibition of the "body language" of the Bush Cabinet. Whenever someone said something Kemp disliked or considered nonsense, he would roll his eyes, obviously discomfited, and shift fitfully in his chair.

At one point, Manuel Lujan, the Secretary of the Interior, observed that perhaps a less visible approach was more appropriate. This prompted an outburst from Kemp (for which he later apologized, noting that he had "the worst body language of any member of the Cabinet").

The meeting concluded with the Domestic Policy Council recommending that the options paper be revised, tightened, and then forwarded to the President with the recommendation that the new Task Force be run by a *staff-level* person (presumably me) and not a more visible Cabinet member (presumably Kemp).

Coming out of the Roosevelt Room, it was evident that Kemp was not at all satisfied. We knew he wanted to be named chairman of the new group and would reject anything smacking of a halfhearted approach. Kemp's irritation finally burst forth in a blistering July 12, 1990, letter to Thornburgh in which he offered his detailed thoughts on the latest revisions to the draft presidential decision memorandum. Kemp reflected on the first war on poverty, noting that it "could not succeed in reducing poverty because it was based on a philosophy of redistributionism and promoted dependency." Economic empowerment was the next logical phase and would succeed because it was premised on "wealth expansion" as well as "access to education, jobs, assets and opportunity; and a strong social fabric."

Kemp was adamant about the Board's future:

> The issue is not *expanding* the Low Income Opportunity Board but giving it the capacity to be effective. This means not only staff but a leader of sufficient stature and authority to articulate the vision within and without the Administration and work with Cabinet Secretaries to ensure that the whole Administration is guided by that vision in managing its current programs and proposing change. Perhaps a Cabinet Secretary ought to lead the effort, with the LIOB staff, as a DPC working group, in a supportive role. As currently constituted, the LIOB could expand considerably and still be ineffective, especially if, as described in the draft memorandum, it simply "encourages private-sector efforts," "develops strategies and research agendas," and "ensures coordination." Sounds like bureaucratizing the effort and sending it to oblivion. The issue is making the effort a high-profile one, and giving the LIOB clout.

Kemp wanted the job all right, and he was 100 percent right to want it, since he saw economic empowerment as "phase two of the war on poverty . . . the logical end of true civil rights enfranchisement." Additionally, he was serving notice to Thornburgh that a tepid approach was unacceptable, at least to him.

Notwithstanding Kemp's general concerns, I was pleased, at least initially, with the revised recommendations headed for Bush. The effort would now be high-profile and would build upon several existing innovations: expanding the Earned Income Tax Credit, improving health services for infants and pregnant women, and promoting Kemp's housing initiatives. Moreover, I had managed to include a section on services integration, an unwieldy bureaucratic term that meant trying to make existing government programs work better for people in guaranteeing greater self-sufficiency and independence. After all, this was a perfect theme for Bush to emphasize. No other president in this century had the background and experience in government that George Bush brought to the presidency. If Bush was predisposed temperamentally to be a managerial President, then he ought to go about the business of managing. The need to "make government work" on behalf of individuals was a theme clearly related to the core concept of economic empowerment and the one that played to Bush's natural strengths.

Before the memorandum went to Bush, the Domestic Policy Council met one more time, on July 25, 1990, at 3:30 P.M. We needed closure on both process and policy, but closure was far from what we got.

HHS Secretary Lou Sullivan opened the meeting by urging that we take an "incremental approach" without a high profile. He clearly didn't want Kemp in the driver's seat. The Task Force, he said, was "more appropriately chaired by a White House official. A Cabinet Secretary would only be a lightning rod." He called for further study of the causes of poverty.

Kemp was squirming. "The time to study this is over. Our efforts should be high-profile, and we've reached a critical mass. We have a political and moral imperative here. If the mayor of Moscow can create enterprise zones," Kemp quipped, "then we can too!" He went on: "This is George Bush's vision. It's like when Lincoln signed the Homestead Act. We need to translate our Lincoln roots into something tangible, something that people can see and believe in."

Kemp and Sullivan had defined the contours of the debate. Others chimed in with comments in one camp or the other, or beside the point. Labor Secretary Elizabeth Dole supported empowerment but rejected the high-profile approach as premature. Energy Secretary Watkins concurred. Education Secretary Cavazos favored putting a White House official in charge. Mike Boskin noted that we were already doing a lot now, and it would be useful to survey this activity as part of an effort to promote better financial management of the federal government. Veterans' Affairs chief Ed Derwinski warned of "god-awful" turf fights and of the need to define clearly what was meant by a "high-profile effort." Darman was absent, but his deputy, William Diefenderfer, asked how we were proposing to pay for this "vision."

Thornburgh and Kemp got the last say. The Attorney General indicated that "our responsibility to the President" was "in arrears. We are here to identify options for him. Moreover, 'high profile' does not necessarily mean 'more money.' We must send forward to the President recommendations, options, and give him a chance to lay out these goals." Our task was clear: sharpen the differences in the options memo, write up the pros and cons on each point, and get it to Bush.

Kemp returned to the high rhetorical road: "We need to get the President to articulate a central theme. We need a holistic approach in addressing despair, drugs, acid rain, Communism, Socialism, poverty. We have to repeat our message: that we have a thematic approach to wage war on the conditions that lead to poverty and broken families."

Few Cabinet Secretaries in the room shared Kemp's enthusiasm. Nonetheless, Thornburgh thought he had a sufficient consensus to proceed. He gave the DPC members a twenty-four-hour turnaround time for getting their changes on the options paper—in their handwriting (i.e., no more leaks)—back to the White House.

Thornburgh sent the final memorandum to the President on August 3, 1990. It came back approved by the President three days later, bearing Bush's initials. To my great delight, aside from the President's signature and his tick marks next to the options he approved, the only other comment on the paper was a series of check marks in the margin next to the paragraph I had written about the need to make government work. Kemp also got the job he wanted.

Thornburgh wrote to the Domestic Policy Council members on September 4, 1990, announcing formally the creation of the new Economic Empowerment Task Force under Kemp's leadership. Our tasks were to advance an overall economic empowerment strategy, identify new initiatives, review existing programs, and find ways to integrate services as part of a more "client-centered" approach. Having Bush's approval, our next step was to put real meat on the bones of the presidentially approved initiative.

Doing so was not going to be easy, because it meant intruding on Dick Darman's budget process, now well under way and headed for closure. Our deliberations could also complicate the ongoing budget deal negotiations. For those reasons, during the latter part of the summer of 1990 through the conclusion of the budget summit negotiations, our group made relatively little substantive progress. We did, however, undertake a series of preapproved background briefings for key reporters, people like Mickey Kaus and Fred Barnes of *The New Republic*, Alan Murray and David Wessel of the *Wall Street Journal*, David Broder of the *Washington Post*, and Jason DeParle of the *New York Times*—in an effort to get more serious coverage of our efforts. When the budget negotiations ended, we were ready to move quickly.

In the meantime, the concern over empowerment inside the White House continued to take on new features.

The White House is an extremely fascinating place. It is also, on occasion, a ridiculous and downright silly place. The reaction to an initiative designed to parallel and complement the work of the Economic Empowerment Task Force, our efforts to establish an "Empowerment Breakfast Group," provides a fine example.

Shortly after my arrival, Cabinet Secretary David Bates left the White House for private law practice. Ede Holiday, then General Counsel to Nicholas Brady at the Treasury Department, succeeded Bates and soon brought her own team to run the Cabinet Affairs Office. Holiday hired a brilliant, cheerful, and energetic lawyer from Treasury, Richard Porter, to serve as Executive Secretary of the Domestic Policy Council. Richard Porter's job was to coordinate for the Cabinet the work—issues papers, options papers and other documents—that ultimately went to the Domestic Policy Council for review.

Richard Porter had worked on the policy staff during the 1988 Bush–Quayle campaign before joining Treasury and had a keen appreciation of our need for a visible, vibrant domestic agenda. He also knew Jim Pinkerton and was thoroughly enamored of the New Paradigm and economic empowerment. So we had another ally, in this case an exceptionally capable one.

Richard Porter, Pinkerton, and I decided to assemble a group of sympathizers from the White House and a few Cabinet departments to meet for breakfast early each Friday morning in a private dining room in the White House Mess. Each week we would invite an outside speaker to address the group and then spend an hour discussing issues relevant to our Task Force agenda. The point behind the breakfasts was obvious: Meeting each week would send a signal throughout the White House complex that there were some two dozen or so aides seriously interested in these ideas. By hearing from some of the country's leading thinkers, we would give ourselves the benefit of fresh, original minds as we shaped our own proposals.

The breakfasts began on September 21, 1990. Stuart Butler, domestic policy director of the conservative Heritage Foundation, was the first speaker. He was followed on successive Fridays by Bill Bennett; Irving Kristol; Jack Kemp; Representative Steve Bartlett, who headed the House Republicans' working group on empowerment; Attorney General Thornburgh; Labor Secretary Lynn Martin; Dinesh D'Sousa; then GOP Chairman Clayton Yeutter; Robert Bork; and many others. The breakfasts were a hit and often drew standing-room-only attendance. A solid core of staffers attended, including individuals from the Vice President's office, speechwriters, the Counsel's office, Public Liaison, Cabinet Affairs, our Office of Policy Development, the Justice and Labor Departments, and the Council of Economic Advisers. Infrequently, an Assistant to the President or even someone from the Presidential Personnel Office would show up.

Word got back to us, however, that Sununu and Darman frowned on our idea, and that's when the silliness started. Hearing about the opposition only inspired us further. I then learned from Richard Porter that Ede Holiday, in deference to Sununu, wanted the name changed from the "Empowerment Breakfast Group" to the "Domestic Policy Reform Breakfast Group." We complied. During this time, Roger Porter accepted an invitation from Richard Porter and me to be our guest speaker one Friday morning. Porter had actually attended the session at which Jack Kemp spoke. However, about the same time Roger Porter accepted our invitation, the word came down from on high (Sununu) that "empowerment" was a dirty word. The next thing we knew, Roger Porter had abruptly declined our invitation—literally at the last minute—and chose not to reschedule. The risk-averse Porter plainly wanted no part of something that Darman and the Chief of Staff disliked. Nonetheless, other senior Administration members—and Marilyn Quayle on one occasion—continued to join us as guests. Roger Porter, whose office was roughly one hundred paces and two flights of stairs away, never showed up again.

With the budget negotiations now over, we were ready to move. The next step was to assemble the Task Force to begin implementing the President's decision. I convened the group without Kemp present and, since the President had endorsed our work, offered Roger Porter an opportunity to address its members to reiterate the President's charge. To my surprise, Porter accepted.

The group met on November 28, 1990, at 11 A.M. in the Roosevelt Room. I opened the session and then turned it over to Porter. The room was unusually full, the meeting well-attended. There was a reason: On November 16, Darman had delivered his speech dividing both Pinkerton and the "New Paradigm." Coming just days after he had concluded the controversial and much-derided budget deal, Darman's remarks ridiculed the New Paradigm's conservative agenda as just so much "neo-neo-ism," a symptom of what the OMB director termed "a perpetual national adolescence" amounting to little more than "sloganeering."

Every leader, Darman had said, tries to do something new and bold, hence the New Deal, the New Federalism, the New American Revolution, the New Realism, several New Partnerships, and two recent New Beginnings. Each approach to solving the country's problems was little more than a "catch-phrase," including the recent efforts within his own party and Administration:

> Republicans, of course, would argue that this is in contrast with the seriousness of their approach to problem-solving—increasingly marketed, by some, as the *New Paradigm*. This label, unfortunately, may be a bit too pretentious for a would-be populist movement. Upon examination, intellectuals might note that four of the New Paradigm's five key principles—market-orientation, decentralization, choice, and empowerment—tend often to collapse into one. And further, the fifth—an emphasis on what works—may in some of the most difficult cases conflict with the other four. So the effete might debate whether the New Paradigm is, perhaps, enigmatically paradigmatic. At the same time, in the real world, others might simply dismiss it by picking up the refrain, "Hey, brother, can you paradigm?"

According to Darman, the "New Thises" and "New Thats" were slogans that took the place of rigorous intellectual analysis. They had little to do with actually solving problems. "They leave undecided most of the hard choices of detailed program design and resource allocation." To Pinkerton, Darman was saying: Go away, little boy, and leave the tough tasks of governing and managing to expert technocrats like me.

But Darman's intellectual hubris and pride in his own experience got the better of his judgment, for he went on to criticize Representative Newt Gingrich, referring in his speech to "new Newtism" as just another aspect of the same catch-phrase intellectual laxity.

That was a major blunder. Gingrich was a darling of the conservatives because he had helped engineer the House defeat of Darman's first budget deal in early October. Darman erred by kicking sand in his enemy's face. As a result, Pinkerton, the New Paradigm, and empowerment attracted far more attention from the media and the pundits than they otherwise might have. The *Wall Street Journal* columnist Paul Gigot blasted Darman for condemning the policies of the 1980s and rejecting the themes that helped get Bush elected President:

> The speech shows contempt for politics based on principle, and by implication the politics that elected President Bush. In the Darman view, the essence of governing is tinkering with mechanisms, not persuading voters; manipulating insiders, not changing the public mind. No wonder he was no match for serious politicians like Democratic Sens. George Mitchell and Robert Byrd.[5]

The fury, however, was not restricted to conservative columnists like Gigot. Within days, Gingrich himself called upon Darman to recant his speech or resign. "If he stands by the written speech of one week ago, I don't see how we can work with a Republican Dukakis. . . . Darman has crossed the Rubicon."[6] Gingrich viewed Darman's attack as leveled against his own party, and Bush would be unable to govern against his own party in Congress. According to Gingrich, Darman "has more feeling for computers than for politicians."[7]

The media attention brought out the White House staff to our November 28 session. Everyone wanted to play in this game. Midway through Porter's ten-minute remarks, the door opened and in sauntered none other than Dick Darman. He hadn't been invited, and certainly no one expected him to show up and sit down in the midst of mere mortal staffers, but he was clearly welcome to join the group. When Porter concluded, I asked Darman if he would like to say anything.

Darman proceeded to tell us why what we were doing was hardly "new." He went on, cynically and caustically, to deride both Pinkerton and empowerment. Darman spoke for some twenty minutes, after which I opened the floor for discussion.

Roughly forty minutes after he arrived, Darman got up to leave. I turned to him and said, "Dick, we want to thank you for joining us this morning. If I'd only known in advance you were coming, we could have sold tickets and used the proceeds for deficit reduction."

The room erupted in laughter, and Darman, clearly not amused, continued on his way out. Fred Barnes learned of the incident and later retold it in one of his *New Republic* columns, no doubt further endearing me to Darman.

Darman's attempt to throw cold water on our empowerment initiative did not deter us. Kemp, who found Darman tedious and politically inept, vowed to continue to take his case for an "economic opportunity" agenda directly to the President himself if he needed to.

A major problem with that strategy, however, was evident to most of us: The President (and most of the Cabinet, for that matter) considered Kemp a blowhard. It was difficult to have a discussion with Kemp, even when only two or three of us were meeting with him alone in his office at HUD. Every time we met with him we got a speech, often the same speech we'd heard during the last visit. A former member of the Reagan Administration and a friend of Kemp put it this way: "The problem with Jack is that his politics are just too glandular."

Kemp's "glandular politics" turned out to be as much of a hindrance as a help. It was Kemp's personality—actually his exuberance—not his ideas, that had prompted his fellow Cabinet members to want someone else in charge of our empowerment agenda. It was also evident, however, that Kemp was an eloquent and convincing spokesman for the Administration and the Republican party on the needs of the country's urban poor. Having Kemp's support and leadership was crucial in withstanding the open hostility of Darman and Sununu when it came to advancing our agenda.

Our nine empowerment principles at the outset of our options paper were reflected in the various budget and legislative proposals that were hammered out prior to the President's 1991 State of the Union message and budget presentation. Ultimately we were able to identify numerous legislative proposals that we could point to as the heart of our empowerment agenda: educational choice; homeownership and expanded tenant management in public housing; job training; a lower capital gains tax; enterprise zones; repeal of the Social Security Earnings Test; repeal of the Davis–Bacon laws requiring workers on federally financed projects to be paid the prevailing wage; targeting Small Business Administration loans to promote entrepreneurial capitalism; reforming the Public Employment Service; restoring the value of the personal exemption; and experimenting with ways to make welfare transitional. Virtually all of these proposals went to the President on December 21, 1990.

Throughout the budget-development process in the late autumn of 1990, Darman went out of his way to make sure that certain empowerment notions—most notably school choice—were reflected in the fiscal year 1992 budget. He quickly realized that his attack on Pinkerton's New Paradigm had backfired, especially among conservatives, who were, and remained, furious with him for the budget deal and Bush's retreat on his "no new taxes" pledge.

Darman even went so far as to stage a makeup session with Pinkerton. One Saturday afternoon he walked down to Pinkerton's Old Executive Office Building suite to discuss their differences. Like his other celebrated effort to mend fences, his overture to Newt Gingrich, Darman's approach was aimed first and foremost at buying time. He needed to recede from the limelight, or else the demands for Bush to replace him would continue to escalate beyond control. This would be a recurring pattern with Darman—his ability to bob and weave, avoiding his critics and the press whenever he ran into trouble—right up to the end of Bush's presidency. Of course none of this actually changed Darman or his views, and privately he spilled his venom on all the Republicans, like Gingrich, who had opposed his budget deal.

Meanwhile, the battle continued inside the White House to influence both the President's thinking and his rhetoric. The most significant public occasion for this was the January 31, 1991, State of the Union address to Congress.

Few ritual activities inside the White House and the Executive Branch account for as much wasted time and energy as the annual State of the Union message. Like awaiting the first leaves falling in autumn, one listens for the first time someone says, "Well, perhaps we can get this into the State of the Union speech." The frequency of such utterances quickens, and usually in late October the battle to have this or that idea, phrase, or policy included in the President's speech begins. As a consequence, recent State of the Union addresses have become themeless listings of programs and ideas that more often bore rather than inspire or inform.

The 1991 address was no different, except that those of us espousing the economic empowerment agenda were also in the fight to get as much as possible of our rhetoric into the text.

To put matters in perspective, it's worthwhile considering the structure of Bush's prior message to Congress, delivered in January 1990. That speech contained a total of 63 paragraphs: 14 were devoted to introductory or general remarks; 20 discussed foreign policy; and 29 addressed a smattering of domestic issues, broken down as follows:

Political system	1 paragraph
Economy, competition, markets	7 paragraphs
Education (including one paragraph per goal)	9 paragraphs
Deficit	3 paragraphs
Environment	3 paragraphs
Miscellaneous legislative	1 paragraph
Social Security	2 paragraphs
Health care	1 paragraph
Crime/community issues	2 paragraphs

With this type of laundry-list format and approach, we could hope at best for no more than a few paragraphs about our proposed domestic antipoverty agenda, especially given the preoccupation with the Persian Gulf conflict. What we got was the following:

Since the birth of our nation, "We the people" has been the source of our strength. What government can do alone is limited—but the potential of the American people knows no limits.

We are a nation of rock-solid realism and clear-eyed idealism. We are Americans. We are the nation that believes in the future. We are the nation that can shape the future. And we've begun to do just that—by strengthening the power and choice of individuals and families.

Together, these last two years, we've put dollars directly in the hands of parents instead of bureaucracies. Unshackled the potential of Americans with disabilities. Applied the creativity of the marketplace in the service of the environment, for clean air; and made home ownership possible for more Americans.

The strength of a democracy is not in bureaucracy. It is in the people and their communities. In everything we do, let us unleash the potential of our most precious resource—our citizens, our citizens themselves. We must return to families, communities, counties, cities, states, and institutions of every kind the power to chart their own destiny, and the freedom and opportunity provided by strong economic growth. And that's what America is all about.

This passage from the President's speech was interrupted by enthusiastic applause four times. Although he didn't use the buzzword "empowerment," Bush had nonetheless laid out and endorsed the basic principles of what we were trying to do through the Economic Empowerment Task Force.

The 1991 State of the Union address was a small down payment on empowerment and a mini-rhetorical triumph for Kemp. We thus pressed for a fuller articulation of the Administration's economic opportunity agenda.

That moment came on February 27, 1991, when Bush spoke to the American Society of Association Executives at the J. W. Marriott Hotel just a few blocks from the White House. His remarks resonated with the type of empowerment rhetoric we'd been urging for months. Bush told the audience:

> Today, our administration is proposing an agenda to expand opportunity and choice for all. It involves more than six major initiatives across the scope of our entire Government: restoring quality education, ensuring crime-free neighborhoods, strengthening civil and legal rights for all, creating jobs and new businesses, expanding access to home ownership, and allowing localities a greater share of responsibility. In its entirety, I believe it represents one of the most far-reaching efforts in decades to unleash the talents of every citizen in America.

As part of his agenda to "assure that every American enjoys the equality of opportunity and access," the President pledged vigorous enforcement of the civil rights laws and refinement of those laws where improvements were warranted. He added: "But legislation that only creates a lawyer's bonanza helps no one. We all know where opportunity really begins. As I said above, it begins with a job."

Flanked by Cabinet Secretaries Kemp, Sullivan, Thornburgh, and Robert Woodson, president of the National Center for Neighborhood Enterprise, George Bush delivered—at least intellectually—the single most comprehensive and coherent statement of his domestic agenda since his "Building a Better America" speech to Congress two years earlier. Not until James A. Baker III resigned from the State Department in August 1992 would a senior Administration official (other than Kemp, who did so daily) deliver such a comprehensive presentation of our domestic policy, one which even linked the successful completion of the Persian Gulf crisis with our needs at home.

There was just one slight problem.

The speech was a flop. Even though he was speaking to a hand-picked crowd of some seven hundred supporters, Bush's remarks received no applause until the perfunctory recognition at the end. He came away not only stunned but irked, and it was clear to us that we were in danger of losing his interest. And we did. We had to wait until June for Bush to make another serious foray into domestic policy themes.

The Marriott speech was not helped by its unfortunate timing. Bush delivered it on the day the Gulf War ended. Nobody cared what he had to say about economic opportunity. Victory was only hours away. So, once again, another domestic message was lost in a sea of good news about foreign policy.

Timing, however, wasn't the only problem with the Marriott speech. The audience of mostly trade association executives had been poorly selected. There was no context in which enthusiasm for empowerment could build. Moreover, people had been kept sitting listening to a series of talking heads before Bush arrived. The audience had been bludgeoned into listlessness and boredom by the time the President had arrived. Bush was just one more talking head who walked into an auditorium and delivered a message.

Remarkably, Bush's White House handlers repeated this goof four months later, when Bush delivered a lengthy speech about volunteerism to some two thousand hand-picked supporters on the White House South Lawn the evening of June 12. After remarks by Sununu's deputy, Andy Card, Bush delivered a speech full of lofty rhetoric about volunteerism and community service. It sounded more like a sermon than a carefully drawn presentation of his overall domestic policy:

> I believe that the people gathered here tonight, under the twilight shadow of our magnificent Washington's Monument, understand this better than most. You are extraordinary Americans, representing thousands of others. You bring to life the genius of the American spirit. And it is through you and with you that we can solve our most pressing problems. Together we can transform America and create whole and good communities everywhere. Tonight, all Americans can help lead the way.

If the speech was a statement of vision—Bush's view of an "America whole and good"—it was equally an admission of failure. The President began his remarks by expressing disappointment, but not surprise, that after ninety-eight days the Congress was still incapable of passing the two bills he'd pressed for immediately after the Gulf War: crime and transportation.

The Leader of the Free World was sad about this, but it was painfully clear that he had no consequences in store for the dilatory Congress: "I thought 100 days was fairly reasonable. And I wasn't asking the Congress to deliver a hot pizza in less that 30 minutes. That would be revolutionary for a Congress."

That one-liner drew laughter, but during the rest of the speech the audience was stone silent until near the end, when Bush said, "Thank God for our teachers!" Only then was the President interrupted by applause.

But his message was clear. After admitting that he couldn't explain Congress's inaction (it was simple: Congress wanted him to fail), he announced that he would turn elsewhere for answers, to the nation's communities:

> The state of our nation is the state of our communities. As our communities flourish, our nation will flourish. So we must seek a nation of whole communities, a nation of good communities—an America whole and good.

Bush laid out his vision of a government that was compassionate and competent, a government that was good and was linked with the free market and the ethic of serving others.

While well-crafted and full of sound policies, the speech was, at best, a snooze. People strolled across the South Lawn on that beautiful summer evening wondering what the point of it all was. This speech was the forerunner of a virtually identical situation that would crop up the following year.

Bush had given the Congress an ultimatum to act, and it had defied him, sticking instead to business as usual, thumbing its collective nose at him and taking its own bloody time. The President would once again give Congress an ultimatum in his January 1992 State of the Union address, and the results would be the same. What emerged in each instance was the image of a weakening President. No arm-twisting. No swearing. No bullying. Just a polite sermon to the faithful. One could hardly have imagined Lyndon Johnson behaving in this way.

Franklin Roosevelt once said that there is "no magic in Democracy that does away with the need for leadership."[8] The problem with George Bush's rhetoric was that it failed to stir even his most devoted followers. It failed to move them because they knew—and even he admitted—that his words were divorced from action. After his Marriott and South Lawn addresses, nothing happened that was any different from what had come before. At issue was the President's credibility.

As the months passed, we believed we had to do something to revive Bush's—and the Administration's—interest in empowerment. Our legislative proposals languished before the Congress, while the White House expressed little interest in making a serious push to get the measures enacted.

Nothing concentrates the mind more than a meeting with the President. So Richard Porter, John Schall, and I went to see Kemp and convinced him that we needed to schedule a meeting with Bush to review our current progress. Everyone agreed, and a Domestic Policy Council session was scheduled for June 20, 1991.

The problem, as always, was the meeting's substance. The fact was, there had been relatively little progress. Eyes would glaze over if we focused too much on "services integration," so we looked for more details to bring before Bush. That left us with recapping the status of our principal legislative initiatives. Our goal was to convince Bush that the Congress was doing nothing to enact his economic opportunity agenda and that he could help by charging Capitol Hill to get moving.

After months of working on empowerment, several of us on the Task Force had concluded that one of the most significant barriers to our achieving a real breakthrough in antipoverty policy was the "poverty trap." The term referred to the fact that the eligibility criteria attached to existing federal programs typically made it impossible for recipients simultaneously to accumulate capital or assets *and* continue to receive benefits. As a result, millions of the poor found themselves "trapped" in poverty, damned if they did save, damned if they didn't.

Kemp was fond of telling about one welfare recipient, Grace Capetillo, who was prosecuted for welfare fraud when she saved some $3,000 to send one of her children to college. She was fined $15,000 and soon found herself back on welfare.

Kemp wanted to place this issue on the agenda with the President on June 20, although the HUD Secretary preferred to discuss the matter in terms of the high implicit marginal tax rates that discouraged work and asset accumulation and encouraged further dependency on federal welfare programs. As Kemp put it, the poor are actually "taxed" at the highest marginal rate of all American citizens. In some instances they pay effective marginal tax rates of 100 percent, because they lose all welfare benefits the moment they begin to accumulate assets. Kemp argued that the situation was patently unfair and had to be changed.

The meeting with Bush was held in the Cabinet Room at 10 A.M. on June 20, 1991. The President opened the session with a surprising endorsement. He referred to our economic opportunity agenda as the "philosophical heart of what we're about" and added that it's simply "crazy" for the press to report the charge that "there's no domestic agenda."

Most of the Cabinet members present said a few words about their own empowerment-related activities. Kemp was the most enthusiastic and outspoken in challenging the status quo, particularly the Democrats who often sought votes in "poverty pimping." Kemp also emphasized the need for tax reform that would reward saving and entrepreneurial risk-taking.

When Bush asked if the states were interested in any of these approaches, Darman responded by explaining that the concept of services integration had really begun in the late 1960s. There was "nothing new" to what was being proposed, although the Congress would clearly see it as a threat to its turf, especially the existing committee structure.

Kemp urged a confrontation with the Congress, especially when it came to what we've gotten for the money spent thus far. "We've spent $2.4 trillion since 1964 on poverty just to maintain dependency. There is a flaw in the system. People are dependent in perpetuity." He then launched into a discussion about the importance of asset accumulation and the need to deal with the high marginal tax rates encountered by the poor—what Darman insisted was more accurately termed the "benefit reduction rate." The hard part of addressing this issue, according to Darman, was that if you removed the benefit more slowly, you might actually encourage more people to come into the welfare system. It wasn't so much a "tax issue" as it was "a design dilemma."

There was a spirited debate for an hour or so, and that was about it. Afterward there was no agreement as to next steps. Bush thanked everyone for their efforts and left the room.

During the summer months, the Administration's economic opportunity agenda again made relatively little progress. While work advanced on services integration, principally under the leadership of HHS Assistant Secretary for Planning and Evaluation Martin Gerry, little else occurred. I became concerned for several reasons. First, by the fall of 1991, roughly one year before the 1992 presidential election, we would need something of substance to show for all our efforts. Second, one of the reasons for meeting with Bush in June was to task departments with including new empowerment initiatives in their planning for the 1993 fiscal year budget. That planning usually began during the summer, and the goal was to influence the policy process early on in each department.

Department budget proposals were due for submission to OMB on September 1. Thus, if we were to influence that process, we had to "infect" the planning well in advance of the due date. That explained why we wanted the June meeting with Bush.

On August 7, I convened our Task Force without Kemp to review the initiatives the members were planning to pursue in the fiscal year 1993 budget. As I feared, there were virtually no new ideas except for a clever idea from the Interior Department to block-grant much of the money administered to Indian tribes by the Bureau of Indian Affairs. It was obvious to Richard Porter, Jay Lefkowitz (Porter's chief aide), and me that we were going to have to devise the next round of empowerment initiatives ourselves.

Lefkowitz and Tom Humbert, Kemp's principal empowerment aide (along with Assistant HUD Secretary Anna Kondratas) prepared two memoranda listing new empowerment initiatives. The themes were derivatives of our earlier work, but now they focused more on asset accumulation by the poor so that they could establish capital or own property as a basis for achieving financial independence from welfare. We wanted to stress ways to remove barriers to people getting off welfare, encourage entrepreneurship, stimulate home ownership, and integrate services while promoting good government. When the list reached sufficient critical mass, we were ready to meet with Kemp to discuss the proposals.

Kemp saw us on Wednesday, October 30, 1991, in the conference room just off his spacious HUD office. He was in a feisty mood, having earlier that day given an address at the National Press Club where he announced that the Administration should abandon the 1990 budget deal because it was constraining our ability to pursue the economic growth agenda that the country badly needed.

Kemp was adamant about two things. First, he rejected Darman's budget deal and saw no reason to be constrained by it. Second, if nothing came of our latest attempt to engineer an economic opportunity agenda, he would resign as Chairman of our Task Force.

"It's just a fraud," he declared. "I'm not prepared to continue as Chairman if we're never going to produce anything." He remarked that he was loyal to Bush and wanted to serve in the Cabinet in a second Bush term, but he was not prepared to continue this "charade."

We reviewed the agenda, and Kemp was satisfied.

"Write it up in a memo by early next week. Let me look at it and then schedule a Task Force meeting before the end of next week. Then we'll take it to the full DPC."

The recommendations of the Economic Empowerment Task Force were reflected almost in their entirety in the fiscal year 1993 budget released in January 1992. More than even the previous year, we had succeeded in having our work accepted, at least nominally, by the President and Darman. The elaborate budget presentation actually included a table in the front section that described our agenda. Under the title "Proposals for Increasing Opportunity, Choice, and Home-ownership," virtually all of our ideas were included under eight sub-headings. We could not have been happier. It looked as if, finally, the Bush Administration was getting serious about pursuing an economic opportunity agenda.

Wrong again.

This time, our carefully developed policies fell victim to personnel changes that ultimately put the Task Force out of business completely. Without it, Jack Kemp lacked an effective vehicle for pushing the empowerment agenda. Without Kemp, other efforts in the Administration were doomed.

John Sununu's departure as Chief of Staff on December 16, 1991, and the arrival of Sam Skinner threw the White House into turmoil. Not only did we have to complete work on the budget and the State of the Union address, both due in six weeks, but we also had to live with the uncertainty associated with Skinner's decision to undertake a top-to-bottom management review of the White House staff.

Gene Croisant, a friend of Skinner's from R.J.R. Nabisco in New York, had undertaken a similar management review for Skinner when he became Secretary of Transportation. Croisant in the past had also acted as talent scout for Skinner, a fact which created considerable unease and uncertainty for almost the entire White House staff at precisely the most intense and difficult time of the year. People were expected to give their utmost each day while simultaneously worrying whether they would have a job in a few weeks. The situation was crazy.

Croisant took his time surveying the White House operation, scheduling appointments to interview almost all the senior staff—Deputy Assistants to the President and above. His findings and recommendations were expected at the end of February 1992.

Rather than streamline Bush's White House operation, Skinner and Croisant did the precise opposite: they layered it. It was evident from my two lengthy discussions with Croisant that whatever influence Porter may have had left would be coming to an end. Either he would be gone or he would find himself superseded by a more forceful and decisive domestic policy czar. On January 31, 1992, Bush announced that the Republican National Committee Chairman, Clayton Yeutter, would be his new Counselor for Domestic Policy.

Yeutter's arrival was a deep embarrassment for Porter. He was moved from his paneled West Wing corner office into a much smaller office across from the men's room, then found himself officially excluded from the new coordinating mechanism that Yeutter had insisted upon as a condition of his taking the job. Bush abolished the Domestic and Economic Policy Councils and replaced them with a Policy Coordinating Group (PCG), so named by the President himself. In Bush's absence, Yeutter chaired the PCG, which consisted of Vice President Quayle, Nicholas Brady, Skinner, Henson Moore (a former U.S. Representative, a former deputy Energy Secretary, and Skinner's new deputy Chief of Staff), and the ever-present Darman. But no Roger Porter. Instead, Porter was put in charge of a "PCG Deputies Group," which met at an intermediate stage to resolve policy disputes before they were brought to the PCG for final consideration.

A clue to the Bush Administration's priorities—in particular its

slavish consistency in elevating form and process over substance—
came when Bush not only established the PCG but also moved
promptly to massage the bruised ego of his Treasury Secretary. Under
the prior structure, there had been both a Domestic Policy Council
and an Economic Policy Council, the former chaired by Dick Thornburgh, the latter by Nicholas Brady. As a condition of taking the
position of Counselor to the President for Domestic Policy, Yeutter
insisted on controlling both policymaking bodies. Brady strongly pro-
tested, and Bush responded by naming him to the PCG and immediately establishing a Working Group on Economic Policy that Brady
would chair. In other words, a rump Economic Policy Council would
continue while the former Domestic Policy Council was abolished,
replaced by the Policy Coordinating Group and whatever array of
substantive working groups and task forces might be established to
address specific policy areas.

But what became of the Economic Empowerment Task Force,
especially now that its parent entity, the Domestic Policy Council,
had been abolished?

There was no serious discussion about reconstituting the Task
Force as a working body under the new regime. Our agenda—so
carefully developed and nurtured through the White House and
agency bureaucracies for almost two years—now sat unattended on a
stump. The new White House team wasn't interested. After the release of the 1993 budget, the Economic Empowerment Task Force
never met again.

One thing that caught the attention of the new command, however, was welfare reform. In November and December 1991 I began
urging Porter (who again was charged with coordinating the themes
for the President's State of the Union address) to include welfare
reform as a critical issue in the President's election year agenda. As
I told Porter in a lengthy memorandum on December 20, 1990,
Ronald Reagan had decried a "welfare monster" in his 1987 State of
the Union address. A year later, Reagan signed the Family Support
Act, the most significant welfare reform in decades. The crisis in the
American family—low-income single mothers, children in poverty,
out-of-wedlock births, high concentrations of urban poverty—meant
that much more still needed to be done. Moreover, a consensus
across the political spectrum was emerging when it came to time-
limited welfare, flexibility, integrated services, meaningful job-

training efforts, and other ideas. We could lead or we could follow. I shopped these ideas around to allies like Bill Kristol and Al Hubbard in Quayle's office, as well as the chief speechwriter, Tony Snow.

In his January 28, 1992, State of the Union address, Bush made a statement on welfare reform that pointedly included a quotation from Franklin Roosevelt unearthed by Jay Lefkowitz to the effect that welfare "must not become a 'narcotic' and a 'subtle destroyer' of the spirit."

Some media critics accused Bush of using welfare reform as the "Willy Horton" issue of the 1992 election year. In fact, welfare signified the failure of many of the antipoverty programs that had evolved over the last thirty years. That failure was reflected in growing rates of dependency, particularly in America's urban centers, where many generations of the same family had now grown up living almost entirely on public assistance. Reforming the welfare system was a key aspect of our economic empowerment philosophy and strategy.

Once again, the Bush Administration's follow-up lacked urgency and seriousness. When I realized the White House had no interest in continuing the Economic Empowerment Task Force, I decided to reconvene essentially the same players under the guise of implementing Bush's welfare-reform agenda. Beginning in early February, we met weekly to develop recommendations for Bush that would advance that agenda. Unfortunately, various personnel changes and the new domestic policy structure inaugurated by Skinner only slowed the process. Instead of having recommendations ready by late March, the process moved at a snail's pace, with relatively little to show for all the effort by mid-May, except for Bush's approval of an innovative welfare reform waiver requested by Wisconsin's Governor Tommy Thompson.

At the same time, welfare reform was becoming a significant campaign theme and was used successfully by Governor Bill Clinton as a "wedge" issue against Republicans. By calling for greater personal and individual responsibility as the guiding principle behind his welfare-reform ideas, Clinton was positioning himself as a new kind of Democrat, one who believed that government programs could not replace individual initiative or greater personal responsibility and empowerment. Clinton was aping Reagan, who had used similar tactics in his 1980 campaign when he attacked "welfare queens." It was a perfect middle-class issue that resonated with commonsense "damn rightness!" Republicans had raised the issue first, but in a remarkable display of ineptitude and "incumbentitis" we managed to fumble this one as well by letting Clinton capture the rhetorical high ground. Clinton had obviously learned far more from Ronald Reagan than we had. He appropriated what should have been our message while we slavishly adhered to bureaucratic buzzwords.

Aside from the fact that welfare reform wasn't going anywhere, the more serious problem was that no one in the country had any idea of what the Bush Administration stood for when it came to welfare reform. We had become caught up in a feckless bureaucratic process in which the President kept emphasizing "waivers." Nobody knew what he was talking about or cared.

Under the new Policy Coordinating Group structure, the Bush White House had also become a paragon of process. Substance was all but abandoned to a relentless pursuit of meetings and memos that did little to advance any definite policy. Nothing was happening.

That is, until Jimmy Carter showed up one day.

In early April, George Bush met with former President Jimmy Carter, who sought Bush's support for his "Atlanta Project." Carter wanted to devote the "rest of his life," as he put it, to doing something to improve drastically the plight of inner-city Atlanta. Carter believed that government services in Atlanta were not working: They were fragmented, inefficient, and poorly targeted. The dollars were there, coming from all levels of government, state, local, and federal, but they weren't working for people.

Jimmy Carter was "the perfect GS-100," a high-level super bureaucrat (the natural GS, or "Government Service," level maxes out at GS-15) absorbed in the minutiae of government policy. He cherished a belief that if properly and efficiently run, government could play an important role in repairing the fabric of urban Atlanta, which in turn could become a model city for the rest of the country. His plea to Bush was to have his Cabinet members work with his team at the Carter Center "on a bipartisan basis" to make this project a reality.

Carter had some sound ideas that were also consistent with our own efforts to promote services integration. And yet when Kemp and others in Bush's own Administration had urged these ideas, the President, along with Darman and Sununu, responded if at all by dismissing their utility. Jimmy Carter now arrived on the scene, and

Bush directed seven of his Cabinet members to meet with the former Democratic President.

Which they did, on April 20, 1992. Accompanied by aides from his Atlanta Project, Carter met with almost the entire Bush domestic Cabinet: Lamar Alexander, Dick Darman, Jack Kemp, Ed Madigan, Lynn Martin, Louis Sullivan, and George Terwilliger, the newly confirmed Deputy Attorney General. Gregg Petersmeyer hosted the meeting in the Council on Environmental Quality's conference room on Jackson Place, just across from the White House on Lafayette Park. Having advised Petersmeyer earlier about Carter's ideas, I was invited to join the session. Roger Porter was there, too.

Carter spoke eloquently and in considerable detail about his future plans for Atlanta. He wasn't seeking additional federal funds; instead, he was looking for innovative ways to allocate and spend federal, state, and local resources more effectively. He called for additional waivers to make federal resources more flexible. In short, he advocated precisely some of the features of our own economic empowerment agenda.

Kemp, the first Administration member to respond to Carter, told the former President that what he wanted was point-for-point what the Bush Administration had already been seeking. It was congressional Democrats, however, who were unwilling to break out of their categorical mentality and turf consciousness to authorize such flexibility. Kemp at one point included in his remarks a joke—something to the effect that Roger Porter "knew a lot about poor people. He met one once." Everyone cracked up, except for Porter who, head down, kept on writing while turning crimson.

Superficially supportive of Carter's goal, Darman nonetheless let everyone know that these efforts had been talked about for more than twenty years, going back to when he was a young deputy assistant secretary at HEW. Still, he and the other Cabinet Secretaries pledged to help Carter advance his Atlanta Project.

Throughout most of the meeting Kemp and I were exchanging glances. Each of us knew what the other was thinking, and afterward, standing outside in the driveway on Jackson Place, Kemp could barely contain his anger.

"Charlie, will you tell me what the hell is going on here? We spend two years trying to advance these ideas inside the Administration and nobody listens. Now, a former Democratic President like Jimmy

Carter—of all people!—waltzes in and we're supposed to set up a damn command center for him in the White House? Are we crazy or what?"

Kemp was absolutely right, and the most plausible explanation was the Bush Administration's penchant for dealing with elites, in this case a former President. Despite the fact that Carter was a Democrat and a failed leader, to whom the media were already beginning to liken Bush himself, he was a member of the most exclusive elite of all, former Presidents, so Bush was ready to give him more than the time of day.

Kemp was appalled on both policy and political grounds. But none of that mattered to Bush. Kemp was left out in the cold for three years, and his ideas were rejected by Bush and his inner circle because their exponent was someone they considered a zealot. Kemp had once challenged Bush for the country's highest office, and now he was viewed as trying to advance a philosophy of government that was eons removed from Poppy's amiable toffs, a world far from Andover, Yale, Skull and Bones, Kennebunkport, and the Alfalfa Club. Bush could identify with Carter, even though the former engineer-turned-peanut-farmer schooled at Annapolis wasn't exactly from the same background. They had both faced the same challenger in Ronald Reagan. Both were world leaders. Both had faced declining opinion polls.

One-term presidencies? That distinct possibility also occurred to some of us.

As Carter's limousine pulled away, Kemp was livid. Two days later he called me back and we talked further. I suggested that, notwithstanding his frustration at the fawning over Carter, he use this opportunity for furthering our empowerment agenda and, more specifically, for setting up a White House working group that would advance the specific agenda items included as part of the President's budget request, which were now lying fallow, unaddressed and ignored. I suggested further that he seek a commitment from Yeutter to create such a group immediately. In fact, I had even sent Porter and Yeutter a note on March 13, 1992, urging that we use the new Policy Coordinating Group process to advance our economic opportunity ideas:

> You . . . might want to give consideration to creating a PCG Working Group to pursue the various initiatives that comprise the President's economic opportunity agenda. . . . The creation of the new PCG mech-

anism provides an excellent forum for continuing the work in this area and for ensuring that initiatives already announced are actually implemented.

As usual, no reaction.

On Wednesday, April 29, 1992, however, an unexpected event in a Simi Valley, California, courthouse changed the landscape for Jack Kemp and our empowerment agenda. An all-white jury acquitted four policemen of charges of police brutality in the beating-arrest of a black man, Rodney King, in Los Angeles. Most of America had seen a home-made videotape, which recorded both King's arrest and the ensuing beatings, some fifty-seven blows in a little more than eighty seconds. Even Bush stated publicly that he and Barbara were "stunned" by the verdict.

If Bush was stunned by the King verdict, his White House operation, once again, demonstrated its inability to respond to the situation with clarity and speed.

Shortly after the verdict was announced, Los Angeles began to burn. Rampages and looting, accompanied by arson and brutal beatings and slayings, occurred on a scale that surpassed even the Watts riots of 1967. America and the world looked on with horror and shame.

One of Bush's first reactions was to assemble the nation's "civil rights leaders"—in this case the usual cast of tired old establishment characters with whom he'd tried to negotiate a civil rights bill in 1991. Interestingly, but not surprisingly, Bush did not invite the *new* civil rights leaders who supported his own empowerment agenda, people like Robert Woodson of the National Center for Neighborhood Enterprise or the talk show host Tony Brown, who advocated an approach to civil rights issues that included Kemp's empowerment philosophy. No, Bush opened the door to the old guard, along with radicals like Representative Maxine Waters, the Watts representative, who openly dismissed economic empowerment as a sham.

The week that began on April 27 had been a rough one for Kemp and his relations with the Bush White House, but by its end Kemp had risen from the flames and ashes of Los Angeles to become the Administration's leading spokesman on the country's urban agenda. That week began with an episode that demonstrated the lack of political clout Kemp really enjoyed within the Bush White House, but it ended with Kemp being publicly used as a band-aid to cover a huge policy gap in the Bush Administration. The particular episode involved here also showed how petty, myopic, and vindictive Bush's internal political operation had become.

One of Kemp's senior aides, deputy assistant secretary Tom Humbert, had announced his intention to resign to run for Congress in Pennsylvania against incumbent GOP Representative William Goodling. Humbert saw a splendid opportunity after it became known that instead of the initial handful of checks he claimed to have bounced at the infamous House bank, Goodling had really bounced some 430, making him among the worst offenders among incumbent House Republicans.

A nine-term representative, Goodling did just that, finding himself poised for reelection with only token Democratic opposition. Humbert decided to challenge Goodling and was able to get his name on the fall ballot as an Independent, which infuriated the Bush White House. Goodling was reportedly one of Bush's earliest supporters. He also served as ranking member of the House Education and Labor Committee, but he had accomplished little when it came to moving the President's education-reform policies through the Democratically controlled House of Representatives.

When Humbert resigned to challenge Goodling, the White House decided to play hardball. It also made a fool of itself.

Another Kemp aide, his Assistant Secretary for Public Affairs, Mary Brunette, announced that she intended to leave HUD later that summer to run Humbert's campaign. Ron Kaufman, Director of Political Affairs at the White House, decided Brunette should get an early start and ordered that she be fired immediately for her treachery in working against a fellow Republican, the mega-check-kiter Goodling. If Ms. Brunette was planning to help Humbert unseat Goodling, she wasn't going to do so from her perch in the Bush Administration. A senior White House aide said: "If you want to describe yourself as a 'Reagan–Kemp' Republican that's fine, but not while you are serving in the Bush Administration."[9]

The reaction was another gratuitous swipe at the conservative faithful and, in particular, the Kemp wing of the GOP. Not only did this boner inflame loyal Reaganites and many conservative Republicans (already skeptical of Bush's *bona fides* dating back to the Trilateral Commission, "voodoo economics," and the 1990 budget deal), but it placed Bush in the position of supporting the status quo come hell or high water. As one congressional incumbent after another—of both parties—succumbed to withdrawal pressure or primary losses resulting from the check scandal, here was the President of the United States striking out boldly in support of one of the GOP's most flagrant check-kiters.

When Jim Pinkerton learned of Brunette's treatment by the White House, he responded promptly and, as always, with principle: he sent Humbert a $200 campaign contribution.

Barely hours later the usually adept Kaufman had to eat his words. Jack Kemp, so long regarded as Bush's dog in the manger, was en route to being rediscovered, again, as the darling of the Bush White House. The Los Angeles riot put not only Kemp but also our entire economic opportunity and empowerment agenda on the front pages of virtually every paper in the country. Now the policies had yet another new title: "George Bush's urban agenda."

Kemp popped up on all the major network television news and morning shows. He was resurrected from Cabinet obscurity to find himself seated at Cabinet meetings immediately next to the President. A first. When Bush visited Los Angeles to tour the riot scene, Kemp rode with him on Air Force One.

Either there is a God for sure, or someone in the White House has an exceptionally wry sense of humor, because on the trip out to L.A. the detailed seating chart for the President's jumbo jet had Jack Kemp placed right next to Roger Porter. The former Buffalo Bills quarterback and former Representative, the most outgoing and gregarious member of Bush's Cabinet, found himself seated next to one of the most uptight members of Bush's senior White House staff. That must have been a fun five hours, especially when Kemp repeated his crack about Porter that he'd delivered in front of Jimmy Carter (this time changing "poor" to "black"): "Ah, yes, Roger Porter knows a lot about black people. I think he met one once." Porter, definitely not amused, reportedly complained, "Jack, it wasn't funny the first time, and it isn't funny now."

Somebody on that flight did talk, however, because the *New Republic*'s Fred Barnes reported that Porter "groused about having to sit next to Kemp on the plane to L.A. and listen to him hold forth."[10] (Imagine what Kemp must have been thinking!) Porter saw the story, and on the evening that I went to tell him that I was planning to leave the White House before the year ended, regardless of the election results, he paused at the end of our discussion to ask if I knew Fred Barnes. I said yes. Porter asked me if I knew who might be the source of the negative stories Barnes had written about him.

Three weeks earlier Barnes had written a piece that had mentioned me and had fingered Porter for allegedly having ignored a direct presidential directive to implement the Supreme Court's *Beck* decision involving the use of union membership dues paid by nonunion members for political lobbying purposes.

Such subtlety.

Porter clearly thought I had been the source in both stories. (I was not.) So I told him that the piece about the trip to California clearly had to have been told by someone who was on the plane, perhaps Kemp himself. Porter insisted that Kemp could not have been the source, then took considerable pains to tell me what a good relationship he thought the two of them had developed.

I didn't have the heart. I just couldn't tell Porter how little Kemp thought of him, of Kemp's references to him as a "do-nothing" and worse. I ended my chat with Porter by volunteering to call Barnes in an effort to set the record straight or at least to get him off Porter's back.

In the meantime, I had sent Kemp some materials suggesting how he might use the new White House process to take the best advantage of this development. I recommended that he propose to Clayton Yeutter establishing a permanent Policy Coordinating Working Group that would have the effect of resuming the work formerly handled by the disbanded Low Income Opportunity Board and Kemp's Economic Empowerment Task Force. I made sure also that Kemp had a copy of the memorandum I'd sent to Porter (with a copy to Yeutter) on March 13, 1992, more than six weeks before the L.A. riots, suggesting the creation of precisely such a working group. Porter's response had been the usual: nothing.

Such a working group was established, however, on May 20, 1992, roughly two weeks *after* Bush's visit to LA. Unfortunately, Yeutter put Porter in charge, which made it unlikely that anything of substance would emerge. The working group's charter was to help develop a "longer-range" urban strategy (whatever happened to empowerment?), and Clayton Yeutter confessed candidly to me that Porter would handle the sub-Cabinet work to avoid Jack Kemp's "hyperactivity." There was a conscious decision this time *not* to involve the

Cabinet for fear that Kemp would try to run it. Just as Kemp was being showcased as a political front man for the Administration's urban agenda, his ability actually to do anything was being scuttled by the White House.

The first meeting, held in the Cabinet Room the following week, was a disaster. Nothing happened other than an affirmation to push for urban enterprise zones in the Congress.

All of this would have been comical had it not been for the seriousness of the entire undertaking. The President appeared intent on pushing his economic opportunity agenda, albeit after having been dragged into the issues—reactively, as always—as a consequence of the carnage and violence that destroyed portions of Los Angeles. Putting Porter in charge of developing new ideas, in view of his previous noninvolvement in this area, was remarkably obtuse.

Some two weeks later Porter was finding relatively little in the way of innovation coming from the Cabinet departments. When he mentioned that at a staff meeting on June 1, I told him it should come as no surprise. We had gone through the identical exercise the previous year, only to learn that we could not expect innovations from our Cabinet-level colleagues. It just wasn't going to happen. So I advised Porter that the only way we could hope to generate additional ideas was for a small group of us in the White House to repeat what we'd done last year: seek out expert advice and develop the initiatives ourselves, then peddle them to the Cabinet members. The latter, confronted with a *tabula rasa* in their own bailiwicks, would no doubt be pleased to react to something coming over from the White House.

I returned from lunch in the Mess one afternoon during this period and found a note on my desk asking me to join Roger Porter in his office, where he was meeting with Michael Sherraden from Washington University in St. Louis. Sherraden had been especially helpful to us in 1991 when we were devising the economic opportunity initiatives in the President's 1992 budget (the same ones we'd neglected until after the Los Angeles riots). Porter had never met Sherraden, the author of an intriguing book entitled *Assets and the Poor*, which Jack Kemp had been praising for months. I had already met with Sherraden on at least three prior occasions and had spoken with him repeatedly on the telephone during the last year, so when I entered Porter's office that afternoon it was like greeting an old friend. Porter was clearly surprised, and I got the distinct impression that he was now racing to make up for lost time. Suddenly asked to do something that he'd studiously ignored for two years, he was obviously scrambling to bone up on the subject.

I joined Sherraden and Porter near the end of their half-hour session and found Porter barely able to stay awake. Because he routinely got no more than three or four hours' sleep, Porter frequently dozed off in meetings. (His nodding off became so flagrant at one meeting with people from outside the White House complex that his Executive Assistant, Bradley Mitchell, excused himself from Porter's office, went out to the secretary's desk, and placed a call to Porter urging him to stay awake!) On these occasions, it was always interesting to watch Porter's eyes. As long as *he* was talking, everything was fine, since he had infinite time and patience for listening to his own observations. But the moment others in the room began talking, his eyelids would narrow perceptibly and his pupils would roll backward in his head— just for a second or two until he caught himself. That would happen often enough to make others in the room aware that he didn't give a hoot about what they had to say.

The Bush Administration's reaction to the Los Angeles riots highlighted the fact that the President cared little about domestic policy. In the wake of the violence and killing, the Administration not only rediscovered Jack Kemp but also decided to begin advocating its own ideas that had been part of the budget request to Congress announced almost five months previously. Porter had been ignoring suggestions that we follow through on those ideas, so nobody had been doing anything in this critical area until Los Angeles began to burn. It was surprising that the Democrats failed to make more of our incapacity for meaningful leadership.

The Bush Administration's failure to advance a New Paradigm agenda soon caught up with it where it counted most for Bush: in the polls and in the politics. On June 5, 1992, the *Wall Street Journal* columnist Paul Gigot, an unabashed Pinkerton admirer and friend, wrote that the rise of H. Ross Perot in the opinion polls and the threat he posed to Bush's reelection were essentially predicted by Pinkerton and reflected a growing public desire for change and, in particular, for a government that worked:

As a young White House aide in 1990, Mr. Pinkerton predicted a "new paradigm" in politics and argued for an energetic domestic reform agenda. For his temerity, the lanky protege of Lee Atwater was ridiculed by budget director Richard Darman and shunned as a prophet without honor. Maybe the Perot movement should be called Pinkerton's Vindication.[11]

The world of domestic politics was changing, and the Bush Administration, shackled by the limited horizons of managing government better, never understood what Peter Drucker termed "the power of the naïve question" when it came to government reform: "If you weren't already doing something, would you start?"[12] The classic example, noted frequently by Pinkerton, was the fact that the U.S. Agriculture Department had some 3,300 employees in 1900. Today there were 3 million fewer farmers than in 1900, yet the Department has 129,000 employees![13]

In the weeks following Los Angeles, the President briefly rediscovered Kemp and his own economic opportunity agenda, but he didn't know what to do with any of it. The left-leaning weekly *The Nation* aptly if cynically summed up the Bush White House's reaction in a clever little poem by Calvin Trillin:

Jack Kemp (A White-Guy Rap)

April

    Jack is dissed by Bush's troops
    Jack's cut out of all the loops.
    White House dudes say Jack's a pain:
    Jack can't tell which stream is main.
    Jack still talks of urban blight.
    Jack forgot the votes are white.
    When the White House has a do,
    Jack's as welcome as the flu.

May

    White House dudes say, "Jack's our man.
    We're behind Jack's housing plan.
    Jack's the greatest. Jack's the top.
    Jack's our favorite photo op.
    Urban program? There's no lack
    (Get the details there from Jack).
    Jack's the coolest of them all.
    We're with Jack, at least till fall."[14]

And it was all true.

We were scrambling through the motions to look responsive to the latest national need (as defined by the tabloid headlines). Had we moved aggressively beginning in 1990, the President would have been far out in front of his critics as well as his Democratic opponents. Even if Congress had failed to enact his proposals, Bush would have occupied the high ground by having fought for these ideas as strenuously as he fought for other initiatives with the Congress, like Israeli loan guarantees or approval to act in the Persian Gulf crisis.

The evening before Gigot's column appeared, the President decided to hold a press conference in the White House East Room. Stung by his now dismal showing in the public opinion polls, the rising popularity of the undeclared presidential candidate Perot, and the defection of the GOP loyalist Ed Rollins to co-manage Perot's campaign, Bush and his advisers decided to make some news and perhaps seize the initiative by sending the President out to confront the press at a prime-time televised news conference, the second such formal conference of his presidency. But Bush had nothing of importance to announce, and all three major television networks declined to air the news conference. Only CNN carried the forty-minute event live, and the President found himself competing head-to-head with "The Simpsons" and "The Cosby Show."

Bush opened the press conference with a brief statement supporting a balanced budget amendment and then fielded questions. It was an average performance during which the President attempted to dispel the idea that he lacked a domestic agenda. He rattled off the list of bills he'd sent to the Congress that were still awaiting action, but once again his litany was unconnected to any overarching vision or theme for the future. As Democratic Representative Rob Andrews said to me at breakfast the next morning, "Charlie, you've got six hundred domestic policies on all sorts of issues, which means, of course, that you don't have a domestic policy at all."

The problem was both a lack of gumption and a lack of focus. As quickly as George Bush rediscovered Jack Kemp after the Los Angeles riots, he put him back on the shelf.

The White House had failed to follow up after Los Angeles in any way that would convince the public (or members of the President's own Administration, for that matter) that he meant business. Shortly after the L.A. riots political analysts told NBC News that the President "seems to say the right things but not really follow through, and you don't know if it's just his heart isn't in it or he doesn't quite connect."[15] By midsummer Kemp was openly showing his disgust and privately expressing his loss of hope.

Of course, there was action. A task force went to Los Angeles and set up an operational base. But the White House never convinced the public that it was on top of the crisis, as it would that fall when it responded to the twin hurricanes in Florida and Hawaii.

Bush's rhetoric, at least, brought a sense of urgency to addressing the concerns raised by Los Angeles. His actions, however, were a different matter altogether. On May 2, 1992, Bush declared Los Angeles a disaster area and moved to provide federal emergency assistance. Two days later he met with his Cabinet and established a Presidential Task Force to handle the problem. Next, on May 8, he announced that some $19 million in "Weed and Seed" funds would go to Los Angeles. "Weed and Seed" is a Justice Department program intended to provide help to neighborhoods in first "weeding" out criminals, gangs, and drug dealers and then "seeding" those same neighborhoods with assistance to rebuild their infrastructure.

In the meantime, debate raged within the Administration and the Bush–Quayle campaign over whether Bush should also propose a major jobs program along the lines of Franklin Roosevelt's Civilian Conservation Corps. Jim Pinkerton was strongly backing the idea, while Darman (no surprise) was arguing that it was crazy. The President rejected Pinkerton's CCC-type approach and instead reiterated the need for Congress to pass an urban aid package that included his enterprise zone proposal. He did not, however, pursue this initiative with sustained energy. By late August 1992 little had happened on Capitol Hill to advance the agenda other than a continued battle between the two parties over how many zones there should be and whether the legislation should also include a targeted capital gains tax cut. The wrangling intensified when the Democrats cleverly added to the legislation a provision that would have made permanent many of the temporary tax increases in the 1990 budget deal that were soon to expire.

Oddly enough, the Bush White House—on the eve of the Republican National Convention in Houston, where a generally conservative group of delegates outraged by the tax increases would be gathering—actually had to debate whether to oppose that last aspect of the pending legislation. GOP supply siders like Kemp were urging the President to reject the budget deal's tax hikes and come out strongly in favor of lower taxes and economic growth. More traditionalist Republicans—the Brady–Darman crowd—wanted to keep the focus on the budget deficit. Politically it was obvious that Bush had to distance himself from Darmanomics if he wanted to nail down his Republican (and Reagan Democrat) base. Given this political necessity, it was remarkable that the Bush White House even flirted with the possibility of accepting such a suicidal proposal as making the tax increases permanent.

This situation was yet another example of Darman's pulling Bush's levers in an effort to salvage the 1990 budget deal. Bush could have indicated that he meant business about the 1990 deal being a mistake by taking a highly visible public position opposing all legislation that sought to make permanent the taxes that were soon to expire. Remarkably, many people inside Bush's own White House were actually unaware that many of the taxes raised in 1990 were set to end in 1993! What better way was there for Bush to repudiate the deal than by vigorously insisting that these taxes expire?

Instead, *per* Darman, virtually nothing was said, and Bush came perilously close to acquiescing in the taxes' extension, which would have been fatal to what little credibility on taxes he may have had left. Had Bush acquiesced, the Democrats would have had a field day: There would be no way Bush could repudiate the 1990 budget deal after having agreed to make permanent taxes that were only temporary. We would have finally surrendered the tax issue to the Democrats, and Bush would have been incapable of resurrecting his core constituents. That Darman and others in the White House could have entertained such a possibility is indeed a remarkable commentary on the state of disarray in the Bush White House on the very eve of the party's Houston convention.

Little more was heard about our empowerment agenda for the remainder of the summer. The Administration's support for urban enterprise zones, the last visible component of that agenda to receive much focus, along with school choice, was obscured by congressional debate about a tax bill. The focus was lost, and nothing ever emerged from negotiations with the Congress.

As for empowerment, all was not over. It would take one final gasp for breath in the waning weeks of the 1992 presidential campaign. Ignored for more than two years, empowerment would be one of the last straws the President tried to grasp before his reelection debacle.

8

In Search of Domestic Policy

"Kinder, Gentler" Gridlock

"Welcome home, Mr. President."[1]

—*The Wall Street Journal*, March 1, 1991

The Persian Gulf crisis occupied the attention of the President and many in the White House almost exclusively from August 2, 1990, through the war's conclusion on February 27, 1991. Virtually the only domestic sideshow during that period was the blustery series of negotiations on Capitol Hill that concluded in the 1990 budget deal. Although most domestic policy initiatives were put on hold until after the fighting, the President's domestic policy staff was busy shaping several initiatives for Bush to announce in his January 29, 1991, State of the Union address.

The odds were good that the bulk of Bush's message to Congress in early 1991 would emphasize the economic, political, and military turmoil associated with the Gulf operations. The challenge for us was to ensure that domestic policy was not slighted in Bush's remarks to Congress.

I began preparing several policy backgrounders for Roger Porter, who once again had been asked by Bush to coordinate input for his 1991 State of the Union remarks. Porter would gather various ideas and, along with National Security Adviser Brent Scowcroft, Governor Sununu, and the President, would prepare an outline to be given to the designated speechwriter, in this case the young and talented Mark Lange.

Bush's 1990 address had stressed several important issues, with domestic policy holding a prominent place and accounting for the bulk of the speech. I considered it critical for Porter to find ways to emphasize certain essential themes and, perhaps most important, to devise a natural segue from the foreign policy worries that were uppermost on people's minds into the domestic agenda that would be the country's natural focus after the Gulf War ended. My December 4, 1990, memorandum to Porter included the following suggestion:

> The transition from foreign to domestic policy ... should emphasize individual freedom, decisionmaking, and choice. Our model of democratic capitalism was what inspired the revolutions in Poland, Czechoslovakia, East Germany, even the Baltics.
>
> This triumph affords us the opportunity to reinforce the values and principles upon which our Republic was also founded.

To highlight my point, I recommended that the speech stress our empowerment agenda as a way to "reinvigorate individual choice in American life." Why not also use the speech to salute the efforts of Polly Williams, Kimi Gray, Shelby Steele, Rubin Greenberg, and other black leaders "who are redefining the ways in which civil rights, educational and housing services, plus anticrime efforts are being delivered"?

I further recommended that the address "emphasize the importance of solid growth incentives as the best way to ensure a sound economy." Any growth message should be accompanied by a strong warning against *re*regulation and should stress the importance of cost-effective environmental rulemaking. The latter suggestion was expressly directed at those in the business and manufacturing sectors of the economy who were beginning to worry about paying the high costs of the Clean Air Act Amendments of 1990.

As usual, I received no feedback from my boss.

The speech that issued from the President's lips on January 29 was a rhetorically acceptable but fundamentally undistinguished address that focused on the pending Gulf conflict. When it got around to the domestic front, it substituted rhetoric for action. Bush claimed that he stood before the Congress and the American people "with an appeal for renewal . . . not merely a call for new government initiatives; it is a call for new initiatives in government, in our communities, and from every American to prepare for the next American century."

Those of us waiting to hear the President call for greater economic empowerment settled for tepid oratory. He spoke of the "individual" as holding the key to our future: "We must return to families, communities, counties, cities, States, and institutions of every kind the *power* to chart their own destiny and the freedom and opportunity provided by strong economic growth."

As he had with many of Bush's other major addresses, Porter sat in the House gallery and added up the number and frequency of applause lines, using a stopwatch. Porter was particularly pleased when Bush said in connection with his determination to win the Gulf conflict, "This we do know: Our cause is just; our cause is moral; our cause is right." Porter favored us at a staff meeting with an account of how he had urged the line on Bush, while Darman had wanted it deleted. (The OMB Director did prevail, however, in deleting another line: "This is democracy's day." Said he didn't understand it.) Of such instances are White House egos made or broken. It was but a small example of the problems inherent in the Bush White House: With no clear guidance on policy from the President, senior aides were sparring over one-liners in the State of the Union text. The problem would worsen by the time the date arrived to start work on Bush's next State of the Union message, which would be his last.

Bush's 1991 State of the Union address was filled with references to doing what was "right." As rhetoric, the President's remarks were uplifting, especially to those of us who'd labored so long to embellish the speech with references to individual opportunity and placing power in the hands of the people. We acted as if we had a license to proceed again.

But after January 29, 1991, virtually nothing happened to make good on the lofty rhetoric. While there was lots of internal activity—Fact Sheets, legislative drafting, speeches, and the like—there was no concerted agenda, no mapping out of a strategy. If there was any agenda at all, it was microscopic.

The President once again called for enterprise zones and Jack Kemp's favorite home ownership policies. Again, no action.

The President endorsed term limits and the elimination of political action committees as a step that "would truly put more competition in elections and more power in the hands of individuals." Big deal, said the Democrats. Bush backed off.

Finally, borrowing a page from the revenue-sharing concept of the 1970s, Bush announced what came to be called the "turnback" proposal through which the federal government would "turn back" to the States some $15 billion in federal programs "in a single consolidated grant, fully funded, for flexible management by the States." Shortly after the speech, Bush aides presented a listing of some two dozen eligible programs to the winter meeting of the National Governors' Association. After reviewing the list, the governors revised it to include more than eighty programs, while staying within the original $15 billion limit. Again, nothing further happened.

The "turnback" proposal was a splendid idea, a concept consistent with the steps taken at the Charlottesville Education Summit to send a clear signal that many of the country's problems had to be addressed outside Washington. By calling for greater flexibility in the way federal money was spent, Bush was also taking a bold step toward ending the "categorical" program mentality that gripped Washington, a mindset that believed there was a program in Washington that could solve every problem in America.

The "turnback" proposal gave Bush a ready-made issue with which to hammer away at the Democratic Congress. They were "Old Paradigm" and he was "New Paradigm," in the sense of offering a fresh approach to government. Of course, Congressional Democrats would hate the idea, because its core theme was to shift power and authority away from Washington and place it closer to the states and the people. Doing so would dilute the focus and the power of the hundreds of Washington-based special interest groups. Had Bush turned this idea into a crusade, he would have been in a far better position to go head-to-head later with Governor Bill Clinton's calls for "reinventing government." The idea was there, but this time pushing it forward wasn't a matter of wallet. It was a matter of will.

The pattern emerging by mid-1991 would later haunt Bush throughout the rest of his presidency. His failure to follow through, to prioritize his goals, and to marshal his resources for a big drive on Capitol Hill undermined a credibility that had already been strained by the 1990 budget deal's reversal of his "no new taxes" pledge.

Yet another example of the Administration's lack of staying power was its handling of capital gains. Bush had called for a capital gains tax cut in his 1990 State of the Union address to "encourage risk-takers, especially those in our small businesses, to take those steps that translate into economic reward, jobs, and a better life for all of us." Having gotten nowhere with the idea for another year, his 1991 address proposed that Fed Chairman Alan Greenspan head a joint commission with the Congress to determine the revenue impact of a capital gains tax cut. When that proved to be a nonstarter and the Democrats ignored him, Bush did nothing. He never even made the Congress's inaction an issue.

Instead, he retreated from the field altogether. Few people realized at the time that the retreat was staged even before the battle had been begun!

Eight days after his State of the Union address, on February 6, 1991, Bush's own Treasury Department, in preparation for the quarterly "Issues Assessment" held by Cabinet Affairs Secretary Ede Holiday, forwarded a memorandum to Holiday listing the department's "highest priorities." This rackup included banking reform, alleviating the credit crunch, modernizing the tax system, the Enterprise for the Americas Initiative, enforcing Iraq–Kuwait sanctions, the Mexican Free Trade Agreement, implementing the Brady debt-reduction plan, and initiating a review of the American insurance industry. Incredibly, barely a week after the President addressed the nation, the document included no reference at all to capital gains or the Greenspan Commission. It was little wonder that few on Capitol Hill took Bush seriously when his own Treasury Department was able to ignore the President's words with impunity.

When the Treasury Department visited the White House on February 11, 1991, to brief officials on its priorities, Deputy Secretary John Robson completed his presentation without once mentioning capital gains. When I pointedly asked during the Roosevelt Room session what had happened to the President's capital gains tax proposal and why wasn't it among Treasury's "major" (or "minor," for that matter) initiatives, I was greeted with an embarrassing silence.

The Bush Administration never understood the political reality of what was at stake in the fight over capital gains. There was no genuine interest on the Democrats' part in the merits of the idea; to them it was a power struggle, nothing more nor less. It took a defeated Democratic presidential contender, former Massachusetts Senator Paul Tsongas, to express in 1992 what the Bush White House never grasped:

> The reasons a lot of Democrats voted against the capital gains tax cut
> is that they preferred to have the issue of class warfare available for
> their own political ends. And having the class warfare option politically
> was more important, in my judgment, to them than looking at how you
> help the economy.[2]

The White House should have been pounding that message home
repeatedly, beginning in 1989.

The principal story of the Bush Administration in 1991 was how a
popular incumbent President who enjoyed almost 90 percent approval
ratings during the first quarter of the year saw his support begin to
plummet to below 50 percent a year later. Three factors explain Bush's
job approval freefall.

First, both Bush and Sununu admitted that domestic policy wasn't
a priority.

Second, the economy continued its downward slide, rallied somewhat by summer's end, but then resumed its decline at an even
greater pace by late autumn.

Third, the President continued to flaunt his foreign policy predilection while ignoring his domestic portfolio. Symptomatic is the fact
that his Cabinet-level Domestic Policy Council failed to meet at all,
on any subject, from July through November 1991. Equally interesting is the fact that beginning in March 1991 through almost the end
of the year, the Republican National Committee and the White House
didn't even bother to take a single political poll. Why bother? The
Persian Gulf victory would surely mean George Bush's automatic
reelection in 1992!

The neglect of domestic policy in 1991 had grown so worrisome to
those of us trying to elevate it as a priority that the Cabinet Affairs
aide, Richard Porter, who served as the Domestic Policy Council's
Executive Secretary, wrote and circulated a note asking "What Has
Happened to the Domestic Policy Council?" The one-page note explained that while the DPC had been active through the 1990–91
budget season (meeting on drug policy, medical malpractice reform,
and infant health concerns), it had "gone underground" after the
various "blowups" with OMB. Now it met, if at all, only at the "sub-
cabinet level." Furthermore, proposed meetings on civil rights, empowerment, border security, and education had been turned down. In
one instance, OMB actively boycotted a session on balanced budget
amendment policy after the budget office itself had requested the

meeting! Numerous "side meetings" held in Sununu's office pre-empted Cabinet-level discussions. The President was rarely involved; Sununu and Darman primarily were calling the shots. Everybody else was excluded.

Richard Porter drew the following, unfortunately accurate, conclusion in his note:

Messages Sent to the Troops

- "Too many meetings" "Meetings for the sake of meetings"
- Can't be trusted—Empowerment
- Don't rock the boat
- Leave it to OMB
- Domestic policy is a problem not an opportunity

He also offered an obvious, but ignored, solution: "We're part of the team—use us!"

With his State of the Union speech behind him, Bush's early post-Gulf rhetoric, however, sounded promising. On February 25 he delivered a major civil rights address to commemorate Afro-American History Month as part of an attempt by Boyden Gray to "redefine" civil rights in terms of economic opportunity rather than litigation. Bush told his mostly black East Room audience:

> Together, we must write a new chapter in the history of civil rights, a chapter that says: Opportunity must replace despair. For opportunity means education, equipping kids with the tools they need to compete in a new century. It means freedom from drugs. Opportunity means jobs, the dignity of work. It means owning your own home, and being safe in it. Opportunity means social programs to keep families together, and health care to keep them strong. And, above all, opportunity means we must treasure and defend the value of every human life. For as Langston Hughes wrote, "There's a dream in this land with its back against the wall; to save the dream for one, it must be saved for all."

The remarks were both well-crafted and, unlike the Marriott Hotel empowerment speech two days later, extremely well-received. Gray had gone to considerable lengths to ensure that the audience consisted of black leaders and others who were enthusiastically supportive of Bush's controversial efforts to chart a course to a new "opportunity" agenda.

A few days later Bush spoke to a cheering joint session of the Congress on March 6, 1991. The President sounded ready for action at home as he called for an end to "politics as usual":

> In the war just ended, there were clearcut objectives—timetables— and, above all, an overriding imperative to achieve results. We must bring that same sense of self-discipline, that same sense of urgency, to the way we meet challenges here at home. In my State of the Union Address and in my budget, I defined a comprehensive agenda to prepare for the next American century.

He then outlined his chief priorities: to get the "economy rolling again" and to enact legislation—energy, crime, civil rights—that will be "key to building a better America" through measures of "reform and renewal."

Then came this curious passage:

> So, tonight I call on the Congress to move forward aggressively on our domestic front. Let's begin with two initiatives we should be able to agree on quickly: transportation and crime. And then, let's build on success with those and enact the rest of our agenda. If our forces could win the ground war in 100 hours, then surely the Congress can pass this legislation in 100 days. Let that be a promise we make tonight to the American people.

Crime and transportation? What about economic growth? And capital gains? And welfare? Or something of substance?

There was no effort to explain what those bills did or why they mattered. The President could just as easily have substituted "education" and "energy" for crime and transportation. There was no inner logic. There was no outer logic either, for that matter. The transportation bill, at least, could have been touted as a massive jobs bill, which it was, but it would be almost another year before the economic pump-priming features of this bill would be stressed. The Congress, as might have been expected, essentially ignored the President's invitation to work together in a sense of national urgency.

If there *was* a domestic agenda, albeit a dormant one, what was it? Most Americans were unaware—and the White House certainly never took the time to apprise them—that even in the midst of the Persian Gulf crisis in early 1991 the President and his domestic team at the

White House and throughout the executive branch were hard at work assembling a series of initiatives, nicknamed "domestic policy rollouts" by the White House, to be unveiled shortly after the President's 1991 State of the Union address. Throughout the spring and summer months, the White House proceeded with a series of these rollouts. Each of those initiatives—on crime, economic growth, the "America 2000" education strategy, health care liability reform, job promotion—went to Congress and then went nowhere, in large part because the Bush White House had no strategy for pursuing those ideas or rallying public support to put pressure on the Congress to achieve them.

After his State of the Union address, Bush sent one piece of domestic legislation after another to the Congress. First, coinciding with the submission of the fiscal 1992 budget, Bush announced his newest national drug control strategy.

Then, on February 5 , 1991, came comprehensive banking reform proposals, the "Financial Institutions Safety and Consumer Choice Act of 1991," intended to reform outdated banking practices by making the nation's banks more competitive and the banking system more innovative.

On February 20 Bush unveiled his "Surface Transportation Assistance Act of 1991," which proposed a $105.4 billion investment over five years to strengthen the nation's transportation infrastructure, including highways, mass transit, and highway safety programs. A massive jobs bill, this legislation if enacted promptly could have had a strong impact in warding off the effects of recession and preventing the double dip that occurred by the end of 1991 (when the bill was finally enacted and signed into law).

That same day Bush transmitted his national energy strategy, intended to ensure a secure, efficient, and environmentally sound energy future for the country by, among other things, reducing our long-term energy vulnerability.

Bush sent his Enterprise for the Americas Initiative to Congress on February 26. Crime legislation went up two weeks later, on March 11, 1991, reiterating the "badly needed reforms" that Bush acknowledged had been sent up to the Congress "two years ago." If those changes were so critical to ensuring safe streets, schools, and communities across America, you would never have guessed it from the Bush Administration's lack of concerted advocacy. More than a year later, as he headed into his fall reelection campaign, Bush would still be calling on the Congress to pass his crime control legislation restoring the federal death penalty (especially for drug kingpins), reforming *habeas corpus* laws to end frivolous appeals, reforming the exclusionary rule, and increasing the penalties for firearms offenses.

The domestic policy rollouts continued throughout the winter and early spring of 1991, and still nothing happened. We rolled them out and let them sit. Contrast that with Desert Storm, where we not only rolled out the tanks, we used them!

Jim Pinkerton had written a superb anonymous memorandum on March 5, 1991, entitled "The 'Lessons' of Desert Storm." Emerging as one of the great White House Cassandras, Pinkerton pointed out that the "President has the opportunity to apply the momentum gained from the successful outcome of the Kuwait crisis toward solving domestic crises." He explained that much of the military's quick success was due to the fact that in the wake of Vietnam, our armed forces had undergone major renovation and restructuring. The "military has chopped away at its tail and its bureaucratic overhang." Taking the same approach domestically would demonstrate that George Bush had a domestic vision: "The time has come, the President can say, for the Congress to move forward on a bold domestic agenda of reform and restructuring, so that our domestic public sector can face challenges as effectively as the Pentagon just did."

Of course, nobody listened, and Pinkerton was once again ignored.

By March, when the former Tennessee Governor Lamar Alexander had succeeded Lauro Cavazos as Secretary of Education, the Administration had begun work on its "America 2000" national education strategy designed to achieve the six national education goals. Bush heard about Alexander's strategy within days after Alexander was sworn in and embraced it immediately. The President spent virtually all of April 18, 1991, at photo-ops related to unveiling Alexander's effort to achieve "break-the-mold" New American Schools, world-class standards of educational achievement, and serious community-wide participation in education reform. This, too, was a characteristic White House pattern: lots of initial hoopla but limited, if any, follow-through with Congress.

By the time the summer of 1991 had arrived, almost a hundred days had passed, and the Congress had failed to enact the two measures Bush had called for in the aftermath of his Gulf War triumph. Did he then take on the Congress for its inability to meet the nation's domestic needs? Of course not.

Two days before the hundred-day deadline Bush delivered a non-televised speech at 8 o'clock at night on the South Lawn of the White House in which he chided the Congress for its failures. He then proceeded to preach a sermon about how America's problems couldn't be solved in Washington anyway, and that future challenges at home required "a nation of whole communities—an America whole and good."

The speech was a *noblesse oblige* special: peppy, preppy, full of star-spangled banter about the importance of community spirit. And beside the point. The speech received almost no press coverage (actually a blessing), but it only underscored how pitifully out of touch the Bush White House was when it came to winning public support for its proposals. It was as if Lyndon Johnson had followed up John Kennedy's assassination and his own 1964 landslide election with a call for the Congress to reform the Small Business Administration. To twist a phrase, we were clueless and gaga.

Inside the Bush White House virtually no effort was made to connect legislative priorities, policy development, and communications outreach through Public Liaison, speechwriting, and presidential scheduling. There were people carrying out each function, but few of them actually worked together in any coordinated way.

The problem was that no one could begin to fight back with a positive Republican agenda, because no one knew what Bush believed in domestically, not even his closest advisers. The White House political affairs director, Ron Kaufman, reportedly suggested that before Christmas in 1991 Bush Administration political appointees should gather together for a pep rally of sorts in Washington's Constitution Hall, a large amphitheater owned by the Daughters of the American Revolution and the scene of similar rallies in the Reagan years, attended by Reagan and most of his Cabinet. After making his suggestion, Kaufman paused to muse about what the White House would have to tell the gathering. Even Kaufman couldn't tell the faithful what we stood for any more.

Perhaps George Bush's lifelong modesty, his inability to engage in self-promotion except when the chips were down and he was in serious political trouble, explains our overall communications failure. At any rate, the contention that Bush lacked a domestic agenda was belied by the facts and the fact sheets. You would never know it, however, if you had to depend on the ability of the White House to articulate a central message and, more importantly, to sustain that message or to frame it in a context that mattered to people. As one Democratic adviser noted, the signal failure of the Bush White House with regard to its domestic agenda was not realizing that persistence was most of the game.[3]

Yet blaming everything on communications was neither accurate nor fruitful. Having in hand discrete pieces of legislation and other proposals that fitted together could have made a full package, but the Bush Administration lacked the intellectual coherence and drive to do so. The political appointees weren't hungry for much of anything. One colleague said: "When the Reagan people came into the Departments and agencies, they knew what they were there to do. The Bush people are different. They show up on the job the first day and sit there waiting to be told what to do. Perhaps the Reagan politicals were too zealous, but at least they wanted to get things done. These people don't see it that way. Their first thought is having the job, not what to do with it."

Jim Pinkerton expressed a similar thought when he acknowledged that for the Bush Administration governing after 1989 amounted to holding a third consecutive Republican term, a fact which made complacency—"incumbentitis"—Bush's biggest enemy. An aimless agenda nursed along by thousands of clueless political appointees wondering what they were hired for only fostered the sense that Bushies lacked a mission and a sense of direction for governing.

Ted Sanders, the Under Secretary of Education, once commented that the political appointees in the Bush Administration were like the "Christmas help in department stores." He intended the remark as a compliment to government career staff and never even recognized how damning this attitude was to his own Administration. His message couldn't have been any clearer: Long after the politicals have come and gone, the career staff will be here running the show. It was as if the politicals didn't matter, and the way Bush was governing, it was increasingly evident that they didn't. Bush might as well never have appointed any political people to his Administration and just let the government run according to the day-to-day concerns of the "year-round help."

The first half of 1991 was characterized by a monumental effort *inside* the Bush White House to prepare and transmit all the legislative proposals noted earlier. While most of them reflected sound policies and principles, they suffered from a debilitating problem: Nobody knew about them, because the Bush White House refused to spend any presidential capital in pressing for their enactment. The public still believed Bush lacked a domestic agenda, but some of us found it especially worrisome that even his political appointees had not a clue as to what the President stood for.

Shortly after arriving at the White House, I was asked by the Office of Personnel Management to participate in the orientation sessions held at the White House for new political appointees, including many at the presidential appointment level who required Senate confirmation. By the early winter of 1991 I had developed a "stump" speech, which I used to present an overview of the Bush Administration's domestic policies. The speech began by linking those principles of choice, competition, and individual initiative that had brought about the collapse of Communism to similar principles that formed the common denominator of what I believed *we* stood for in the Bush Administration. What I called the "foreign side" of the house was characterized by the "revolutions of 1989," which represented a triumph of choice and the decision by individuals to reinvent their governments, their economies, and their social systems based primarily on free market, capitalist, and decentralized models. The "domestic side" of the house could be summed up by Bush's "economic empowerment" agenda, which represented an effort to "reinvigorate participatory democracy" here at home.

In addition to our proposals on school choice, childcare, housing, civil rights, and crime, I would, over time, extend the list to include our voucher model for health care reform and even structural changes like term limits and reforms of the laws governing political action committees. Those last two were relevant because so many Americans failed to participate in our political process, in part because they felt their votes didn't matter.

I concluded by arguing that our foreign and domestic policies in the Bush Administration *were* connected by this common thread of individualistic democracy. America had helped inspire those revolutions of 1989, and our mission at home was to ensure that we remained faithful to those same principles that had animated millions of freedom-loving people around the world. Those countries had rejected command-and-control bureaucracies, and we should do all we could to ensure that our own country continued to live by those principles as well.

I test-marketed these ideas in scores of speeches in Washington and around the country, to the political faithful in the orientation sessions, and to others who were less politically oriented. Many thousands of people had heard this speech, and on almost every occasion the reaction was extremely positive. Heads would nod in agreement.

The reaction from Bush political appointees, however, was noteworthy for one consistent feature. Each time I delivered my observations, I always heard from people in the audience, either in the question period afterward or later by phone or letter, that they had never heard this message before and that it laid out for them what Bush was really trying to accomplish domestically. Couldn't we get this message out more forcefully? Some people asked me point blank: Why is this the first time we've heard this overview coming from the White House?

An excellent question, one that pointed to the failure of our communications apparatus to keep our own appointees informed, to say nothing of the American public.

The triumphant return of American troops from the Persian Gulf spawned a series of jubilant homecoming parades across the country, continuing through the spring and into the summer. Bush seemed invincible. His popularity approached 90 percent. The brief economic downturn supposedly occasioned by Saddam Hussein's invasion of Kuwait and the corresponding threat to world oil reserves in Saudi Arabia would now surely end. As the troops returned and the euphoria continued throughout the summer, the Bush White House grew smug with the expectation of certain reelection by a grateful public. People in the White House were so optimistic about their futures that even Roger Porter, one of the world's most cautious men, stopped renting and bought a house in McLean, Virginia. All the auguries pointed to a second term.

A few storm clouds, however, were beginning to gather on the horizon, even as early as mid-March 1991. A CNN/Gallup poll of 1,018 adults, conducted March 7–10, showed the President scoring a record 87 percent overall approval rating. On "personality" factors—active, confident, warm, steady, sincere, and so on—the range was from 83 to 91 percent. He received similar high marks for his handling of foreign policy.

On social and economic issues, however, the numbers looked much different and trended in an altogether different direction. Some 63 percent approved of his handling of race relations, but the numbers kept dropping quickly as you moved from the environment (54) and education (53) to crime (47), abortion (40), the poor (38), health care (34), and poverty/homelessness (27). On the economic front, only 31 percent approved of his handling of the budget deficit.

In retrospect, it can be said that George Bush's greatest triumph, his Persian Gulf victory, ironically sowed the seeds of his 1992 defeat. Soaring popularity and months of diversion from domestic issues, in combination with a sluggish economy, caused the Bush White House to put off until far too late addressing the political and policy disaster of the 1990 budget deal. If Darman's deal was an abscess infecting George Bush's presidency, the Gulf War euphoria served as the anaesthetic that masked the pain for months. Absent that victory, George Bush might have been forced to confront his error well before his reelection campaign had begun. Instead, the Gulf War only deepened the belief in the Bush White House that we were the right people to be in charge, as the American people knew and understood, and that the privilege of governing was ours as a matter of right.

By November 1991 the climate had changed dramatically as the President sustained one stunning defeat after another on the domestic front. But the first inklings of those difficulties had come much earlier in the year as civil rights began to reappear as an issue with a vengeance. The principal domestic issue of the second half of 1991 would turn out to be a brutal public battle between the White House and the Congress over civil rights.

Perhaps no other area of domestic policy illustrates the inherent confusion and the crazy-quilt inconsistency of the Bush Administration's policymaking apparatus more vividly than civil rights. Our policy—if you could call it that—emerged in fits and starts, and almost invariably in response to some stimulus from outside the Administration.

The Democrats would introduce their own civil rights bill. We had to respond.

The press would uncover that for a decade Republicans themselves had tolerated and even promoted a practice known as race-norming. We again had to respond.

While we publicly favored tolerance, civility, historically black colleges and universities, and the United Negro College Fund (to which George Bush had been a loyal contributor ever since his days at Yale), we were ultimately unable to articulate or implement a consistent policy that went farther than reflexive opposition to racial quotas. Some even wondered whether our chronic inconsistency might somehow stem from a subconscious desire for atonement after the Willie Horton ads that appeared during the 1988 presidential campaign. Once again, we were hopelessly inconsistent and confused, the inescapable result of an Administration lacking in first principles and clear direction.

Shortly after Bush's February 25, 1991, speech on Black History Month and his February 27, 1991, speech on economic opportunity, Boyden Gray sent the President a March 22 memorandum in which he urged a redefinition of traditional civil rights policy to include, first and foremost, education reform. The memorandum, as well as both speeches, continued to elaborate the point Gray had articulated for Bush the previous October in the President's message to the Senate explaining his veto of the Kennedy–Hawkins civil rights bill. Coming off the Gulf War victory, Gray believed that the President was in a solid position to challenge the traditional Democratic and civil rights establishment views:

> Every indication is that we are in a stronger position than we were last year. Kennedy is having trouble finding co-sponsors, for example, and hasn't even introduced a bill. As your views on this issue become clearer and more persuasive, we may well see increasing attacks from our opponents. If this happens, it will reflect their weakness more than their strength.
>
> I believe that education reform should continue to be the flagship of your equal opportunity package. This is consistent with your goals as the Education President, and it makes sense as policy: improvements in education promise to have the most direct and lasting effects on the problems that the Democrat civil rights bill pretends to address, namely, full and equal participation in the job market.
>
> For example, every increment of additional schooling translates directly into better employment prospects for blacks and whites. What's more, as education levels go up, the absolute differences between black and white unemployment rates narrow; for college graduates, black and white unemployment rates are almost identical.
>
> The chance to make real progress is therefore enormous. Fewer than one-fourth of the students who enter the D.C. public schools ever graduate from the 12th grade. Bill Coleman told me this is why he wants a civil rights bill that *forbids* employers to require high school

diplomas. Catholic schools, however, do much better with all children, including minorities. One study, for example, showed that black seniors at Catholic high schools were three times more likely to graduate from college than black seniors at public schools. Colin Powell therefore seems to have a more positive approach than Bill Coleman when he tells every kid who writes to him, "Stay in school." ...

All of this is well-known as a matter of education policy, of course. The important thing is to make it clear that the best educational policy is the best civil rights policy as well.

Gray was determined to pursue a color-blind civil rights policy that opposed quotas, unnecessary litigation, and more expansive group rights theories while strongly favoring individual initiative, merit, and academic achievement. That was why education figured so prominently in his strategy. Equal opportunity would be guaranteed, and the existing civil rights laws would be vigorously enforced; but quotas, race-norming, and a host of other numerically based affirmative-action strategies would be rewritten or dropped.

Only two days after the Gulf War ended, a *Wall Street Journal* piece by Alan Murray and David Wessel stated that now the President could turn his attention to domestic problems, "problems that critics from both ends of the political spectrum say he has ignored for too long."[4] After cataloguing the President's plate of domestic issues, including the economy, health care reform, and his opportunity agenda, Murray and Wessel quoted a former Carter domestic policy adviser, Stuart Eizenstat, to the effect that the "issuance of the domestic agenda the very day he's announcing the end of the war is another indication of the blind spot this administration has for domestic leadership."[5] They concluded their story by noting that the "Democrats are pressing their civil rights bill again, the same one that Mr. Bush vetoed last year. The White House has yet to find a successful way to advance its counter-proposal without appearing insensitive to minorities."[6] Boyden Gray's strategy was to execute an end-run around this situation by redefining the entire issue as a matter of empowerment, educational opportunity, and, ultimately, achievement.

The establishment civil rights leaders with whom Gray was negotiating, however, knew precisely what was at stake. Gray noted with candor after Bush's failed reelection bid that leaders like Bill Coleman and Vernon Jordan were pressing for a civil rights bill designed to guarantee numerical proportional representation in the workforce. The press, he said, wouldn't call their bill a quota bill, but that's precisely what it was. Gray termed it "demonically quota-oriented" and noted that Vernon Jordan actually bragged about never having read the text.

To understand what was really happening in civil rights in the Bush Administration by late 1991, however, one must first go back to a critical event that happened during George Bush's first year in office.

The heated debate over civil rights legislation that developed by the fall of 1991 was, in the end, inextricably connected with the makeup of the U.S. Supreme Court, and that is precisely why the nomination of Clarence Thomas to succeed Thurgood Marshall became so controversial, even before the confirmation process became preoccupied with the sexual harassment allegations raised by Anita Hill. The reason Congressional Democrats were seeking legislation in the first place had to do with their determination to reverse through legislation a 1989 Supreme Court decision called *Wards Cove Packing Company* v. *Antonio. Wards Cove* had overruled an eighteen-year-old precedent, *Griggs* v. *Duke Power Company*, which had held that the 1964 Civil Rights Act precluded employment practices that had discriminatory effects as well as practices that were intended to discriminate.

Chief Justice Warren Burger had written *Griggs*. His opinion essentially codified what the civil rights lawyers called "disparate impact" analysis: Whenever employment patterns showed an underrepresentation of minorities relative to their distribution in the population, this statistical showing could be used as the basis of litigation challenging employers for their apparent underhiring of minorities. Under *Griggs*, employers bore the burden of proof to demonstrate that the "disparate impact" of their hiring practices was not discriminatory but rather resulted from legitimate—that is, business-related—reasons.

Conservatives had long opposed the *Griggs* reasoning as supportive of group entitlements and racial quotas. Discrimination, many of them argued, should be eliminated wherever actual instances occurred but should not be *inferred* merely on the basis of some statistical showing. "Hiring by the numbers" was all too likely to result in hiring by quotas, a practice many conservatives deemed an example of intolerable and unconstitutional reverse discrimination.

Wards Cove changed all of that. The Supreme Court's five-to-four ruling reversed the previous approach to proving discrimination by modifying disparate impact analysis as a basis for litigation and by shifting the burden of proof for proving discrimination from the employer to the aggrieved party. Writing for the majority, Justice Byron White declared that "a plaintiff must demonstrate that it is the application of a specific or particular employment practice that has created the disparate impact under attack." In short, the mere presence of a statistical imbalance in the workforce relative to the surrounding population was insufficient for a suing plaintiff to proceed with a *prima facie* case. Under the Court's new standard, such cases would readily be dismissed.

Civil rights groups were outraged. Assisted by Senator Edward Kennedy and other liberal Democrats, they supported legislation to overturn *Wards Cove* and to reinstate the *Griggs* burden of proof.

Congressional Democrats believed they could enact their bill and either force Bush not to veto a popular civil rights measure or, if he did, muster sufficient votes to override his veto. In the meantime, Bush had signaled that he wanted to sign a civil rights bill. He never really explained *why* he wanted to do so, however, or what he wanted the bill to accomplish. Here were the makings of yet another muddle—ostensibly good intentions totally divorced from any underlying rationale or substance or willingness to fight.

The President could not have things both ways. If he opposed disparate impact analysis, he should have been wholly satisfied with *Wards Cove*; nothing more needed to be done. If *Wards Cove* was wrong (which he implied by repeatedly announcing that he wanted to sign a bill), then presumably disparate impact analysis (and quotas) were acceptable. This kind of intractable confusion was what prompted so many skeptics on both the right and the left to conclude, almost in exasperation, that Bush really didn't want a bill at all, but instead wanted to keep alive a key issue—opposition to quotas—that would help reelect him in 1992.

Led by Kennedy and Representative Augustus Hawkins, congressional Democrats passed a civil rights bill, S. 2104, in the fall of 1990. Bush vetoed the legislation on October 20, labeling it a "quota bill." In his veto statement, the President explained: "Throughout congressional consideration of this bill, I have said repeatedly that I want to sign a civil rights bill this year that addresses certain Supreme Court decisions regarding employment discrimination." He was willing to compromise, but not on quotas. Noting that he had already signed into law the Americans with Disabilities Act, "the most sweeping civil rights bill in 25 years," Bush decried quotas because they "foster divisiveness and litigation, set group against group, minority against minority, and in so doing, do more to promote legal fees then [*sic*] civil rights." But at the same time, Bush signaled a willingness to accept a reversal of the *Wards Cove* provision that had shifted the burden of proof and the defendant's having to justify the "business necessity" of a particular practice in a disparate impact case.

The same day he vetoed the Kennedy–Hawkins bill, Bush transmitted his own proposal to the Congress. Two days later he sent a carefully worded message to the Senate explaining the reasons why he opposed S. 2104. In addition to racial quotas, Bush offered numerous technical reasons for opposing the bill: needless incentives for litigation, unwise changes in court procedures, unacceptable retroactivity, and the awarding of attorneys' fees. The final paragraph of his message, drafted by Boyden Gray, was one of the earliest efforts to redefine civil rights as going beyond the narrow confines of employment discrimination and the Democrats' efforts to reverse *Wards Cove*:

> In order to address these problems, attention must be given to measures that promote accountability and parental choice in the schools, that strengthen the fight against violent criminals and drug dealers in our inner cities; and that help to combat poverty and inadequate housing. We need initiatives that will empower individual Americans and enable them to reclaim control of their lives, thus helping to make our country's promise of opportunity a reality for all. Enactment of such initiatives, along with my Administration's civil rights bill, will achieve real advances for the cause of equal opportunity.

Introduced late in the congressional session, the President's bill was destined for oblivion. There was not a prayer that Democrats would turn tail and pass an Administration-sponsored bill. Nonetheless, the President's signal that he *would* sign a civil rights bill reversing aspects of *Wards Cove* was a worrisome prospect for conservatives and for some in the business community. It was evident to many that the Administration had failed to articulate a convincing rationale for simultaneously opposing quotas while acquiescing in a reversal of *Wards Cove*.

The good news for Republicans and the Administration was that Congress shortly thereafter adjourned. As concerns continued to mount over the prospect of fighting in the Persian Gulf, such domestic controversies as the battle over civil rights legislation took a back seat to national security matters. They did not, however, disappear altogether, and in a handful of areas controversies kept cropping up in ways that would illustrate the lack of firm principle underlying the Administration's civil rights policymaking.

As already mentioned, in late December 1990, Assistant Secretary of Education for Civil Rights Michael Williams announced that racially based minority scholarships were inconsistent with Title VI of the Civil Rights Act of 1964 and were therefore illegal. The uproar over Williams's ruling ultimately forced the Bush Administration to suspend the Williams decision, which amounted to a retreat.

The failure of the Bush White House to back Williams illustrated not only the unprincipled nature of decisionmaking in the West Wing but also a desire that issues of racial justice be left vague and unresolved. Sununu and company just wanted the whole mess to go away.

Meanwhile, other opportunities arose for civil rights confusion at the White House. The Department of Justice was litigating a case it had initiated under the civil rights laws against the all-male Virginia Military Institute, founded in 1839. The Department's civil rights division brought the lawsuit, claiming that single-sex education was both bad and discriminatory, and that "diversity"—in this case the admission of women—was mandated by law. It was incredible that those arguments were being advanced by Bush Administration lawyers while other senior Administration officials were openly decrying the kind of "political correctness" that sacrificed individuality for mandated conformity.

The federal district judge hearing the VMI case sided with the school and rejected the government's argument with the observation that "VMI truly marches to the beat of a different drummer." Some weeks later, President Bush himself went on the warpath against political correctness in a speech delivered just days after his own Justice Department had decided to appeal the trial judge's ruling!

As if that were not sufficient confusion for everyone, the President further remarked that he saw "some merit" to efforts in Detroit to establish a number of special public schools attended exclusively by young black males. There was no principled way—no explanation short of a political one—to reconcile the Justice Department's VMI appeal with the President's personal endorsement of single-sex, racially segregated public schools.

Left with egg on its face, the Justice Department, now headed by Acting Attorney General William Barr, decided to continue its appeal, albeit on extremely narrow grounds and without needlessly pointing up the glaring inconsistency with the President's remarks. When I asked Barr about Justice's position at one of our quarterly Cabinet Affairs review sessions on October 1, 1991, he acknowledged the problem and said that Justice would make only modest revisions in its position on appeal lest the Court of Appeals have a problem with the Department's reversing its prior position.

Barr's concern was that the Department of Justice's reversing itself in mid-lawsuit might appear too unsettling for the court to contemplate. Admit error in the initial decision to prosecute VMI? Never. Quietly ignoring the case and downplaying the prior position was the more appropriate tactic. Hence Barr said that while his attorneys couldn't withdraw the appeal (a notice had already been filed with the appellate court), the Justice Department had no desire to highlight the discrepancy with Bush's position and would instead concentrate on a narrow, hypertechnical position. Again, everybody just wanted the matter of the discrepancy to fade away.

But error would be acknowledged just a few short weeks later, not in the VMI litigation but in a case pending before the Supreme Court. In fact, the government would reverse itself in a legal brief, this time at the direct command of the President.

In *Ayers* v. *Mabus*, the Department of Justice had filed a "friend of the court" brief in a higher education desegregation case involving the State of Mississippi. At issue was whether Mississippi had completed its obligations under the Constitution and federal law to desegregate its state-run colleges and universities. The Justice Department's *amicus* brief was written by Ken Starr, the soft-spoken, widely admired former federal appeals court judge who was also rumored to be on the GOP short list for a future Supreme Court appointment.

Starr's brief sided with civil rights groups in concluding that the State of Mississippi had not yet completed its desegregation obligations and had more work to accomplish before it would be in compliance with the law. But Starr noted further that achieving future desegregation would *not* require the state to spend an equal amount of resources on its Historically Black Colleges and Universities (HBCUs) as it did on its non-HBCUs. Once again, civil rights groups went through the roof, particularly the heads of the country's HBCUs and the President's own Advisory Board on HBCUs, headed by a former Howard University president, James Cheek.

Cheek and others called the White House and ultimately held an HBCU Advisory Board meeting, which Bush attended, in the West Wing. The HBCU leaders told the President that if the Supreme Court adopted his Solicitor General's arguments, states would no longer feel compelled by law to maintain public support for the non-private HBCUs. That was an overstatement, but it was framed as an issue that struck at the heart of George Bush's patrician background. Ever since his days at Yale, where he had headed fundraising campaigns for the United Negro College Fund, Bush had publicly and zealously supported black education. The HBCU college presidents were blunt: Mr. President, how could you let your own Department of Justice file a brief whose position, if adopted, would undermine the financial support that you yourself have devoted a lifetime to securing?

Once again, as with the negotiations over civil rights legislation, the President turned to Boyden Gray and directed him to resolve the matter as quickly as possible. Gray faced three alternatives: submit the Solicitor General's brief as written, reverse course 180 degrees and change the brief, or seek some compromise that assured the HBCUs of the Administration's support.

Andy Card, Sununu's deputy, convened a meeting to review the options. Card, a pragmatic former state legislator from Massachusetts and a key 1988 Bush campaign operative, asked why we couldn't just change the government's brief. Gray and one of his assistants, Nelson Lund, explained that doing so, particularly before the Supreme Court, was virtually unprecedented and would undoubtedly engender stories in the legal trade press and the national media about how the White House had reversed its own Solicitor General. As for sticking with the brief, Card learned that some Advisory Board members were planning to resign (on the eve of the Clarence Thomas confirmation vote in the Senate) and hold a press conference denouncing the President's and his Administration's lack of support for black colleges.

The search for a middle ground produced this idea: Was there some assistance or financial support that the federal government could pledge that might compensate for whatever diminished state funding might be forthcoming were the Supreme Court to adopt the Solicitor General's position?

Card again asked what was so wrong with the Solicitor General's reversing himself when he filed his forthcoming reply brief.

"It's never been done before," Gray said. His aide, Nelson Lund, reiterated that forcing the Solicitor General, in effect, to eat his words would foment a series of unflattering stories in the press. "We'd look ridiculous," Lund said. Moreover, such a decision would establish a terrible precedent for influencing, and presumably undermining, the integrity of the Solicitor General's legal judgment on the basis of blatant political calculations.

When the meeting broke up, Card instructed Tom Scully of OMB to prepare a series of cost options that could be offered the HBCU presidents. The rationale was to buy them off by promising to hold them harmless in the event the Supreme Court's ruling placed their future state funding at risk.

But there were no dollars to be had. When Card and Boyden Gray went to brief Bush, the President himself decided to grant the Board's principal wish. He took the highly unusual step of directing the Solicitor General to reverse course and drop the argument made in his brief filed earlier that summer.

Overlooked at the time, however, was the fact that the President's unprecedented action had the effect of accepting the principle of separate but equal education funding that had been rejected in 1954 when the landmark Supreme Court case of *Brown* v. *Board of Education* overturned the Nineteenth Century holding of *Plessy* v. *Ferguson*. Historically Black Colleges and Universities were to remain legally separate institutions but would be deemed second-class schools unless they received "equal" levels of financial assistance. Furthermore, implicit in Bush's decision was a message that undercut the rest of his education position, namely, the education establishment's message that higher spending was the key to achieving better academic performance.

The confusion was deepening. With minority scholarships still a pending issue and the *Mabus* and VMI cases evolving in curious and inconsistent directions, the Administration kept wrestling with yet another quota-related civil rights issue, which, with its rudderless civil rights agenda, it found impossible to resolve. This time the issue came from the Labor Department and involved the practice of race-norming, or within-group scoring, in the evaluation of the General Aptitude Test Battery (GATB).

Through its Employment and Training Service, the Department of Labor had long administered a test used by hundreds of state employment offices and thousands of businesses across the country in determining the qualifications of applicants for what are basically blue-collar jobs. GATB scores were then forwarded to participating businesses, which used the rankings to select among potential candidates. Scoring well on the GATB thus increases an individual's chances of being considered for employment. Those not performing well normally fail to make the "cutoff" and never reach the interview phase.

Unbeknownst to most political officials even in the Reagan Administration, the Department of Labor began acquiescing in GATB race-norming during the early 1980s. "Race-norming" meant that companies received, instead of participants' raw scores, "normed" scores, which reflected a candidate's performance not relative to all other test takers but relative only to people in his or her same minority. Thus, blacks competed only against blacks, whites against whites, and so on. The practical results of race-norming were that GATB rankings, which were provided to prospective employers without any explanation that a candidate's score might have been the result of within-group scorings, left a misleading impression of an individual's actual performance on the test. Proponents of race-norming argued that without it many minorities would have been precluded from even being considered for employment, since their scores were sometimes too low to make the employers' cutoff for interviews.

When the practice first came to light in the second Reagan term, the Department of Justice's Civil Rights Office, then under the leadership of William Bradford Reynolds, tried to halt it as inconsistent with existing law (which it was). Although Reynolds never succeeded in stopping race-norming, the Labor Department—to allay concerns about the validity and reliability of the GATB (one of the most frequently administered tests in America)—asked the National Academy of Sciences to study the test in detail. In 1989 the Academy issued a book-length report concluding that GATB was basically a reliable test which actually *overpredicted* the success of blacks. This surprising (and often overlooked) conclusion meant that even without race-norming the GATB was already biased in favor of blacks. When race-norming was added, the bias was further enhanced!

The Labor Department, like the White House itself, was in a quandary over what to do. Some argued that if race-norming were to be banned, the GATB should be discontinued. We should begin afresh by devising a more accurate test that would predict an individual's employment prospects. The problem with that approach was that the GATB was one of the most validated tests in the history of American testing. Scrapping the GATB would send a strong negative signal when it came to the reliability of tests generally, particularly at a critical moment when the President's education reform agenda was calling for more nationwide testing of schoolchildren.

At the same time, race-norming could scarcely be justified under existing civil rights laws. Labor Secretary Martin proposed suspending the test until further work could be done. White House Counsel Boyden Gray and others felt strongly that scrapping the test was the wrong way to go. Gray won out, and the Labor Department was ultimately instructed to prepare a Notice for the *Federal Register* explaining that the practice would be eliminated.

The emergence of race-norming as a critical civil rights issue brought the wheel full circle. The dilemmas posed by administering the GATB also highlighted the Bush Administration's education testing agenda at the precise time when testing also emerged as a major controversy in negotiations over the civil rights legislation. The focus was suddenly intense. Congressional Democrats were falsely accusing the Bush Administration of wanting to require a high school diploma as a prerequisite for someone to qualify as a janitor. Both Education Secretary Lamar Alexander and Evan Kemp, head of the Equal Employment Opportunity Commission, sent letters to the Congress denying this claim and contending that the Democrats' version of the bill would not only foster employment quotas but also would undermine the ability of employers to demand standards of performance and excellence when it came to hiring decisions. In other words, the debate over testing and race-norming took center stage in the debate about what constituted, for purposes of the proposed civil rights statute, a legitimate "business necessity" entitling an employer to select legitimately one candidate over another.

Negotiations over the civil rights legislation had dragged on through most of 1991 but came to a dramatic head after the nomination of Clarence Thomas to the Supreme Court. It was just a matter of days after the bruising congressional hearings over Thomas's fitness to serve on the Supreme Court that Bush suddenly—and surprisingly— announced that he would sign the civil rights bill negotiated by Republican Senator John Danforth, the man who happened to be Thomas's mentor as well as his chief sponsor and advocate in the Senate. The White House reasoned that it was best to get the entire race and quota issue out of the way as quickly as possible, especially in light of the prospect that David Duke, a state legislator and former Grand Wizard of the Ku Klux Klan, was expected to make a strong showing in his effort to become the next Republican Governor of Louisiana. Bush was beginning to have his fill of race and civil rights issues.

But the issues refused to recede, and Bush, Boyden Gray, and others in the Administration found themselves having to explain why what had always been dubbed a quota bill now, suddenly, after only modest textual changes, was no longer a quota bill.

To heighten the confusion, the same week that George Bush agreed to the Danforth-sponsored civil rights compromise, he also issued an Executive Order designed to curb excessive litigation. The Order applied to federal government litigation, and one section called upon government departments and agencies not to transmit proposed legislation to the Congress without first ensuring that all the principal statutory terms had been defined. The point was to reduce needless litigation over what those terms actually meant. Just a few days earlier, Bush had been out trumpeting his civil rights compromise in which both sides had agreed *not* to define "business necessity," leaving this essential aspect of the bill up to the courts to clarify. None of it made any sense. As one aide put it, there was an "irreconcilable conflict" between the two initiatives.

Conservatives were disgusted. By the end of October Patrick Buchanan was criticizing "moderate Republicans" who, "to salve their stricken social consciences . . . sell down the river the people who elected them."[7] According to Buchanan, not only would the new civil rights law result in quotas but it "throws away one of the Republican Party's winning arguments: We oppose reverse discrimination, and we will stand up to the special interests."[8] Then he expressed a growing concern that was on the minds of many Republicans who were now wondering what the Bush White House was really doing:

With the Thomas victory, the GOP had the Democrats divided, defeated, on the run. How sweet it was! With a chance to turn victory over Kennedy & Co. into rout, Mr. Bush rushed out to cut a deal, and give back his ill-gotten gains. Unable to believe their good luck, Mr. Kennedy and Mr. Mitchell are now mocking the man who made it possible. Is there a clinical term to describe a terror of winning?[9]

Bush's White House Counsel saw the law differently, and a few days before the Rose Garden signing ceremony Gray claimed in a *Washington Post* column: "We won, they capitulated."[10] He went on to explain that Bush had "won a clean victory for equal opportunity" without resorting to racial quotas.[11]

A "clean victory" it was clearly not. Few really accepted Gray's explanation, especially not the conservative wing of the GOP, which was still fuming over the previous year's "sellout" over taxes. So, as if to underscore his point, Gray decided to draft a presidential directive to be announced in the signing statement accompanying the civil rights bill. The new directive would have required federal agencies to examine their programs involving hiring and personnel practices (including EEOC enforcement and guidelines) to ensure that they not foster quotas, preferences, or other illegal practices. Gray's policy was indeed sound. It was also consistent with his view that quotas were absent from the civil rights law Bush was about to sign.

As the draft directive was circulated for clearance to Cabinet Departments, its contents were leaked to the press on the eve of the Rose Garden ceremony. At least three Cabinet members—Labor Secretary Lynn Martin, Transportation Secretary Sam Skinner, and HHS Secretary Louis Sullivan—whose staffs had earlier cleared the policy now opposed the directive and urged that it be scrapped.

It was. The President's signing statement was rewritten with the proposed directive deleted. Then, to make matters worse for Bush politically, he felt the need to go out of his way in his remarks to reaffirm his belief in affirmative action.

What did it all mean?

It meant mass confusion once again.

Writing in the *Washington Post*, William Raspberry offered the following insight into what was going on:

If Bush favors affirmative action, why would Gray, his friend and long-time adviser, be preparing an executive order that would wipe it out?

The only answer that makes sense to me is that Gray (who opposes affirmative action) had reason to believe that Bush didn't care that much one way or the other. Thus Bush's decision *not* to issue the executive order was political, not principled, and it made him seem wishy-washy.

Nor is it just on the race-relations front that Bush appears to be marching without benefit of a drummer. He appears to have no clear sense of what to do about the U.S. economy or any set of principles to guide him.[12]

Raspberry had a point. A pattern was now emerging, and it was not especially reassuring to the American public. The President who barely nine months ago had acted with swift certainty and purposiveness against foreign aggression was now uncertain what to do at home about the lingering recession. He reversed course over extending unemployment benefits and then flip-flopped on what he really meant about banks lowering their credit card interest rates, which provoked a heated and, what was worse, public shouting match between John Sununu and Ann Devroy, the *Washington Post* White House correspondent. Since April, when Sununu's proclivity for using military aircraft for personal and political business became public, the White House Chief of Staff had been on a long, slow slide to political ineffectiveness and ultimate oblivion. As Bush himself was taking more heat for the economy, Sununu increasingly became the focal point of critical stories indicating that the White House was in disarray.

It was. With the 1992 election drawing closer and the President's approval rating having dropped nearly forty points to approximately 50 percent, GOP leaders were getting very nervous. Some of them were saying that Sununu was the problem and had to go.

And go is what he ultimately did. On December 3, 1991, while traveling with Bush to Florida on Air Force One, Sununu resigned as Chief of Staff. Transportation Secretary Sam Skinner was named to succeed him on December 16.

All things considered, George Bush's third year as President was a disaster. A year that had begun with a successful military operation halfway around the world, confirming Bush as the commanding presence among world leaders, now ended with his entire Administration in disarray on just about every front.

At the beginning of the year, many of us were optimistic that we would both announce and vigorously pursue an economic opportunity agenda that, in addition to redefining civil rights, would become the cornerstone of our entire domestic policy strategy. The rhetoric, at least, was in place, but what was needed was concrete action, a relentless and concerted drive to press those policies home with the Congress and the people. This strategy offered the President a ready-made formula for linking American successes around the world—most notably the collapse of Communism—with a vibrant domestic agenda that promoted individual choice and decisionmaking.

None of it ever happened.

During 1991 Bush had two splendid moments—the Gulf War victory and the Clarence Thomas confirmation—after which he could have pressed forward with a domestic agenda that would put Democrats on the defensive. He threw away both opportunities. Why?

No one was closer to the President on civil rights or on the effort to redefine civil rights as economic opportunity than Boyden Gray. A few weeks after Bush lost his reelection bid I asked Gray what had happened to that effort. It seemed as though it all just stopped, faded away, after the bruising battle to confirm Clarence Thomas. The usually thoughtful Gray just shrugged his shoulders. "I don't know why," he said. But he went on to add that after the budget deal, except of course on issues that were directly in his jurisdiction, like executive branch ethics and judicial selections, he found his access to the President "drastically curtailed." This was a remarkable disclosure from a man who had served as George Bush's attorney for almost twelve years.

Boyden Gray was not alone in this regard. With the exception of Darman and Sununu, most of the President's senior policy advisers rarely had direct, unfettered access to the President. Roger Porter had been elbowed aside by Darman and essentially drifted into irrelevancy, preoccupied with his note-taking and the preparation of endless White House fact sheets. Without strong backing from Porter, our capable Office of Policy Development staff was essentially ineffective.

As Assistant to the President for Cabinet Affairs, Ede Holiday had scarcely a word to say about substance. Holiday had initially been highly receptive to our empowerment initiatives until Sununu and Darman expressed their disapproval. She failed to support Michael Williams in the minority scholarships issue and refused to back one policy issue after another, from auto insurance reform to empowerment. Holiday had an excellent staff but failed to deploy it for any purpose except as earpieces to pick up the latest tidbit from the various Cabinet departments and agencies. Mike Boskin at one point reportedly became so frustrated at his lack of access to Bush that he threatened Sununu with his resignation. Connie Horner, a staunch conservative with solid principles and good policy sense, became marginalized and compartmentalized as the head of Presidential Personnel after Chase Untermeyer's departure.

If the 1990 budget deal was a disaster that alienated the Republican party's political base, including millions of Reagan Democrats who had crossed over to vote for Reagan and Bush in 1980, 1984, and again in 1988, then the events of 1991 proved to be a different kind of disaster. Now George Bush was in serious danger of splitting that portion of the GOP base which considered social issues, most notably the opposition to racial quotas, critical.

Once again the President had nothing positive (at least politically) to show for his efforts. The Rose Garden signing ceremony for the civil rights bill only outraged establishment civil rights leaders, who had easy access to the national media. Bush had acquiesced to a bill that had indeed reversed aspects of *Wards Cove*, and conservative commentators were quick to explain that his efforts meant both more lawsuits and a resort to quotas—exactly the opposite of what the President had promised.

Other than in the Persian Gulf, the Bush White House was unable to mount a sustained offensive on anything during 1991. The stunning and rapid victory in liberating Kuwait served to underscore the Administration's incompetence and indecisiveness at home. For the first time in more than a decade, a Republican White House found itself divided, defensive, and disheartened. The 1992 presidential campaign was a mere six weeks away.

9

Campaign Mode

Ready to Fight?

"HURRY UP PLEASE ITS TIME"

—T. S. Eliot, *The Waste Land*[1]

The victory seemed as splendid as it was complete: On October 15, 1991, the United States Senate confirmed Judge Clarence Thomas to the Supreme Court. The vote was 52 to 48. Bush's second nominee to the Court picked up all but a handful of the Republican Senate votes and a sufficient number of Southern Democrats, who were well aware that 1992 was an election year and that many of their states had large black populations.

The Thomas victory afforded Republicans and the White House— now just a little more than a year out from election day—an opportunity once again to take the offensive domestically. It was time to begin thinking about what the President often called "campaign mode." Washington was perceived as stuck in a political "gridlock" in which unresponsive politicians of both parties refused to put aside partisan differences for the country's good. For Republicans, still a minority in the Congress but with control of the executive branch, the real issue was whether we were ready to fight.

The Thomas confirmation hearings—similar in many respects to the ill-fated 1987 Senate hearings on Appeals Court Judge Robert H. Bork, nominated by Ronald Reagan to the Supreme Court—highlighted four serious problems with the judicial confirmation process as it had evolved when the Republicans controlled the White House and Democrats held the Senate. Confirmations had become intensely political, had degenerated into embarrassing and needless character attacks, reflected fundamental differences on policy that were used (not even covertly) as a pretext for challenging a nominee's fitness, and involved inordinate delay that had a negative impact on the entire process, the institutions, and the individuals involved. As Judge Bork was later to write in his own memoir of his confirmation experience, "One effect of the political struggle over my nomination was to heighten awareness of what was at stake, and the effects may be seen everywhere."[2]

The former judge's assessment of his own frustrating experience was equally applicable to what was happening to Clarence Thomas, *as well as to the entire Bush Administration*, some four years later. The White House, however, hadn't figured this out yet.

By the end of 1991 the pundits were diagnosing the problem as "gridlock." With the executive and legislative branches controlled by different parties, the argument went, the country's business just wasn't getting done. The Republican solution was obvious: elect more Republicans to Congress. So was the Democrats': put one of them in the White House. Given this approach, it was far easier for Democrats to focus their resources on electing one of their own to the presidency than it was for Republicans to elect several dozen new Members to the House and roughly eight new GOP Senators. Republicans, however, were beginning to fall into a dangerous trap by acquiescing in the "gridlock" diagnosis. Democrats found it far easier to blame one Republican President for the country's woes and thereby deflect any responsibility from themselves. Their task was much simpler; ours was enormous.

Which was all the more reason for not accepting their diagnosis. The issue was *not* gridlock, which somehow implied a flaw in our political system. "Gridlock" did, however, describe the result. By the end of 1991 what was at issue was nothing more than a good old-fashioned partisan Washington power struggle, which actually had begun in earnest in 1989, when Senate Majority Leader George Mitchell had succeeded in blocking the President's capital gains tax proposal.

Judge Thomas's experience provided legitimate reasons for questioning the conduct of the Senate's judicial confirmation process. The President planned a major speech shortly after Thomas was sworn in, which would have given him an occasion to call for reform of the process. The President's speech was also an opportunity to lay the groundwork for ensuring a more accountable Congress. His message could include proposals for the Congress to police itself in matters of check-kiting, confirmation delays, exempting itself from certain legislation, term limits, PAC reforms, unpaid restaurant bills, and failure to complete appropriations bills on time.

Bush did give a speech, and the White House—at least for a brief time—decided to withhold sensitive FBI background reports from Senators but then retreated when the Congress responded by further delaying confirmations. Once again the Bush White House blinked. We were all bluster and no follow-up, no hardball. Had we but made a case for our own more than reasonable reforms and then proceeded with one recess appointment after another, we would have brought the Senate to the table. The power struggle over judicial nominations continued through 1992, and the result was that George Bush left office in January 1993 with dozens of unfilled federal judgeships. Overnight the new Democratic Administration would be able to appoint a significant percentage of the entire federal judiciary.

The Thomas win gave us momentum to forge ahead with our domestic agenda. Having frittered away this same opportunity after the Persian Gulf War and then again after the civil rights bill debate, we now had a third chance. With the 1992 election looming, would we once again blow it, or would we finally manage to drive home our message now that the Democrats were politically wounded?

On Monday, October 28, 1991, I arrived at the White House with a relatively light schedule, a rarity, which meant that I had some time in the morning to catch up on reading. As it turned out, I read two speeches before lunch. One was a draft speech that the President was planning to give later that week at a political rally in Houston. I was to review the text and make whatever suggestions might be necessary before it was put in final form for Bush to review.

The other speech was one delivered the previous week by Governor Bill Clinton, the youngest of the then-declared Democratic candidates for President. He had spoken at Georgetown University, where he had been an undergraduate almost thirty years before.

To my surprise, I found myself applauding Clinton's rhetoric and (as usual) dismayed at yet another unimaginative draft prepared for Bush. Except for some perfunctory Reagan and Bush bashing—decade of greed, selfishness, the rich getting richer, etc.—Clinton's speech was one I would have been proud to deliver myself. I would have been even prouder if George Bush had delivered Clinton's speech. His call for a "New Covenant" in America contemplated "empowering" individuals instead of establishment bureaucracies and constituted a notable departure from the traditional Democratic special-interest pandering. Clinton emphasized themes that some of us, including chief speechwriter Tony Snow and one of his able colleagues, Dan McGroarty, had long urged on Bush.

Was it possible the Democrats were waking up, at last?

More to the point, were we Republicans beginning to appear increasingly like the Leonid Brezhnevs of the 1990s, resisting reforms at every turn, reacting passively to events rather than leading with bold strokes and courageous vision?

Bush's remarks talked bravely about how we were on the side of democracy, but the rhetoric just wasn't convincing, especially measured against the reality of his domestic and foreign policies.

What about Croatia and its faltering democracy, being ruthlessly exterminated by Serbia, the last hard-line Communist outpost in Eastern Europe? The Bush Administration was silent.

What about those brave young human rights activists in China? Bush had consistently undermined their striving for freedom and democracy by blindly granting the Chinese government preferential trading status, again with virtually no progress to show for it.

And what about our support for Boris Yeltsin which emerged only when Gorbachev appeared to be totally spent politically? Again, we didn't lead; we followed.

When Bush talked about economic growth, I could barely suppress a chuckle. Why had he remained virtually silent about capital gains for months? Why did he respond to the recession in late 1991 only after some of his wealthy friends lectured him about the perils they faced from the credit crunch? We had, after all, transmitted an economic growth package to the Congress in early 1991, not to mention similar proposals in 1990 and 1989.

But that's all we did. We proposed, while Senate Majority Leader George Mitchell and other congressional Democrats disposed. They said no, and we politely walked away from the battlefield. The word was getting around Washington: Nobody would pay a price, political or otherwise, for blocking George Bush.

By contrast, Governor Clinton's speech drew essential connections between the triumph of Yeltsin in Russia, the freedom of the Baltic states, the collapse of Communism, and the need to ensure the vitality of our own economic and political structures at home. His themes, if not his very words, were precisely the points I'd been trying to get into Bush's rhetoric for months:

> We should be celebrating. All around the world the American Dream— political freedom, market economics, national independence—is ascendant. Everything your parents and grandparents stood for from World War II on has been rewarded.

Clinton then called for

> . . . a New Covenant that will challenge all our citizens to be responsible. The New Covenant will say to our corporate leaders at the top of the ladder: We'll promote economic growth and the free market, but we're not going to help you diminish the middle class and weaken the economy. We'll support your efforts to increase profits and jobs through quality products and services, but we're going to hold you responsible to be good corporate citizens too.

And then, in a line that could have come straight from Ronald Reagan or Jack Kemp, Clinton used the "e" word so hated by Sununu and Darman: "I want to make government more efficient and more effective by eliminating unnecessary layers of bureaucracy and cutting administrative costs, and by giving people more choices in the services they get, and *empowering* them to make those choices."

Clinton also emphasized reinvigorating volunteer and other participatory institutions, a notion not at all dissimilar to George Bush's own "Points of Light" theme. As Clinton put it: "We want to be part of a nation that's coming together, not coming apart. We want to be part of a community where people look out for each other, not just for themselves."

That same day, the *Wall Street Journal* ran a front-page story about the precious little time George Bush actually devoted to domestic, as distinguished from foreign, policy. Michel McQueen and John Harwood had conducted interviews with some two dozen White House aides and had reviewed the President's public calendars and schedules to describe "a president who rarely misses a chance to dabble in international matters, but who rarely seizes a chance to take the initiative on domestic policy."[3]

In recent weeks the President had instituted a series of morning "domestic policy briefings," usually held shortly after nine, with Darman, Porter, Boskin, and Sununu. It was evident to the staff, however, that those sessions were cosmetic, orchestrated principally to create the impression that the President really cared about domestic issues. The decision to undertake these sessions was obviously provoked by outside criticism. It was characteristically and quintessentially reactive.

Little ever came from those sessions. They appeared to be essentially *ad hoc*, with Porter taking to the meetings whatever issues of the day his staff had suggested to him either the night before or earlier that same morning at our own OPD staff meetings. On one occasion, borrowing a page from Reagan's second Chief of Staff, Don Regan, Porter even solicited jokes from us to take to the meetings and share with the President. (We didn't have any for him.) As far as we could tell, no coordinated strategy, by way of shaping a sustained and coherent domestic policy agenda, ever came out of the sessions.

Unfortunately, the strong impression created over time was that George Bush governed the way he golfed. The point was to get through the day with maximum speed: start early, engage in a lot of frenetic activity, fill up the appointments calendar, but basically do so with relatively little purpose or direction. From all of his endless activity, the public apparently was supposed to decipher what mattered and what didn't.

Let the American people figure out what we were all about, that was our attitude. For that matter, why not let our own political appointees do the same? With the election now staring us in the face, such an attitude was the height of hubris. We in the West Wing were reluctant salesmen who, having convinced ourselves, saw no need to convince others. We also had no fundamental idea of the product we were selling.

No wonder there was confusion among rank-and-file Republicans as to what Bush ultimately stood for. That confusion escalated to near panic on November 6, the day after the incumbent Senator Harris Wofford of Pennsylvania (appointed by Governor Casey to fill the seat of Republican John Heinz, who died earlier that summer in a tragic plane–helicopter crash) trounced the former Bush Attorney General, Dick Thornburgh. Thornburgh managed to win just 44 percent of the vote, a figure virtually equal to the lead he had held over Wofford just three months before the special election.

It was, at last, wake-up time at 1600 Pennsylvania Avenue.

Or was it?

As Chairman *pro tem* of Bush's Domestic Policy Council, Thornburgh had been a surrogate for the President himself. Democrats maneuvered successfully to portray the Thornburgh–Wofford race as a referendum on Bush's domestic agenda and a dry run for the 1992 presidential campaign. The Democrats were test-marketing the themes they hoped to use the following November: middle-class fairness, welfare reform, tax *cuts*, health care reform, and, above all else, change. They were even trying out two seasoned but otherwise nationally unknown campaign advisers, Paul Begala and a wily Louisianan, James Carville.

True to form, Thornburgh's approach to his campaign was like the Bush Administration's attitude toward health care: hunker down, avoid controversy, run out the clock, say as little as possible, and coast to the finish on your massive lead. If Bush could do it and retain a high approval rating, then so could Thornburgh, who had amassed a commanding lead in the polls that summer.

The problem was that Thornburgh had nothing to say to the voters, except that he was a clubby member of Washington's power elite. While Thornburgh may have known his way around the capital's "corridors of power," as he put it, he failed to advance an agenda that real people cared about.

After Thornburgh's loss, recriminations flew all over the White House. Some blamed the messenger—Thornburgh lacked charisma and was a lousy candidate. Others began to realize that you can't run an effective campaign when you have nothing to talk about but process. Bill Bennett correctly warned Republicans after the Thornburgh loss that you can't expect to win an election simply by just "showing up." Republicans had to stand for something.

That advice was not uniformly welcomed, because it suggested that something might be amiss. It prompted others to emphasize the races where Republicans had not only won but had done so handily: Mississippi, where the GOP upset the incumbent Democratic Governor Ray Mabus, and New Jersey, where both houses of the state's legislature shifted to the GOP in a crushing reaction against Democratic Governor Jim Florio's tax hikes and income redistribution schemes to finance equalized educational expenditures across the state. But those were sideshows. The real spotlight was on Pennsylvania's early referendum on George Bush, and anyone who thought otherwise was just kidding himself.

The White House Director of Political Affairs, Deputy Assistant to the President Ron Kaufman, was one of those who tried to find a positive message. An amiable and exceedingly capable political operative who was also Deputy Chief of Staff Andy Card's brother-in-law, Kaufman saw the 1991 election results more favorably. "This was the best off-year election for Republicans in years," he explained at a Department of Labor retreat held by Secretary Lynn Martin and her senior presidential appointees at Airlie House, an hour away from Washington in the Virginia countryside. It was the week after the 1991 election, the Veterans Day federal holiday. Kaufman was also a realist. He did not discount or disregard the strong negative message that Pennsylvania voters had sent, but he chose to emphasize the positive implications of the strong GOP finishes in the New Jersey and Virginia legislatures and in the Mississippi gubernatorial contest.

Kaufman acknowledged, however, that the Bush White House had not done a good job in "getting out the message" about what we stood for, and it was clear that now was the time to "repackage" those themes. As he put it, "I promise you, I can assure you that you'll see that message begin to emerge during the next several months as the election campaign begins in full." He went on to say that part of the difficulty thus far had been the absence of a national campaign because the President had not yet formally declared his candidacy for reelection. This comment, of course, made no sense whatever, unless, of course, one subscribed to the view that campaigning and governing were two wholly unrelated activities.

In retrospect, this *was* an important moment. Here was the White House political director innocently announcing what others would turn into the campaign's *modus operandi* for the next eleven months: Don't worry, just wait. More specifically, wait until the President comes roaring back in January with a dynamite State of the Union address.

While Kaufman made it sound as if Republicans were fighting with one arm tied behind their back, he went on to assert that when the presidential campaign began in earnest, "we've got the better people, the better talent, and more resources." He predicted a massive electoral win for the President in 1992 with the pickup of huge numbers of open and other seats in the House, while probably breaking even in the Senate. He pointed to Bush's recent political speeches in Houston and Dallas, where he went to kick off fundraisers for the '92 campaign, as evidence of how emotional Bush could be when he got wound up and began attacking the Congress.

The twenty-five or so senior officials from the Labor Department were not convinced by Kaufman's optimism. Many were even openly skeptical. The problem was that everything Kaufman said about Republican presidential prospects—"better people, better talent, and more resources"—was also true of Thornburgh's race in Pennsylvania.

Most people in the room saw a disjunction between Kaufman's projections about our future effectiveness and the experience we'd already had with our past. The question, framed bluntly, was this: Why, after almost three years in office, have we failed to govern in a way that emphasized what we are for as Bush Republicans? Do we only articulate these themes when running for office and not implement them once we actually hold power?

Our basic problem derived from the fact that so many Bush Republicans, including the President, saw "campaign mode" and "governing mode" as two separate and unrelated activities, two apparently contradictory habits of mind. For too many of the people around the President, the "grasping" was far more entertaining than actually "holding" the prize.

Kaufman predicted that the 1992 campaign would be waged against the Congress, which I found both laughable and likely. Once again we would avoid stating what we stood for and define ourselves totally by reference to the other party. The model Kaufman was alluding to was Harry Truman's 1948 campaign against a "do-nothing" Congress. But we were a "do-nothing" Administration! How could Bush effectively run against the same Congress with which he was, on a daily basis, ready to cut deals to compromise many of the positions that had carried Ronald Reagan through eight years of his successful presidency?

The last two months of 1991 marked the nadir of George Bush's presidency—that is, until his defeat a year later. For starters, he was

reaping the economic political fruits of the budget deal he had negotiated the previous year. And, as the recession both lingered and
deepened, his Administration's unparalleled indecisiveness on virtually everything—health care, unemployment benefits, tax cuts for the
middle class, dealing with the recession, recognition of Croatia and
Slovenia, the trade imbalance with Japan, and the decline of Mikhail
Gorbachev followed by the rise to power of Boris Yeltsin in Russia—
painted a picture of an Administration totally adrift. By the end of
November almost everyone at 1600 Pennsylvania Avenue had just
one thing in mind: Let's hustle the Congress out of town as quickly
as possible. The President would then have nearly a two-month
breather (Congress would return for business in late January 1992)
and could get his act together in time for his State of the Union
address in late January and the release of his fiscal year 1993 budget.

Even this strategy, however, failed to bring unity to Republicans
inside the Administration and on Capitol Hill. Mavericks like Jack
Kemp and House Minority Whip Newt Gingrich urged the President
to call Congress back into session after Thanksgiving and hold their
feet to the fire until they passed Bush's economic growth package to
address the recession. The trouble with this scenario was that Bush
and his advisers had no idea what they wanted. They feared keeping
the Democrats around and providing them with a continuing forum to
beat up on the President. Senior-level White House aides were furious at the House Republicans who were publicly urging the President
to keep Congress in session. Roger Porter referred to their strategy as
an attempt to "shoot themselves in the feet."

Kemp and Gingrich were right. Bush's failure to take prompt action
on the faltering economy left the impression that he didn't care much
about the problem or, if he did, had no idea what to do about it. For
some of his advisers, both characterizations were correct. The "wait-
until-January" mindset was taking hold.

Dick Darman, finding the national whining over the recession
laughable, did all he could to prevent Bush from taking action before
late January. After all, action on the economy in late November or
December would preempt Darman's big show in early February 1992,
when his budget would be released. He also feared engaging in new
negotiations over his much-loved (by himself) budget deal.

By delaying two more months, Bush made it virtually impossible
for any steps he might take toward bolstering economic growth and

recovery to have a positive impact on his reelection prospects. Given the nature of election-year politics, a late January 1992 announcement of Bush's economic agenda would face an intransigent Democratic Congress unwilling to take steps that might make Bush look good or strengthen his reelection hopes. Should the economy worsen, Congressional Democrats and the party's 1992 presidential candidates could continue to blame everything on excesses from the Reagan–Bush years.

By early December 1991, one other event worked against a timely and preemptive announcement of Bush's economic strategy: the resignation of his Chief of Staff, John Sununu. The arrival of Transportation Secretary Samuel K. Skinner at the White House on December 16 would mean several more weeks spent trying to hammer out not only a campaign organization that would now be seriously tested against the Pat Buchanan challenge in New Hampshire but also a White House staff organization that would deal with the twin problems of a failed communications strategy and an overly timid and inert domestic agenda. Unfortunately, as 1992 arrived, the principal focus was on the former. Bush's policies were deemed sound; his message was failing to get out to the media and the American people, that's all.

The President's long-awaited State of the Union address on January 28, 1992, was billed as the speech of all speeches. It would have to be: By delaying action on the economy for almost ninety days, the President had allowed expectations to rise to an almost unattainable level. Not only that, but the speech, as the first major public product of the new West Wing under Skinner, was expected to set the stage for the coming year's reelection campaign. The address was bound to be a letdown.

And it was. While many of the policy proposals were sound—the ninety-day regulatory moratorium, repealing the luxury tax on boats and planes, tax credits for first-time homebuyers, targeted investment incentives, accelerated federal spending, reducing the capital gains tax—they did not add up to a credible package. The President who just a year earlier had acquiesced in a tax *increase* was now urging Congress to reduce taxes on middle-class families. Even the President's unilateral action to reduce the federal withholding tax immediately was written off as a gimmick. Pay it now or pay it later, the tax owed was still the tax owed. Most Americans would not count that as money in the bank.

Politically, it was evident that the Bush economic plan was designed for one thing: to end the economic recession at last and guarantee the President's reelection. Congressional Democrats, accordingly, had every incentive to stall. Most of the blame would stick to the one President, not the 535 members.

Bush outlined his economic growth package and challenged the Congress to pass it . . . by March 20.

Now, where had we heard this before? The mind behind that ultimatum should have asked itself what reason there was to think a Democratic-controlled Congress would act in fewer than sixty days to rescue the economy (and, just coincidentally, George Bush's presidency), when the previous year it had failed to act during the hundred days Bush gave it? Once again, the President had made an idle threat. For the economic growth zealots who, like Kemp, Gingrich, and Vin Weber, had been urging him to act months before, the President's message, in effect, was this: Now that you've waited since last November, let's all wait together until March.

The situation could be described as a George McClellan syndrome in reverse. Abraham Lincoln was prepared to go forth and do battle at the outset of the Civil War, only to find himself stymied by a reluctant general. Bush, on the other hand, had loyal troops and more than a few generals raring to go, but consistently refused to fight. The troops, in the meantime, were beginning to worry as the February primary season arrived and sample polling data indicated that Bush would face a significant challenge from Pat Buchanan in New Hampshire.

A few days after Bush's State of the Union address, on January 31, 1992, an entertaining and revealing episode took place in the White House Mess. Much to everyone's surprise, John H. Sununu, still on the payroll as a "counselor" to Bush with Cabinet rank, accepted an invitation from Richard Porter to attend one of our Friday morning "Reform Breakfasts." After months of sending signals that he didn't like the term "empowerment" and frowning on our efforts, Sununu agreed to be our guest exactly one month before leaving the White House to become a consultant and a commentator on CNN's "Crossfire."

He had dropped a few pounds, but otherwise Sununu had not changed much in the six weeks since being replaced by Skinner. Sununu began his breakfast discussion with a sermon of sorts on the theory behind the Bush Administration's domestic agenda. The theory, it turned out, really was to have no domestic agenda. To put it differently, the agenda was a nonagenda. The nation didn't really need to have much done for it, at any rate not in Washington.

Sununu singled out the 1989 Charlottesville Education Summit with the nation's governors as a potent signal to the country that solutions to its ills did not begin or end in Washington. The states and localities—particularly in education, but in other areas as well—should become accustomed to playing a more central role in addressing those problems.

The speaker went on to explain (ever the engineer!) how one of the most unfortunate modern scientific developments was the invention of air conditioning. Before the air conditioner arrived in Washington, Congress used to leave town for the summer, which meant that elected representatives could do less damage to the body politic and at the same time were forced to spend more time back home among their constituents. Today, Congress was in session virtually year round, and members went to considerable lengths to avoid returning to their districts.

Sununu's intense dislike for the Congress was hardly news for those of us sitting around the table in the Mess. What was surprising was how his antipathy extended to our supposed Republican allies, especially those conservative Republicans, including HUD Secretary Jack Kemp, who opposed the 1990 budget deal. By Sununu's reckoning, those Republicans were irresponsible. They failed to grasp the essential difference between what you had to do in governing the nation and what he termed "bumper sticker conservatism," which went no further than mere sloganeering.

As an example of "bumper sticker conservatism," Sununu pointed to the inability of people like Gingrich and Kemp to understand the politics of the capital gains tax, which they continued to advocate like robots, ignoring the fact that a tax credit—which Sununu argued *could* have been achieved with their support—was a much more effective and feasible economic approach.

At that point a note of low comedy was introduced. Sununu began to calculate by way of illustration just how a tax credit, as distinguished from a capital gains tax cut, would work. He invited the listeners to consider how a $50 profit from the sale of a capital good would be treated under both approaches. In the process he managed to demonstrate an inability to calculate in his head a relatively simple number. Working his way through his own example, Sununu got gummed up in his own arithmetic, which prompted a colleague to observe after the breakfast: "Wasn't it just amazing that this supposed member of Mensa [the select club for supposed geniuses] couldn't figure in his head twenty percent of fifty?"

When Sununu had concluded his opening remarks, I asked him to comment on a series of stories in the media speculating over whether the Bush Administration's main problem was its policies or its communications process.

"Governor," I asked, "some people in the media say our problem is with our domestic policies; still others say it's our failure to communicate adequately with the public. What do you think? Is it one of those? Both? Neither?"

To the amazement of just about everyone around the table, Sununu's answer was "neither." He proceeded to explain that our policies were sound and that we'd made a significant effort to inform the American people about them. The problem was that people didn't understand. It was a remarkable display of denial. To listen to Sununu, the nation's affairs were in wonderful shape. Either people were too dumb to absorb that fact or, like Newt Gingrich and Jack Kemp, they were unable to free themselves from the simple-minded sloganeering of "bumper sticker conservatism."

Richard Porter asked Sununu what he thought had happened to his reputation among conservatives since his arrival in Washington in January 1989. After all, Sununu had once been the darling of the conservatives, the keeper of the true faith in an Administration that without him might lapse into a terminal pragmatism of trilateralists. What had happened? How had it come to pass that Sununu was now so vilified by everyone?

Once again, Sununu wasn't the problem. His answer elaborated on the "you don't get it" theme, reinforced with the "bumper sticker mentality" comment. Conservatives like Kemp and Gingrich failed to appreciate the subtleties associated with governing. Campaigning for office, actually holding office, and—even more important, Sununu noted—actually accomplishing something required more than rigid adherence to a few litmus-test propositions. Running the federal behemoth meant that you couldn't fall on your sword every time a critical political issue surfaced. Occasionally you had to negotiate with the enemy to accomplish something that was headed in the direction in which conservatives wanted to go. (I thought to myself: "Okay.

Now I get it. Like the budget deal that raised taxes, increased spending, didn't touch entitlements, and crippled the President?")

Sununu's one-hour performance at breakfast that morning summarized his often stormy tenure as Chief of Staff. After starting off with a strong statement of conservative themes and principles, it degenerated into what all of us had come to expect: open contempt for Congress, name-calling, bullying, and boorish behavior calculated more to prove his own brilliance and toughness than to advance genuine intellectual discussion and understanding of the issues.

One of the more entertaining moments came when Sununu and Todd Buchholz, a clever and witty lawyer-economist who was a member of the Economic Policy Council staff and author of the well-received book *New Ideas from Dead Economists*, bantered over economic policy. A fairly interesting debate over Bush's economic policy had barely gotten under way when, in response to some dissenting opinion from Buchholz, Sununu exploded: "That's horseshit!" With diplomacy like that, it was no wonder Sununu had alienated more than half the Cabinet, substantial numbers of our Republican allies in Congress, and most of the White House staff. Not only had he outlived his usefulness to Bush, but it was now clear he had been temperamentally unfit for the job in the first place. Buchholz later remarked: "Sununu and Darman considered themselves Jupiter and Saturn while treating the rest of us as Uranus."

The following Monday morning, February 3, 1992, I had breakfast in the Executive Mess. When I walked in, Sam Skinner was dining alone at the round open staff table. He was soon joined by his new deputy, former Representative and Energy Department Deputy Secretary Henson Moore. Skinner welcomed Moore on his first day at the White House. Then he turned to me and said, "Charlie, you've been here for a while. Why don't you give Henson some sense of how things are being perceived around here, particularly among the midlevel and junior-level staff."

There are two significant things to note about that exchange with Skinner. First, here was the White House Chief of Staff sitting at the staff table having breakfast in his shirtsleeves at 7 A.M. In my nearly two years at the White House, I had *never* seen Sununu dining at the open staff table. Second, Skinner seemed genuinely interested in hearing what others thought, in seeking their appraisal of how things were going since his arrival there in mid-December.

So I told Skinner and Moore that the mood among the staff was uncertain. People were frankly worried about their futures, but otherwise there was a sense that things were possibly starting to turn around, because there was a recognition that what we'd tried in the past was not working—George Bush was still faltering in the public's eye. Then I shared with them the episode from the previous Friday, when Sununu concluded that our problems included neither policy nor communications. There was a brief moment of silence as Skinner and Moore looked at each other in disbelief. Then Skinner said, "That's why we've got problems!"

Sam Skinner's arrival at the White House was intended to fix those problems. It didn't. That's understandable, because the problems weren't essentially in personnel, although it soon became evident that many of our problems could be traced to the impact of one particular personnel choice.

Skinner had asked his friend Gene Croisant, a personnel consultant from RJR Nabisco, to undertake an intensive two-month study of what was wrong with the Bush White House. Croisant discerned that our difficulties were twofold: policy *and* communications. Croisant became well versed in the dysfunctional aspects of the Bush White House. He knew that Roger Porter bottled up his own staff and himself, and that virtually every office was dominated by OMB and Darman.

A prudent manager would have moved promptly to eliminate those difficulties by means of a radical, perhaps even painful, restructuring of the White House staff. Instead, Skinner moved very slowly, in part because his own arrival came at perhaps the worst possible time for a full shakeup. Not only did Skinner face the daunting task of preparing an election-year State of the Union address and a budget for a floundering president, but he also had to resolve the policy debate over the Administration's health care plan and oversee the startup of the Bush–Quayle 1992 reelection campaign. Even if Skinner had wanted to clean house, the practical question of who would then get the work done militated against any fundamental reforms in process or personnel.

With one notable exception. Dick Darman.

There is no doubt in my mind that Skinner had Darman's number and wanted him gone. In fact, I was told that Skinner had planned to name Republican National Committee Chairman Clayton Yeutter as the new OMB Director but found his way blocked. George Bush would not dump Darman. Skinner's fatal first mistake had been to accept the job without assurance that he had carte blanche to remove or reassign anyone inside the White House complex.

Skinner had been warned about Darman. One friend, an alumnus of the Nixon, Ford, and Reagan White House staffs, went directly to a Skinner aide and told him bluntly: "You guys are gonna have to watch your backs as long as Darman's around. At first he'll be sugary sweet, but the moment you aren't watching, he'll drive in the knife."

Croisant also led me to believe that he was keenly aware of the problems created for Bush by Darman's dominance within the White House complex. At one point during my second interview with him I made an offhand reference to the way in which budgets in the Administration tended to drive the policymaking process. He immediately cut me off, politely but firmly: "No, policy should always drive the budget." I took this as at least a hint that Darman's influence would be on the wane.

I was wrong. The much ballyhooed management review only resulted in a layering of the White House staff. No one was fired, a few were reassigned, and Darman was only briefly cauterized. Unfortunately for Skinner—an honest, decent man who tried extremely hard—the whole endeavor came to represent weakness and indecisiveness, an impression that clung to the former Transportation Secretary throughout his White House tenure.

Skinner's changes only made the entire operation more cumbersome. Resolution of virtually every issue became harder to achieve. After repeated unsuccessful efforts to recruit an outside communications czar, Skinner turned to Marlin Fitzwater, the veteran press spokesman, and enhanced his coordinating role over the disparate and diffuse White House communications operation, which by then included Dorrance Smith (the award-winning former executive producer of ABC's *Nightline*, who served as director of media relations and worked with outside-the-Beltway media), David Demarest (nominally Director of Communications, which had included the Public Liaison outreach office), and Fitzwater's own press office, which handled the daily relations with the White House press corps and the national media. The only structural change Skinner effected was to reduce Demarest's role by limiting him to supervising the speechwriters and, in February 1992, bringing on board Sherrie Rollins, wife of the Bush critic Ed Rollins, to head the consolidated Public Liaison and Intergovernmental Affairs operations. Instead of streamlining the communications operation, Skinner actually increased the number of players whose views would have to be considered, making it even more likely that the White House would not speak with one voice. In view of the critical importance of ensuring smooth and synchronous communications between the White House and the nascent Bush campaign, this management structure for communications proved a disaster.

Skinner took a similar tack when it came to domestic policy, although his paramount goal here was to name a domestic policy czar who could serve as an effective counterweight to Darman. What he *should* have done was demand permission from Bush to fire Darman, which would have taken the wind out of Pat Buchanan's sails long before the *Crossfire* commentator could embarrass Bush in the New Hampshire primary. While Darman's loss would have minimally complicated completion of the fiscal 1993 budget and the Administration's health care reform proposal, keeping him around only heightened resentment among conservatives. His notorious stealth in preparing the budget, moreover, came close to causing yet another firestorm of criticism—once again over raising taxes—that could have seriously wounded the Bush presidency going into a highly charged election contest.

The January 1992 budget message was intended to unveil the details of the President's long-awaited health care reforms. Darman had crafted the message by himself, without bothering to share it with anyone. Representative Bill Gradison somehow learned that the President's plan strongly resembled the Heritage Foundation's proposed approach of tax credits (or health vouchers) combined with a so-called tax cap, which had the effect of taxing the value of employer-provided health benefits. Gradison went directly to Bush and sounded the alarm. The policy was actually sound. Darman, however, lacked the political sense and the bargaining skills to frame or time the policy appropriately. He hadn't consulted with our Republican allies in Congress. Republicans had been taking the heat for having raised taxes to the tune of $175 billion in the 1990 budget deal, and now Bush was on the verge of doing it again, this time indirectly through the "tax cap" on health benefits. The budget had gone to the printers when Skinner halted publication and ordered Darman to destroy several thousand printed copies and rewrite the introduction, omitting the tax cap and any details as to how the Administration would propose paying for its suggested changes.

It is simply inconceivable that Darman had gotten so far on his own with a major policy proposal without anyone else in the Bush White House sounding the alarm. A senior Bush adviser outside the White House, who had been counseling concerned GOP members of Congress on health policy and who was instrumental in helping avert Bush's near disaster, commented that Darman had been allowed to develop his ideas solo, with no input or second-guessing from elsewhere in the White House complex. No one had known what Darman was up to, and when the Bush adviser blew the whistle about Darman's plan to Bob Teeter, the Bush–Quayle campaign chairman and pollster, he looked the other way. Had Gradison not gone directly to Bush, which resulted in Skinner's stopping the presses, Bush would have found himself having to defend yet another Darman-inspired tax increase on middle- and upper-income Americans less than a month before the New Hampshire presidential primary.

In December 1991 several Congressional Republicans had also written to Skinner urging that the President appoint a domestic czar who could bring a sense of purpose and coherence to the domestic policymaking process in the White House. Skinner did just that on January 31, 1992. Although unwilling to name him as Darman's replacement, Bush announced that Clayton Yeutter would be designated Counselor to the President for Domestic Policy. In Yeutter's place at the RNC, Bush would finally appoint a trusted and capable friend, Rich Bond, a consultant, political activist, and Lee Atwater protégé. Yeutter would carry the needed clout and would be a counterweight to Darman at the White House, while freeing the RNC position for someone who—like his mentor and friend, the late Lee Atwater—would bring a street-fighter's skills and smarts to the party during the coming election.

Naming Yeutter as Bush's domestic policy czar raised a question: What would happen to Roger Porter? Although Yeutter's arrival at the White House could easily have meant my own departure or reassignment, I was delighted that someone would be coming on board who could give direction to a policy development process that had languished.

The handwriting was on the wall for Porter, who was being layered in terms of his access to the President and with respect to his policymaking role. Yeutter was scheduled to report for duty on Tuesday, February 18, 1992, the day of the New Hampshire primary.

On the Thursday before Yeutter's arrival, Porter broke his silence to comment on the new appointment. At the daily OPD staff meeting he announced that, to the best of his knowledge, Yeutter's arrival would have relatively little effect on our office and staff. That was more dismaying than reassuring. Porter would remain in his current position and would keep his title, including that of Director of the Office of Policy Development. (Titles, after all, mattered very much to him. The longer, the better.) Nothing in life—or at the White House—was ever certain, of course, but Porter told us he thought we could probably sleep more comfortably at night. OPD would remain intact.

But some things *were* changing with Yeutter's advent. Most noticeably, Porter had to vacate his corner West Wing office and move 50 feet down the hall. Yeutter wanted to make a point by displacing Roger Porter.

On his second day in the White House, the day after the disastrous New Hampshire primary, in which Pat Buchanan racked up some 37 percent of the vote against Bush, Yeutter called a staff meeting in his new (Porter's old) office.

Yeutter sat at the head of the conference table, where Porter used to preside. Porter sat to his left. Pinkerton was no longer there, having joined the Bush–Quayle campaign some eight weeks before. The rest of the staff filled up the conference table and the adjacent sofa. Yeutter began the meeting by asking "Rog" to introduce each of the staff members and to say a little about the areas in which they specialized. After going around the table, Porter explained to Yeutter how well-received the OPD work product was and, to make his point, distributed the most recent White House fact sheet, released the day before, on the Administration's research and development policies.

When Porter had finished his introductions and had proudly handed Yeutter a copy of the four-page fact sheet, Yeutter began his remarks. The contrast with Porter's preoccupation with trivia could not have been more apparent. First off, Yeutter welcomed everyone and let us all know explicitly that we worked for him, which presumably meant Porter as well. Touching upon the general significance of the

New Hampshire results, he said that Bush, after all, had won and won handily. At the same time, he acknowledged that all was not well with the Administration and the President's reelection effort. Conservatives perceived us as having lost our way, and the American public by and large had no idea what we stood for. We needed to identify a handful of governing themes à la Ronald Reagan, hone them, and then use them to guide our policy initiatives. Reagan had placed emphasis on lower taxes, less government, and more defense. Bush needed to do the same thing, to be more like Reagan. Yeutter then invited each of us to submit to him a two-page memorandum describing the Reagan-type themes to be emphasized during the coming months. In other words, we were to figure out what the Bush Administration stood for.

We were delighted. At last, we thought, we had an opportunity to get through the blockade Porter had erected between the OPD staff and the Oval Office.

I decided to make my memo candid. I did not explicitly call for Bush to fire Darman, but I advised Yeutter that the President "should repudiate the budget deal (or at least stop talking about it)." The budget deal

> . . . sticks in people's craws, enrages conservatives, and, frankly, hasn't worked. Let the Democrats brag about it. (Very few do these days.) Even the much-noted spending caps won't put a positive spin on the matter: after all, a critic could say that we bought and paid for those caps by swallowing the largest baseline increases in domestic discretionary spending in more than a decade (and then added annual inflation-based increases to that base). And with all that, Senator Byrd continues to call for more spending.

We also needed to "draw a line in the sand on taxes and spending" as a way of reestablishing the antitax, anti-big-government base that bonded and sustained the GOP since 1978. Frankly, it didn't even matter any more whether Bush could do so and sustain a veto. We were losing our base and needed to move rapidly to solidify it. Finally, we needed to find a way to rekindle the natural optimism of the American people. One way to start was to dispel the notion that Reagan–Bush policies had benefited only the wealthy. They hadn't, and we were now paying the price for having left unchallenged for more than a year the Kevin Phillips view of America.

I urged Yeutter to press for domestic themes that would also have an echo in our foreign policy, themes based upon our central principles of efficient government at the service of individual liberty. We had learned from the newly emerging democracies that individual freedom works. Those countries looked to America as a model for free political institutions that respond to the popular will, to market-driven economic organization, and to a social structure that respects and nurtures families, churches, and civic life. This powerful message should remind Americans that what we have been doing all these years has worked, that we should continue in that direction (in part by minimizing and streamlining government), and that we should seek ways to reform and restructure to meet new challenges.

The concluding paragraph of my first memo to Yeutter offered the following recommendation:

> Just as the world has changed in the last four years, so America has changed. We face new challenges calling for fresh, creative approaches at home and abroad. In the latest issue of *Foreign Affairs*, David Gergen warns of America's missed opportunities at home and abroad. A new book by Clinton adviser David Osborne and Ted Gaebler is entitled *Reinventing Government* and calls for an American "perestroika" which will transform the public sector through introducing an entrepreneurial spirit. This message and these themes are ours for the taking if we are able to see the world with new eyes.

But we weren't, as it later turned out.

My advice to Yeutter harked back to the simplicity of Ronald Reagan's presidency, which from start to finish was embodied in six words: lower taxes, less government, strong defense. The Reagan appointees knew those themes by heart and—broad though they may have been—relied upon them to animate and direct day-to-day policy implementation within the Administration.

George Bush's difficulties stemmed from a perception by the public (and many in the conservative GOP base) that he had reversed course on the first two Reagan themes. He had repudiated his "read my lips" pledge and had permitted government spending and regulation to increase, with depressing effects on the economy. Those steps had impaired Bush's credibility. People no longer knew what he stood for or what he would do with four more years in the White House. As for defense, the world had changed in ways that permitted—indeed, some would say, dictated—altering the country's national defense priorities. Reagan's "strong defense" theme could now be modified, precisely because the Reagan–Bush policies *worked*. The GOP could bask in the credit while moving promptly to establish new Bush–Quayle priorities for our future security.

The following week Yeutter called me into his office. In the middle of a discussion on other substantive issues, he generously thanked and complimented me for the memorandum. He was refreshingly encouraging about the Administration's future ability to speak with clarity and vigor when it came to laying out an agenda. I was pleased that Yeutter was at least listening. Our new domestic policy czar seemed to welcome frank advice on the Administration's "big picture."

My optimism collapsed, however, when Yeutter told us a little later that "jobs, family, peace" were to be the marching orders, apparently the handiwork of Deputy Chief of Staff Henson Moore. That framework made no sense. It was political pablum. Who in the country could disagree with "jobs, family, peace"? They were just nouns. No action was implied. How, exactly, were we going to go about securing "jobs, family, peace"? Many of us in the White House wanted to know. So did the American people.

For some time I had been urging Yeutter, Skinner, and others throughout the White House complex to read a new book on politics by the Scripps-Howard reporter Peter Brown, *Minority Party: Why the Democrats Face Defeat in 1992 and Beyond*. The title sounded like good news for Republicans, but actually it wasn't. Brown had analyzed in concise and focused detail why the Democrats kept losing presidential elections. His assessment provided the Democrats—if they chose to follow his script—with a roadmap of what they needed to do to win. His strategy had already been ratified, in fact, by the success of Paul Begala and James Carville in running Harris Wofford's Senate campaign in Pennsylvania. Brown's expectation, however, was that the Democrats wouldn't heed his advice.

In a March 2 memorandum to Clayton Yeutter headed "Presidential Leadership After March 20, 1992," I presented the following conclusion:

As Peter Brown writes in *Minority Party*, "With the exception of environmental awareness, virtually every major change in American politics [over the last 25 years] has been Republican—tax cuts, less government spending, a more traditional approach to social issues, or a stronger defense. The only Democratic initiatives have been targeted to the poor and minorities." (Page 322) This message of change becomes more difficult to sustain with each new day of incumbency. And yet, given the challenges we face at home and abroad, it is essential that we not become wedded to the status quo. A solid "damn right" agenda will reinvigorate our natural supporters and define our differences with the Democrats.

It would have been so easy to develop this message early in 1992, but there was no interest in the Bush White House. All Bush had to do was lay out for the public not only what he opposed (taxes, spending, government regulation) but also what he favored, versus what the Democrats favored:

I'm for	*They're for*
1. education reform	1. more $$ for the status quo
2. childcare credits	2. government-run day care
3. family values	3. political correctness
4. safe streets	4. endless due process
5. banking reform	5. a 1930s-era system
6. capital gains cuts	6. taxing everything in sight
7. energy reform	7. command-and-control policies
8. legal reform	8. more lawsuits
9. welfare reform	9. welfare dependency
10. regulatory reform	10. more regulations
11. health care reform	11. play-or-pay, top-down, anti-market solutions, socialism
12. term limits	12. sinecures that preserve incumbency
13. PAC reform	13. $$ for votes

The American people would have had a clear-cut choice between two widely varying menus. The President could have highlighted the differences further by explaining that, after all, the party in charge of the Congress for almost half a century has been *theirs*, not *ours*. The

Democrats in Congress were trying to saddle George Bush with the failure of their model for governing America. Bill Clinton clearly understood this. (Tom Harkin, incidentally, did not). In Clinton's case, though, until he won the Democratic party's nomination he could not totally forsake the typical left-leaning Democratic special interests, which explained his leftward tilt on school choice (favoring only public school choice to secure the endorsement of the National Education Association) and welfare reform (backpedaling by saying he'd oppose New Jersey's innovative welfare reform plan). Once nominated, however (I wrote to Yeutter on March 11), "Clinton's exclusive target will be George Bush. If we haven't captured the high ground of reform by then, our belated efforts will ring hollow and sound like 'me too.' "

What we ultimately did capture and hold aloft with consummate pride was the high ground of process. We were running the White House like a seminar at Harvard's Kennedy School of Government.

Before the end of February Skinner had completed his final White House staff reorganization. On February 24, 1992, Bush signed a memorandum announcing the creation of the Policy Coordinating Group to "facilitate the coordination of domestic policy." Bush named Yeutter the PCG's Chairman *pro tempore*.

Yeutter wasted no time in making the new configuration operational. When the Cabinet meeting adjourned the morning the PCG was announced, Yeutter convened a meeting with the Office of Policy Development staff to explain the structure and the resultant new assignments. While OPD would remain intact, some of its functions and reporting relationships would be slightly different. French Hill, a former Treasury aide who served as Executive Secretary to the now defunct Economic Policy Council, would handle the Executive Secretariat functions of the new PCG and its working group on domestic economic policy (chaired by Treasury Secretary Brady). Hill and Porter would also work together in staffing the new deputies committee, and Hill would assume the economic policy responsibilities on the OPD staff formerly handled by economist Larry Lindsey, now a Federal Reserve Board Governor.

Under the new structure, Yeutter intended to confine Porter to "administration," but Porter continued to behave as if Yeutter's arrival had changed nothing. Instead of expediting decisions, Porter still managed to bottle up the work being produced by OPD. Yeutter found Porter hopeless to deal with and referred to him as the "sink."

Health care expert Gail Wilensky (brought on in February to replace Pinkerton) found Porter so fatuous that almost from the beginning of her White House days she categorically refused to attend his staff meetings. She would attend an OPD staff meeting with Porter in the room only if Yeutter chaired the meeting.

The final White House restructuring came at a critical period during the early primary season. Pat Buchanan was bashing Bush openly and relentlessly for his retreat from Reaganism, but actually that was working to Bush's advantage. Had Buchanan's insurgency not developed and expanded beyond the New Hampshire primary, the Bush White House most probably would have dismissed its impressive New Hampshire showing as a fluke and resumed its dreamlike slumber until the August 1992 convention. Buchanan woke us up—at least momentarily—and started to get us focused on what was needed to revive and revitalize the Republican conservative base.

The immediate reaction to Buchanan's perceived threat was to return to the verities of Ronald Reagan's two successful terms: lower taxes, less government, and strong family values. Of course, it was hard to tell just how much of this discovery of Reaganism was due to a change of heart and how much to the growing political problems Bush faced from the insurgent Buchanan campaign.

On Yeutter's first day at work, Buchanan racked up 37 percent of the vote against Bush in New Hampshire. The White House senior staff expressed concern about the President's poor showing but did little. Their cockiness lasted until the Buchanan "protest" phenomenon began to show up in other primaries around the country. Some 30 to 35 percent of Republican voters were now sending Bush a message the White House could not ignore: They were fundamentally displeased with the direction of his presidency and the result of his policies after three years in office. This vote did not necessarily translate into a vote *for* Buchanan. The commentator's presence on the ballot seemed to account for only six to seven extra points, as evidenced by the South Dakota primary, where "uncommitted" received some 30 percent of the vote, with only Bush's name on the ballot.

The disheartening trend continued. On March 3, 1992, I sent Yeutter a memorandum entitled "Some Thoughts on the Anti-Bush Vote." My point was, I thought, obvious: The New Hampshire and South Dakota primaries suggested that nearly a third of GOP voters wanted to send the President a message. They were not voting *for* Buchanan so much as protesting Bush's apostasy on two issues: his position on taxes and spending, and the perception that he again caved in to the Democrats on affirmative action and quotas. I told Yeutter that the protest vote would substantially diminish if the President were to repudiate the budget deal and stake out a positive position opposing taxes while calling for spending restraints and reductions that would return Republican stalwarts to the fiscal policies that had sustained the Reagan coalition since 1978.

The President needed also to develop a new "defining" or "wedge" issue that would resonate with the same people who were upset about affirmative action and quotas. This was not a suggestion to play the "race card" but rather a proposal to identify the President with a limited set of values issues that would rejuvenate the faithful who were appalled at his signing of the 1991 Civil Rights Act. I suggested welfare reform, personal responsibility, and safe schools and communities as issues to be stressed:

> Buchanan's message emphasizes the fallout from the budget deal and reiterates various fundamental values, but it then turns wholly negative in the areas of trade, immigration, and foreign policy (all of which are strong suits for George Bush). For these reasons, Buchanan's message by itself will not wear well over time. The President can win back the protest vote relatively easily by plucking from his side—sooner rather than later—the various thorns that are causing some of his natural supporters to limp along rather than sprint with him to nomination and reelection. The sooner we get the issues of taxes and spending corrected and begin to emphasize tough-minded pro-family and personal-responsibility values, the sooner we will offer those protest voters a real reason for returning to the fold.

The most important "damn right" move would be for George Bush to repudiate the budget deal. On March 3 Bush in fact did precisely that by concluding publicly that the deal "probably wasn't worth it." The language was graceless, and the reference was plainly to the *political* (as distinguished from policy) grief the "no new taxes" flip-flop had caused the President, yet this frank admission was the beginning of our healing the wounds caused by Nick Brady's and Dick Darman's disastrous fiscal and budgetary advice.

By then the self-imposed March 20 deadline was looming, and both the press and the public were beginning to wonder what, if anything,

George Bush would do in the face of congressional inaction. The answer should have surprised no one, because he did in 1992 the same thing he had done the previous year: He gave a speech.

Yeutter had always encouraged candor, so I decided to tell him what I really thought about our new direction. We were running around the White House with a contentless, verbless agenda of "jobs, family, peace," which inspired confidence and commitment in no one. The President had just been deeply wounded politically in the New Hampshire primary and was headed for his self-imposed March 20 deadline looking extremely weak. Trying to be both tactful and critical, I sent Yeutter a memorandum on March 11, 1992, entitled "Defining Our Future":

> Our three themes—jobs, family, and peace—are sound. They do, however, have one major difference from the Reagan approach. Reagan's emphasis on low taxes, less government, and more defense had an ideological cutting edge which our three themes lack. Some people actually favored *more* government, *higher* taxes, and *less* defense. Some still do. The last decade has proven their judgments profoundly wrong. One would be hard-pressed to find anyone who disagreed with the importance of jobs, family, and peace. The question is how you get there—the roadmap—and we might want to consider sharpening this message in ways that differentiate our roadmap from the Democrats'.

Cam Findlay, a top Skinner aide with whom I'd shared my thoughts, agreed completely. He wrote back:

> The most important point—that "jobs, family, peace" are things no one, including Dems, would disagree with—is being lost in the course of our message/speech discussions. That point is certainly lost on Henson [Moore].
>
> I believe strongly that Clayton is the best vehicle to sharpen our message, to mix a metaphor, for two reasons: (1) because he is in a position to develop & propose next-term initiatives; and (2) because he understands your point better than any Assistant-to-the-Prez level person around here.
>
> If we use "jobs, family, peace" as no more than a set of baskets to drop 1989–92 accomplishments into, we're dead.

By the early spring of 1992 Americans were by and large feeling unsettled. While the lingering recession was not especially deep, it had been unexpectedly long. Moreover, the collapse of Communism had removed a "certainty" that had been part of our world outlook for half a century. Americans were now unsure of the future; the defense industry was downsizing; white-collar workers were losing their jobs; the future was suddenly looking less bright than the past. This offered George Bush a splendid moment to exercise leadership at home, because the fundamental unease related essentially to the need for a future roadmap. I wrote to Yeutter that

> . . . some people perceive government as ignoring them, being unresponsive, or being corrupt. The House banking and post office scandals are examples of these problems and are reminiscent of the bureaucratic arrogance that brought down the *apparatchiks* in the former Soviet Union. . . . There's a sense of confusion and uncertainty about the future—a troublesome, nagging worry that past certainties (*e.g.*, the "Evil Empire," safe streets and schools, rising living standards, job security) have changed and that the future will be dangerous and uncertain. Rapid technological change, with its corresponding impact on the labor force and the economy, only reinforces this fear. At the same time, the opportunities for leadership in such circumstances are substantial at home and abroad.

What was needed was a President who could first explain what was happening and then present a roadmap for how to deal with all these changes. "Perhaps an emphasis on 'domestic renewal' will help us define more vividly our differences with the Democrats. The President can begin this message by making the political point that our opponents do not want us to succeed. That's understandable; it's what partisan politics is partially about."

The Democrats' partisan politics, of course, were costing lost opportunities for millions of Americans. The best person in the country to explain all that would be the President. Doing so would also serve his own partisan desire to win reelection.

We were now less than two weeks away from the March 20, 1992, deadline that the President had given the Congress to enact his economic growth agenda. By now it looked more than likely that the Congress would ignore the deadline or, perhaps even worse, would pass legislation that tied some of the President's economic proposals to a tax package unacceptable to the White House. Congressional Democrats were taking advantage of the time not only to drag out any action (thereby delaying any stimulative effect until after the November election) but to work and rework the "fairness" issue along the lines of class warfare over who should pay more taxes.

Come March 20, all eyes would be on the President. Was he prepared to take on the Congress?

If the Congress *did* send him an unacceptable economic package he should swiftly veto it, preferably on national television. To do so, however, meant that he had to begin preparing the rationale for that action ahead of time. We needed to line up our congressional allies to help turn the "fairness" issue in our favor. After all, "fairness" had been a loser for both Jimmy Carter and Walter Mondale, but since 1989 Republicans—the White House in particular—had done a terrible job of explaining why Republican policies benefited everyone in the 1980s and would continue to do so in the future. The President needed to explain also that he had done his best when it came to unilateral actions to stimulate the economy through accelerated grants, accelerated transportation spending, and the altered withholding tax. His message would be: We've done our part since January. Congress hasn't.

Based on a suggestion made to me by Martin Anderson, a Hoover Institution economist and former Reagan domestic policy adviser, I also recommended to Yeutter that the President convene a meeting with outside economic advisers to solicit their advice on interim measures the President could take in the face of congressional intransigence. A meeting with people like Milton Friedman, Paul McCracken, George Shultz, Bill Simon, Jim Miller, Murray Weidenbaum, and Beryl Sprinkel, many of whom had been systematically ignored by the Bush White House for almost four years, would send a clear signal that these conservatives and their beliefs were welcome at 1600 Pennsylvania Avenue. (Such a meeting actually took place several months later, on August 13, when it was so late and so private as to have none of the desired effect. Interestingly, Skinner, Brady, Boskin, Yeutter, and Roger Porter attended, but Dick Darman pointedly boycotted the session. During the meeting, Skinner and Brady ardently advocated a national value-added tax as a way to raise money. On the eve of the Houston Convention, two of Bush's senior advisers were *still* advocating tax hikes!)

Above all else, however, the President needed to act. He could not let the March 20 deadline come and go as he had with the previous year's hundred-day challenge to the Congress. He needed to be seen actively engaged in promoting the economic recovery through unilaterally indexing the capital gains tax or invoking the line-item veto and allowing the courts to decide the fine legal question of whether it was constitutional. A *Wall Street Journal* editorial headline advised Bush on February 20, 1992: "Now Do Something."[4]

We also had to find ways to energize our base supporters. It had been a long time, I told Yeutter, since we had pursued compelling initiatives that would prompt people to sit up and say, "Now he's showing them!" In my view, there were several things the President could do to make Congress the issue:

- Continually remind the public of Congress's inability to govern itself (check-kiting, over-the-counter cocaine sales at the House post office, bloated staff, late appropriations bills, franked mail, etc.)
- Support term limits and PAC reforms
- Send legislation to Congress subjecting it to the various rules and regulations from which it has exempted itself but imposed on the rest of the country (this was subsequently done in a *pro forma* way but never emphasized or pushed as a priority)
- Use the recess appointment process to name a new administrator of the Office of Information and Regulatory Affairs to bolster further the impact and seriousness of the regulatory moratorium
- Implement the Supreme Court's *Beck* decision (which restricted the use of labor union dues for political purposes)
- Implement the Labor Department's homeworker regulation immediately (Vice President Bush had called for this in *October 1988* and it still hadn't happened!)
- Propose congressional reforms that would centralize the appropriations process (I'd been urging this reform for months as the necessary prerequisite for making any meaningful headway against entitlement spending.)
- Consider reinstituting the President's rescission authority
- Press for a balanced budget amendment
- Call for a cap on entitlement spending, to be accompanied by the appropriate reconciliation legislation
- Freeze domestic discretionary spending (this would have meant breaching the 1990 budget deal!)

- Continue to highlight welfare reform
- Promulgate a risk-assessment, risk-management Executive Order to deal with high regulatory burdens
- Get tougher on street crime and, in particular, violence in the schools

Adopting some or all of the above proposals would have energized our base and might have convinced Americans once again that we were the party of *change*, that we favored individuals' (versus government's) ability to *choose* for themselves, and that we wanted a limited government that *cares* about empowering people and that works.

Another option Bush had for taking on a recalcitrant Congress was to veto the legislative branch appropriations bill. Mike Horowitz and California Representative Chris Cox urged this tactic on the Bush White House throughout the spring and summer months of 1992. Darman, however, rarely missed an opportunity to avoid confronting the Congress. While Bush had been made aware of this approach (it was contemplated for inclusion in his August 1992 Houston acceptance speech), the idea never materialized.

By March 20 George Bush's overall job approval rating had fallen to 39 percent, and two Democratic presidential contenders, Bill Clinton and Paul Tsongas, scored better in polls than Bush when matched up one-on-one against the incumbent. The public was quickly losing faith in the President. In his January State of the Union speech he had promised a domestic equivalent of his Persian Gulf "line in the sand" if Congress failed to enact his economic growth plan. Would he deliver? If so, what?

March 20 arrived, and the President woke up that morning to a letter in the *Wall Street Journal* signed by nineteen prominent conservatives, most of whom had served in senior positions in the Reagan–Bush Administration.[5] Among the signers were Gary Bauer, Reagan's former domestic adviser; former OMB Director Jim Miller; Dan Oliver, former Chairman of the Federal Trade Commission; and former senior Reagan Justice Department officials Charles Cooper, Ted Olson, and Richard Willard. The letter suggested numerous unilateral actions Bush could take if faced with Congressional intransigence. Among their recommendations were indexing capital gains, establishing a capped regulatory budget, liberalizing capital requirements to ease the credit crunch, and instructing agencies and departments to ignore nonbinding congressional report language that had not been codified into statute. Of course, by the time the letter appeared in print, the language of Bush's speech, scheduled for delivery that afternoon, was already set.

The President delivered his remarks to a crowd of some two hundred Administration officials, including Cabinet members and White House staff, and GOP congressional supporters assembled in the East Room of the White House. After the dramatic buildup to this date since January and the express analogy to the Gulf War, many wondered whether (and some of us even hoped) we would soon find ourselves at war with Congress.

Nope. It was all the same old talk and virtually no blueprint for action. No one should have been surprised, because the principal author of the March 20 speech, Darman's aide Bob Grady, was the same person who had written much of the State of the Union message. The President decried the Congress for its devotion to "PACs, perks, privilege, partisanship, and paralysis" but did little more than outline portions of his existing proposals to reform health care, education, and the legal system, and to promote more international trade. We could concentrate long enough to devise a catchy alliterative phrase, but we couldn't for the life of us follow up on any of it.

As for what he would actually *do* given Congress's nonresponse, why the leader of the Free World (one of Roger Porter's favorite phrases) was going to *propose* to eliminate sixty-eight budget items for a whopping total of $4 billion! Incidentally, approximately $3 billion of that was accounted for by canceling two Seawolf submarines, which Bush had already announced he would eliminate. Those sixty-eight would be the first in a series of proposed "line-item rescissions" that reportedly added up to a potential total of some 1,300.

So, no line item veto. No unilateral indexation of capital gains. No legislation branch appropriations veto. No red meat. No "damn right" anything. Practically nothing that was guaranteed to stir the glands of anyone other than a green-eyeshade OMB budget examiner. But what should we have expected, when once again a key Darman protégé had been put in charge of the text?

Was there any serious follow-up to the March 20 speech, tepid though it was? Not really. The sixty-eight rescissions went to Congress and were never heard of again. To my knowledge, none of the remaining contemplated 1,300 rescissions ever left the Old Executive

Office Building. Bush did send up legislation, drafted by Boyden Gray's office, that subjected the Congress to laws it had imposed on others but from which it had exempted itself. That legislation also went nowhere.

Accompanying the March 20 speech was, as usual, another White House fact sheet. It was called "Major Administration Legislative Initiatives That Have Not Received Favorable Congressional Action." Basically it was a compendium of all our legislative proposals— economic growth, education, crime, energy, banking, health reform, trade, economic opportunity, government reform, and civil justice reform—that had gone nowhere in the Congress, partly for the usual political reason: Congress wasn't going to help out George Bush in an election year. But another reason was our own reluctance to go on the hustings and drive this message home to the American people. Instead we issued fact sheets that nobody cared about.

The President had repeatedly contended that it was wrong to say he lacked a domestic agenda. As he explained it, *our* agenda was different from *their* agenda. That was true, but we never used our agenda offensively, never twisted enough arms, inflicted sufficient political pain, or made our opponents sweat to secure passage of our goals. As a result, members of Congress just ignored the Bush White House. If George Mitchell could block the President on capital gains and still get free weekend rides home to Maine on Air Force One, why act differently? We were able to sustain almost three dozen vetoes before it was all over, but after a while people grow tired of hearing politicians brag about what they didn't accomplish. Our essentially reactive and negative posture was reinforcing the notion that Washington was in "gridlock" and that serious change was needed to get things moving again.

"Jobs, family, peace" never cut it, notwithstanding the President's stilted comment after the March 10, 1992, primary that "the voters of eight States have declared their support for my proposals on behalf of jobs, family, and peace." So we moved on to stressing our "change" program, our agenda for reforming America. Someone in the White House or the campaign coined the phrase "five pillars of reform" to encompass our plans for health, education, legal, welfare, and government reform. Then someone else observed that Islam, too, had "five pillars," so this theme was dropped.

Throughout April the President described himself in several

speeches as an agent of "change" but presented very little of substance or novelty to show what he meant. People could also sense intuitively that he wasn't comfortable with this tack. Even Clayton Yeutter basically admitted to David Broder of the *Washington Post* that Bush was maneuvered into brandishing a "change" agenda because Bill Clinton was beginning to make headway by emphasizing the same themes.[6]

The White House was now seen as bouncing around from one issue or message to another. When the message was "jobs, family, peace," everybody tried to come up with lists—"matrices" they were called—that included everything Bush had proposed or achieved that could be fitted into one or more of those three categories. A similar exercise went on when the message was switched to the five "pillars of reform." Cam Findlay was right: We were "dead" all right, brain dead.

None of those agendas was ever taken seriously inside the White House. They were viewed as part of a search for a theme, a message, a slogan, something—anything—that would carry us through the 1992 campaign. By late spring Americans were beginning to catch on to the game. Too many patterns were becoming evident, but perhaps the most damaging was the inability or unwillingness to follow through on an issue or a message.

Whenever we attempted to make good on an earlier commitment, we did so in ways that failed to move even our own most loyal constituents. Take welfare reform. Here was a potential "wedge" issue, which, if handled adroitly, would have given us the upper hand over Clinton on a commonsense issue like personal responsibility. We could have nailed Clinton for his welfare waffle when he refused to endorse New Jersey Assemblyman Wayne Bryant's welfare reform law, which Governor Florio ultimately signed into law. Instead the President, as he traveled around the country or made speeches in Washington, talked about welfare "waivers."

It was all process, divorced from results. Only a political scientist or a state welfare official could care about "waivers," but still the staff sent Bush out on the road to talk about things that made no sense to ordinary folks. With a little less than three months to go before election day, here was the President out on the hustings, speaking to the conservative American Legislative Exchange Council convention in Colorado Springs with all the passion, vision, and dynamism of a bureaucratic bean counter:

I know everybody at ALEC likes light reading. Now here is a midsession review [prepared by OMB], and in it, it tells exactly and specifically how to get this budget deficit down. It's been sitting up and
languishing in the Congress, who do not want to make the tough
decisions that I have recommended year after year. I urge you all to go
out to your nearest bookstore, hopefully getting it at a discount, and
read this program. You'll be impressed because it is ALEC philosophy.

The disease was incumbentitis. We spent the summer of 1992 still
looking for the cure.

Had it been handled properly, a serious government reform agenda
could have helped the President in the 1992 campaign. It was also the
right thing for him to champion. Our courts were overburdened, and
justice was too often delayed. The executive branch administered
hundreds of programs that didn't work. The Congress seemed incapable of doing much of anything, including governing itself. Why not
have the President seize the high ground and propose meaningful
structural reforms for all three branches?

I sent Roger Porter a memo to this effect. It began with what I
thought was a helpful passage from James Q. Wilson's book, *Bureaucracy:*

> Over many years, government has become entwined in elaborate man-
> agement control systems and the accretion of progressively more de-
> tailed administrative procedures. This development has not produced
> superior management. Instead, it has produced managerial overburden.
> . . . Procedures overwhelm substance.

Wilson, a political scientist, was quoting from a 1983 report from the
National Academy of Public Administration.[7] Reading that paragraph
months later, I realized that it could just as easily have applied to the
Bush White House in 1992.

In late May I came across an article in the London *Times Literary
Supplement* by the prominent neoconservative Irving Kristol. Headed
"America's Mysterious Malaise," the essay presented a compelling
analysis of why America appeared to be in a funk despite having won
the Cold War and having endured a comparatively mild recession.
Referring to "an acute sense of insecurity among our middle classes,"
Kristol explained how America's academia had been gripped by "a
kind of apocalyptic fever" and the media had become filled with all

sorts of "alarmist chatter" about our declining competitiveness and the consequent need for an industrial policy. In fact, the godfather of the neocons noted, the economy wasn't all that bad (our computer and textile industries, and even the stock market, were doing comparatively well). What had happened was that the industrialized democracies had finally achieved their goal of the previous fifty years. With the collapse of Communism, there was the promise of "greater affluence and economic security." Kristol summed up: "getting what you want can turn out to be a disillusioning experience."[8]

According to Kristol, both the United States and Western Europe were suffering from a "revolution of shattered expectations" after having succeeded far beyond our wildest dreams. That didn't mean life was perfect by any means: There were still crime and drugs, a growing underclass, rampant sexual promiscuity, and consequent sexual diseases that far too often proved fatal. Kristol ended his essay with the following observation:

> The centre is not holding. While our politicians, left and right, are pasting band-aids all over that centre, expanding national health insurance or privatizing it or whatever, the citizenry is turning anti-political. The new distinctive feature of our modern democracies is the contempt of this citizenry for their governments and their politicians. They demand more and more of their governments, since they have been taught that this is their democratic duty, but at the same time they expect less and less. Deep down, very deep down, there is a free-floating anxiety that our secular civilization, along with the ideologies that have created it and sustain it, are edging glacier-like to some sort of crisis. Since life imitates art, we can expect some kind of "postmodern" politics, one that distances itself from the very building blocks of modernity—rationalism, secularism, science, technology and representative government. There ought to be little doubt that the story of the twenty-first century will be the story of this crisis.[9]

But in the shorter perspective, the story of 1992 turned out to be the story of H. Ross Perot, not exactly what Kristol meant, but close.

Kristol's insights about what was happening in the country were some of the most perceptive I'd found, and I circulated the piece widely among my "usual suspects." Yeutter and Roger Porter, as well as many on the OPD staff, thought he had struck a nerve. Our goal, in many respects, was to position the President first to explain and then to deal with the forces Kristol had identified, and the most immediate and demanding context for doing so was our preparation for the challenge from the antipolitician Ross Perot. If we couldn't understand collectively what Kristol was trying to say, there was no way we would be able to tap into the sentiments that Perot was awakening across the country.

Aside from being a new face and a nonpolitician, Perot appealed to people because of his basic simplicity. His rhetoric was straightforward, direct, and declarative. It was also positive and forceful, whereas Pat Buchanan's in the primaries had been negative. Perot's bottom line was readily grasped. It wasn't mealy-mouthed: "If you don't like [whatever], then don't vote for me." Bill Bennett had spoken with similar cadences and emphases—and to similar effect—when he was Reagan's Education Secretary and Bush's drug czar.

George Bush had spoken that way once too—in his August 1988 acceptance speech at the New Orleans Convention. But he didn't any more.

Bush's rhetoric was sometimes rambling, lawyerlike, and unpersuasive. It was homogenized almost to the point of being meaningless. The President's words didn't lack content, they lacked passion. (Remember "no net loss of wetlands"?) The columnist Morton Kondracke, in a piece printed on May 28, 1992, included an apt quote from a White House aide: "The nervous-Nellyism around here is not to be believed. . . . Anything that happens that people might pay attention to, they view as a flap. It is distasteful to these people to say anything strong. They think that a declarative sentence is merely an opportunity to make enemies, not to lead."[10]

Perot was gaining followers because people saw him, at the time, as decisive and as displaying leadership. The precise details didn't matter, because at least he claimed to be a leader. I was convinced that people found Perot attractive for many of the same reasons they found Ronald Reagan appealing: an almost earnest cheerfulness, tempered with determination, integrity, and drive.

Perot also made clever use of symbolic statements, a tactic never mastered by our own communications people. Perot never attacked Clinton directly, for example, on the issue of alleged marital infidelity. What he said was more devastating than a frontal assault: "Who can trust a man if his wife can't trust him?" and "I wouldn't have an adulterer in my Cabinet."

Part of Perot's appeal also stemmed from his mastery of the "Cin-

cinnatus phenomenon," the appeal of the citizen-leader who reluctantly walks away from his plow to perform unsought government service. By contrast, George Bush's lengthy resumé of public service was a study in irrelevance, easily dismissed by Perot, particularly when he quipped that he had no personal experience in running up a four-trillion-dollar deficit. Perot understood precisely what Kristol had identified about the country's "mysterious malaise": the growing disdain for professional politicians, the burgeoning support for term limits, and the expected high turnover in the House of Representatives.

We, on the other hand, spent too much time trying to wow people with our mastery of mind-numbing detail. We would point to the number of domestic policy speeches given by the President or the number of new initiatives undertaken, as if quantity proved anything at all. With the new Policy Coordinating Group process up and running, issues weren't getting decided, so instead many White House aides were tasked with preparing lists of initiatives, accomplishments, legislative proposals—you name it. None of this went anywhere, of course, but it chewed up countless thousands of hours of staff time.

Meanwhile, Perot was out on the hustings whipping up the faithful with his own "damn right" appeal. Our supporters, for the most part, were wandering around shaking their heads and muttering, "Damn shame."

In early June I was repeating to Clayton Yeutter what I had already written to him in March: The President was unpopular because of the economy and his incumbency. I mistakenly thought that the economy would correct itself by late July. It did, actually, but few people noticed the fact until four weeks after the election. Anyway, the incumbency issue was much harder to address:

> The only way to change this is for the President to state clearly how he intends to use his incumbency to alter the status quo in America. His message should have a double edge to it: America is working and growing, but she also needs reforms in many key areas. . . .
>
> Our challenge is to structure the themes on which George Bush will run. Most of the time we do it backwards: first we assemble the details and point to an emerging theme. We should be identifying cutting-edge themes and then filling them out with the details.

We should be going after the trial lawyers, welfare bureaucracy and deadbeats, the health care bureaucracy, the "educrats" and others, I wrote, special interests should be challenged. Doing so would help the President's message hit home.

I was not alone in my chronic memo-writing. Others in the White House complex were venting their frustrations in the same way. Jay Lefkowitz, Richard Porter, David McIntosh, and a few others were hard at work trying to figure out a way to break through the barriers so that we could move forward. The former chief speechwriter, Tony Snow—a highly skilled writer who was ignominiously dumped from his position to make way for a young kid who had previously worked for the Kentucky Fried Chicken company and who excelled at drafting one-liners—produced memo after memo, along with draft op-ed columns, with excellent suggestions for turning around the President's polling data.

Was anybody listening?

Of course they were. Clayton Yeutter read, and thanked us for, every suggestion sent forward. But in all honesty, Yeutter was not the problem. Of the people I worked for and with in the Bush White House, Yeutter had perhaps the keenest grasp of what was wrong and how it needed fixing. But nothing ever happened.

It was becoming increasingly evident to me by late June that Yeutter himself was gradually being cut out of the loop as, once again, Richard Darman was elbowing his way back to the center, diminishing Sam Skinner personally, and ultimately emerging triumphant with the return to the White House of his friend and mentor, Secretary of State James A. Baker III.

One afternoon in early July Yeutter called me into his office and asked me to prepare a comprehensive list of Bush's major legislative proposals. The list was to indicate which ones had been enacted and which were still awaiting action by the Congress. Rather than start from scratch, I thought I'd first see if the compilation might not already exist elsewhere in the complex.

Our legislative affairs office did not keep such a list. Then I thought of OMB and called an old friend, Bernie Martin, whom I'd known for almost a decade. Martin was Darman's senior career staffer in the legislative area. As I suspected, Martin indeed had the list. I told him I needed it to respond to a specific request from Yeutter. Martin said, "Sure, Charlie, I'll be glad to share it with you. But let me just check first with my higher-ups to make sure there's no problem."

A few hours later Martin called me back. I could tell from the sorrowful tone in his voice that he was thoroughly disgusted. "I have the information you requested, but I've been told from the very highest level in OMB that I can't release it. It's not available for distribution. That person also said if anyone had any further questions they could take the matter up with Dick Darman directly."

So it was Darman basically saying to Yeutter: "Screw you, Clayton."

That's how far the Bush White House had degenerated with only four months to go before the election: the Director of OMB refusing to share a purely factual document with the Counselor to the President! When I told Yeutter what had happened, he just shook his head in disgust. We never got the list.

The rest of the summer of 1992 was bizarre indeed. Nothing was happening at the Bush White House. We were getting pummelled in the media day after day, watching our initiatives get bottled up in the Congress, and yet we were doing nothing about it.

What was going on? Where was the campaign? Did Bush really want to be reelected?

I was still not convinced that the senior folks at the White House knew what was going on, so I decided once again to do the only thing I could to try to influence matters: pepper Clayton Yeutter with unsolicited, but always welcomed, advice. As it turned out, none of it ever mattered.

Washington had settled into what I called " 'kinder, gentler' gridlock" between the Congress and the President.

Candidate Ross Perot was scoring points against both Bush and Bill Clinton by claiming that only someone like himself—an outsider—could fix matters. As with the onset of the recession, George Bush needed to explain to the American public *why* there was gridlock, but he refused to do so. Our political system wasn't flawed. The Democrats were just bound and determined to keep George Bush from succeeding in any area of his domestic agenda. Bush had a golden opportunity to lay the groundwork for demonstrating who was responsible for the situation, but he chose not to. Once again, when he finally did get around to bashing the Congress for blocking his agenda, his message sounded craven and contrived, as if it had been lettered on cue cards for him to read.

The first week in July, Clayton Yeutter again asked the OPD staff for more "bold ideas." I was delighted to comply, but a little concerned: Isn't it rather late to be still looking around for major campaign issues? The second thought I had was that none of this mattered anyway as long as the President was determined not to fight back against his critics until the Houston Convention, set for the middle of August. This strategy was folly: It gave Bill Clinton and the Democrats almost four weeks to bask in the glory of their own convention, criticize George Bush, and dominate the national media.

Which is precisely what they did. We sat tight, meanwhile, convinced that when Perot dropped out of the race on July 16, most of his voters would return to the Republican fold, which they did not. On or about July 16, 1992, Bill Clinton surged ahead of George Bush in one-on-one opinion surveys. From then through the November 3 election Bush never recovered.

Inside the White House, our policy office kept churning out suggestions for initiatives that ultimately went nowhere. Finally, frustrated beyond my own ability to preserve even a modicum of tact, I shot off a memorandum to Yeutter on July 7 urging that Darman be fired and replaced with John Cogan, an economist at the Hoover Institution and a former OMB Deputy Director at the end of the Reagan Administration. By that time it was apparent to most observers that Bush's real problems had little to do with policy and everything to do with credibility. He lacked it.

Even though the President had called the budget deal a "mistake," the policies enshrined in the deal remained in place, as did its architects. It was time, I wrote, to repeal the deal.

Another week of inaction went by, and I wrote to Yeutter again, basically reviving the list of suggestions made in the *Wall Street Journal* by various Republicans on March 20. I even threw in a new one offered by the former OMB Director Jim Miller: that Bush threaten to veto each and every appropriations bill that reached his desk if it didn't contain authority for a line-item veto. Both Reagan and Bush had repeatedly called for a constitutional amendment granting the President such authority, but it could be achieved faster if the Congress were to enact it as part of appropriations legislation. The idea also had the virtue of making the President legislatively relevant. Congress, after all, still needed the President's signature on appropriations bills.

Nothing happened, and a few days later I figured out why. Most of those suggestions—and I was not the only one in the White House thinking along these lines—would have required a vigorous campaign against the Congress, and guess who nixed that idea? Once again, Darman was engaged in negotiations with the Democrats in a last-ditch effort to salvage the President's economic growth agenda in the context of yet another major piece of tax legislation. After all, he favored acquiescing in legislation that would have made those same taxes *permanent!*

Any political novice could have sorted out what was happening here. The Democrats had not the slightest desire to give George Bush anything. Their goal was to run out the clock. The fact that we would even contemplate making the 1990 taxes permanent convinced me then and there that we did not deserve to win reelection. In the scenario actually being considered Bush, having praised the budget deal in 1990 and 1991 and called it a mistake in March 1992, in August would be making permanent many of the taxes that, under the terms of the budget deal, were due to expire shortly. And people wondered why the President had little credibility with the public?

On the day after Bill Clinton's acceptance speech at the Democratic Convention, I sent Yeutter an analysis of Clinton's rhetoric. I was struck by the fact that so much of Clinton's language was similar to what we'd been advocating (halfheartedly) in the Bush Administration. The question I put to Yeutter was whether Clinton would succeed in convincing the American public that *he* was the real agent of change for America's future.

Something strange is happening here, and the only way I can describe it is that our own rhetoric, our own policies are in danger of being turned back against us. If this happens, it will be because we have been far too timid in advocating and following through on the ideas in which we believe.

Some examples. Consider the rhetoric in Clinton's speech—a speech that is really little more than an extended (and tedious) version of his "New Covenant" speech first delivered at Georgetown University in October 1991. Clinton spoke of: an "entrepreneurial economy," "free enterprise," "economic opportunity," "change America," "putting power back in your hands," "putting the government back on your side," "opportunity for all Americans," "rewarding hard work," "a government that works for [people]," "change the way government does business," "[t]here is not a program in government for every problem," "we've got to make [government] work again," "a government that offers more empowerment and less entitlement," "[a] government that is leaner, not meaner; a government that expands opportunity;" "We offer opportunity. We demand responsibility," "common community," "make change happen," "Opportunity. Responsibility. Community."

What is especially frustrating is that several of us here have worked hard to associate the President with an empowerment/opportunity/responsibility agenda, only to watch Clinton move in and steal our themes. Recall that in 1988 we claimed that "We are the change." . . . Somehow we've forgotten that message, perhaps because we've gotten less hungry as incumbency has worn on. If anything needs to *change* in the next few weeks, it is this attitude.

Once again, there was little movement inside the Bush White House or the Bush campaign. The President had decided not to launch his campaign in earnest until after Houston, and that was all there was to say on the subject. For those of us who had been waiting since the previous November, the message was: "Wait some more."

Change was coming to the White House, however. With Bush's popularity still dropping, rumors circulated that Skinner would soon be replaced by the President's best friend, Secretary of State Jim Baker. And that is exactly what happened on Sunday, August 16, when Baker and his team were sworn in that evening after returning from Houston.

The real question was whether anything would change even then, or whether it was already too late for Jim Baker to rescue George Bush one last time.

10

Omens of the Reckoning

But you pretend and I pretend
That everything is fine
And though we should be at an
    end
It's so hard admittin'
When it's quittin' time

—Mary-Chapin Carpenter

Lee Atwater had always said that the Republicans would lose one presidential election before the end of the century. Given Atwater's reputation for political acumen, those words could have been unsettling. But some took comfort in assuming that they couldn't apply to George Bush. The smart money was on a loss in 1996 if Dan Quayle won the GOP nomination as Bush's heir apparent.

In September 1991 a *Wall Street Journal* article had begun in a breezy, comforting tone: "Confident Republican strategists think the most important question about President Bush's 1992 re-election campaign isn't whether he will win it, but rather what kind of victory it will be."[1] Bush had planned to coast to reelection, accepting a near-certain coronation by an adoring populace, forever thankful for his splendid Persian Gulf victory over Saddam Hussein. His stunning triumph over Iraq, however, was soon diminished by Saddam's continuation in power and his persistent nose-thumbing at both Bush and the various teams of United Nations inspectors charged with ensuring that Iraq's nuclear and biological weapons capability was dismantled. Domestically, meanwhile, the economy failed to show the aggressive growth needed to restore confidence and prosperity in the months running up to the November 3, 1992, election.

The first omen caused a knot in the stomach, particularly for those who gave any credence whatever to numbers as precedents. The RNC statistician David Hansen's sobering figure, shared with some of us on October 17, 1991, was beginning to hang over the Bush White House like an ominous thundercloud: Since 1948 no incumbent president had won reelection when the growth rate in real disposable income per capita the autumn *before* the election had been 2.3 percent or below. In October 1991 that number wasn't even close to Hansen's minimum. Under Bush's stewardship, the growth rate was *minus* 1 percent!

The second omen only served to ratify and reinforce the first: Right track–wrong track polling data showed an astounding 80 percent of those surveyed believing that the country was headed in the *wrong* direction. Although Bush continued to enjoy a modest lead over Clinton in the polls through the first week of July 1992, more and more stories in the press were suggesting that the incumbent was headed for the rocks. His "negatives" in the polling data were alarmingly high and showed no signs of budging.

By the early summer of 1992 George Bush's political fortunes had shifted dramatically from the near 90 percent approval rating he enjoyed coming off the Persian Gulf War. Having kept Pat Buchanan's insurgency to a minimum, Bush failed to take seriously the third-party assault launched by a fellow Texan, the billionaire H. Ross Perot. While Perot could never deliver a knockout blow and actually win, his persistence served to highlight Bush's own feckless performance as President.

Perot was no longer an idle threat. By the end of May 1992 the entrepreneur and political maverick was already ahead of Bush in one national opinion poll and occasionally leading the President in a handful of important states, including Texas and California, which accounted for much of the GOP's Electoral College lock. The possibility that Texas, George Bush's adopted home state, could conceivably fall into the column of its native-born candidate was an embarrassment.

The likelihood of a serious three-way race in which Perot stood to outperform the Independent ticket of John Anderson in 1980 had the professional politicians rethinking their election scenarios. Bush might have to campaign in every state and make repeated forays into Texas, while Clinton could reap substantial gains in the South. States that traditionally were written off in the GOP electoral calculus—New York, Michigan, and even Massachusetts—suddenly had to be reappraised by the Bush campaign. If the Sunbelt base comprising California, Texas, and Florida (which together counted for 111 electoral votes, nearly half of the 270 needed for victory in the fall) was suddenly up for grabs, then twenty-plus years of GOP campaign strategy, dating back to Richard Nixon's celebrated Southern strategy of 1968, now required prompt and serious reevaluation.

Late May's polling data brought dreadful news to the Bush campaign. In addition to the right track–wrong track figures, Bush was shown finishing third in California, and Perot was seen as taking away more support from the President than from the Arkansas Governor. New political fault lines could be detected. If sustained, they pointed toward a remarkably volatile political year characterized by pervasive distrust of government generally and politicians in particular.

By June 1 nearly fifty House of Representatives incumbents, a postwar record, decided voluntarily not to seek reelection, many because of revelations about the House post office and bank scandals. There was a sense throughout the country that the old order not only was passing but was being swept away by massive discontent. The time for excuses was past.

Earlier efforts by the Bush Administration's Young Turks to effect a paradigm shift in domestic policy, which had gotten nowhere, were now having dramatic and unexpected echoes. It appeared that a paradigm shift in political alignments was under way.

The Bush White House experienced a rude shock when the news arrived that the Republican loyalist Ed Rollins, director of Ronald Reagan's 1984 reelection campaign and former political director of the Reagan White House, was considering an offer from the Perot camp. With more than twenty years of devotion to GOP politics behind him, Rollins was the quintessential Reaganite. The fact that he would entertain the idea of working for a third party candidate side by side with Hamilton Jordan, Jimmy Carter's Chief of Staff, illustrated how serious the Republican rift was becoming.

No doubt Rollins's flirtation with Perot stemmed from his perception that George Bush was failing to lead the country. He might also have spotted a chance to exact a measure of revenge for the way Bush, Sununu, and Darman had vilified him after the 1990 budget deal. It was Rollins, after all, who had urged GOP congressional candidates to break with the President over the budget deal. Subsequently Bush had pressured Rollins out of his job as head of the National Republican Congressional Committee. The idea that Rollins would even consider (let alone accept) an overture from Perot was particularly galling to the Bushies in light of the fact that Rollins's wife, Sherrie, now held a senior position in the Administration as head of Bush's Office of Public Liaison.

During this period, most of the people around the President in the West Wing could not comprehend his continued slippage in the polls. After all, the strategy had called for Bush's popularity to rise in lockstep with the recovering economy. Its failure to do so left the President and his advisers in a quandary. Once again they found themselves confused. In that condition, they were able to convince each other that inaction was still the "prudent" approach. People could not fathom why Bush's numbers weren't turning around, and the excuses offered just reinforced the public impression that Bush and his advisers were totally out of touch with the country. As things turned out, the public was right.

Another indicator of the President's growing irrelevance was an unidentified senior White House official's response in the *Washington Post* to the polling data's right track–wrong track indicators and the perceived lack of any domestic agenda: "Obviously, something is wrong here and our message is not getting out. Bush has given 20 percent more domestic speeches this year than last and 40 percent more than Reagan did in this period, and people still say we don't have a message. We do have a good message, but people just aren't getting it."[2] No doubt this spokesman also failed to understand why the most sustained applause at the 1992 Houston GOP convention was reserved for former President Ronald Reagan. As an Administration, we were rapidly beginning to resemble the American education system we kept hoping to reform: We were manifesting a profound ability to do less with more, and then brag about it. The country wanted results, and we just bragged about inputs.

The anonymous official who made that assessment about the number of Bush's domestic policy speeches was probably David Demarest. While fine for internal consumption, these figures made the

Administration look ridiculous, as if doubling or tripling the number of speeches (or perhaps raising one's voice) would be enough to solve a problem. We were back to where we had been six months previously, at the end of 1991, when the debate had been about whether the President's difficulties stemmed from poor policies or inadequate communications. It was no wonder that the press once again began to speculate about another White House shake-up.

What was happening to George Bush in the late spring of 1992 was a political reckoning, an accounting for more than three years of failure to advance with any consistency, credibility, or conviction a coherent, compelling domestic agenda. To make matters worse, a remarkable degree of cynicism about government was abroad in the land. So Bush was rapidly drifting into political irrelevance, hence the plaintive cries about numbers of speeches and similar beside-the-point attempts to justify previous inaction. They were an attempt to react to a growing public dissatisfaction, but they served only to highlight earlier failures.

The clearest example of the phenomenon was Bush's effort to advance an urban agenda in the wake of the Los Angeles riots triggered by the acquittal in the Rodney King case. The more he argued the necessity of his plan, the more obvious it became that he was simply reacting to the situation, not demonstrating leadership.

The Los Angeles riots started on April 29, 1992, but it took Bush almost a week to get around to visiting L.A. When Hurricane Andrew slammed into south Florida in late August, on the other hand, leaving a quarter million people homeless, Bush (at the insistence of his new Chief of Staff, Jim Baker) diverted Air Force One from a political trip in Connecticut to inspect the storm damage in Florida. Perhaps coincidentally, by that point many Republican political strategists had written off California, conceding the state to the Democrats' electoral column for November. Meanwhile, Florida, a traditionally solid Republican state, was still very much in play. Bush was now doing everything he could to keep it that way.

The response to Hurricane Andrew and Bush's perfunctory concern about Los Angeles occurred at different times, which is important in explaining the President's widely divergent reactions to the two crises. One must understand that George Bush is essentially a man of many modes. His tendency was to compartmentalize not only his staff but himself.

The two most significant Bush modes are his governing mode and his campaign mode. In Bush's mind, the nitty-gritty boorishness of campaigning for office was wholly distinct from the lofty business of actually governing the nation. What you had to *say* to get elected had no real bearing on or relationship to what you subsequently *did* once elected. That modal mentality explains how Bush could so cavalierly jettison his "read my lips" pledge not to raise taxes and then mock his own vow by telling the media to "read my hips" when he was out jogging one day. That was then, this is now.

While more and more supporters were urging Bush to fire back at Clinton before the GOP convention, Bush just said no. The more he was pushed, the more he refused, noting that he would not begin his "campaign mode" until arriving in Houston for the convention. After all, he told his senior aides, he was right about Buchanan fizzling and Perot dropping out of the race, so you could trust his instincts about when to begin his attack on Bill Clinton and the Democrats.

This scenario took no cognizance of the country's mood. People were tired of waiting. The economy was not rebounding, and Americans were rapidly growing weary of George Bush. Unemployment figures were still high and included a huge jump (three tenths of 1 percent) in July, just on the eve of the Democratic convention in New York. Bush's personal popularity was still headed downward, dropping below 30 percent in July. The right track–wrong track polling suggested further that people were focusing on another Bush mode—his "incumbency mode"—and were not especially pleased with what they saw.

Campaigning in 1988, Bush had faced the relatively simple task of defining his differences from his Democratic opponent and his Republican predecessor. As far as he was concerned at that time, his past was a virtual *tabula rasa*. Not so in 1992. Bush could not run against Bush. His "campaign mode" would be constantly assessed in light of his 1988 promises ("no new taxes," "18 million new jobs") and his four-year record in office. The public and even some of his supporters were becoming fed up with Bush's stubborn hesitation to enter the fray. Perhaps more significantly, his reluctance to engage Clinton only reinforced his critics' claim that he was a passive, out-of-touch President who "just didn't get it."

In his excellent study of the collapse of Detroit's car industry, *The Reckoning*, the Pulitzer Prize journalist David Halberstam describes a Motor City filled with highly paid executives who, even when warned in the early 1970s, fail to comprehend the challenge they were facing from burgeoning Japanese competition coupled with the growing scarcity and cost of Middle Eastern oil. Detroit was

> . . . a place of people who had made their way up by taking as few risks as possible and never letting their eyes waver from the bottom line. Innovation cost money and entailed risk, and they had little stomach for it. The three main Detroit companies believed that they were fiercely competitive with each other. . . . The more important the issue, the less they competed and the longer they waited for someone else to take the first step, lest it be a mistake.[3]

When it came to the aides surrounding George Bush (as well as Bush himself), the parallels with Detroit's car executives in the early 1970s were remarkably similar—long before the ironic symbolism of Bush's jaunt to Japan with the country's top auto executives in tow. No one was prepared to take a risk, lest it spark some national (or even internal White House) controversy. What Halberstam concluded about the ruling class in Detroit applied precisely to Bush's status-quo, establishment-oriented White House. As Halberstam expressed it, "Those who had the most power had the least passion."[4]

People outside the White House—most notably loyal Republicans—could not fathom what was happening or understand why Bush was refusing to fight back against the growing attacks from Ross Perot and the likely Democratic nominee, Arkansas Governor Bill Clinton. They would call to ask what was going on. Why wasn't Bush responding? Why wasn't he laying out an agenda? Does he really want to win? Does he really want to run? Is he sick?

While Bush was holding his fire, his Vice President wasn't. On May 19, Dan Quayle delivered a major speech on personal values and responsibility. The speech also contained a brief but poignant criticism of the television sitcom *Murphy Brown*, which, Quayle complained, glorified the principal character's out-of-wedlock childbirth. Quayle's unambiguous denouncing of the fictitious character's decision to have the baby as a single mother once again brought confusion to the West Wing. The President and Marlin Fitzwater backed off from the Vice President's remarks, but only after considerable debate. It was, after all, a popular television sitcom they were talking about. The situation was reminiscent of the flap that had occurred in May over the relationship of many Great Society programs to the LA riots. The White House couldn't even agree with itself.

Ironically, Quayle's assertiveness prompted the observation that no longer was the young Vice President behaving like a deer frozen in the glare of oncoming headlights. Quayle was marching forward with one initiative after another; it was now the Bush West Wing that responded in fits and starts. Bush had become the deer. Columnists and others openly joked about Quayle dropping Bush from the ticket!

How could this situation have befallen an individual so well-prepared for the presidency of the United States, one who had served closely with Ronald Reagan for eight years?

Of modern Presidents, George Bush assumed office with perhaps the best resumé, the best experience, and the best set of historical circumstances. His stewardship of the presidency, however, revealed an inability to see beyond today, a fundamental failure to grasp the significance of the world around him—its changes as well as its challenges—and to seize the ring of leadership that would enable America to take real advantage of the accomplishments its people had worked so long to achieve.

For those reasons, the Bush presidency will be seen as a caretaker presidency, a transitional period in which Bush's own incumbency was spent drawing down the capital invested by his predecessor, Ronald Reagan. Having devoted the better part of seven decades to opposing Soviet Russia and Communism's brutal and murderous excesses, we emerged in 1991 victorious but disoriented, unsure of our ability to lead by moral suasion, to compete vigorously in an economically interdependent world, and to redeploy our domestic priorities and our economy in ways to meet the future. We had emerged from a dark tunnel in our twin wars against fascism and Communism only to admit to the world that we had no clue as to where to head next. A sluggish economy and Bush's disdain for rhetorical flourishes did not help matters. People were losing patience with the President's repeated procrastination. By the time he realized his political career was at stake, few were willing even to listen to him.

The week before the Democratic convention in New York marked a turning point, for that was the critical moment when Bill Clinton first tied and then began to surpass George Bush in almost all the major national opinion polls. After a near-flawless convention in New York City, Clinton opened a lead of almost thirty points in some polls. The Bush camp, clearly worried by the numbers as well as its own tracking polls, began to wake up. The talk in Washington turned to yet another White House staff shake-up. Chief of Staff Sam Skinner would be replaced by Secretary of State James Baker. As in 1988, it would be Baker to the rescue—which by itself said reams about the difficulties Bush had in managing his own White House.

By July 1992 it was apparent that something drastic had to be done to reverse Bush's continued slippage in the polls. The Bush–Quayle campaign operation was not meshing with White House decisionmaking, and more and more of the blame was falling on Skinner. Bringing back Baker was a last-ditch effort designed to save Bush's presidency.

Bush was reluctant to jettison Skinner for several reasons. First, dumping yet another Chief of Staff, particularly with the election scarcely more than three months off, would look like desperation, reminiscent of the personnel shuffle Jimmy Carter had tried with no real success. Second, Baker had already held the job (under Reagan), was happy at the State Department, and was engaged in sensitive peace negotiations in the Middle East. Democrats, of course, came to Baker's "rescue" by complimenting his performance and lamenting disingenuously that his departure would not only jeopardize American diplomacy but establish an unseemly precedent of politicizing foreign policy should Baker move either to the campaign or back to the White House. Some thought they did protest too much. After all, the same James Baker had left Ronald Reagan's Treasury in August 1988 to save the earlier Bush campaign from foundering.

Bush remained silent about any possible White House shake-up and actually discouraged such speculation. Rumors flew nonetheless, especially during the week of the Democratic convention, when Bush and Baker vacationed together at the Secretary's Wyoming Ranch.

Inside the White House, meanwhile, few doubted that Baker would replace Skinner as Chief of Staff. The only question was when. The first unmistakable sign of the change came in early July, when I happened to be reviewing the President's daily personal schedule—not the long-range schedule issued to just a few senior White House aides, but the one with an even more limited circulation that presented the minute-by-minute breakdown of Bush's days. Clayton Yeutter's executive assistant, Chris Sheehan, dropped by my office to discuss a scheduling question. She happened to have the next three days of the President's schedule, which we went over together looking for the event at issue.

To my utter shock, I saw that at eight o'clock each morning when the President was in Washington he was receiving a "domestic update" from Dick Darman! Those briefings had previously been conducted by the Chief of Staff. Now they were being handled by Darman alone! From what I was able to learn, neither Skinner nor Yeutter attended the sessions. I remembered what Debbie Steelman had told me just a few months before: Sununu had actually recommended to Bush that he name Darman Chief of Staff. When it came to domestic policy matters, that was, in effect, what had now happened.

Had the President lost his mind? At this point, with his conservative base straying from the GOP fold and flirting with a Perot vote or no vote at all, Bush had chosen to rely almost exclusively on the architect of the 1990 budget deal that remained the source of most of his political and policy problems. Congressional Republicans were now openly calling for Darman's departure, and so were conservatives all across the country. So Bush responds by giving him even greater access and responsibility?

I was stunned. I knew Bush was stubborn, but I was certain he wasn't stupid.

To me it meant something else. Bush simply must be in agreement with Darman's view that the 1990 budget deal was *not* a mistake, at least as a matter of policy. The agreement may have hurt Bush politically and wrecked his overall credibility, but it was now a certainty that the President himself, whatever regrets he may have expressed, must be convinced that what he did in November 1990 was in the country's best interests.

What I would later call "Darman's coup" went mostly undetected and unreported by the media. It was also not widely known within the White House. When I shared the information with friends, the reaction was always amazement. When I first asked Boyden Gray if Darman's new role meant Darman was now effectively Chief of Staff, he said "yes," but when I put the same question to him a few hours later, he backed off a bit.

"Boyden, were you really serious about Darman now being the Chief of Staff?" I asked.

"It's not that bad, Charlie. It just reflects that the President is fed up with Yeutter." He didn't elaborate, but it was apparent that Bush was now relying almost exclusively on Darman when it came to domestic policy, a fact which obviously signaled Bush's preparation for a Baker return to the White House. After all, Darman had served as Baker's deputy when the latter was Reagan's Chief of Staff and his Secretary of the Treasury. With a staff of nearly six hundred, Darman was the 800-pound gorilla in the White House complex. He refused to share anything with anybody, which meant that he was well positioned to crowd out his rivals. He now had Bush's ear all to himself.

Clayton Yeutter could not have been pleased at that development, although he never acknowledged it or commented on it. While Bush may have become "addicted" to Darman because of his ready access to information and his facile manipulation of policy, the absence of Yeutter from the 8 A.M. briefings meant that Bush was deprived of perhaps the soundest judgment to be had in the White House. In the weeks ahead this would show to the President's detriment.

Inside the White House, the only questions during July and early August were when Baker would leave the State Department and whether he would take up residence in his old West Wing office or be located on Fifteenth Street at Bush–Quayle headquarters. Baker would not have a say in answering at least the latter question.

Under the new ethics-in-government rules, had Baker left government to join the campaign, he would have been precluded from conferring with senior government officials on policy matters. (This was the same ethics restriction Bill Bennett had pointed to as his reason for declining the chairmanship of the Republican National Committee.) That limitation would have made it impossible for Baker to have run both the campaign and the White House, so the only option available for Bush was to replace Skinner with Baker. Darman's closeness with the Secretary of State would further reinforce and finally cement Darman's grip on Bush's faltering presidency.

On July 30, 1992, a little more than two weeks before the Houston convention opened, I had lunch with the RNC Chairman, Rich Bond, in the White House Mess. According to a mutual friend, Bond was no fan of Darman, so I took the occasion to share with the party chairman my concerns about Darman's looming reincarnation.

"First of all, Rich, if Darman sticks around between now and January 1993, he'll be the one writing the first budget and list of policy priorities for the President's second term. And remember, Bush will have only three budgets; his fourth will be a lame duck budget going into the 1996 election. So it's important what happens in his first budget that OMB will be preparing between now and Thanksgiving."

Bond nodded both agreement and concern. I added that I'd concluded, with considerable reluctance, that it was now too late to fire Darman. Doing so would seem a Carteresque act of desperation. Bond concurred.

So what could be done? I had an idea. Why couldn't Bush just announce that he was assigning the preparation of his first budget and policy priorities of his second term to someone other than Darman? Keep Darman around (only because dumping him was embarrassing at this late stage), but announce that, beginning September 1, 1992, the fiscal 1994 budget would be prepared by three fresh faces: John Cogan, a Hoover Institution economist and former Reagan OMB deputy director; the economist Tim Muris, a Jim Miller protégé; and Vin Weber, the departing Minnesota Representative (as well as an outspoken Darman critic).

I concluded my proposal: "Rich, it's simple. We keep Darman but just take away his toys. Doing so sends the signal that Bush is serious about a new direction and that he genuinely regrets the 1990 budget deal. After September 1, OMB will be under new management!"

Bond bolted upright in his chair. "Charlie, I like it. It's a great idea." He nodded toward Clayton Yeutter, who was sitting two tables over from us in the Mess. "Have you told it to Clayton yet?"

"Not yet. I just thought of it." By all means, Bond said, tell Yeutter as soon as possible.

I did. After our lunch I decided to put the idea in writing, a risky step in view of Darman's notorious vindictiveness. But, as I wrote the memo, I came to realize that I would have welcomed being fired. It would have put me out of my misery.

Yeutter never responded to my note, the gist of which I had also faxed to Jack Kemp, knowing that he and Weber were close allies. Yeutter had no obligation to respond, and I certainly didn't expect him to. But the next morning I saw Rich Bond again, this time at the session of our Domestic Policy Reform Breakfast Group. When I met him in the West Wing basement to escort him to the breakfast, I handed him a copy of the memorandum I'd sent Yeutter.

Unbeknownst to me, Bond had gone directly from our lunch the day before to meet with Sam Skinner and, he said, to tell the Chief of

Staff my idea. Bond was sure that unless he had misunderstood Skinner, or unless Skinner was lying, the Darman problem "had been taken care of." Whatever Skinner had said, Bond was absolutely convinced that Darman's days were numbered.

As events evolved, of course, it was Sam Skinner whose days were numbered. Darman *had* been taken care of. By August the betting was that the long-expected White House shake-up would occur just before the Houston convention. I predicted it would happen on Wednesday, August 12, but I was wrong—by one day.

On August 13 Bush announced at the morning senior staff meeting that Baker would resign as Secretary of State, effective August 23, and join the White House as Chief of Staff the following day. Skinner would move to the RNC as the ceremonial "General Chairman."

Yeutter told the policy development staff the news at our 8:45 A.M. staff meeting in his office. Sitting to his immediate left, I could clearly detect that Yeutter was troubled by the President's decision. Nonetheless, his trademark broad smile accompanied his upbeat and positive gloss on the shake-up when he told us his own plans were uncertain. He had no intention of staying on without a substantive role; on that point he was emphatic. One possibility would be to move to the campaign as a super-surrogate for the President on the campaign trail. That turned out to be the position offered him, and accepted with his characteristic grace and dignity, which was remarkable in light of the shabby way he'd been treated in recent weeks.

Baker and his entourage lost no time in taking over, at least their office space. The following afternoon Porter dropped by to inform me that "the Baker people" would be needing my office, so I'd have to leave the West Wing for the Old Executive Office Building. Fine with me.

The Baker transition had to be painful for Porter, perhaps even more so than Sununu's departure and his layering by Clayton Yeutter. Baker brought with him four top assistants. Janet Mullins, his legislative aide at State, now would oversee Ron Kauffman's political activities. Dennis Ross, a foreign policy expert, would become Assistant to the President for Policy Planning. Marlin Fitzwater gleefully relinquished his title as Counselor for Communications so that Margaret Tutwiler, formerly Baker's spokeswoman at State, could assume full control over White House (and, presumably, campaign) messages.

Most galling to Porter, I would guess, was the naming of Bob

Zoellick as Deputy Chief of Staff. Zoellick, a low-key, cerebral 1988 campaign operative, had been one of Porter's students years before at the Kennedy School. Earlier in the Bush Administration Porter had refused to attend a meeting at State when he learned that it would be held in his former pupil's office. Porter had remarked, Zoellick was a perfectly fine "teaching assistant," but the meeting would have to be held in *his* office in the White House. Now, not only did Zoellick occupy a first floor West Wing office just paces down the hall from the Oval Office, but he was, effectively, Roger Porter's boss!

Bush's decision to replace Skinner with Baker was positively received by most people in the White House, at campaign headquarters, and, surprisingly, by conservatives. Gone were the worries that Baker was a nonideological "pragmatist." By this point, with Bush still nearly thirty points behind Clinton in some polls, Republicans were willing to try anything to turn things around.

While Bush was, as always, gracious in praising and thanking Sam Skinner for his help, most of the blame for the latest round of White House "disarray" was reserved for Skinner. But the problem wasn't the Chief of Staff; it was the Chief of State.

In fairness to Sam Skinner, the former Transportation Secretary never had a chance to install his own team and to run the White House the way he'd wanted. It was clear that Skinner was just another one of the hired help. He would never develop the relationship with the President that would enable him to stand up to Jim Baker or Dick Darman. To his credit, however, Skinner himself recognized the shortcomings of the White House operation in the summer of 1992 and took the lead in urging Bush to bring back Baker.

Someone looking at this situation objectively from outside the White House might have asked George Bush the following question: "Mr. President, first you blamed the Congress for your troubles. Now you're blaming your staff. When are you going to look in the mirror and blame the one person who's responsible for your predicament?"

It is a pity no one put that question directly to the President. It is a pity this President didn't ask it of himself.

In the Bush White House under Skinner's management, issues were seldom decided promptly, if at all. Whereas John Sununu just said "no" to almost everything, under Skinner you couldn't get a decision without going through a cumbersome and frequently elaborate process. That, however, was not altogether Sam Skinner's doing.

Unable to rid himself of many of Sununu's holdovers, stuck with Darman, and apparently lacking sufficient authority to decide matters unilaterally, Skinner presided over an unwieldy operation in which decisions were vested not in him as Chief of Staff but in the Policy Coordinating Group, chaired by Clayton Yeutter in Bush's absence, on which the Chief of Staff was but one of five members. Decisiveness was sacrificed for collegiality. It therefore came as no surprise that the return to the White House of Jim Baker and his four key aides established a close-knit decisionmaking process in which collegiality was sacrificed for decisiveness.

The difficulties encountered by the Skinner-run White House were also reflected in the Bush–Quayle campaign itself and in the relationship between the campaign and the White House. To begin with, the complicated Policy Coordinating Group structure, established under Skinner primarily as a buffer against Darman's domineering personality, only meant decisions weren't made or, if they were, emerged slowly and fitfully. On those rare occasions when decisions were reached, the White House had no idea how to capitalize on them.

A senior campaign official recalls observing Henson Moore, then Skinner's deputy, taking notes during a political dinner at which Haley Barbour, a political operative and former Reagan political affairs director, was speaking. While Barbour emphasized the importance of picking a set of key themes and stressing them repeatedly, Moore was observed studiously writing and underscoring in his notepad, "Stress themes." Back at the White House this translated for a while, unfortunately, into the mechanistic formula "jobs, family, peace."

Part of the difficulty in running the 1992 reelection campaign was that it was not 1988. When Bush had sought the presidency as Vice President, he didn't have to worry about the White House. The campaign organization was capable of making decisions without having the difficulty of also coordinating them with some other entity. Now, in 1992, nothing was getting done, and to complicate matters even more, the campaign organization found itself hamstrung by what many considered to be overly stringent interpretations of ethics requirements by the White House Counsel's Office. Those interpretations had the effect of hindering the ability of the White House and campaign operations to move quickly and coordinate their overall activities.

The other difficulty faced in 1992 was that the campaign chairman,

Bob Teeter, according to one senior campaign official, provided little direction or management to the daily operations: "No one could get in to see Bob. At the White House there was absolute ineptitude. The people there were either brain dead or incompetent. No one had a clue as to what the hell was going on. Given the vacuum at the White House and the indecisiveness at the campaign, these factors only highlighted Bob's shortcomings" as a manager.

And then there was Dick Darman. The effect of his influence at the White House had been to stifle innovation. The activist staffers at the second and third tiers found themselves cut out. This same chilly climate carried over to the campaign, where, one official recalled, there was "no atmosphere of openness and intellectual dynamism." Darman apparently accomplished the same thing with his involvement in the Bush–Quayle campaign.

Both the Bush White House and the reelection campaign had received extensive briefings from two Conservative party members who had played a leading role in British Prime Minister John Major's come-from-behind win over the Labour party candidate, Neil Kinnock. Among the tactics employed successfully by the Conservatives was to brand their opponent as a big taxer and spender. They coined the slogan, "In Come Labour, In Come Taxes," for example, as an indication of what a Kinnock victory would mean. More precisely, they were able to "cash out" in specific, quantifiable terms exactly what a Kinnock victory would mean for *higher* new taxes for people at various income levels. The tactic proved highly effective in the closely fought U.K. election.

While a similar strategy would have been nearly impossible for George Bush after the 1990 budget deal, Bill Clinton offered the President and his campaign a splendid opening to raise a related concern. Clinton's budget numbers just didn't add up; he could not possibly pay for all his proposals without either drastic spending cuts or significant tax increases that would hit middle-class Americans. Once Clinton had made that gaffe, several in the Bush campaign urged Bush to go on the offensive, explaining precisely how the Democratic challenger's numbers were mistaken.

Jim Cicconi and others in the Bush–Quayle campaign had prepared detailed analyses of Clinton's numbers, only to find themselves stonewalled in their ability to use them by Darman, who succeeded in blocking their release for more than six weeks. Finally, in exasperation, Cicconi had printed a sliding table, similar to what the Conservatives had used in Britain, showing the specific tax effect of Clinton's proposals for American households with middle incomes and above. The message of the Cicconi table couldn't have been any more direct: "In Come Clinton, In Come Taxes." The campaign printed thousands of charts for distribution, but they were not disseminated in earnest until the waning days of the reelection effort, when it was too late to make a difference.

Given a sluggish economy and a record that his Democratic rival repeatedly described as the "worst since Herbert Hoover," Bush's *noblesse oblige* mindset was not only irrelevant but becoming positively offensive. While Democratic liberals were pining for a Clinton Administration that would restore the "legitimate role" of government in addressing the nation's ills, even conservative activists—the faction of the GOP most often associated with Jack Kemp—were carping at Bush's inaction. By late July, as Bush slumped further in the polls and found himself running behind Clinton in *every* state but Utah and one or two others, party regulars were growing frantic at Bush's insistence on not beginning his campaign before the Houston convention.

But there was nothing concerned Republicans could do about the President's intransigence. Everyone had to play by Bush's rules and wait.

Once again, for the third time in 1992, waiting produced little reward and now, with the clock running out, little chance of success. Bush's Houston acceptance speech bombed, which should have been no great surprise to anyone who knew it was primarily the work of the same Darman protégés who had put together the January State of the Union message and the March 20 speech when Congress missed Bush's deadline for action on his economic agenda. The party faithful in Houston and across the country made sure the President got an opinion poll "bounce" from Houston, but the momentum had evaporated within a week. Bush was still trailing Clinton in almost every poll by double-digit amounts ranging from ten to twenty points.

The Republican convention bolstered the party's conservative base (which essentially captured the 1992 platform with its strong antiabortion, religious, and family values planks) but alienated many women, moderates, and Reagan Democrats, the latter representing crucial swing voters that Bush had to pick up and hold to win the November election. The message that emerged was one of strident exclusiveness rather than the inclusiveness of the Kemp wing of the party. After a cloying night of ill-tempered rhetoric about family values and Pat Buchanan's well-crafted but exceedingly inflammatory and negative speech, the GOP found itself alienating old allegiances instead of forming new ones. And by waiting so long to make his case, Bush handed Clinton one more advantage.

Expectations were high for Bush's acceptance speech, but aside from a few clever one-liners ("I bit the bullet [on Iraq] while my opponent bit . . . his nails"), the address was memorable mostly for its policy gimmicks: the vague allusion to across-the-board tax cuts in a second Bush term and a "checkoff" on the IRS tax return for individuals wanting to ensure that up to 10 percent of their tax payments would be used to reduce the national debt. Once again Bush had failed to deliver on "the vision thing." He had not laid out a coherent or credible policy for a sustained economic recovery. His Houston acceptance speech was not enough to sustain his basic message through the fall campaign. Moreover, as Michael Barone of *U.S. News & World Report* told a group of White House aides three weeks before the election, had Bush given a better speech in Houston, he would have overshadowed the negatives that had arisen earlier in the convention from Buchanan, Pat Robertson, and others. Instead, the message coming out of Houston lacked clarity.

Announcing his forthcoming resignation at the State Department on August 14, Baker gave what many commentators termed the most coherent statement about George Bush's presidency and why he should be reelected that had been articulated to date. Conservatives cheered Baker's reference to "principles, values, and ideals." New Paradigmers were pleased when he spoke of the need to "empower" the poor. Of such crumbs was optimism made.

When Baker spoke of building "on the fundamentals of lower tax rates, limits on government spending, greater competition, less economic regulation and more open trade" as a way of "unleash[ing] tremendous private initiative and growth"—a clear allusion to the Reaganism that had helped elect Bush in 1988—it was a sure signal that Baker knew Bush had to regain the initiative on taxes and spending to have any prayer of being reelected. Baker also explained the connection between our foreign policy and the conservative domestic agenda. He made the link abundantly clear:

> America must have appropriate new approaches for the changes at home, just as we have launched new policies to manage the changes abroad.

We must concentrate on the interrelationship between domestic and foreign policy, and between economic and security policy. . . . So I have decided to resign as Secretary of State, effective August the 23rd, to work with the President to help develop a second-term agenda that builds on what has been achieved and that fully integrates our domestic, economic and foreign policies.

Baker's remarks upon leaving State won high praise—higher than every other speech delivered by his boss, the one running for reelection. The apparent contrast was obvious, but nobody seemed to mind. People in the Administration as well as in the media heralded Baker's remarks as the most coherent statement of George Bush's "vision" to emerge from the Administration in almost four years.

Baker's speech proved to be a trial run for Bush's Detroit Economic Club address, delivered a month later on September 14. Written principally by his new deputy Chief of Staff, Bob Zoellick (also responsible for Baker's), it mimicked substantially the framework of Baker's own remarks. Bush echoed Kemp in calling for "entrepreneurial capitalism that grows from the bottom up, not the top down." Paul Gigot of the *Wall Street Journal*, noting that the President was embracing a "Reaganesque populist economic theme," appropriately called Bush's speech "at least a rhetorical victory for the reform agenda that conservatives have long sought from the White House."[5]

But by the time the President gave his coherent Detroit Economic Club speech, nothing was working to move the numbers—poll as well as electoral—in Bush's favor. He had lost the election. A few days earlier, on September 9, I drew up a list of key predictors that broke in Bush's favor versus those favoring Clinton. As I told a few close friends at the White House, it was clear to me that the President would go down to defeat in November. No one disagreed with my analysis or my conclusion. The President and the campaign had waited too long to crystallize a winning message. Even if he had stuck to the themes of his Detroit Economic Club speech, people weren't listening any more, and his campaign would never achieve the necessary lift it needed to get off the ground. By mid-September, people were beginning to deliberate on whether they could accept a Clinton presidency.

For all its Truman-style rhetoric in August about running against a "do-nothing" Congress, the Bush White House did almost nothing to challenge the legislative branch. Bush rejected entreaties that he unilaterally exercise a line-item veto when reviewing congressional appropriations bills headed his way. He talked a good game against Congress, but when it came to real action, he just signed the appropriations bills Congress sent to him.

On the same day Bush gave the best speech of his campaign in Detroit, UPI reported polling data showing the incumbent President with a solid lead in only two states, Indiana and Utah, for a mere 17 electoral votes. Only ten other states, with 76 electoral votes, were leaning his way.

Accompanying the President's remarks in Detroit was a twenty-nine-page campaign document prepared by Zoellick, Darman, and Bob Grady entitled "Agenda for American Renewal." The "Agenda" included multiple references to "empowerment," including the following:

> First, start with the basics: We are a nation of special individuals, not special interests. Individuals gain primary strength, protection, and inspiration from their families and communities, not the legal system or Government social services. People find their friends and their enjoyment in voluntary association with one another, not in some bureaucrat's paint-by-numbers dream. . . .
> We prefer a hand up to a handout. We want to empower people to make their own choices, to break away from dependency.

It was all good stuff, the right stuff, the sound conservative Republican principles of less government, lower taxes, reduced regulation, and economic growth. But it was too late. George Bush's Detroit speech and his "Agenda for American Renewal" could and *should* have been delivered almost two years before. All of the ingredients— the rhetoric, the ideas, the detailed programs, the restructuring of the legal and educational systems, welfare reform, economic opportunity —had been part and parcel of the policy emphasis so many of us in his own White House had been trying to bring to light since back in 1990.

By the fall of 1992, however, the American public had tuned out George Bush. Some may have listened to his words and his belated rhetoric, but the vast majority of the public (evidenced by adding up Clinton's and Perot's poll numbers) had no reason to expect the underlying momentum of a second Bush term to be any different from that of the first. Many of us in the White House had reached the same conclusion. George Bush's own admission that he had two "modes," one for governing and one for campaigning, further eroded his fundamental credibility. He had lost the moment, and lost it so completely that his last few weeks on the campaign trail found the President lurching almost randomly from one proposal to the next without rhyme or apparent reason in an almost pathetic parody of what he should have been doing in 1990. It was as if he had suddenly discovered many of the good ideas that had never made it to fruition before and was now announcing them frantically and without conviction. It was like trying to build a mansion in two weeks by standing on the lot and throwing fistfuls of nails at stacks of lumber.

An example of presidential panic was the decision in early October to announce the automobile insurance reform that had percolated inside the White House for nearly two years. It was a sound idea that had been carefully reviewed and had long been ready for adoption by the Administration. I first raised the proposal with Roger Porter and others in the fall of 1990, after receiving a detailed briefing by its sponsors, Mike Horowitz, the former OMB General Counsel, and University of Virginia law professor Jeff O'Connell. Sununu didn't like the idea, however, because a modest federal preemption of state law would be required. The plan was to authorize liability insurance contracts in which the insured party voluntarily waived his right to sue for standard pain and suffering and punitive damages. In exchange for the waiver, the insured's liability premium would be reduced by 60 to 70 percent—the equivalent of a $30 billion nationwide tax break. The proposal's effect was to price out the real cost of the tort lawyer's fees in each premium and then offer people a choice as to which type of coverage they wanted. As a matter of policy, this proposal was also consistent with such other Bush reforms as school choice, childcare vouchers, and Kemp's homeownership plans. When Bush finally announced it out of the blue at a campaign stop in New Jersey on October 16, the idea was lost on his audience, received no serious coverage by the media, and was eclipsed by a band of hecklers who rattled Bush during his speech. The plan was never mentioned again.

Inside the Bush White House the characteristic indecision continued. For the umpteenth time during the Administration there was a debate about whether or not Bush should index the capital gains tax rate unilaterally through regulation. He decided not to, despite compelling arguments supporting his authority from a former Reagan Assistant Attorney General, Charles Cooper.

Cooper was a friend of the Administration who was trying to help. Instead of having his views warmly considered, he was all but shunned. In advance of making public his analysis, Cooper shared it with officials in the Bush Justice Department, urging them to pick it apart and show him where he was wrong or had missed something. Cooper never heard a word back. When I invited him to speak at our Friday Empowerment Breakfast the week *after* his advice had been rejected, I learned that Communications Director David Demarest had called Ede Holiday in Cabinet Affairs, furious that Cooper was invited to the Mess. Cooper came anyway. Those were the serious issues on the minds of some of the Assistants to the President eight weeks before the election.

When I learned of Demarest's reaction to the Cooper invitation I was inspired to redouble my efforts to please. Larry Kudlow, who had served as David Stockman's chief economist and was now at Bear, Stearns in New York, had published a boldly critical article about the Bush Administration's economic policy in the September 6, 1992, Business section of the Sunday *New York Times*. Kudlow urged Bush to fire Brady and Darman as a way to "break the stranglehold on change and new ideas" in the Administration.[6] Great idea! So I invited Kudlow for the following Friday's breakfast.

Kudlow readily accepted. He opened his remarks by mentioning that this was the first time he'd been back in the Mess in years. As he walked through the White House gates that morning, he had thought of requesting Secret Service protection, considering his recent article. He then took note of the Bush Administration's inexplicable "aversion to rhetoric." The White House even refused to allow good spokesmen to go on television to rebut the Democrats' critiques of the Reagan–Bush years. Kudlow also indicted the Administration's four-year budget record. We should have been promoting more direct business investment, capital incentives, and ways to cut the federal budget deficit to make room for more tax cuts, he said. No one in the room disagreed.

While the Presidency is an institution, it reflects what each incumbent brings to the job, the various personal traits that reflect the character of the person sitting in the Oval Office. Ronald Reagan may have gone horseback riding on Wednesdays and given almost six times *fewer* press conferences in his first term than Bush did, but the aides minding the store knew precisely the direction in which he was heading, whether he was on a horse or behind his desk. Bushies, by contrast, lacked a blueprint. Their recipe for success was action for the sake of action.

The prospects that any of this would have changed beyond 1992 were unlikely, and that is why George Bush became a one-term President. He posted the worst reelection performance by an incumbent Republican President since William Howard Taft in 1912. The fact that this Yankee-born patrician ran third behind the Southerners Clinton and Perot in one of his three "native" states, Maine, only underscores the electorate's massive commitment to an agenda for change going beyond rhetoric and White House fact sheets.

In the month leading up to November 3, 1992, a truly remarkable number of White House aides at all but the top levels would openly admit among themselves that we didn't deserve to win. They were right. We wanted to win, of course, but we weren't hungry enough.

The Bush White House increasingly became trapped in a myopic inability to look beyond the limits of its own mindset. As the 1992 presidential campaign heated up, Democrats like Bill Clinton began to advocate "New Paradigm" solutions to domestic problems, such as time-limiting welfare and reducing the size of government bureaucracy. Bush and his White House advisers remained enshrouded in their own bubble, trying to rerun the 1988 campaign, playing by the rules of the 1990 budget deal, and avoiding innovation, creativity, and, above all else, risk. The most senior levels of the Administration seemed emotionally and intellectually drained. There was no evident desire to do much of anything but secure Bush's reelection. Our fascination was in the courtship, not in the marriage. It was, after all, the Republicans' third successive term in office; the momentum and enthusiasm of the Reagan years had faded.

To win, George Bush needed to reinvigorate his government. Doing so required what the modern art critic Kirk Varnedoe calls "a fine disregard for the rules" of the game of governing. George Bush's team needed a fresh perspective and a new pallette. What he got instead was the same old brushes, colors, and canvas. The team was still standing in the identical place, its perspective unchanged, trying to paint the same old picture.

Internationally, by comparison, the rules of the game had changed dramatically, and Boris Yeltsin's leadership in Russia and the new Commonwealth of Independent States was a bold example of not

responding to change but making change happen. The response from
the United States continued to be characterized by backchannel leaks
from the State Department questioning whether Yeltsin would succeed. At home as well as abroad, Bush favored the status quo, whether
the issue was one of policy or of personality. He demonstrated an
unwavering preference for the known over the unknown. Contemplating bold initiatives was unthinkable.

The Bush White House was incapable of developing Varnedoe's
"fine disregard" for the rules of the game of politics. The President,
after all, had played them well all his life to reach the pinnacle of
power in the Western world. His natural reserve and caution had
served him admirably throughout his political life, and he saw no
reason to begin rocking the boat now. Moreover, he had surrounded
himself with people just like himself, men of primarily inherited
wealth who themselves were quite comfortable with things as they
were. Capitalists, yes. Entrepreneurs, no. Small wonder, then, that
many of us urging greater change in the Administration were, like
Clinton, heavily influenced by David Osborne and Ted Gaebler's
Reinventing Government, which preached entrepreneurial government.[7]
The President's senior advisers, on the other hand, wanted to play it
safe. If the economy just turned around, even modestly, they reasoned, Bush would win reelection, especially since the Democrats,
leaving out New York's Governor Mario Cuomo, could put up no
candidate to match Bush's national stature and experience—or so the
Republicans expected. If that calculation had proved true, by the way,
it did not bode well for the future of the Republican party and its
presidential prospects in 1996.

Some of us recalled an event from late in 1991. In December a
magazine article was circulated throughout several White House offices. It just showed up one week on lots of people's desks. It was by
a former Jimmy Carter speechwriter, James Fallows, and had run in
two issues of *The Atlantic* in 1979. Its title was "The Passionless Presidency: The Trouble with Jimmy Carter's Administration." Another
omen.

The parallels between Carter's lifeless and rudderless Administration and Bush's addled White House operation were uncanny. The
workaholic George Bush, whose passion for endless motion—regardless of direction—on the golf course, in his cigarette boat, as well as
day to day in the White House was now being compared to the

technocratic Carter, who immersed himself in the minutest of policy details, not to mention scheduling of the White House tennis court. It was understandable that the decade-old Fallows piece found avid readership in the Bush White House.

Fallows could have been describing us. He wrote of a President whose "positions are correct; his values sound" and yet he could not "explain his goals, and thereby . . . offer an object for loyalty larger than himself."[8] Bush's central message during the 1992 reelection campaign was a call for loyalty to his own person, as witness the statement: "This election is about trust. Who do you trust to sit in that Oval Office?"

While the Bush Administration prided itself on dozens and dozens of fact sheets on issues ranging from "fast track" negotiating authority to energy policy, wetlands, spotted owls, and school choice, it lacked conviction, priorities, and a sense of mission. We had become an Administration of foxes and fact sheets. We had no hedgehogs.

Carter had suffered a similar disability. He had lists (not arguments) and saw his role as picking from the menu presented to him. In Bush's case, however, policies became Administration policies not because Bush chose them but because they just sort of happened. They welled up from below instead of issuing from some governing philosophy or ideology coming from the Oval Office (as with Ronald Reagan). This process describes how most of the issues Bush chose to talk about in the 1992 fall campaign—health care, civil justice reform, welfare reform, public *and* private school choice—came into being. They weren't felt passionately; they were merely on a list handed to him by someone. The President was ultimately led to each one of them by staff work that intermittently bubbled up from below. It appeared to be his conscious choice not to embrace them with zeal, enthusiasm, or conviction. The American people could feel it. They knew it.

So Fallows's depiction of *his* boss could just as easily have been written about ours, as it relates to Sir Isaiah Berlin's description of the fox:

> I came to think that Carter believes fifty things, but no one thing. He holds explicit thorough positions on every issue under the sun, but he has no large view of the relations between them, no line indicating

which goals (reducing unemployment? human rights?) will take precedence over which (inflation control? a SALT treaty?) when the goals conflict. Spelling out these choices makes the difference between a position and a philosophy, but it is an act foreign to Carter's mind. He is a smart man, but not an intellectual, in the sense of liking the play of ideas, of pushing concepts to their limits to examine their implications.[9]

Similarly, Bush wanted to be the education President, the environmental President, and the economic growth President. When it turned out that being the environmental President was also making him the regulatory President and, consequently, *not* the economic growth President (because of the high cost of his regulatory initiatives, involving the Clean Air Act, wetlands, and the Americans With Disabilities Act), Bush was in a quandary as to what to do. He would ask his Chief of Staff, "Surely we are not *re-regulating*?" He had never inquired deeply enough into these priorities to determine whether they were mutually attainable or whether there was any inherent conflict. When they did conflict, he didn't know what to do.

Fallows said of Carter, "He thinks he 'leads' by choosing the correct policy; but he fails to project a vision larger than the problem he is tackling at the moment."[10] Both men tended to be good rather than effective. In Carter's case this was possibly excusable: He had been a one-term Governor with virtually no experience of the federal government. In Bush's case, it was not: He brought to the presidency a stellar resumé with nearly a lifetime of experience in senior federal positions. Moreover, his top staff—Darman, Scowcroft, and Porter—had cut their teeth in the Nixon and/or Ford administrations. Darman and Porter even taught government process together at Harvard's Kennedy School before joining the Bush Administration. There was, at least on paper, no excuse for the Bush Administration's ineffectiveness.

As President, Jimmy Carter favored "stability, harmony, and order" in his White House. No one was rewarded for superior service or penalized for failure. According to Fallows, Carter "created an administration in which . . . people were more concerned with holding their jobs than with using them."[11] Ditto for Bush.

Carter and Bush believed deeply in establishing a world of hierarchies around them. Fallows describes how the Carter White House resembled a feudal system in which everyone had his or her place in the Great Chain of Being. While such a world was orderly, it was also, Fallows wrote, "stagnant." Bush similarly adhered to his own sense of presidential hierarchy and internal harmony.

Bush expressed his preference for harmony over discord in his 1988 acceptance speech at the New Orleans GOP Convention when he spoke of America as "a nation of communities, of thousands and tens of thousands of ethnic, religious, social, business, labor union, neighborhood, regional and other organizations, all of them varied, voluntary, and unique." Once in office, he gave flesh to this concept—his "Thousand Points of Light" pledge—by establishing an Office of National Service in the White House and a Points of Light Foundation to give recognition to examples of civicmindedness all across America. It was all consistent with Bush's long-ingrained sense of *noblesse oblige* and his firm belief, as he expressed it in June 1991, in an America "whole and good." But because he hated bickering, he stood by idly while the Democratic Congress blocked most of his legislative proposals.

George Bush had inherited the world, literally. Ronald Reagan had left the Bush Administration the strongest record of peacetime growth in the nation's history. From a military and geopolitical standpoint, the country had never been stronger. Within ten months after Ronald Reagan's retirement, the Berlin Wall had collapsed, and by 1990 the Soviet Union and most of its empire had effectively committed suicide. Drawing on Reagan's military arsenal, George Bush assembled a splendid coalition that rolled back aggression in the Persian Gulf. As Bush himself was fond of noting: missions defined, missions accomplished.

So how does an incumbent President with a near 90 percent approval rating lose reelection to a man frequently referred to by RNC Chairman Rich Bond as "the failed governor of a small state"?

A few weeks before November 3 I found a button from George Bush's 1988 campaign. Its message was simple and short: "We are the *Change!*" Seeing that slogan gave me a laugh, particularly in view of the prominence "change" had come to have during the 1992 election campaign.

What had happened to "We are the *Change!*" between 1988 and 1992? The answer to that question explains why George Bush was a one-term President.

The party of new ideas had become the party of incumbency.

Many Republicans now took for granted the "electoral lock," the Southern bloc, and Republican control of the executive branch. Their complacency was reinforced by the President's own high approval ratings through the first half of his term. Yet it's fair to say that for the first two years of the Bush Administration we were still spending down Ronald Reagan's inheritance. Even though the actual policies being implemented in many respects were really at odds with Reagan's core philosophy, the country had not yet woken up to the fact that under George Bush's stewardship federal spending (along with the deficit) was spiraling upward, taxes would start creeping up again, and regulatory policies would impose billions of dollars of new burdens on the public. This was "change," all right, but the wrong kind of change. Most of the country rejected it as "small change." We had been hoping for better.

The cumulative effect of these deviations from Reaganism, combined with the disastrous 1990 budget deal, split the Republican national coalition and contributed to the lingering recession that began in mid-1990. It was not a particularly deep recession (unemployment never reached the peak level during Reagan's 1981–82 economic downturn), but it was unusually long and affected many white-collar service workers for the first time in our history. In the past, recessions had touched primarily the manufacturing sector; now it was mid-level management that was feeling the pinch.

The collapse of Communism, moreover, meant the loss of a "certainty" the nation had taken for granted for half a century. The Soviets were no longer our enemy. For the first time, the multibillion-dollar defense industry would begin to shrink in both output and employees in the wake of the dramatic downsizing called for by the Soviets' demise. Many things that Americans had long taken for granted were now changing rapidly, some in ways that would mean a stronger nation, others in ways that the public found unsettling. The country needed sound leadership that was capable of doing two essential things: explaining why the changes were happening and charting a future course to address them.

What the American public got from us instead was slavish adherence to the status quo and an unwillingness or inability to explain all the major developments in a context that Americans could fathom. The country saw its sixty-eight-year-old President traveling the land expressing his own bewilderment and calling 1992 "weird, weird, man." And "weird" was not what people wanted or needed to hear, because it translated very simply into something else: I don't understand either. The President's shrill rhetoric further underscored the growing perception that his Administration was incapable of charting a course for the future. If you yourself don't understand your own environment, how can you lead your fellow citizens?

And yet I can see some of my former White House colleagues who might be reading this passage today shaking their heads and wondering how I can write what I've just written. (I recall Boyden Gray, shortly after the election, saying that there were so many "remarkable, and yet unremarked" aspects of the Bush Administration.) Have I somehow forgotten that we *did* have lots of serious proposals for change—in welfare reform, health care, education, housing, childcare, etc., etc.? That we accomplished a new Clean Air Act, civil rights and disabilities laws? Of course I haven't.

But those last three examples probably hurt the President politically more than they helped, as each came to be associated with more regulation, more lawsuits, and more costs imposed on the taxpayers. I worked on many of these ideas and proposals, but to any of my dismayed former colleagues I would add one vital rejoinder: Having a list of proposals and an arsenal of fact sheets is not the same thing as having an agenda accompanied by the driving force to do something with it. Our proposals—many of them excellent—were but pieces of a puzzle that nobody bothered to assemble. Our communications strategy was little more than an *ad hoc* series of staged events disconnected from any overarching strategic message. As quickly as we made a policy, we "unmade" it by botching the way it was communicated or bottling it up by finding endless reasons why we shouldn't risk doing it. And, of course, some of our policies—on the budget and on regulations, for example—were wrong. As things evolved, "We are the *Change!*" became nothing more than "campaign mode" thinking. It never managed to infect the way in which the Bush Administration actually chose to govern, until the last month of the campaign, by which time it was too late.

Shortly after George Bush was defeated, Bill Bennett said in the *New York Times* that we had lost because we were tired and had run out of steam and ideas. He was wrong. *Some* people in the Administration were, indeed, tired, but they had been tired twelve years ago, some even sixteen years ago. They were the people around George

Bush in the upper echelon of the White House who had elevated process over substance, crowding out and holding back the Administration's "Young Turks" who were pushing hard for a more activist, growth-oriented economic and domestic agenda. For many of those quintessentially establishment figures, the world had changed so quickly in four years as to leave them ill-equipped to respond to events. Unable to respond, they were equally incapable of anticipating, let alone understanding, so they chose to cling to old familiarities. Stick to tried and true. Above all, don't rock the boat.

We had policies, programs, and proposals, dozens of them, but that's precisely why we did not have a domestic agenda in the Bush Administration. Proposals were advanced, but in many instances, not far enough. There was no focus and little follow-up. Rarely was there a willingness to fight for something, whether capital gains, school choice, or urban enterprise zones.

How to explain all of this? Was it due to the personalities? Partially. There were people in the Administration who, like Darman, wanted the stage all to themselves, and others like Roger Porter, who just refused to fight and were shoved aside. An environment of real teamwork never really evolved among people who fundamentally did not trust one another. The West Wing was filled with lots of tennis players, but tennis is mostly one-on-one. It's not a team sport. The result was gridlock—gridlock *within* the White House itself.

For four years we had a government that lacked interest in its own domestic policies. Was this the natural result of being (at least nominally) "conservative" Republicans? Hardly. Many, like Pinkerton and the Young Turks, were passionately concerned that Bush's accomplishments had little to do with the conservative ideas. We believed in small government and fewer programs. George Bush did, too, in theory, but in practice he presided over an expansion in the size of the executive branch and the largest growth in federal spending in almost thirty years.

The problem was the glaringly visible gap between our rhetoric and our reality. When the President owned up, the American people caught on. They were tired of politicians who promised one thing but did another. They wanted "campaign mode" and "governing mode" to come together. Only the future will tell which political party was really listening.

11
Looking Beyond

"Don't look back."

—Roger B. Porter,
November 4, 1992

The advice struck some of us as peculiar.

The day after George Bush's loss to Bill Clinton, Roger Porter convened his Office of Policy Development staff in Room 476 of the Old Executive Office Building.

Reading awkwardly from prepared notes, Porter began by explaining to us that he'd been through transitions before, notably when Gerald Ford lost to Jimmy Carter. His best advice was to put it behind us, "Don't look back."

If people followed Porter's advice, history would never be written. Errors of analysis or judgment and personal foibles that altered the country's direction would never be exposed. More important, in the future there would be only books by people like Porter to tell the story.

Besides, George Bush's loss to Bill Clinton took real talent. It wasn't accidental. People had to work exceedingly hard to bring down a President who in early 1991 had achieved the highest approval ratings in modern polling history. Now he would be grouped in the history books with three other twentieth-century presidents who had

337

failed to be reelected: William Howard Taft, Herbert Hoover, and Jimmy Carter.

I have tried to describe how George Bush's disastrous loss happened. Perhaps now it's worth a moment or two to look beyond, to reflect on what it all means, especially for the Republican party.

The Bush Administration held power in America at a particularly critical time. Change dominated the headlines around the world, but inside the White House the dominant theme was caution, coupled with a desire to do as little as possible domestically.

That did not have to be. We must hope it will be different in the future.

It was no secret that George Bush's favorite President was Theodore Roosevelt. Not only did TR's portrait hang in the Roosevelt Room, but Bush placed another portrait of his hero in the Cabinet Room, in the space where Ronald Reagan had once hung Calvin Coolidge. The attraction was obvious: Teddy Roosevelt was both an environmental President and a notoriously activist President, and it was abundantly evident that George Bush thought of himself in similar terms. The reality, however, was altogether different.

In the first volume of his biography of Franklin Delano Roosevelt, *The Crisis of the Old Order*, Arthur M. Schlesinger, Jr., describes how Teddy Roosevelt had once written in his autobiography about "two opposing theories of the Presidency":

> One, which he called the Taft–Buchanan school, took the view that the President could do nothing, no matter how necessary it was to act, unless the Constitution explicitly commanded the action. The other, which T.R. called the Jackson–Lincoln school, looked on the President as duty-bound to do everything that the needs of the nation demanded where the Constitution did not explicitly forbid him to render service.[1]

TR saw himself as a continuation of the Jackson–Lincoln tradition, and Schlesinger quotes him accordingly: "I believed in invoking the National power with absolute freedom for every National need, and I believed that the Constitution should be treated as the greatest document ever devised by the wit of man to aid a people in exercising every power, necessary for its own betterment, and not as a straitjacket cunningly fashioned to strangle growth."[2]

In his own autobiography, *Looking Forward*, George Bush wonders openly how he would have handled the question correspondent Roger Mudd put to Teddy Kennedy in 1980: "Why do you want to be President?" Bush at first mused over the various answers previous American leaders might have offered, and of his model Bush wrote: "Teddy Roosevelt might have told Mudd that he was *a man with a mission*, to save America's soul, and the White House was a 'bully pulpit.' "[3] Amusingly, candidate Bush speculated that Franklin Roosevelt would have been unable to answer this question since, according to the columnist Walter Lippmann, FDR was little more than a "pleasant man who, without any important qualifications for the office, would very much like to be President."[4]

Now, on the eve of his second presidential bid in 1988, here is what George Bush wrote about how he would have handled Mudd:

> By May 1, 1979—the day I announced my candidacy—if Roger Mudd had asked why I was running for President, my answer would have been: first, because I didn't see any Roosevelts or Eisenhowers running; second, because we needed a great deal better than Jimmy Carter's best to solve the serious problems that faced our country both at home and overseas; and finally, because I believed that by experience in government and business, as well as by philosophy and temperament, I was the best-qualified candidate on the scene to lead America in the 1980s.[5]

This response is remarkable for its lack of conviction: "I'm running because I don't see anybody else around who's on a par with FDR or Ike; Carter was a failure; and I want the job." And Bush lacked the self-knowledge to quote Lippmann's criticism of FDR!

By August 1988, however, George Bush was ready at the New Orleans GOP convention to embrace his own image of Teddy Roosevelt by saying of himself in his memorable acceptance speech: "I'm a man who sees life in terms of missions—missions defined and missions completed." The rhetoric was as sound as it was lofty, but it was once again "campaign mode," and the words were easily forgotten when it came time to govern. George Bush's rhetoric—in 1988 and again in 1992—adopted the themes and aspirations of the Jackson–Lincoln–Teddy Roosevelt model, but the reality of his governing record was decidedly in the mold of Buchanan and Taft.

Woodrow Wilson once said that the "President is at liberty, both in law and conscience, to be as big a man as he can. His capacity will set the limit. . . . The Constitution bids him speak, and times of stress and change must more and more thrust upon him the attitude of originator of policies."[6] Not so with our Administration. In fact, far too often the aim seemed precisely the opposite. In the White House, George Bush was surrounded by gifted and loyal aides who saw our time at the helm as an opportunity to achieve something, to defend Reagan's triumphs, to build on them toward an entrepreneurial economy and a government that emphasized empowering individuals. They were the ones inside the White House who were repeatedly urging a more activist agenda. Time and time again their efforts were rebuffed, ignored, belittled, demeaned, and dismissed.

As Dennis Ross, a Baker aide from the State Department brought to the White House in August 1992 to replace Clayton Yeutter and Roger Porter in domestic policy, explained after the 1992 election, for months the Bush White House had discarded ideas not on the basis of their merit but on the basis of who had proposed them. That George Bush allowed this situation to happen, that he permitted himself to be surrounded by senior aides who cut him off from alternative views and courses of action, will be remembered as his biggest tragedy as President.

Had George Bush truly emulated his role model, he would have moved aggressively and promptly on several fronts. The activists in the Cabinet, the White House, and the Congress urged him repeatedly to index the capital gains tax through administrative rulemaking; implement the line-item veto, leaving it to the courts to tell him whether he was right or wrong; challenge the Congress to reform itself; enforce the Supreme Court's *Beck* decision; effectively repeal the Davis–Bacon law through Executive Order; make recess appointments in the face of unwarranted congressional delay; pursue relentlessly an economic growth and empowerment agenda to include welfare reform; veto the legislative branch appropriations bill; take stronger measures to support families; and press repeatedly and seriously for the various legislative proposals that he had sent to Congress and which were languishing without action or attention from the Democratic majority.

By pursuing some or all of those initiatives early on, George Bush could have strengthened the role of the presidency vis-à-vis the Congress and enhanced his own reelection prospects. He also could have built upon the twin principles of lower taxes and reduced government spending that constituted the core of Reagan Republicanism. Instead, his steadfast reluctance to exercise presidential authority at home to its full potential, along with the political and policy disaster of the 1990 budget deal, led to the collapse of the premises on which the GOP had been headed toward majority party status. We neither shored up our bases by defending what Ronald Reagan had achieved nor moved forward aggressively to build upon his accomplishments.

Prior to Reagan's election, the national Republican party had been more or less the functional equivalent of a green-eyeshade OMB budget examiner, saying to the Democrats who had controlled the Congress: "OK, go ahead and spend, but we're gonna do our best to keep spending levels down and reduce the tax burden on the American public." It was a naysayer's job, for which Republicans received hardly any political credit. And until Reagan's arrival, the GOP enjoyed relatively little success. The party seemed destined for a permanent minority status.

The advent of supply side economics changed things for Republicans. Supply side theory opened up new vistas for Republicans: the Reagan-era tax cuts meant that the GOP could now offer something positive to *its* constituents, going in effect head-to-head and dollar-for-dollar with the Democrats and paying for it to boot. The only problem was that the second half of the equation—spending restraint—never materialized, as the Democrats in Congress worked assiduously to maintain the spending levels of the various federal programs essential to their own constituents. The GOP deserves criticism, too, for not pushing harder for the necessary spending cuts.

By 1990, however, the political system in the country had done its job relatively well. It had produced an apparent policy stalemate between the two major parties, but most Americans seemed quite comfortable with it anyway. The public appeared perfectly content with *both* lower taxes *and* higher Social Security payments.

At the same time, there was a vague unease across the land about the need to address hopelessness, health care, crime, and the environment, and those issues were never approached in any systematic or specific manner. Incumbent Senator Harris Wofford trounced Dick Thornburgh in the 1990 Pennsylvania Senate race by raising the issue of health care. Wofford said nothing specific and offered few details but was seen as fundamentally more "caring" than his opponent.

Budget directors like Stockman and Darman were unprepared to accept the status quo. Above all, they were unwilling to admit that supply side theory might actually have worked. (Tax revenue did increase even with the 1981 tax cut, but Congress refused to make good on the spending restraint.) Instead, they engineered an effort to return the GOP to its pre-1981 condition by acquiescing to higher taxes (ostensibly to lower the deficit) while giving scant attention to efforts to restrain federal spending. With that approach, Republicans reverted to the same essentially naysaying role vis-à-vis the Democrats they had played *before* Ronald Reagan was elected President. With Bill Clinton now in the White House and proposing to revert to traditional Democratic tax-and-spend policies, the risk for Republicans is substantial if the party continues to pursue the pre-1981 approach. If it does, it is almost guaranteed to retain minority status in perpetuity, as it can never within this framework outbid its Democratic opponents.

That is what the 1990 budget deal was all about, and it explains why George Bush was a one-term President. Darman's deal yielded George Mitchell levels for taxes and entitlement spending and Robert Byrd levels for domestic discretionary spending. Once again, there were no real spending cuts. George Bush got only one thing out of all this: early retirement.

In retrospect, George Bush will be seen as a transitional President. From the very beginning of his Administration, there was a noticeable lack of clarity when it came to setting the country's future direction. Bush's was a presidency of lowered expectations—more "will than wallet" was how he expressed it on day one in his inaugural address. As it turned out, there was not much of either. His agendaless Administration represented a coda in American political life.

Ronald Reagan, by contrast, had been a hedgehog among the foxes. His central vision of America's future was simple and clear: lower taxes, less government, and stronger defense. To accomplish his goals, he pursued strategies of decentralization, deregulation, and denationalization. Power increasingly devolved toward the states and individuals, and away from Washington. Reagan issued a "Federalism Executive Order" in a calculated effort to codify this trend and to rein in the scope of the federal government itself.

Likewise, Reagan's pursuit of deregulatory initiatives (spearheaded by then Vice President Bush) complemented his brand of "New Federalism," minimizing the burdens imposed on the people—states, local governments, individuals, and corporate America—so that free markets and competition could flourish. Wherever possible, problems were to be disaggregated and not approached as if some overarching grand national scheme could solve them: It was far better to let problems be addressed in thousands of communities all across America. As a hedgehog, however, Reagan had a profound belief in and appreciation for the foxes when it came to the detailed solutions.

George Bush, on the other hand, entered the White House as Ronald Reagan's heir apparent but lacked his driving vision. He was a fox who believed in quiet competence and the steady, day-to-day tick-tock management of the affairs of government. His much-vaunted handling of the Persian Gulf Crisis demonstrated consummate bureaucratic skills aptly summed up by verbs like "collaborate," "coordinate," and "organize." The only difference was that the objective in the Gulf—restoration of the status quo prior to Saddam Hussein's invasion of Kuwait—was indeed critical, but it required relatively little imagination. It defined itself. Domestically, we needed more than a clockmaker's love for detail. The times required imagination and drive.

Reagan was almost always prepared to stake out his policy positions by defining his differences from his opponents. By contrast, Bush and most of his White House aides (many of whom had long government pedigrees) preferred to define areas in which they and their adversaries could agree while often denigrating their natural allies. Over time, this stance caused the Reagan coalition to fray and ultimately collapse. The Bush Administration stood for little as a matter of principle when it came to domestic policy. The President caved in repeatedly, first on taxes, then on quotas in the civil rights bill, on spending, on regulatory policy, and on capital gains tax reduction. In the meantime, the Bush White House sat idly by while its Democratic opposition in Congress ran out the clock.

As for the President's legislative agenda, the limits of whatever advances he might make were determined by the willingness of the Democrats to go along. Bush would rarely risk a veto override. If he knew he lacked the votes to sustain his veto, he simply refrained from exercising it. That permitted the congressional Democrats to score big victories, while it drove Bush's conservative supporters crazy time after time.

In the end, the American people figured this out. As the Bush

campaign in 1992 lurched from one message to the next, totally incapable of maintaining any focus, it was obvious that all the public was
getting was rhetoric designed to reflect the findings from the latest
focus group. This wasn't leadership. It was "campaign mode"—only
this time the public's collective memory of the previous four years
and of George Bush's overall record was pretty accurate.

Arthur Schlesinger once wrote that American history was subject to
certain cycles. Had he been correct, Vice President Bush, following in
the footsteps of most of his predecessors, excluding Martin Van Buren, would have retired as Michael Dukakis assumed the presidency
in January 1989. While Schlesinger's theory of cycles has never manifested itself with perfect predictability, there does appear to be a
recurring theme or cycle between two strong currents that often run
throughout American history: the current of centralized government
authority and the current of denationalization. It is not an exaggeration to conclude that the strongest leaders in American history have
emerged in the context of trying to resolve those competing trends.

Alexander Hamilton placed his faith in a strong national government, whereas Thomas Jefferson favored an agrarian democracy. The
American Civil War involved a bitter conflict between forces of union
and disunion. More recently, Franklin Roosevelt and Lyndon Johnson
exhibited a routine faith in the ability of the national government to
get things done. According to Joseph A. Califano, Jr., of Lyndon
Johnson's Administration, Johnson's "Great Society" was a continuation of the New Deal impulse with its creation of new federal laws
for civil rights, student loans, "child nutrition, truth-in-packaging, bail
reform, mine safety, urban mass transit, national parks and seashores,
clean rivers, international education, auto, tire, and highway safety"—
and much else.[7]

By contrast, beginning with Reagan our goal was to decentralize
authority away from Washington, in part because of the belief that
states, localities, and individuals could better address the issues that
really mattered. That approach was not necessarily wrong; indeed, I
believe it was, and remains, correct, given the failed record of centralized bureaucracies during the last half-century. Under George
Bush, we just never managed to pursue it with sufficient vigor. Many
of our proposals would have undone New Deal and Great Society
approaches in favor of more decentralized approaches that would empower nongovernment actors.

Our weakest Presidents have been those who managed the office of the presidency without clear views, one way or the other, about this central question of our history and national character. Reagan believed with all his heart and soul that government had grown too big and too bloated. It had to be reduced, tamed, and made responsive to the needs of the people. Bush, on the other hand, was all over the lot, exhibiting an inconsistency that deprived his Administration of intellectual coherence and consistency.

For example, on the one hand he briefly advocated a "turnback" proposal in January 1990 (basically greater revenue-sharing with the states) but simultaneously acquiesced to imposing additional state mandates through huge expansions in the federal Medicaid program (a significant portion of which the states paid for). The pattern repeated itself when, in November 1991, he suddenly woke up to the fact that on his watch government regulation was setting new records for being burdensome. What did he expect, after all, in the wake of bills like the Clean Air Act, the new Civil Rights Act, and the Americans With Disabilities Act? The same style manifested itself in matters of spending.

Where Reagan had a few simple guiding principles that all his appointees knew, Bush had nothing, except perhaps a devotion to process and the allegiance of literally hundreds of friends he had made throughout his many different careers in government and private industry. That lack, more than anything else, explains the many instances when the White House was hit with some complex or controversial policy issue and found itself stunned, unable to reach a consensus on what the right action should be.

In the Bush White House, there was little if any encouragement of competing views, no real opportunity to dissent from conventional wisdom. Califano had described a White House where LBJ had "turned the Oval Office into a parade ground for competing views."[8] By contrast, Bush became increasingly isolated. He had surrounded himself on the domestic side with advisers who were either passive and timid or so fundamentally insecure that they could not bear to have the President hear views different from their own. Elsewhere, his National Security Adviser, Brent Scowcroft, was secure enough in his relationship with the President to feel comfortable in occasionally sending memos to Bush from NSC staffers who disagreed on an issue. That just didn't happen on the domestic side. Few people were able to get through to George Bush's Oval Office, which remained until the end dominated on domestic issues by Dick Darman.

In December 1991, the *New York Times* reported that the Bush Administration suffered from "oxygen depletion," a comment that proved more prescient than I thought at the time. Deprived of sufficient oxygen, an individual first becomes light-headed and dizzy—dazed—and then falls unconscious. Califano's "parade ground for competing views" never existed when it came to domestic policy in the Bush Administration. The responsibility, however, can only lie with the President, who could have opened the door to his Oval Office far wider than he did.

American Presidents tend to be either conviction Presidents or managerial Presidents. Recent American history confirms that conviction presidents—FDR, Truman, Kennedy, LBJ, and Reagan—often enjoy more successful administrations. Managerial presidents—Nixon, Ford, Carter, and Bush—are, at best, placeholders. At their worst they are overwhelmed by those around them, who are able to manipulate the internal processes of the White House to their own ends.

But whether the country has a conviction President or a managerial President at the helm, it is absolutely essential to have people in senior government positions, especially at the White House, who are fundamentally comfortable with themselves and who manifest a basic core of self-esteem, dignity, integrity, and confidence. Ronald Reagan, perhaps the quintessential conviction President of this half-century, displayed both an unwavering sense of purpose and a basic sense of personal security. It was Reagan, after all, who could sign a movie poster depicting himself and the chimpanzee Bonzo with the following inscription: "I'm the one with the watch."[9]

George Bush, a genuine war hero who had risked his own life to save his friends and his country in World War II, had the self-assurance, honesty, and integrity for the job but fundamentally lacked conviction in defining what he wanted to achieve and where he wanted to lead the country. The absence of conviction does not necessarily mean a flawed or failed presidency, but it does leave the office of the presidency open to manipulation by those around the President who have an agenda of their own or, just as damaging, no agenda other than to develop the process of decisionmaking with themselves at the center.

People who are essentially insecure and uncomfortable with themselves have no business holding senior government positions. They approach the exercise of political power as a zero-sum game even with their supposed "friends" and allies. They see it as a means of filling up the empty spaces they face within their own lives. Politics is their cover, affording them the grand illusion of self-esteem and self-importance. There was no room on the White House stage for a Roger Porter, who, albeit politely and without staying power, might have challenged others for undisputed reign over domestic policy. A Newt Gingrich was dismissed as "dishonest," a Trent Lott called "irrelevant" for daring to challenge the White House's brilliance. A Jack Kemp was vilified as the biggest hypocrite of them all.

For George Bush, success in the presidency was managing the affairs of the country in a prudent and judicious fashion. That he did relatively well. The goal was little more than maintaining order. I do not believe, however, that he either understood ideas or felt comfortable with them. One of his senior aides even suspected that Bush was mildly dyslexic, hence his preference for almost constant motion and athletic activity to more reflective pursuits. Unlike Ronald Reagan, who was a voracious reader—Martin Anderson called him a "closet bookworm"—George Bush never appreciated how ideas could be deployed as part of an agenda to bolster, sustain, and advance nearly twelve years of Republican-led successes.

The Bush presidency began with an understandable desire to do things differently from Ronald Reagan. As one senior presidential aide put it, the goal was to "take some of the rough edges off Reaganism." That desire explained phrases like "kinder, gentler" and an avowed goal to address matters involving the environment, civil rights, and the rights of the disabled. Those may have been reasonable aspirations, but—and this is precisely the point lost on the Bush Administration—they could have been carried out by men and women with consistent ideas, conviction, and passion.

Bush could have pursued all of those goals while simultaneously emphasizing the importance of cost-effective regulation and the need for less litigation. Instead, he acquiesced in solutions that ran counter to his predecessor's philosophy of government. When people balked, Bush was trapped in the middle, caught in a political and philosophical muddle from which he could not extricate himself. His failure to articulate a consistent governing philosophy and his lack of conviction on taxes cost him his credibility. Nothing could be more revealing than 1992 opinion polls that showed George Bush's economic recovery plan receiving higher ratings than Bill Clinton's in blind comparisons. Once people learned which was Bush's, however, Clinton's scored better.

The primary thrust of the Bush Administration should have been to build on Ronald Reagan's successes, not to dissipate those triumphs by allowing Reagan's critics to recast what happened during the 1980s and ignite the fires of class warfare. There is a tendency to explain the collapse of the Bush Administration as having to do with the "end of an era," the fact that George Bush was the last American President— its last Cold War leader—to be born in the period of the Great Depression and to have fought in World War II. With the collapse of Communism, the critics say, there will now be a natural desire of the country to refocus on domestic matters, to turn to a new generation for leadership.

Unfortunately, matters aren't that simple. After all, Ronald Reagan's policies covered two fronts, domestic and foreign. At home he enshrined the importance of lower taxes, less government, sound monetary policy, traditional family values, and a strong national defense. Abroad he maintained the pressure on the Soviet Union until it collapsed of its own internal contradictions. The British intellectual Noel Annan has written, "Perhaps it was even the threat of star wars Reagan had conjured up that brought about Gorbachev's demarche."[10] While the collapse of Communism will undoubtedly mark the signal event of the last half-century, its occurrence was by no means divorced from the policies Ronald Reagan advocated domestically. In fact, the two mirrored each other quite remarkably.

Efforts to reduce the size and scope of government, to make government accountable, and to turn more power and authority over to people and take it away from government are what led to the phenomenal economic growth in America during the 1980s and the collapse of one totalitarian regime after another around the world. The utter failure of centralized bureaucracy as a model for organizing governments, people, and businesses was abundantly clear to the oldest man ever to hold the presidency. It was also perceived by dozens of younger democrats—Vaclav Havel in Czechoslovakia, Lech Walesa in Poland, Ognian Pishev in Bulgaria, and Yegor Gaidar in Russia, to name but a few—who were determined to bring freedom and capitalism to their nations.

We may speak of the "end of an era" with the demise of the Cold War, but there is a remarkable and refreshing continuity between the ideas of octogenarians like Ronald Reagan and a younger generation abroad that understands his governing philosophy perhaps even better than many in America do today. It was no accident that the Republican party under Reagan garnered a majority of the "youth" vote in America, just as it was no accident that by 1992 George Bush would forfeit that vote to Bill Clinton. In each instance, success or failure had nothing to do with age and everything to do with ideas.

The 1992 election was not a rejection of Republican principles. In fact, Bill Clinton remains a minority president who received only 43 percent of the popular vote, a figure even lower than the vote Michael Dukakis won in 1988. Many Perot voters were disillusioned Reagan Democrats fed up with George Bush's departures from Reaganomics. Add their votes to those Bush received from GOP stalwarts and you have a sizable majority that opposes big government intervention and distrusts the ability of unaccountable centralized bureaucracies to manage a welfare state.

My conclusion is that the Bush White House operated in an all-pervasive confusion in which rhetoric and reality went their separate ways. Instead of offering the American public a clear agenda that differed dramatically from the Democrats', Bush Republicans blurred their differences with their opponents, sacrificing ideology and principle for compromise. The result: an evisceration of the GOP's previous "lock" on such critical pocketbook issues as spending, the budget deficit, and the economy in general.

The 1992 postelection polling data confirmed these observations beyond any question. Bill Clinton did not win so much as George Bush simply collapsed, on virtually all fronts. The repudiation was profound and total.

Among his base of self-described Republicans, Bush lost eighteen percentage points from his 1988 showing. The same trend was true with conservatives, with whom his vote count was fifteen points lower. While Bush got 48 percent of the critical Northern union vote in 1988, he won only 24 percent in 1992.

And then there were three stunners:

Of those *Reagan Democrats* who'd gone for Bush in 1988, only 28 percent did so four years later. Clinton picked up a remarkable 53 percent of 1988 Reagan Democrats, and 54 percent of 1984 Reagan Democrats. The Independent candidate, Ross Perot, carried 22 percent of 1984 Reagan Democrats, while Bush received a mere 24 percent.

Take *military veterans*, who make up 18 percent of the voters and among whom the former war hero George Bush was almost certain to do well. He lost here, too. Clinton, the so-called "draft-dodging, dope-smoking, philanderer," beat him 41 to 37 percent!

As for *people who'd voted for him in 1988*, George Bush managed to retain a mere 58 percent of them.

While George Bush's support was collapsing, the Democrats had used the 1992 election to position themselves well among younger and first-time voters. For the first time since 1980, the Democrats won more of the "youth vote" than the Republicans. First-time voters went 46 percent for Clinton, 32 percent for Bush, and 22 percent for Perot. The incumbent President also managed to lose to Clinton in *all* age groups.

The electorate's rejection of George Bush the President did not, however, mean that Americans rejected George Bush the man.

In polls about the personal qualities of the candidates, Bush trumped Clinton decisively on matters of experience, judgment, trustworthiness, and convictions. But Clinton destroyed Bush on the two qualities that mattered most in deciding for whom to vote: "will bring about needed change" and "has the best plan for the country." On the former, Bush scored a paltry 5 percent to Clinton's 67 percent. As for the best plan, Clinton outpolled Bush 58 to 17 percent. Not surprisingly, Bush won handily when the qualities involved "process" but lost miserably when the comparison turned to action and change for the country.

Stepping away from candidate comparisons and judging the two parties' overall performance, we see from the 1992 election that Americans viewed the Democrats as offering better positions on the economy, the budget, education, and health care. Bush effectively lost the first two issues in 1990 when he compromised away the traditional GOP high ground in the 1990 budget deal. In education, although the President made repeated attempts at elementary and secondary school reform, he had nothing to say about postsecondary education, which millions of American families worry about. On health care, his Administration was virtually silent until the end.

If it confirmed anything, the 1992 election confirmed the fact that ideology matters. The issues being debated by the candidates do not have to be at ideological extremes, but when the voters perceive no convincing difference between the two major parties, there will be a net movement *toward* candidates like Clinton and Perot, who at least appear to offer something new and different.

In the wake of Bush's humiliating loss, there will probably be a tendency for some in the GOP to look inward, in every sense of the word. First, there may be the temptation to retreat into isolationism in foreign policy and exclusionary attitudes domestically. Doing so would be a mistake of gigantic proportions. As the world grows increasingly diverse, America cannot sit on the sidelines and watch. Our policies in areas as different as international trade and immigration will determine not only our standard of living but also what kind of people we will be. Closed borders in either instance will limit our role in the future.

Second, there will be a flurry of prominent former GOP officeholders heading to various think tanks, old and new, across the country. There they will think the great thoughts and ponder the future of the party and what it should stand for in order to make a comeback by 1996. Those efforts will all be to the good. They are needed to create new political capital. As Bill Bennett was fond of saying about education reform, we already know what works: less government, lower tax rates, sound money, traditional family values, and a strong national defense. The challenge is to go out and do it! We need more retail-level politicians, Republicans who ply their ideas in the statehouses, county councils, and city halls across the land. They are now in short supply.

People around the world have lost faith in government because centralized bureaucracies have failed to deliver what they promised. In exchange for either greater authority over the people (as formerly in Eastern and Central Europe and the former Soviet Union) or higher rates of taxation (as in the United States and Western Europe) governments promised to provide a variety of goods and services. Sometimes, when the delivery is accomplished by *de minimis* bureaucracy and accountability for results is maintained, government can succeed. In other instances, government has become a dysfunctional monopoly which actually delivers bad services and impedes consumer choice and satisfaction. The future lies not with more government but with seeking ways to redefine a legitimate role for government in the delivery of certain services, while freeing the private sector and individuals (through lower taxes and fewer regulations) to compete and innovate whenever possible.

We also need a strong government to ensure the enforcement of our civil rights laws so that people are not discriminated against as they seek to educate their children or earn a living for themselves and their families. But we do not need more of a government-sponsored and government-encouraged system of rules and regulations that encourages needless litigation as a way of seeking a better life. For most Americans today, the successes of the civil rights movement mean that their future lies not in trying a case in a courtroom but in having a good job, being able to save for their future, sending their children to a good school free of drugs and violence, being able to own their own home, and walking down local streets free of crime. As Lord Annan has noted presciently, "The rage to do good by legislation could lead to a paradise for censorious busybodies and lawyers."[11] Politicians who bear this advice in mind will prosper. Those who ignore it will find themselves bucking history and an impatient electorate tired of excuses, lawyers, and doubletalk. The people will replace them.

The model for the future of the Republican party should be a party that maximizes individual choice and personal responsibility while redefining and minimizing the role of government in people's lives, one that simultaneously reaches out to mainstream America while including minorities and, particularly, our country's youth. Ironically, George Bush embraced part of this agenda, at least rhetorically, throughout much of his presidency. It was there in his first speech to Congress on February 9, 1989, and it was present in his September 16, 1992, Detroit Economic Club speech. He was correct when he stated at the end of the second presidential debate in 1992 that one of the key differences between himself and his opponents was his desire to "empower" people to make decisions for themselves. But having articulated the premises for this agenda as well as several good ideas for achieving it, his presidency wandered all over the lot when it came to trying to deliver. There was no staying power. Oddly, he secured passage of a major civil rights bill in 1992 but received a smaller share of the black vote than he had in 1988, barely exceeding Ronald Reagan's share.

To succeed, conservative leaders must not lose sight of the importance of linking their policies and prescriptions with the people. The strength and the success of Ronald Reagan lay in his ability to keep his ear close to the ground, always able to sense the mood of the people as well as their needs. He was a conviction President who, while secure in his own persona, embodied a populist movement that was first and foremost bottom-up. After all, Washington didn't find Ronald Reagan; it was the other way around. Reaganism's emphasis on lower taxes was born out of the populist revolt that began with Howard Jarvis in California. It later gained advocates in Washington— Jack Kemp, William Roth, Vin Weber, and others—who sought federal legislation to further those dreams.

In the wake of George Bush's defeat, the Republican party will now seek a new generation of leaders. But those leaders cannot be drawn solely from the party's intellectual elite. The future—and this applies as well for the Democrats having been taken over by the supposedly more conservative Democratic Leadership Council and its assortment of serious-minded "policy wonks"—lies with those politicians who are best able to link reform ideas with popular sentiment in an effort to remake government, reduce it wherever possible, and ultimately, where there is a legitimate role for government, make it work for people.

The biggest challenge for Bill Clinton in governing is, oddly enough, the same one faced by the Republicans who must now play the role of "loyal opposition": Can ideas be linked with action in ways that disempower government bureaucracies and continue the world-wide trend toward empowering individuals to make decisions for themselves? Whether the specific policy concerns school choice or marginal tax rates, the heart of the matter is, Who decides, individuals or the government? The temptation after years spent in the political wilderness will be for the policy wonks and lawyers now in power to forget where their roots really lie and head for the security of the Old Paradigm belief that government does, after all, know best.

For Republicans, the mantle of leadership will more than likely fall to those who, like former Representatives Jack Kemp, Vin Weber, and Dick Cheney, champion an activist and inclusive party that strives to redefine the role of government while simultaneously stressing the principles of market economics, empowerment, and the fundamental importance of individual choice and freedom. These are approaches that build on and strengthen the Reagan legacy. The tragedy of the Bush Administration was its inability to advance these ideas beyond the occasional rhetorical flourish and turn them into concrete reality for the American people.

The good news for the future of the Republican party is that today its outer strength is consistent with the internal logic of its own philosophy. Innovations are being made in statehouses and local governments across the land—in the work of governors like Tommy Thompson of Wisconsin, Carroll Campbell of South Carolina, John Engler of Michigan, Jim Edgar of Illinois, and William Weld of Massachusetts, and mayors like Bret Schundler of Jersey City, New Jersey. These are not just leaders who, whatever the differences, preach sound cultural values and personal responsibility plus the need for welfare and school reform (although we need those, too); they are people who help shape, and are in turn shaped by, a popular consensus to find practical solutions to everyday problems. It's retail politics at its very finest. The national Republican party must now disperse far out across the land and tap into the innovative and entrepreneurial spirit that is the genius of the American people. In the end, all of this will be good for the party and for the country. We will return renewed and refreshed, with governing and campaigning united as one.

Epilogue

November 3, 1992, was one of those splendid Indian summer days so rare in Washington, D.C. The weather in the capital had been dull and dreary for weeks, reflecting in some respects the gray pallor that had settled on George Bush's reelection campaign. But on election day the dawn broke with a singular clarity and crispness followed by a deep warmth and brilliance as the day progressed. There was no more haze or daze. The American public was about to render its verdict on our performance, and it was more likely that they would see things clearly and see them whole.

Shortly after lunch I dropped by Roger Porter's office in the West Wing to tell him I intended to resign that afternoon, effective three days later. There was no need to wait around any longer. Sitting behind his desk, he muttered something about how, looking back, he "might have been more aggressive in some things." He didn't say what. I didn't ask. It was time to go.

I wrote four letters that day. One went to the President indicating that I was resigning and thanking him for the opportunity to serve in his Administration. Another went to Jack Kemp, who'd always been a supporter and mentor; a third went to Lauro Cavazos. Both had been extremely kind to me, and I wanted to express my appreciation. My last official act after nine years in government was to send a letter of thanks to Ronald Reagan.

Would I miss the White House? Not particularly. It was a time of both incredible excitement and personal frustration. I was grateful for the experience, but I was ready to move on. So many wonderful opportunities were lost, including George Bush's ability to enter American history as a great President.

What I would sorely miss, however, was the daily contact with friends and colleagues who had worked tirelessly to achieve a different outcome. We had failed, not because our ideas were wrong, but because George Bush had allowed his presidency to be defined by people who were either fundamentally insecure or inherently timid and passionless, devoted to an in-box mentality that worshiped process over progress.

What mattered most, however, was that we had tried. And there were lots of key players who would be around for the future, household names like Lamar Alexander, Bill Bennett, Lynore and Dick Cheney, and Jack Kemp; foresighted policy intellectuals like John Cogan, Chris DeMuth, Connie Horner, Mike Horowitz, Bill Kristol, Larry Lindsey, Peggy Noonan, Debbie Steelman, and Vin Weber who believed deeply in the efficacy of ideas; and future stars like Jim Cicconi, Austen Furse, Jay Lefkowitz, Lee Liberman, Nelson Lund, Mary Matalin, Dan McGroarty, David McIntosh, Jim Pinkerton, Richard Porter, John Schall, John Schmitz, Tony Snow, Michael Williams, and others of the "Young Turks" of the Bush Administration or campaigns who someday would be back.

Near the end of World War II, on the brink of military success, Winston Churchill had offered an observation that was equally applicable to those who had worked so hard for a different outcome in the Bush years. To paraphrase Churchill: "We had all come together, and had stayed together, as a united band of friends, in a very trying time. History would recognize this."[12]

NOTES

Introduction

1. Martha Sherrill, "Leave It to the Beavers: The Frenzied Pace of the White House Workaholics," *Washington Post*, May 29, 1990, p. C–1.
2. Maureen Dowd, "Bush's Adviser on Domestic Policy: The Perfect Man to Process Details," *New York Times*, March 29, 1990, p. A–18.

Chapter 1. Doing It Differently

1. George Bush with Victor Gold, *Looking Forward* (New York: Bantam, 1988), p. xii.
2. Peggy Noonan, *What I Saw at the Revolution: A Political Life in the Reagan Era* (New York: Random House, 1990).
3. Id. at 301–2.
4. John Yang, "For Bush's Speech: A New World Order," *Washington Post*, June 22, 1991, p. A–10.
5. Ann Devroy, "High-Level Government Jobs Reserved for Bush Supporters," *Washington Post*, January 14, 1989, p. A–1.
6. Isaiah Berlin, *Russian Thinkers* (New York: Viking, 1978), p. 22.
7. *Ibid.*
8. Bush, *Looking Forward*, p. 29.
9. *Ibid.*, p. 22.
10. *Ibid.*
11. Lou Cannon, *Reagan* (New York: Putnam, 1982), p. 32.
12. Martin Nolan, "George Bush: Will He Now Say Who He Is?" *Boston Globe*, May 25, 1992, p. 8.
13. David Broder, "A Penchant for Dealing with Elites," *Washington Post*, July 31, 1991, p. A–21.

14. Bush, *Looking Forward*, p. xii.
15. *Ibid.*
16. Arthur M. Schlesinger, Jr., *The Age of Jackson* (New York: New American Library, 1945), p. 42.

Chapter 2. *Playing Tennis: It's All Form*

1. P. G. Wodehouse, *Very Good, Jeeves!* (Harmondsworth: Penguin Books, 1957), p. 18.
2. Maureen Dowd, "Bush's Adviser on Domestic Policy: The Perfect Man to Process Details," *New York Times*, March 29, 1990, p. A–18.
3. Speech entitled "The Challenges of the Presidency in the 1980's," delivered at Brigham Young University on October 9, 1980.
4. Roger B. Porter, *Presidential Decision Making: The Economic Policy Board* (Cambridge and New York: Cambridge University Press 1980), p. 83.
5. Fred Barnes, "Logjam," *The New Republic*, May 11, 1992, p. 10.

Chapter 3. *"You've Been Darmanized"*

1. Philip Larkin, "Toads," *Collected Poems* (New York: Farrar, Straus & Giroux, 1988), pp. 89–90.
2. Marjorie Williams, "The Long and the Short of Richard G. Darman," *The Washington Post Magazine*, July 29, 1990, pp. 10, 14.
3. *Ibid.*, pp. 13–14, 29.
4. Paul Gigot, "Parting Shots: It's Better in Bulgaria," *Wall Street Journal*, November 29, 1991, p. A–6.
5. Terry Sanders, *Energy in the Executive: The Case for the Strong Presidency* (New York: Free Press, 1992).
6. Stuart Auerbach, "Bill Gives Rostenkowski a Way to Settle Accounts," *Washington Post*, October 9, 1991, p. F–1.
7. Albert Karr and Michel McQueen, "Unlike Reagan Aides, Many Bush Officials Expand Regulation," *Wall Street Journal*, November 27, 1989, p. A–1.
8. Warren Brookes, "Will Iago Win Again?" *Washington Times*, December 17, 1991, p. F–1.
9. Jonathan Rauch, "The Regulatory President," *National Journal*, November 30, 1991, pp. 2902–3.
10. Editorial, "President Darman," *Wall Street Journal*, November 6, 1991, p. A–18.
11. Bob Woodward, "Origin of the Tax Pledge," "No-Tax Vow Scuttled Anti-Deficit Mission," "Primary Heat Turned Deal Into a 'Mistake,'"

"The President's Key Men: Splintered Ties, Splintered Policy," *Washington Post*, October 3–6, 1992, p. A–1.

Chapter 4. Darmanomics at Work: "We Can't Lose"

1. Alan Murray and Timothy Noah, "Perot's Plan Is Called Model of Good Sense, Bad Economic Timing," *Wall Street Journal*, September 29, 1992, p. A–1.
2. Donald Lambro, "Economic Distress in Wake of Higher Taxes," *Washington Times*, October 24, 1991, p. G–4.
3. Lawrence Lindsey, *The Growth Experiment: How the New Tax Policy Is Transforming the U.S. Economy* (New York: Basic Books, 1990), pp. 127–28.
4. *Budget of the United States Government*, Fiscal Year 1991, p. 20. Emphasis in original.
5. *Ibid.*, p. 21
6. Kevin Phillips, *The Politics of Rich and Poor: Wealth and the American Electorate in the Reagan Aftermath* (New York: Random House 1990), p. 165.
7. *Ibid.*, p. xxii.
8. Paul Gigot, "Mr. Darman Reveals Himself Once and for All," *Wall Street Journal*, November 23, 1990, p. A–8.
9. Bob Woodward, "Primary Heat Turned Deal into a 'Mistake,' " *Washington Post*, October 6, 1991, p. A–1.
10. *Budget of the United States Government*, Fiscal Year 1991, p. 19.
11. *Budget of the United States Government*, Fiscal Year 1992, p. 9.
12. *Ibid.*
13. Paul McCracken, "The Big Domestic Issue: Slow Growth," *Wall Street Journal*, October 4, 1991, p. A–14.
14. George Will, "Who's Better Off These Days?," *Washington Post*, October 31, 1991, p. A–21.
15. Warren Brookes, "Why Job Growth Has Come to a Standstill," *Washington Times*, October 10, 1991, p. G–1.
16. Christopher Brown, "June Fools," *New York Magazine*, November 4, 1991, p. 20.
17. *Ibid.*
18. Mark Shields, "A Pitch to the Middle Class," *Washington Post*, November 7, 1991, p. A–23.
19. John Yang and Ann Devroy, "Administration Considering Tax Rebate of up to $300," *Washington Post*, November 18, 1991, p. A–1.
20. Editorial, "Economic Incompetents," *Wall Street Journal*, November 18, 1991, p. A–16.

21. Michael Wines, "Bush Has No Plans for Major Efforts to Revive Economy," *New York Times*, November 19, 1991, p. A–1.

5. The "Ed-chew-KAY-shun President"

1. David Kearns and Dennis Doyle, *Winning the Brain Race* (Washington, D.C.: Institute for Contemporary Studies, 1988), p. 13.
2. Cited in Mark Duffy and Dan Goodgame, *Marching in Place: The Status Quo Presidency of George Bush* (New York: Simon & Schuster, 1992), p. 82.
3. Robert Pear, "U.S. May Alter Student Lending to Skirt Banks," *New York Times*, January 7, 1991, p. A–1.
4. Jack Anderson and Michael Binstein, "Banks That Bank on Student Loans," *Washington Post*, February 16, 1992, p. C–7.

6. The Week Bush Fired Cavazos: Sununu Knows Best

1. Andrew Rosenthal, "Struggle at White House," *New York Times*, December 20, 1990, p. A–1.
2. Julie Miller, "Williams Charts a New Agenda for Rights Office," *Education Week*, September 5, 1990, p. 1.
3. *Ibid.*

7. Empowerment and the "New Paradigm"

1. Thomas Kuhn, *The Structure of Scientific Revolutions*, 2d. ed. (Chicago: University of Chicago Press, 1970), p. 158.
2. *Ibid.*, pp. 92–93.
3. *Ibid.*, p. 113.
4. Robert Pear, "Administration Rejects Proposals for New Anti-Poverty Programs," *New York Times*, July 6, 1990, p. A–1.
5. Paul Gigot, "Mr. Darman Reveals Himself Once and for All," *Wall Street Journal*, November 23, 1990, p. A–8.
6. E. J. Dionne, Jr., "Gingrich Calls for Darman to Resign," *Washington Post*, November 29, 1990, p. A–20.
7. *Ibid.*
8. Arthur M. Schlesinger, Jr., *The Crisis of the Old Order* (Boston: Houghton Mifflin, 1957), p. 482.
9. Maralee Schwartz, "Kemp Aide Fired on White House Orders," *Washington Post*, April 29, 1992, p. A–4.
10. Fred Barnes, "Unkempt," *The New Republic*, June 1, 1992, p. 11.
11. Paul Gigot, "Perot Proves One Bush Man Right All Along," *Wall Street Journal*, June 5, 1992, p. A–10.

12. *Ibid.*
13. *Ibid.*
14. Calvin Trillin, "Jack Kemp (A White-Guy Rap)," *The Nation*, June 1, 1992, p. 737.
15. Reported in *White House News Summary*, May 8, 1992, p. B–7.

8. In Search of Domestic Policy: "Kinder, Gentler" Gridlock

1. Alan Murray and David Wessel, "A Very Popular President Now Faces Plenty of Troublesome Domestic Issues," *Wall Street Journal*, March 1, 1991, p. A–4.
2. Testimony of Paul Tsongas before the House Budget Committee, September 24, 1992.
3. "White House Bulletin," December 11, 1991.
4. Murray and Wessel, "Very Popular President."
5. *Ibid.*
6. *Ibid.*
7. Patrick Buchanan, "Pre-emptive Surrender?," *Washington Times*, October 30, 1991, p. F–1.
8. *Ibid.*
9. *Ibid.*
10. C. Boyden Gray, "Civil Rights: We Won, They Capitulated," *Washington Post*, November 14, 1991, p. A–23.
11. *Ibid.*
12. William Raspberry, "Bush's Missing Drummer," *Washington Post*, November 25, 1991, p. A–21. Emphasis in original.

9. Campaign Mode: Ready to Fight?

1. T. S. Eliot, "The Waste Land," *The Complete Poems and Plays 1909–1950* (Harcourt, Brace & World, 1962), p. 41.
2. Robert H. Bork, *The Tempting of America: The Political Seduction of the Law* (New York: The Free Press, 1990), p. 349. Emphasis added.
3. Michel McQueen and John Harwood, "Bush's Schedule Shows He Spends Little Time on Domestic Concerns," *Wall Street Journal*, October 28, 1991, p. A–1.
4. Editorial, "Now Do Something," *Wall Street Journal*, February 20, 1992, p. A–14.
5. Letter, "What Bush Must Do After His Deadline," *Wall Street Journal*, March 20, 1992, p. A–14.
6. David Broder, "Bush Seeking Mantle of 'Reform' Candidate," *Washington Post*, April 3, 1992, p. A–1.
7. James Q. Wilson, *Bureaucracy: What Government Agencies Do and Why*

They Do It (New York: Basic Books, 1989), citing "Revitalizing Federal Management: Managers and Their Overburdened Systems," National Academy of Public Administration report, November 1983, pp. vii–viii, 8.

8. Irving Kristol, "America's Mysterious Malaise," *Times Literary Supplement* (London), May 22, 1992, p. 5.

9. *Ibid.*

10. Morton Kondrake, "Who Will Rescue This Presidency?," *Roll Call*, May 28, 1992, p. 23.

10. Omens of the Reckoning

1. Harwood, "Bush's Dominance Going into '92 Has Strategists Advising He Play Hardball for GOP in Congress," *Wall Street Journal*, September 4, 1991, p. A–14.

2. Ann Devroy, "Mosbacher Said to Urge White House Shake-up," *Washington Post*, May 3, 1992, pp. A–1, A–11.

3. David Halberstam, *The Reckoning* (New York: Avon, 1987), p. 22.

4. *Ibid.*, p. 24.

5. Paul Gigot, "Baker Bids to Give Bush Economic Vision," *Wall Street Journal*, September 18, 1992, p. A–1.

6. Lawrence Kudlow, "The Darman–Brady Record of Failure," *New York Times*, September 6, 1992, p. F–11.

7. David Osborne and Ted Gaebler, *Reinventing Government: How the Entrepreneurial Spirit Is Transforming the Public Sector* (Reading, Mass.: Addison-Wesley 1992).

8. James Fallows, "The Passionless Presidency," Part 1, *The Atlantic*, May 1979, pp. 33, 34.

9. *Ibid.*, p. 42.

10. *Ibid.*, p. 43.

11. *Ibid.*, Part II, June 1979, p. 76.

11. Looking Beyond

1. Arthur M. Schlesinger, Jr., *The Crisis of the Old Order* (Boston: Houghton Mifflin, 1957), p. 483.

2. *Ibid.*

3. George Bush with Victor Gold, *Looking Forward* (New York: Bantam Books, 1988), p. 189. Emphasis added.

4. *Ibid.*

5. *Ibid.*, p. 191.

6. Schlesinger, *Crisis of Old Order*, p. 483.

7. Joseph A. Califano, Jr., *The Triumph and Tragedy of Lyndon Johnson* (New York: Simon & Schuster, 1991), p. 122.

8. *Ibid.*, p. 123.

9. Reported in Lou Cannon, *Reagan* (New York: Putnam, 1982), p. 378*n*.

10. Noel Annan, *Our Age: English Intellectuals Between the World Wars—A Group Portrait* (New York: Random House, 1990), p. 448.

11. *Ibid.*, p. 450.

Epilogue

1. Martin Gilbert, *Winston S. Churchill, vol. VIII, Never Despair 1945–1965* (Boston: Houghton Mifflin, 1988), p. 27.

Index

Abortion, 37, 112
Abrams, Elliott, 23
ACT scores, 137
Adams, Sherman, 183
Adoption, 37
Affirmative action, 258–259
Agenda for American Renewal, 163, 326
Air traffic controllers, 102
Alexander, Lamar, 16, 38, 39, 131, 142, 150–153, 159, 161, 181, 218, 240, 256, 356
Allied Services Act, 191
Alternative teacher certification, 133
America: What Went Wrong? (Bartlett and Steele), 117–121
"America 2000," 16, 142, 151, 159, 161, 163, 240
American Bar Association, 42
American Enterprise Institute, 172
American Federation of Teachers, 126
American Medical Association (AMA), 42–43
American Society of Association Executives, 207, 208
Americans with Disabilities Act, 31, 67, 70, 73, 76, 250, 332
"America's Mysterious Malaise" (Kristol), 298–301
Anderson, Jack, 156
Anderson, John, 309

Anderson, Martin, 9, 10, 23–24, 27, 29, 292, 347
Andrews, Rob, 152–155, 228
Annan, Noel, 348, 352
Annenberg, Walter, 16
Antipoverty strategy, 189–196, 216; *see also* New Paradigm/empowerment model
Archer, William, 87
Armey, Dick, 87, 114
Ashcroft, John, 46, 47
Assets and the Poor (Sherraden), 225
Atlanta Project, 217–219
Atlantic, 82
Atwater, Lee, 170–172, 281, 307
Augustine, Norman, 16
Automobile insurance reform, 327
Ayers v. *Mabus* (1991), 252–254

Bailey, Thomas, 31
Baker, James A., III, 5, 16, 19, 53, 55, 57, 183, 207, 302, 306, 311, 315, 317, 319, 320, 324–325
Banking reform, 235, 239
Barbour, Haley, 321
Barnes, Fred, 44, 45, 200, 204, 223
Barnhart, Jo Anne, 193
Barone, Michael, 324
Barr, William, 252
Bartlett, Donald L., 117–121

Bartlett, Steve, 201
Bates, David, 200
Bauer, Gary, 27, 45, 294
Beales, Randolph, 143, 144
Beck, Harry, 44
Beck decision, 43–45, 223, 293
Begala, Paul, 269, 285
Bell, Terrell, 128–129, 137
Bennett, Robert, 172–173
Bennett, William, xiii, 8, 19, 23,
     77, 127–129, 137, 146, 147,
     165, 171–176, 182, 201, 269,
     300, 317, 335, 356
Bentsen, Lloyd, 37, 113
Bergalis, Kimberly, 17
Berlin, Sir Isaiah, 8, 331
Bertini, Catherine, 193
Binstein, Michael, 156
Black, Charles, 171
Blake, Frank, 66
Blumstein, James, 68
Bond, Rich, 98, 281, 317–319,
     333
Bork, Robert, 172, 263–264
Boskin, Michael, xvi, 28, 53, 74,
     75, 78, 88, 109, 198, 261, 268,
     292
Boston Globe, 15
Bradford, David, 118
Brady, Nicholas, 10, 17, 52–54, 81,
     88, 91, 95, 99, 214, 215, 287,
     289, 292
Brady, Phil, 33
Brand, Betsy, 193
Branstad, Terry, 134
Breeden, Richard, 66, 95–96
Brock, Bill, 170
Broder, David, 17, 200, 297
Brookes, Warren, 71, 74, 77, 78,
     110–111
Brown, Peter, 285–286
Brown, Tony, 220

Brown v. *Board of Education*
     (1954), 254
Brunette, Mary, 221–222
Bryant, Wayne, 297
Buchanan, James, 339
Buchanan, Patrick, 37, 44, 45, 95,
     257–258, 273, 274, 280, 282,
     288, 289, 300, 308, 312, 324
Buchholz, Todd, 277
Buckley, William F., 13
Budget deal of 1990, 10, 52, 53,
     56, 58, 59, 62, 64–66, 70, 79,
     81, 88–89, 91–92, 94–114,
     116, 121, 213, 229, 234, 289,
     310, 316, 334, 339, 341, 342,
     350, 389
"Building a Better America"
     speech (February, 1989), 7–9,
     66–67, 132, 141, 193, 207
Bureaucracy (Wilson), 298
Burger, Warren, 248
Burns, Scott, 93
Bush, Barbara, 14, 57, 144
Bush, George
     as ambassador to China, 20
     antipoverty policy and, 189,
          198, 199
     background of, 14–15
     Beck decision and, 44–45, 340
     "Building a Better America"
          speech (February, 1989),
          7–9, 66–67, 132, 141, 193,
          207
     capital gains tax and, 90,
          107–108, 115, 234–236,
          264, 327, 340
     Cavazos firing and, 167–169, 182
     children's television legislation
          and, 11–13
     civil rights and, 177, 183, 207,
          220–221, 237, 245–254,
          257–261, 289, 352

coalition-building and, 5, 10
collapse of communism and,
17–21, 266, 329–330
Congress, relations with, 10–11,
209–210, 240–241, 265,
291–296, 304, 325–326, 340
credit card interest rates and,
113, 259
crime control legislation and,
239–240
Darman and, 53, 57, 80–82, 279,
316–317
defining difference from Reagan
administration, 1–3, 9, 14,
24, 347
Detroit Economic Club speech
(September, 1992), 325,
326, 352
education policy and, 16–17, 39,
126–145, 155–164, 240
elitism and, 16–20
empowerment and, 186,
206–208, 211–213, 230
family issues and, 46, 47
"Golden Rules" of, 6, 7, 24
government regulation and,
66–75, 78, 332, 345
health care policy and, 30,
42–43, 280
Hurricane Andrew and, 311
Inaugural Address, 6, 7, 9–10,
193, 342
King verdict and, 220
Looking Forward, 1, 14, 21,
338–339
Los Angeles riots and, 220, 222,
224–226, 228, 311
Marriott Hotel speech
(February, 1991), 207–208,
237
minority scholarships and, 179,
181, 183

1990 budget and, 52, 53, 56, 79,
81, 96–113, 116, 229, 234,
289, 310, 316, 334, 341,
342, 350
1988 election and, 2, 9, 86, 97,
125–126, 133, 187, 300,
312, 333, 339
1992 election and, 20, 81, 82,
95, 121, 162, 216, 282, 283,
288–290, 297, 298,
300–306, 307–314, 321–337,
348–351
"no new taxes" pledge, 2, 7,
56–57, 88, 92, 94, 95,
97–99, 101, 104, 234
Persian Gulf War and, 21, 39,
40, 231, 233, 236, 244, 245,
260, 261, 307, 333, 343
popularity of, xi, xviii, xix, 11,
109, 227, 244–245, 294,
306, 308, 310, 311
South Lawn speech (June,
1991), 208–210, 241
speechwriting operation and,
3–4
State of the Union address
(1990), 206, 232–233, 235
State of the Union address
(1991), 205–207, 231–235
State of the Union address
(1992), 216, 273–274
"turnback" proposal and, 234
veto strategy and, 10–11, 13–14
visit to Japan, 123, 313
welfare reform and, 215–216,
297
as workaholic, xiv, 330–331
Yeltsin and, 18–19
Bush, George W., Jr., 175
Bush, Neil, 94
Butler, Stuart, 201
Butts, Tom, 151, 154

Byrd, Robert, 52, 55, 99, 106, 203, 342
Byron, Christopher, 111

Califano, Joseph A., Jr., 344–346
Calio, Nick, 11, 157
Campbell, Carroll, 135, 139, 354
Camp David, 17
Cannon, Lou, 15
Capetillo, Grace, 210
Capital gains tax, 89, 90, 107–108, 115, 204, 234–236, 264, 327, 340
Card, Andy, xv, 32, 208, 253, 254
Carpenter, Mary Chapin, 307
Carter, Jimmy, xvii, 2, 24, 61, 72, 109, 126, 158, 182, 217–219, 292, 309, 315, 330–332, 338, 346
Carville, James, 269, 285
Cavazos, Lauro, xiii, xiv, 58–60, 127–131, 136, 138, 144, 147, 148, 165–169, 178, 181, 182, 198, 240, 355
Chapa, Chino, 59, 167–169
Charlottesville Education Summit (1989), xiii, 133–135, 138, 142, 234, 275
Cheek, James, 253
Cheney, Lynore, 356
Cheney, Richard, 183, 353, 356
Childcare, 95–96, 105, 243
Children's Television Act of 1990, 11–13
China, 20, 266
Churchill, Winston, 356
Cicconi, Jim, 30, 33, 48, 49, 67, 79, 91, 95–96, 322–323, 356
Citicorp, 113
Civilian Conservation Corps, 228
Civil justice reform (legal reform), 40–43

Civil rights, 67, 112, 176–179, 183, 207, 220–221, 237, 243, 245–261, 289, 352
Civil Rights Act of 1964, 248
Title VI of, 177–178, 180, 251
Civil Rights Act of 1991, 73, 177, 289
Clean Air Act Amendments of 1990, 47–48, 67, 70, 73, 75, 76, 232
Clinton, Bill, 22, 234
acceptance speech, 305–306
background of, 162–163
education policy of, 134, 135, 139, 162, 287
New Covenant speech (October, 1991), 265–267, 306
1992 campaign, 216–217, 294, 297, 301, 304–306, 308, 309, 313, 314, 322, 323, 325, 326, 328, 337, 348–351
welfare reform and, 216–217, 287
Wharton speech (April, 1992), 119–120
Clinton, Hillary, 45
Coalition-building, 5, 10
Coats, Dan, 141
Cogan, John, 63, 304, 318, 356
Coleman, Bill, 246, 247
Coleman, Tom, 154
Commerce Department, 109
Commission on America's Urban Families, 46
Communism, collapse of, 17–18, 96, 260, 267, 291, 299, 334, 348
Compromise, 14, 22, 23
Concerned Educators Against Forced Unionism, 144
Conference Board, 110

Congressional Budget Office, 104, 148
Coolidge, Calvin, 1, 338
Cooper, Charles, 294, 327–328
Council of Economic Advisers, 110
Council on Competitiveness, 66, 67, 70, 73, 75, 77, 78
Cowper-Cowles, Sherard, 88
Cox, Chris, 294
Crime, 42, 238, 239–240, 294
Crisis of the Old Order, The (Schlesinger), 338
Croatia, 20, 266
Croisant, Gene, 120, 214, 278, 279
Cuomo, Mario, 330
Cutler, Lloyd, 102

Damus, Bob, 102
Danforth, John, 257
Danzansky, Steve, 60–61
Darman, Kathleen Emmett, 55
Darman, Richard G., xvi, 5, 8, 10, 17, 23, 35, 48, 88, 136, 218, 228, 268, 272, 292, 303–305, 332, 336
    Bush and, 53, 57, 80–82, 279, 316–317
    character of, 52, 54–55
    direct loan program and, 148–150, 154–159
    empowerment and, 191, 192, 194, 202–205, 213
    Gingrich and, 202–203, 205
    government regulation and, 66–74, 76, 77
    health insurance legislation and, 62
    management style of, 60–62, 64
    Moynihan's Social Security proposal and, 89–91

National Press Club speech (November, 1990), 51
    1990 budget and, 52, 53, 56, 58, 59, 62, 64–66, 70, 88–89, 91–92, 94–95, 98–107, 121, 229, 289, 342
    1993 budget and, 280–281
    1992 election and, 81, 322, 326
    in Reagan administration, 52–55
    religion and, 55
    Skinner and, 278–281
    staff at OMB, 62–64
    Woodward series and, 81–83
Davis-Bacon law, 204, 340
Death penalty, 42
Deaver, Mike, 5, 9, 128
Defense spending, 2, 64–65
Deficit reduction, 91–92, 96, 97, 99, 102, 103, 105, 110, 112, 121, 148–149
Demarest, David, 5, 6, 8, 131, 160, 279, 310, 328
DeMuth, Chris, 68, 356
DeParle, Jason, 200
Derwinski, Ed, 198
De Soto, Hernando, 19, 188
Detroit Economic Club speech (September, 1992), 325, 326, 352
Devroy, Anne, 259
Diefenderfer, William, 63, 198
Direct loan program, 147–159
Disparate impact analysis, 248–249
Dolan, Tony, 4
Dole, Elizabeth, 198
Domestic Policy Council, 189, 190, 194–200, 210, 214, 215, 236
Donatelli, Frank, 98
Dowd, Maureen, 28
Doyle, Dennis, 125, 142

Drucker, Peter, 226
D'Sousa, Dinesh, 201
Duderstadt, James, 151
Due diligence, 149
Dukakis, Michael, 1, 344, 349
Duke, David, 257
Durenberger, David, 155
Dyer, Jim, 80
Dziewanowski, Kazimierz, 19

Earned Income Tax Credit, 47,
  197
Economic empowerment: *see* New
  Paradigm/empowerment
  model
Economic Empowerment Task
  Force, 195–207, 210, 212,
  213, 215, 216, 224
Economic Policy Board, 34
Edgar, Jim, 354
Educational Excellence Act of
  1989, 141
Education Department, xii, 58–60,
  126, 137, 138, 146–149, 151,
  153, 154, 167, 174, 175,
  177–181
Education policy, xiii, xiv, 16–17,
  39, 126–145, 155–164, 240,
  287
Education Week, 176
Ehrlichmann, John, 27
Eizenstat, Stuart, 27, 247
Eliot, T. S., 54, 263
Emerging Republican Majority, The
  (Phillips), 93
Empowerment: see New
  Paradigm/empowerment
  model
"Empowerment Breakfast
  Group," 19, 200–201, 328
Engler, John, 354
English Rule, 41, 42

Enterprise for the Americas
  Initiative, 235, 239
Enterprise zones, 224, 230, 233
Entitlement reform, 103–105,
  121
Environmental policy, 47–48, 63,
  67, 70, 73
Etzioni, Amitai, 188
Exclusionary rule, 42, 240
Executive Order 12291, 69
Executive Order on the Family,
  45, 46
Eyckoff, Kathryn, 57

Fahrenkopf, Frank, 170
Fair Deal, 2
Fallows, James, 330–333
Family issues, 45–47
Family leave policy, 31–32
Family Support Act of 1988, 215
Farnan, Patty, 46
Farrell, Mike, 152
Federal Communications
  Commission (FCC), 11, 13
Federal Financing Bank (FFB),
  147
Feldstein, Martin, 10, 57, 86
Fiesta Bowl issue, 177–181
Financial Institutions Safety and
  Consumer Choice Act of
  1991, 239
Findlay, Cam, 76, 78, 290, 297
Finn, Checker, 38, 142
Fitzwater, Marlin, 108, 115, 167,
  279, 313, 319
Florio, Jim, 152, 270, 297
Ford, Bill, 151, 157
Ford, Gerald, xvii, 5, 27, 28, 34,
  346
Four Quartets (Eliot), 54
Fourth Amendment to the
  Constitution, 42

Friedman, Milton, 292
Furse, Austen, 32, 356

Gaebler, Ted, 188, 284, 330
Gaidar, Yegor, 348
Geiger, Keith, 38, 39
General Accounting Office
    (GAO), 104, 148
General Aptitude Test Battery
    (GATB), 255–256
Gephardt, Richard, 55
Gergen, David, 284
Germanis, Peter, 191
Gerry, Martin, 118, 193, 212
Gerstner, Lou, 16
GI Bill, 145
"GI Bill for Children," 143
Gideon, Ken, 118
Gigot, Paul, 99, 203, 226
Gilder, Josh, 4
Gingrich, Newt, 10, 14, 57, 87,
    98–100, 114, 170, 193,
    202–203, 205, 272, 274–276,
    347
Ginsburg, Douglas, 68
"Golden Rules," 6, 7, 24
Goodling, William, 138, 221–222
Gorbachev, Mikhail, 18–20, 266
Gore, Al, 121, 162
Government regulation, 66–78,
    118
Grace, Peter, 81
Gradison, Bill, 280, 281
Grady, Bob, 8, 47, 63, 295, 326
Gramm, Wendy, 68
Gramm-Rudman-Hollings bill, 86,
    92, 101–104
Gray, C. Boyden, 31, 44, 66,
    74–76, 78, 172, 179, 237,
    246–248, 250, 253, 254,
    256–260, 316, 335
Gray, Kimi, 232

Great Society, 2, 187, 193, 344
Greenberg, Rubin, 232
Greenspan, Alan, 108, 235
Greider, William, 82
Gridlock, 264, 296, 303
Griggs v. *Duke Power Company*
    (1971), 248, 249
Gross National Product (GNP),
    85, 86, 109
Grove City College v. *Bell* (1984),
    176, 177
Grove City legislation, 176–178, 180
Growth Experiment, The (Lindsey),
    86–88, 93
Gun control, 112

Habeas corpus law, 42, 240
Haig, Alexander, 103
Halberstam, David, 312–313
Hale, Janet, 63
Hamilton, Andrew, 344
Hansen, David, 308
Harkin, Tom, 287
Harper, Ed, 27, 29
Harrison, William Henry, 21
Harwood, John, 267
Havel, Vaclav, 348
Hawkins, Augusta, 249, 250
Head Start, 62, 160
Health and Human Services,
    Department of, 46, 62
Health Care Financing
    Administration, 30–31
Health care policy, 30, 42–43, 280
Health insurance legislation, 62
Heckler, Margaret, 64, 166, 168
Heinz, John, 111, 269
Helms, Jesse, 141
Heston, Charlton, 44
Higher Education Act
    Amendments of 1992,
    146–148, 150, 151, 157–159

Higher Education Act of 1980, 158
Hill, Anita, 248
Hill, French, 287
Hills, Carla, 30
Historically Black Colleges and Universities (HBCUs), 253, 254
Holen, Arlene, xviii, 63
Holiday, Ede, 32, 70, 76–78, 154, 168–169, 179, 200, 201, 235, 260–261, 328
Home ownership, 204, 233
Hoover, Herbert, xvii, 1, 2, 338
Horner, Connie, 261, 356
Horowitz, Michael, 23, 102, 294, 327, 356
Housing and Urban Development, Department of, 63
Housing starts, 111
Howard, Bob, 63
Howard, John, 43
Hubbard, Alan, 40, 41, 73, 216
Humbert, Tom, 212, 221–222
Hunt, Jim, 141
Hurricane Andrew, 311
Hussein, Saddam, 40, 307

Inaugural Address (Bush), 6, 7, 9–10, 183, 342
Inflation, 109, 110, 111, 115
Insurance industry, 235
Interest rates, 110, 113, 115, 259

Jackson, Andrew, 21, 22, 339
Jackson, Karl, 20
James, William, 186
Jarvis, Howard, 353
Jefferson, Thomas, 133, 344
Johnson, Lyndon B., 2, 210, 344–346
Jordan, Hamilton, 309

Jordan, Vernon, 247–248
Justice Department, 63, 104, 251–253

Kamarck, Elaine, 188
Kassebaum, Nancy, 141
Kaufman, Ron, 221–222, 241, 270–271, 319
Kaus, Mickey, 200
Kean, Tom, 38, 63
Kearns, David, 16, 38, 125, 142
Keating, Charles, Jr., 173
Keating Five investigation, 172–173
Kemp, Evan, 256
Kemp, Jack, 8, 14, 17, 54, 82, 83, 93, 96, 100, 114, 116, 119, 193–199, 201, 204, 207, 210–213, 217–229, 233, 272, 274–276, 318, 323, 325, 347, 353, 355, 356
Kennedy, Edward M., 146, 158, 176–178, 246, 249, 250, 258, 339
Kennedy, John F., 2, 346
Kennedy, Nancy, 167
Kid-vid legislation, 11–13
Kilberg, Bobbie, 32
Kildee, Dale, 152
King, Martin Luther, Jr., 176
King, Rodney, 47, 220, 311
Kinnock, Neil, 322
Klawsner, Michael, xv
Kleinberg, David, 105
Komer, Richard D., 179
Kondracke, Morton, 300
Kondratas, Anna, 47, 193, 212
Kozyrev, Andrei, 19, 20
Kristol, Bill, 20, 40, 45, 61, 76, 179, 216, 356
Kristol, Irving, 19, 201, 298–301
Kudlow, Larry, 63, 328

Kuhn, Thomas A., 185, 186
Kuttner, Hans, xv, 36, 46

Laboratories of Democracy
    (Osborne), 188
Labor Department, 44, 116,
    255–256
Labor unions, 43–44
Lange, Mark, 232
Larkin, Philip, 51
Lefkowitz, Jay, 44, 76, 154, 212,
    216, 302, 356
Levey, Jonathan, 117
Lewis, Michael, 94
Liar's Poker (Lewis), 94
Liberman, Lee, 356
Lincoln, Abraham, 274, 339
Lindsey, Lawrence, xiii, xv, 69,
    86–88, 93–95, 97, 105, 118,
    122, 153, 287, 356
Lippmann, Walter, 339
Literacy, 144
Looking Forward (Bush), 1, 14, 21,
    338–339
Los Angeles riots (1992), 47, 220,
    222, 224–226, 228, 311
Losing Ground (Murray), 187
Lott, Trent, 347
Low Income Opportunity Board,
    189–191, 194, 195, 197,
    224
Loyola University of Chicago,
    58–59, 64–65
Lujan, Manuel, 196
Lund, Nelson, 253, 254, 356

Mabus, Ray, 270
MacLaine, Shirley, 1, 21, 22
MacRae, Jim, 68–69, 72
Madigan, Ed, 218
Magnet schools, 133
Major, John, 322

Marriott Hotel speech (February,
    1991), 207–208, 237
Marshall, Thurgood, 248
Martin, Bernie, 302–303
Martin, Lynn, 57, 98, 201, 218,
    256, 258, 270
Matalin, Mary, 171, 356
MBNA, 113
McClellan, George, 274
McClure, Fred, 11
McCracken, Paul, 110, 292
McGroarty, Dan, 266, 356
McIntosh, David, 302, 356
McQueen, Michael, 266
Mead, Emily, xv
Medicaid, 105, 345
Medical malpractice legislation,
    30, 42
Medicare, 42, 105
Meese, Edwin, 5, 9
Merit schools, 133
Metzger, Leigh Ann, 17
Mexican Free Trade Agreement,
    235
Milken, Michael, 94, 119
Miller, Jim, 62, 68, 292, 294, 305,
    318
Miller, Julie, 176
*Minority Party: Why the Democrats
    Face Defeat in 1992 and
    Beyond* (Brown), 285–286
Minority scholarships, 177–181,
    183, 251, 260
Mitchell, Bradley, xv, 225
Mitchell, Dan, 61
Mitchell, George, 5, 47, 90, 99,
    108, 203, 258, 264, 266, 296,
    342
Mitchell, Nancy, 61–62, 118
Mondale, Walter, 89, 292
Moore, Henson, 214, 277–278,
    285, 290, 321

Moore, Kate, 118, 131
Moss, Dorothy, 42–43
Moynihan, Daniel Patrick, 89–91, 113, 114
Mullins, Janet, 319
Muris, Tim, 318
Murphy Brown, 313
Murray, Alan, 200, 247
Murray, Charles, 187

Nathan, Joe, 38
Nation, The, 226
National Academy of Sciences, 255
National Board for Professional Teaching Standards, 141
National Education Association, 126
National Education Goals Panel, 136, 138–139
National Endowment for the Arts and Humanities, 112, 174
National Journal, 71–73
National Labor Relations Board, 44
National Review, 13, 61
National Science Scholarships, 133
National Security Council, 18, 19
"Nation at Risk, A" (Bell), 129, 130, 137
Nelson, Rae, xv, 144
"New American Schools," 142
New American Schools Development Corporation (NASDC), 16–17
New Deal, 2, 187, 344
New Frontier, 2
New Ideas from Dead Economists (Buchholz), 277
New Left, 192, 193
New Paradigm/empowerment model, xviii, 51, 185–230

New Republic, The, 44, 200, 204, 223
Newsweek, 143
New World Order, 20
New York Magazine, 111
New York Times, 13, 28, 61, 119, 121, 148, 178, 190, 194, 200
1990 budget deal, 10, 52, 53, 56, 58, 59, 62, 64–66, 70, 79, 81, 88–89, 91–92, 94–114, 116, 121, 213, 229, 234, 289, 310, 316, 334, 339, 341, 342, 350, 389
Niskanen, William, 10
Nixon, Richard M., 93, 111, 191, 309, 346
Nofziger, Lyn, 10
Nolan, Martin, 15
"No new taxes" pledge, 2, 7, 56–57, 88, 92, 94, 95, 97–99, 101, 104, 234
Noonan, Peggy, 4, 125, 356
Nutrition Labeling and Education Act, 73

O'Connell, Jeff, 327
Office of Information and Regulatory Affairs (OIRA), 68–73, 75–78
Office of Management and Budget (OMB), xii, 51, 62–64, 69, 104, 105, 116, 149–150, 152, 154, 236–237
Office of National Drug Control Policy, 172, 174
Office of National Service, xviii, 333
Office of Policy Development (OPD), 23–24
    Porter as head of, 30–49
    staff of, xv–xvi, 30–33, 36
Office of Public Liaison, 3, 5, 158–159, 310

Oliver, Dan, 294
Olson, Ted, 294
O'Neill, Paul, 38, 39
Osborne, David, 188, 284, 330

Panetta, Leon, 55
Payroll tax, 89
Pear, Robert, 148, 150, 190, 194
Pell, Claiborne, 145
Pell Grants, 145, 152, 153, 155,
    156, 158
Pennsylvania Senate race (1991),
    111–113, 268–271, 285, 341
Perot, Ross, 98, 121, 226, 227,
    299–301, 303, 304, 308–309,
    312, 313, 326, 329, 349, 351
Persian Gulf War, xviii, 20, 21, 39,
    40, 106, 107, 208, 231, 233,
    236, 244, 245, 260, 261, 307,
    333, 343
Petersmeyer, Gregg, xvii-xviii, 9,
    28, 131, 218
Petri, Tom, 156
Philadelphia Inquirer, 116–119
Phillips, Kevin, 93–94, 113, 117,
    283
Pieler, George, 59, 148, 167
Pierce, Samuel, 63
Pinkerton, Jim, xv, xvi, 8–9, 23,
    25, 32–33, 36, 40, 51, 57, 58,
    97, 123, 131, 153, 154,
    185–188, 191–193, 200, 202,
    203, 205, 222, 226, 228, 240,
    242, 282, 336, 356
Pishev, Ognian, 19, 348
Plager, Jim, 68
Plessy v. *Ferguson* (1896), 254
Points of Light Foundation, 333
"Points of Light" theme, 267,
    333
Policy Coordinating Group
    (PCG), 214, 215, 217, 220

Political action committees, 243,
    293
*Politics of Rich and Poor, The:
    Wealth and the American
    Electorate in the Reagan
    Aftermath* (Phillips), 93–94
Pollution Prevention Act, 73
Pork-barrel spending, 59, 60,
    64–66
Porter, Richard, 40, 178, 193, 200,
    201, 210, 212, 236, 237, 302,
    356
Porter, Roger B., xiii, 8, 24–25, 88,
    105, 116–119, 136, 179, 180,
    218, 222–224, 244, 268, 272,
    292, 327, 332, 336, 337, 347,
    355
  adoption policy issue and, 37
  Baker transition and, 319–
    320
  children's television legislation
    and, 12–13
  civil justice reform and, 40–43
  Darman and, 35, 52, 53, 69, 72,
    154, 155
  education policy and, 131, 132,
    135, 138, 140, 144,
    154–156, 159
  empowerment and, 190, 191,
    201–202
  environmental legislation and,
    47–49
  family issues and, 45–47
  family leave policy and, 32
  government regulation and,
    71–72, 74–76
  hands on staff, 32
  as head of Office of Policy
    Development, xvi, 30–
    49
  1990 budget and, 97–98
  PEPAC and, 38–39

presidential speeches and,
33–34
State of the Union address
(1991) and, 231–233
tennis mentality of, 28–30
urban strategy and, 224–225
as workaholic, xiv-xv, 36
Yeutter transition and, 214,
281–282, 287–288
Poverty rate, 85
Poverty trap, 210
Powell, Colin, 247
Presidential Decision Making
(Porter), 34
Presidential elections
1836, 21
1988, 2, 9, 86, 97, 125–126, 133,
187, 300, 312, 333, 339
1992, 20, 45, 81, 82, 95, 121,
162, 216–217, 282, 283,
288–290, 294, 297, 298,
300–306, 307–314, 321–337,
348–351
Presidential Task Force on
Regulatory Relief, 66, 68, 69
Presidential veto, 10–11, 13–14
President's Education Policy
Advisory Committee
(PEPAC), 38–39
Public Employment Service, 204
Putting People First (Clinton and
Gore), 121

Quayle, Dan, 19, 20, 41, 42, 61,
66, 73, 75–77, 87, 162, 214,
307, 313–314
Quayle, Marilyn, 201

Race-norming, 245, 247, 255–256
Racial quotas, 176, 183, 246,
248–250

Rahn, Richard, 56–57
Raspberry, William, 258–259
Ravitch, Diane, 38
Reagan, Ronald, xi, xix, 3, 104,
284–285, 310, 328–329, 338,
346, 347, 353
background of, 15
children's television legislation
and, 12, 13
coalition-building and, 5
economic policy and, 2–3, 7,
85–88, 93, 106
education policy and, 126
family issues and, 45
foreign policy and, 20, 21
government regulation and, 66,
72, 342–343
popularity of, 14, 109
priorities of, 2, 23–24, 342
speechwriting operation and, 4
welfare reform and, 215, 216
Recession, 109–111, 116, 334
Reckoning, The (Halberstam),
312–313
Regan, Don, 23, 258
Reilly, William, 35, 63, 182
Reinventing Government (Osborne
and Gaebler), 188, 284, 330
Republican National Committee,
170–175, 182
Reynolds, William Bradford, 23,
255
Richardson, Elliot S., 55, 191
Robertson, Pat, 45, 324
Robinson, Peter, 4
Robson, John, 235
Rogers, Ed, 168
Rolling hold, 142
Rollins, Ed, 10, 14, 55, 98, 170,
227, 280, 309–310
Rollins, Sherrie, 279–280, 310
Romer, Roy, 139–140

Rooney, Pat, 39
Roosevelt, Franklin D., 2, 3, 94, 133, 210, 216, 228, 338, 339, 344, 346
Roosevelt, Theodore, 133, 338–339
Roper, William L., xiii, xvi, 30–31, 189
Ross, Dennis, 319, 340
Rostenkowski, Dan, 59, 60, 64–66, 111, 113–114
Roth, William, 353
Roukema, Marge, 155

Saiki, Pat, 98
Sanders, Ted, 58, 59, 148–150, 152, 242
SAT scores, 137
Schaerr, Gene, 75
Schall, John, 40, 191, 210, 356
Schlesinger, Arthur M., Jr., 2, 22, 338, 344
Schmalensee, Richard, 189–191
Schmitz, John, 47, 76, 356
Schneider, Claudine, 98
School choice, 131, 162, 163, 204, 205, 230, 243
School discipline, 143–144, 163
Schundler, Bret, 354
Scowcroft, Brent, 18, 231, 345
Scully, Tom, 63, 149, 154, 155, 157, 254
Seidman, L. William, 34–35
Serbia, 266
Services integration, 197–198, 210–212
Shanker, Al, 38, 39, 144
Sheehan, Chris, 315
Sherraden, Michael, 188, 225
Shields, Mark, 112
Shultz, George, 292
Sieg, Andy, 24

Simon, Paul, 155
Simon, William, 10, 292
Skinner, Samuel K., 24, 44, 45, 120, 123, 144, 166–167, 213–214, 216, 258, 259, 273, 277–281, 285, 287, 292, 302, 306, 315, 316, 318–321
Small Business Administration, 204
Smith, Dorrance, 279
Smith, Peter, 97
Snow, Tony, 40, 216, 266, 302, 356
Social Security Earnings Test, 204
Social Security taxes, 3, 89–91, 114
Sole-source grants, 58
Sorensen, Ted, 2
South Lawn speech (June, 1991), 208–210, 241
Soviet Union, 18–20
Speechwriting, 3–4, 33–34
Sprinkel, Beryl, 10, 57, 292
Starr, Kenneth, 41, 252
State Department, 18, 20
State of the Union address
    1990, 206, 232–233, 235
    1991, 205–207, 231–235
    1992, 216, 273–274
Steele, James B., 117–121
Steele, Shelby, 232
Steelman, Debbie, 57, 81, 356
Stockdale, James, 162
Stockman, David, 23, 62, 63, 81–82, 91, 104
Strauss, Annette, 46
Structure of Scientific Revolutions, The (Kuhn), 185, 186
Student loan programs, 145–147
Sullivan, Louis, 54, 62, 198, 207, 218, 258
Sundquist, Don, 57

Sununu, John H., xvi-xviii, 5, 10, 23, 24, 32, 33, 52, 57, 60, 67, 88, 136, 165, 268, 274–278, 320, 327
   Bennett's withdrawal as RNC chairman and, 172, 173, 175, 182
   Cavazos firing and, 166–169, 182
   childcare and, 96
   Darman and, 53, 54
   education policy and, 133–135
   empowerment and, 191, 201, 204
   environmental legislation and, 48–49
   Fiesta Bowl issue and, 179–180
   management style of, 182–183
   Moynihan's Social Security proposal and, 89–90
   1990 budget and, 70, 77, 79, 95–99, 101
   Republican conservatives and, 169–171, 173
   resignation of, 123, 213, 259, 273
Supply side economic theory, xv, 2, 56, 57, 85–87, 89, 91, 93, 106, 341
Supreme Court of the United States
   Ayers v. *Mabus* (1991), 252–254
   Beck decision, 43–44, 223, 293
   Grove City College v. *Bell* (1984), 176
   Wards Cove Packing Company v. *Antonio* (1989), 248–250, 261
Surface Transportation Assistance Act of 1991, 239

Taft, William Howard, xvii, 329, 338, 339
Taxes, 2–3, 10, 85, 87–91, 93–99, 101, 103–109, 111, 113–115, 122, 204, 229, 234–236, 264, 327
Tax Reform Act of 1986, 107
Teacher awards, 133
Teeter, Bob, 57, 96, 131, 156, 281, 322
Television commercials, 11–13
Term limits, 243, 293
Terwilliger, George, 218
Thatcher, Margaret, 87–88
Thomas, Clarence, 175, 179, 248, 257, 260, 263–265
Thompson, Tommy, 155, 162, 216, 354
Thornburgh, Dick, 111, 189, 194, 195, 197, 199, 201, 207, 215, 269, 271, 341
Thurmond, Strom, 170
"Toads" (Larkin), 51
Tobin, James, 85
Toch, Tom, 148
Todd, James, 43
Transportation, 238, 239
Treasury Department, 108, 235
Trillin, Calvin, 226–227
Trucking industry, 118
Truman, Harry, 2, 271, 346
Tsongas, Paul, 235–236, 294
"Turnback" proposal, 234
Tutweiler, Margaret, 319

Ukraine, 20
Unemployment, 111
Unemployment benefits, 109, 259
United Negro College Fund, 183, 245, 253
United We Stand (Perot), 121
Untermeyer, Chase, 261

Valis, Wayne, 5
Van Buren, Martin, 1, 21–22, 344
Vander Jagt, Guy, 114
Varnedoe, Kirk, 329, 330
Very Good, Jeeves! (Wodehouse), 27
Veto strategy, 10–11, 13–14
Virginia Military Institute,
    251–252, 254
"Voodoo economics," 2, 97

Walesa, Lech, 348
Wall Chart, 137–139
Wallop, Malcolm, 141
Wall Street Journal, 44, 45, 67, 71,
    80, 99, 115, 200, 203, 226,
    247, 267, 293, 294, 307
Wanniski, Jude, 82–83
Wards Cove Packing Company v.
    Antonio (1989), 248–250, 261
Washington Post, xiv-xv, 52, 54–56,
    66, 82, 114, 121, 200, 258,
    310
Washington Times, 61, 71, 74, 80,
    119–120, 188
Waste Land, The (Eliot), 263
Watergate, 93
Waters, Maxine, 221
Watkins, James D., 198
Waxman, Henry, 73
Weber, Vin, 14, 17, 87, 114, 193,
    274, 318, 353, 356
Weidenbaum, Murray, 10, 67, 292
Weinstein, Allen, 19–21
Weinstein, Harris, 118
Weld, William, 354
Welfare reform, 189, 215–217,
    294, 297
Welfare Reform Act of 1988, 189

Wessel, David, 200, 247
Wharton School of Finance an[d]
    Commerce, 119
White, Barry, 131
White, Byron, 249
White House Fellows, 28–29
Whitmore, Kay, 16
Wilensky, Gail, 288
Will, George, 110
Willard, Richard, 294
Williams, Marjorie, 54–56
Williams, Michael, 166, 175–181[,]
    183, 251, 260, 356
Williams, Polly, 39, 162, 232
Willkie, Wendell L., II, 172
Wilson, James Q., 298
Wilson, Woodrow, 339–340
Winning the Brain Race (Kearns
    and Doyle), 125
Winston, Chriss, 4
Wodehouse, P.G., 27
Wofford, Harris, 111–113,
    268–269, 285, 341
Wolf, Frank, 114
Woodson, Robert, 207, 220
Woodward, Bob, 54, 56, 81–83,
    104

Yeltsin, Boris, 18–20,   266,
    267, 329–330
Yeutter, Clayton, 53, 120, 163,
    201, 214, 215, 220, 223–[ ]
    278–279, 281–285, 287–29[ ]
    297, 300–305, 316, 317, 318,
    319, 340
Yugoslavia, 20

Zoellick, Bob, 319–320, 325